Levinas and Medieval Literature

Levinas

and

Medieval Literature

*The "Difficult Reading" of
English and Rabbinic Texts*

Edited by Ann W. Astell & J. A. Jackson

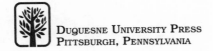
DUQUESNE UNIVERSITY PRESS
PITTSBURGH, PENNSYLVANIA

Published in the United States of America by
DUQUESNE UNIVERSITY PRESS
600 Forbes Avenue
Pittsburgh, Pennsylvania 15282

Library of Congress Cataloging-in-Publication Data

Levinas and medieval literature : the "difficult reading" of English and rabbinic texts / edited by Ann W. Astell and J. A. Jackson.
    p. cm.
  Includes bibliographical references and index.
  Summary: "Twelve essays take the unique approach of connecting Christian allegory, talmudic hermeneutics, and Levinasian interpretation, as authors put into dialogue the ethical philosophy of Emmanuel Levinas with a variety of English and rabbinic writings from the Middle Ages, thus illuminating what it means to classify medieval texts as profoundly ethical"—Provided by publisher.
  ISBN 978-0-8207-0420-3 (cloth : alk. paper)—ISBN 978-0-8207-0421-0 (pbk. : alk. paper)
  1. Ethics in literature. 2. English literature—Middle English, 1100–1500—History and criticism. 3. Rabbinical literature—History and criticism. 4. Lévinas, Emmanuel—Ethics. 5. Literature and morals. 6. Religion and literature—History—To 1500. I. Astell, Ann W. II. Jackson, J. A. (Justin A.), 1972–
  PR275.E77L48 2009
  820.9'38—dc22

                                                      2009001681

∞ Printed on acid-free paper.

Contents

Acknowledgments

The idea for this collection was inspired by sessions held two years in a row at the International Congress on Medieval Studies in Kalamazoo, Michigan in 2004 and 2005. We want to thank the organizers of those Congresses for accepting our proposals for special sessions on the topic "Levinas and Medieval Literature." The response to the calls for papers, the papers delivered, and the ensuing discussions made it clear that a significant number of medievalists were drawn to the writings of the twentieth century philosopher Emmanuel Levinas and discovering surprising connection between his ethical aesthetics, on the one hand, and medieval poetics and ways of reading, on the other. At the suggestion of Susan Wadsworth-Booth, director of Duquesne University Press, we issued a follow-up call for contributions to this collection. While some of the essays included were delivered in a preliminary form as conference papers and subsequently revised and expanded, others were composed specifically for this volume. None of the essays have appeared in print elsewhere.

We thank Susan Wadsworth-Booth for her vision in foreseeing this collection as a valuable contribution both to Levinas and medieval studies. We are very grateful to the two readers for Duquesne University Press—Gary D. Mole (Bar-Ilan University, Israel) and David P. Haney (Appalachian State University)—who responded carefully to the manuscript, providing us with extremely helpful, detailed, and insightful comments in their reports, and who recommended its publication. The individual essays and the collection as a whole are much stronger, thanks to their guidance. The staff at Duquesne University Press has also worked with great attentiveness and expertise, for which we wish to express our gratitude.

We want to thank the many people—family, friends, our colleagues and students at Purdue University, Hillsdale College, and the University of Notre Dame—who have shared our interest in this work and offered their moral and personal support. A special thanks to Jena, Sophia, and Lydia for allowing Justin to leave for days at a time to work on this collection. Joyce Coleman generously shared with us a trove of images from medieval manuscripts depicting people engaged in "difficult reading." Thank you, Joyce! We as editors want to acknowledge too the generous cooperation and patience of the individual contributors with whom it has been a pleasure and an inspiration to work.

Finally, we would like to thank Emmanuel Levinas, whose spirit has been very much alive in our exchanges as we worked together and whose thought has so deeply enriched ours.

Abbreviations

Works listed are primary texts by Emmanuel Levinas. Abbreviations used in individual essays for works by other authors are listed in the notes of that essay.

AE   *Autrement qu'être ou au-delà de l'essence*. La Haye: Martinus Nijhoff, 1974.

AT   *Alterity and Transcendence*. Trans. Michael B. Smith. New York: Columbia University Press, 1999.

AV   *L'Au-delà du verset: Lectures et discours talmudiques*. Paris: Les Éditions de Minuit, 1982.

BPW   *Basic Philosophical Writings*. Ed. Adriaan Peperzak, Simon Critchley, and Robert Bernasconi. Bloomington: Indiana University Press, 1996.

BV   *Beyond the Verse: Talmudic Readings and Lectures*. Trans. Gary D. Mole. London: Athlone, 1994.

CPP   *Collected Philosophical Papers*. Trans. Alphonso Lingis. Pittsburgh: Duquesne University Press, 1998.

DF   *Difficult Freedom: Essays on Judaism*. Trans. Seàn Hand. Baltimore: Johns Hopkins University Press, 1990.

DL   *Difficile liberté. Essais sur le judaïsme*. 2nd ed. Paris: A. Michel, 1976.

DVI   *De Dieu qui vient à l'idée*. Paris: Vrin, 1986.

EE   *Existence and Existents*. Trans. Alphonso Lingis. Pittsburgh: Duquesne University Press, 2001.

Eel   *Éthique et infini*. Paris: Fayard, 1982.

EI   *Ethics and Infinity*. Trans. Richard A. Cohen. Pittsburgh: Duquesne University Press, 1985.

EN   *Entre nous: Thinking-of-the-Other*. Trans. M. Smith and B. Harshov. New York: Columbia University Press, 1998.

GCM   *Of God Who Comes to Mind*. Trans. Bettina Bergo. Palo Alto: Stanford University Press, 1998.

HS   *Hors sujet*. Saint Clement: Fata Morgana, 1987.

IRB   *Is it Righteous to Be? Interviews with Emmanuel Levinas.* Ed. and trans. Jill Robbins. Stanford: Stanford University Press, 2001.

LR   *The Levinas Reader*. Ed. Seàn Hand. Oxford: Basil Blackwell, 1987.

NT   *Nine Talmudic Readings*. Trans. Annette Aronowicz. Bloomington: Indiana University Press, 1994.

OB   *Otherwise than Being or Beyond Essence*. Trans. Alphonso Lingis. Pittsburgh: Duquesne University Press, 1998.

OS   *Outside the Subject*. Trans. Michael B. Smith. Stanford: Stanford University Press, 1996.

PN   *Proper Names*. Trans. Michael B. Smith. Palo Alto: Stanford University Press, 1996.

QT   *Quatre lectures talmudiques*. Paris: Éditions de Minuit, 1968.

TA   *Le Temps et l'autre*. Montpellier: Fata Morgana, 1979.

TI   *Totality and Infinity*. Trans. Alphonso Lingis. Pittsburgh: Duquesne University Press, 1969.

TO   *Time and the Other*. Trans. Richard A. Cohen. Pittsburgh: Duquesne University Press, 1987.

Before the Face of the Book
A Levinasian Pre-face

Ann W. Astell and J. A. Jackson

In an Anglo-Saxon riddle, the Bible speaks, alive as a book after its death as an animal's skin. It describes its killing by an enemy, its washing in water, its drying in the sun, the scraping off of its hair, its being cut with a sharp knife, its inscription with a pen, its binding, its rubrication with blood-red letters, its illumination with gold, its great usefulness to humanity. At the end of its cryptic autobiography, it teases out a guess from the auditor. "Ask what I am called," the riddle entreats, "My name is famous."[1]

In the fourteenth century Middle English poem *Piers Plowman*, a mysterious character named Book suddenly appears in a dream vision: "Then there was a man with two broad eyes; / Book that good father was named, a bold man of speech."[2] That personified Book, too, is the Bible.

The "two broad eyes" of the Book of Books recall yet another bookish, medieval face. In Dante's *Purgatorio,* on the plateau where sinners are purified of gluttony, the pilgrim encounters emaciated human faces, on whom the very name of man (in Italian, "omo") is inscribed through the sinking of the eyes in their sockets and the protrusion of the cheekbones, eyebrows, and nose: "their eyes seemed like a ring that's lost its gems; / and he who, in the face of man, would read / OMO would here have recognized the M."[3]

Does the book have a face? Is the face a book? The Middle Ages clearly answered "yes" to both questions, even as it related them. The face of the medieval book, like the face of man, recalls the mortality of every human being, the suffering one has already endured, the death each person will one day encounter, as well as the anticipated afterlife. The book faces its reader as a memento mori, even as the face of every human being appears, in its nakedness, as a book with two eyes. Its vulnerability, as interpreted by the great twentieth century philosopher Emmanuel Levinas (1906–1995), presents at once a temptation to murder and a divine commandment: "Thou shalt not kill." "The Torah is given in the Light of a face," he writes. "Seeing the other is already an obligation toward him" (*NT* 47).

The present volume is not, to be sure, the riddling Book, not the two-eyed Book of Books, nor is it written on once-living skin, on parchment or vellum. It has no human face of its own to haunt the memory or to disturb the conscience, no face like the starved faces of Dante's souls, who, following Virgil's ghost, might declare, "Non omo, omo già fui" (Not man; I once was man).[4] But it is, in its own way, vulnerable. A preface, therefore, comes before its face and the opening of its pages.

A reader might, after all, object, first of all, that there is an anachronism in "Levinas and Medieval Literature" that is unjustifiable (even by invoking Levinas's own anachronic "time of the Other"). What does a modern philosopher like Levinas have to do with medieval literature? Better put, what can sustained reflection on the work of Levinas contribute to the understanding of medieval texts? And conversely, what can medieval sources (and medievalist resources) contribute to the study of Levinas's philosophy?

Certainly, Levinas cannot be said to have influenced the literature of the Middle Ages, but his writings—as the essays in this collection show—can truly alter our reception, our reading, of that literature. Of equal importance is the discovery that the literary works of the medieval period can illumine our understanding of the Levinasian oeuvre—its characteristic style, method, and themes, as well as its profound resistance to thematization. This is so, moreover, not just in the sense that Levinas indubitably read the literary works of medieval authors and was influenced by them, often in unacknowledged ways.

Rather, despite manifest differences, the literature of the Middle Ages stands in a startling, close proximity to Levinas's own.[5]

What allows for this approximation across centuries is a third entity, which exists prior to the Middle Ages, to Levinas, and to us—namely, the sacred Scriptures. Like medieval authors, Levinas accords a special status to the Bible. His writings may, indeed, be regarded as an original, modern, philosophical extension of the ancient biblical commentary tradition—its "translation" from "Hebrew" to "Greek."[6] Levinas explains: "Every philosophical thought rests on pre-philosophical experiences, and...for me, reading the Bible has belonged to these founding experiences" (*EI* 24).

Medieval authors, too, looked to the Bible as the text that served (in various ways) as the model for, and the actual beginning of, their own compositions. Geoffrey Chaucer, after all, did not hesitate twice to apply to his *Canterbury Tales* the words used by Saint Paul in Romans 15:4 to describe the Hebrew Scriptures: "All that is written is written for our doctrine."[7] A survey of medieval *accessus ad auctores* (the formulaic introductions to classical authors used in the arts curricula in medieval universities) indicates that literary writings were understood to teach virtue (directly and indirectly) and were regularly classified as pertaining (in philosophical terms) to ethics,[8] the very field that Levinas celebrates as the first philosophy.[9] As William Franke notes, for Dante and Levinas alike, "It is in ethics that the significance of any kind of knowledge is realized."[10]

If ethics can serve as an anachronistic connection between Levinas and writings from the Middle Ages, is there not a second, aesthetic objection that can still be raised to the very conjunction "Levinas and Literature"? Levinas's key essays on literary and visual art—"Reality and Its Shadow" (1948) and "The Servant and Her Master" (1966)—describe artistic expression as shadowy (and therefore enigmatic and allegorical), servile, passive, and feminine. Not surprisingly, commentators have found it difficult to present Levinasian aesthetics positively, even when they note Levinas's appreciation of specific writers (for example, Proust, Blanchot, Shakespeare, Dostoevsky) and recall that he uses similar terms to describe the ethical subject accused before the face of a commanding, transcendent Other.[11] The accusative and the imperative are, for Levinas, functions of language experienced as a saying (*le Dire*). Gerald Bruns observes, "The ethical and the poetic are evidently species of saying (*le Dire*) in contrast to the propositional character of the said (*le Dit*), yet neither are translatable to the other, and in fact they are in some sense at odds with one another."[12] Indeed, Jill Robbins has asserted that "Levinas's philosophy cannot function as an extrinsic approach to the literary work of art, that is, it cannot give rise to an application," due to the "incommensurability between Levinas's ethics and the discourse of literary criticism."[13]

The literary criticism of the Middle Ages, however, unlike that of modernity, arguably understood the work of art in a manner akin to Levinas's philosophy. Strongly tied to the materiality not only of manuscripts but also of human bodies, the literature of the medieval period was read aloud or sung, usually to a listening group of people, who responded with sounds, gestures, and interpretive commentary.[14] For Levinas, as Bruns explains, "The sound of words is an ethical event, which Levinas does not hesitate to characterize as *critique,* not only because others interrupt me in making themselves felt, setting limits to my autonomy, but because *even when I myself* speak — even in self-expression — I am no longer an 'I,' am no longer self-identical, but am beside myself."[15] In answer to the question "Is self-expression only the manifestation of a thought by a sign?" Levinas answers no; self-expression is always already dialogic: "By the proffered word, the subject that posits himself exposes himself and, in a way, prays" (*OS* 149).

Writing about the ancient "psalms of David . . . the prayers of Israel," Levinas remarks, "They have become the liturgy of the nations. They trace out, in our space, the way leading from the most intimate interiority — to beyond all exteriority" (*OS* 131). This way across time and peoples is possible, in Levinas's understanding, not only because of a diachrony within time itself, but also because of the Oral Torah of the Jews: "Parable and homily (genres known by philologists, but which appear minor to them) have stored the treasures of Jewish thought and spirituality. . . . The Talmud and its commentaries, and the commentaries on these commentaries . . . prolong (while stabilizing in writing) a very ancient oral tradition from which the Bible emerged and in which, for a Jew, it breathes" (*OS* 130). From the perspective of this Jewish (and, to a large extent, also historically Christian) experience, the Bible as a book is and remains a saying, a word (*verbe*), that thrives in the intersubjective space of the community: "In the Jewish reading, episodes, figures, teachings, words, letters, receive — through the immediate meaning, as if it were transparent — other innumerable meanings" (*OS* 130). The Bible, precisely because its literal meaning is not transparent, generates the literary as a commentary upon itself and as an extension of its own opaque, mysterious, material, and spiritual speech.

In Levinas's writings about the Scriptures themselves and rabbinic exegesis, his approach to these texts is, as Levinas says, "a one-way movement, steep: to the sources, to the old books which are forgotten and difficult, in a strenuous, laborious, and severe study."[16] In his talmudic study, Robbins avers, "the distinction between the philosophical and the non-philosophical writing is not absolute," neither in Levinas's own writing nor in the ancient texts themselves.[17] Neither is this biblical "literature" (for so Levinas calls it) subordinated to his philosophy.[18] Rather, its letters, its words, its images possess a quality that Levinas elsewhere names (in reference to the literary writing of Maurice Blanchot) a "prior transcendence" that "precedes . . . perception."[19]

Medieval exegetes and authors, too, struggled with "old books," their difficult sayings, their "prior transcendence," and thus their meaning for present experience. Chaucer's narrator in *The Legend of Good Women* famously (and ironically) clings to books "Thurgh whiche that olde thinges ben in minde" (line 18). If all the "olde bokes" were lost, he observes, lost would be the very key of remembering: "Yloren were of remembraunce the keye" (lines 25–26). Without them, not only the history of this world and the witness of past experience may be forgotten, but also heaven and hell. Memory itself, as Mary Carruthers has shown, is named a compendious book in the medieval arts of memory — indeed, a book of knowledge and of life, analogous to (and participant in) God's own.[20] For Dante, the Celestial Rose itself is an encyclopedic book, whose petals are bound together by love (*Paradiso* 33:85–87).

In "Difficult Reading," the first essay in this collection, Valerie Allen offers a systematic exposition of the ways in which Levinas's reading and writing reflect and continue (albeit in a modern, post-Holocaustal key) the tradition of medieval understandings and practices of the Book. In many respects, she argues, Levinas's ethical reading has more in common with the medieval monastic tradition of reading than it does with modern philosophical traditions, yet Christian biblical hermeneutics has often rejected Jewish biblical interpretation as blind literalism. It seems to Allen that Jewish reading, however much it shares affinities with phenomenology and medieval monasticism, preserves something of the irreducible and nontransferable. In this, it embodies the preoccupation we find in Levinas's work with the wholly other. Allen convincingly shows that the writings of Levinas—relentlessly moral and ethical in their insistence upon each one's "infinite responsibility" for the Other—reinvigorate our understanding of the texts of the Middle Ages. "We *are*," she writes, "because we read and *as* we read."

Like Allen, Susan Yager emphasizes what is irreducible to cognition, both in Levinas's own writings and in medieval literature. In her essay, "Levinas, Allegory, and Chaucer's *Clerk's Tale*," Yager shows that medieval allegory, properly understood, is not the (Coleridgean) allegory from which Levinas properly distanced himself in his 1948 essay, "Reality and Its Shadow."[21] Medieval allegory, she argues, is truly a speaking "otherwise" than the declaration of facts and beliefs; instead, it figures an expressive invocation, commensurate with Levinas's own distinctive manner of writing and thinking. "It is possible to come near to—or, in a Levinasian sense, ap-*proximate*—definitive meaning in allegory, but never possible to reach it," according to Yager. "In Levinasian terms, we may say that the allegorical resists determinate meaning, resists totalization . . . there is always more *to* allegory, always a surplus that exceeds any particular take or interpretation." In support of her thesis, Yager deftly surveys a range of medieval literary passages—from Langland's *Piers Plowman,* medieval lyric, *Everyman, Pearl,* Chaucer's *Book of the Duchess* and *Troilus and Criseyde*—analyzing their affinity to

Levinas's own use of personification, grammatical metaphor, paradox, sentence fragments, paranomiasia, etymologies, and the characteristic Levinasian conjunction *comme si* (as if). She concludes with a brief treatment of Chaucer's *Clerk's Tale* that underscores its resistance to any single reading (including, especially, Petrarch's), its properly allegorical nature, and its ethical implications.

Taken together, the essays by Allen and Yager provide a theoretical grounding for the project of the collection as a whole, giving a kind of indispensable, introductory, reading lesson. The following essays—those by Eileen Joy, Alexander L. Kaufman, Daniel Kline, James Paxson, J. A. Jackson, and J. Allan Mitchell—each bring Levinas's philosophical work in conversation with a specific work of medieval English literature and its themes. In the final cluster of essays, Cynthia Kraman, Sandor Goodhart, Ann W. Astell, and Moshe Gold focus on Levinas's talmudic commentaries as critical and literary approaches to medieval literature that can, in turn, affect ours.

The essays by Eileen Joy and Alexander L. Kaufman share a concern with the monstrous and the maternal. In her essay, " 'In his eyes stood a light, not beautiful': Levinas, Hospitality, *Beowulf*," Joy takes up the problematic relationship between ethics and politics in Levinas's thought, especially as those two realms are joined in the single image of the home (or mead-hall) with its two facades: one opening inward, toward the secrecy of the domicile, and the other opening outward, toward the street, the wilderness, its strangers, and the hospitality due to them. She considers "Levinas's philosophy of hospitality in relation to the *terroristic* figure of Grendel [and Grendel's mother] in the Old English poem *Beowulf*," in order to explore "the vexed connections between ethics, violence and sovereignty, as well as between ethics and politics, both in the Middle Ages and in our own time." In her analysis of *Beowulf*, hospitality proves to be "a form of politics—a politics, moreover, that has its breakable limits, evidenced by the poem's digressions into stories about violence erupting within the very site of reception that makes hospitality possible at all—the hall itself."

Evoking another monstrous figure who, like Grendel and his mother, inhabits a liminal space in the medieval landscape, Kaufman in his essay, "There is Horror: *The Awntyrs off Arthure*, the Face of the Dead, and the Maternal Other," calls attention to the frightening ghost of Queen Guinevere's mother and sets this ghost before and beside the Shakespearean ghosts to which Levinas frequently alludes. Suffering in Purgatory, the deceased mother suddenly appears before her terrified daughter (called Gaynour in the *Awntyrs*) to beg for her help. The poem, Kaufman argues, tests the notion of one's infinite responsibility for the Other by extending it to the dead and by reversing the mother-child relationship. Called to mother her own mother, to care for her beyond the grave, Gaynour is first plunged into a space that resembles the Levinasian *il y a*—a nightmarish, womblike space from which she can emerge, reborn as a subject, only through the acknowledgement and acceptance of an inescapable responsibility from which she would prefer to flee. Mapping Levinas's serial references to the *il y a* in his major writings against the sequential parts of the romance, Kaufman highlights the narrative development of Levinas's own thought. Kaufman compares and contrasts the medieval poet's exploration of the debt owed by the living to the still-living dead to Levinas's opening memorial dedication of *Otherwise Than Being* to the victims of the Holocaust, including six of his own relatives.

Like Kaufman, who focuses attention on Gaynour's predicament as the daughter of the deceased, Daniel T. Kline also privileges the position of the child—in this case, the biblical Isaac. In his essay, "Doing Justice to Isaac: Levinas, the *Akedah,* and the Brome Play of *Abraham and Isaac*," Kline first seconds and extends Levinas's critique of Søren Kierkegaard's treatment (in *Fear and Trembling*) of the *akedah* (the binding of Isaac) in Genesis 22. Then, attending to "the voice of Ysaac" and "the ethical demands he makes upon his father" in the Brome *Abraham and Isaac,* Kline argues that "the Brome play is, in some ways, more Levinasian than Levinas himself," in the way it extends the ethical relationship between Abraham and God to include Isaac (and Sarah) as a "third party." Kline considers "not simply the face of the Other as ethical demand, but the inevitability of the third, the Other of the Other—in this case, Isaac, the marginalized, spectral child—as the basis of sociality and ethics."

The next two essays—those by James J. Paxson and J. A. Jackson—focus precisely on the face. In "The Personificational Face: *Piers Plowman* Rethought Through Levinas and Bronowski," Paxson explains how Levinas's Face "can illuminate some aesthetically over-determined and semiotically intransigent images" in medieval literary allegory, in particular, a key moment in William Langland's monumental *Piers Plowman*, when a personified Anima speaks. In doing so, Paxson compares and contrasts Levinas's notion with some other modern theorizations of the face—specifically, what he terms "the deManian cult of *prosopopeia*" and "the Deleuzean notion of machinal 'facialization'." Most importantly, Paxson finds an unexpectedly dialogue-partner for Levinas in "the rationalist employment of the perceived human face in the 'scientific humanism' of poet, philosopher, mathematician, and historian of science, Jacob Bronowski."

Whereas Paxson features the face of Langland's Anima, Jackson looks to the face of the visionary Pearl-Maiden in his essay, "The Infinite Desire of *Pearl*." Taking seriously the potential prophetic, revelatory role of literature identified by Levinas in *Ethics and Infinity*, Jackson demonstrates the ways in which *Pearl* is already working through the simultaneity of the irreducible divine-human/human-human relationship that concerns much of Levinas's own writing. Jackson's analysis focuses on desire and a medieval notion of the *imitatio dei*, which leads him ultimately to argue that "rather than simply naming divine being as such, the poem depicts an *otherwise than being*, named as the Kingdom of God itself. This is a kingdom composed of individual beings engaged in an infinite substitutionary relationship, a relationship where each individual utters an in infinite 'after you' to every Other individual." The poem's depiction of this ongoing substitutionary relationship, what Jackson names as "an *agapeistic* envisioning of agape," quite literally "takes up and stages the very problematics of Being recognized by Levinas by performing for the reader Levinasian excessiveness, infinite desire." This substitionary relationship, Jackson observes, forms the very liturgical body of the Lamb of Revelation, which then defines the earthly body of the Church and each individual person within that body, a vision which ultimately deconstructs the categories of worship and charity, demonstrating how each category is simply an extension of the other.

Like Jackson, who finds in *Pearl* a Levinasian critique and a redefinition of medieval desire, J. Allan Mitchell explores Levinas's complex attitude toward the erotic, especially as it serves to illuminate Chaucer's *Troilus and Criseyde*. In "Criseyde's Chances: or, Courtly Love and Ethics About to Come," Mitchell considers the theme of love's adventure and, on that basis, reconsiders "the potential moral dimensions of fortune in *Troilus and Criseyde*." He draws support for his analysis from Levinas, who is "particularly sensitive to the way love adumbrates the ethical relation by virtue of its fortuitousness, future contingency, exteriority and anteriority to the active will." As Mitchell understands it, "Erotic love is for [Levinas] not just an ethical moment in the life of lovers; it is a prototype of the ethical relation engendering human experience." Since Levinas "has in mind medieval arts of love and cultivated desire," when he writes about the erotic, "it is perhaps not surprising to discover that Chaucerian love as presented in *Troilus and Criseyde* is profoundly ethical in the errant sense articulated by Levinas." Mitchell's comparison of Levinas and Chaucer reveals, however, that Chaucer gives greater scope to the exploration of "the *gendering* of the ethical relation." "Troilus may reap the rewards of his passive subjection," Mitchell observes, "but what about the woman's erotic adventure? To whose advantage is it to elevate *her* lack of agency to a virtue?"

Cynthia Kraman's essay, "The Wound of the Infinite: Rereading Levinas through Rashi's Commentary on the Song of Songs," stands in close conversation both with Jackson's essay (interested, as it is, in the Levinasian Infinite) and with Mitchell's (given its concern with erotic love and gender). Answering, in part, to feminist criticism of Levinas, Kraman explores Levinas's view of Eros as an *infinition* by configuring it, in its positive and negative aspects, to Rashi's verse-by-verse commentary on the biblical Song of Songs. "Medieval commentators like Rashi, who relentlessly allegorize the Song of Songs, teach us," Kraman argues, "to read Levinas as a less exclusionary philosopher than his critics have held him to be." Like Rashi, Levinas understands Eros and related phenomena—insomnia, indolence, night, light—*in bono et in malo* (in good and bad senses), according to Kraman. What appears to be a categorical exclusion (of the feminine, for example, from light) is but a point in an exegetical pattern of thought that engages in a continual, meditative review of things from opposite perspectives, in order to see it differently or otherwise. Light, Kraman reminds us, is not always good.

Like Kraman, Sandor Goodhart situates Levinas in the company of the rabbis. In his essay, "'A Land that Devours Its Inhabitants': Midrashic Reading, Emmanuel Levinas, and Medieval Literary Exegesis," Goodhart argues that reading Levinas, as he reads the rabbis, as they read the Torah, makes it possible for us to "rediscover the contexts from which medieval literature appears to have come. From this hermeneutical perspective, the reader is able to recognize continuities with the ancient world in which *allegoria* as translation extends what in fact midrashic thought of the rabbis was already practicing." Looking over the shoulder of Levinas, as it were, as he performs his talmudic reading of a passage in *Tractate Sotah* concerning Deuteronomy 1:22 ("That they may explore the land for us") and related passages in Numbers and Isaiah, Goodhart responds to Levinas by noting and expanding midrashically upon a gap in Levinas's own commentary. The rabbinic interpellation of a "ladder to ascend to heaven" in a passage from Numbers 13:20, which literally refers to the Israelites' "going up" to take possession of the land of Canaan, spurs Levinas to ask how the land itself might be "a ladder to heaven." Levinas's question and brief commentary leads Goodhart to extend his thought (and that of the rabbis) midrashically. The "ladder" in this way becomes, for Goodhart, an image of the proper, rabbinic reading of Torah at different "rungs" or "levels," that is, as translated into different contexts, not excluding the "messianic politics" of "universal justice." According to Goodhart, then, when Levinas reads (Oral) Torah about Torah, he reads about his own reading, performing in the present the ancient Jewish practice that helped to generate the *lectio divina* of the Christian monasteries and the *scala perfectionis* after which the medieval monks strove.

Like Goodhart, Ann W. Astell examines one of Levinas's talmudic readings, "Toward the Other," in her essay, "When Pardon is Impossible: Two Talmudic Tales, Chaucer's *Pardoner's Tale,* and Levinas." Imitating the technique of the rabbis, who used stories to comment on the questions raised by other stories (what Levinas terms a "paradigmatic method"), Astell adds Chaucer's famous tale about avarice and sudden death to the Talmud's two tales of Rab as a third, belated exemplum and a new narrative "climate" in which to explore principles concerning forgiveness. "Rubbing" them together, she argues that all three tales "uphold (albeit from opposite directions) the firm conditions attendant upon forgiveness, conditions that can make forgiveness an impossibility in the present, while yet referring to...a responsibility to and for the other, that exists prior to all offense and all pardon, that cannot be annulled, and that maintains the offended and the offender in an inescapable relationship to one another." Noting that Levinas interprets the unforgiven character, Rab, as both a "Levinasian hero" and a "Heideggerian figure" (and thus a "figural bridge" between the two), she discovers a similar alterity within Chaucer's Pardoner, whose Heideggerian "anxiety toward death" gains expression in his tale. Exploring the themes of impotence, futurity, passivity, and pardon in the portrayal of the Pardoner, she concludes with an examination of the penitential Parson's tale and of Chaucer's retraction as ethical substitutions enacted on the Pardoner's behalf to elicit the reader's own performance of pardon.

Kraman seeks to understand Levinas's work as a performative extension of Rashi's. Goodhart and Astell each perform a medievalist, midrashic extension of Levinas's own rabbinic performance by adding to it different voices that speak in conversation with Levinas, but otherwise than he—those of the Christian monks and Chaucer, as well as their own. In his essay, "Those Evil Goslings, Those Evil Stories: Letting the Boys Out of Their Cave," Moshe Gold goes one step further. Imitating Levinas, but seldom quoting him, Gold dares to comment on a talmudic text (the story of Rabbi Shimon bar Yochai in a cave), upon which Levinas wrote no commentary, by pairing it with a tale from Boccaccio's *Decameron,* rubbing the two medieval tales together to awaken the life within them, the life that speaks to human lives even today. Both tales, Gold argues, are "retellings of the allegory of the cave (from Plato's *Republic*)" that serve to "reevaluate the Platonic good beyond being," thus anticipating in an uncanny way Levinas's own later reappraisal of it. Adept at (but resistant to) the scholarly conventions that would reduce Levinas's work (all too quickly) to a said, Gold endeavors, in his own voice, to "speak hyperbolically, performatively, in excess of propositional clarity." The result is a breathtaking "critical rub" that does "not sacrifice stories as reductive examples of philosophy," but which recognizes their power to awaken "the love of wisdom" that is philosophy's own aim.

As the final word in this volume, Gold's essay sums up well what this collection as a whole has sought to accomplish. *Levinas and Medieval Literature: The "Difficult Reading" of English and Rabbinic Texts* is not a study of Levinas's writings on the literary texts of the Middle Ages. There are, practically speaking, no such writings, except his all-important commentaries on talmudic tales — texts which have seldom been recognized as "literary." It is not a set of essays that try to apply Levinas's philosophical insights one-directionally to works of medieval literature that are said to illustrate them. Instead, the two "ands" in *Levinas* and *Medieval Literature: The "Difficult Reading" of English* and *Rabbinic Texts* imply a dialogical approach that (weirdly, perhaps, but engagingly) performs a contemporary resurrection that allows Levinas, medieval authors, and the exegetes of old to speak to each other, using proper names.

2

Difficult Reading

Valerie Allen

CONSUMING THE BOOK

Whereas Russian was the language that Levinas initially spoke with his family, the first language he learned to read was Hebrew. Contrary to the sequence of most children's acquisition of a language, namely, from oral to literate, Levinas read Hebrew before he spoke it. Moreover, the feel he developed for the "extraordinary presence of its characters" (*EI* 23; *EeI* 18)[1] and for its heavy *lettres carées* (square letters) was ordered more to the pictorial than to the phonetic, more to the visual and tactile than to the aural (*NT* 9; *QT* 22). Those square letters become animated and responsive to the ministrations of talmudic exegesis: "It's really M. Chouchani who taught me this way of blowing (*suffler*) on the text in order to set it alight. There is a Talmudic passage that goes: 'The words of sages are like glowing embers.' Why 'embers' and not 'fire'? Because you need to blow on them to rekindle them."[2] The flame ignites and dwindles according to the respiratory rhythm of the interpreter's exegesis.[3]

The work of Levinasian ethical reading is intrinsically kinetic, an encounter between text and reader involving motor reflexes, bellows-action, nose, hands, cheeks and, as it transpires, feet. Levinas speaks of one Raba, "buried deep in study," who "rubbed" [*frotter*] his foot so hard while he was thinking and reading that blood spurted out from it (*NT* 46–47; *QT* 101–02). We are reminded of the work of medieval tanneries and scriptoria in turning a flayed pelt into a page, of the traces of blood and grease the page retains, and the scraping of it when the scribe makes a mistake. In the same fashion, Levinas agitates the text to arrive at the life it conceals. And such abrasion yields hidden sweetness, for the talmudic texts, responsive and plastic, give off their own distinctive "secret perfume" (*NT* 55; *QT* 120).

The terms in which the square letters are described are as gustatory as they are olfactory. Smacking his lips over the Scriptures, Levinas announces that a new reading of the Talmud "tastes good" (*NT* 79; *QT* 169–70). We can trace a similar Christian tradition of gustatory exegetics that insistently corporealizes the spiritual. The pun in the opening of the Vulgate Psalm 44: "Eructavit cor meum verbum bonum" (my heart has brought forth a great theme) was a favorite monastic jocularism, *eructavit* literally meaning "belched" or "vomited." Indeed, Bernard of Clairvaux preaches an entire sermon on this and other spiritually fragrant belches.[4] Holy meditation or "rumination" takes its vocabulary directly from chewing the cud [*ruminare*]. Peter the Venerable, in chapter 20 of *De Miraculis,* speaks of one Brother Benedict, who "tirelessly chews the holy cud of the Scriptures in his maw" [os sine requie sacra verba ruminans].[5] Richard of Bury exhorts: "First you ought to eat the book with Ezechiel, so that the belly of your memory may be sweetened on the inside."[6] Scripture is not recited so much as it is munched (the texts were mumbled aloud even when reading in solitude). Indeed, the entire incorporation of the word seems to occur in the digestive tract, from alimentation even to excretion.[7]

More is at issue here in the relationship between talmudic and patristic exegesis than the mere commonality of an Old Testament and some metaphors of eating. For all their differences, Christian monastic and talmudic tradition—at least as represented by Levinas—share deep-seated traditions about the discipline of reading and the advent of the Book. Both clearly share a sense of the corporeality of reading, but beyond that, a sense of the violence and "affliction" entailed in the act. Peter of Celle's "On Affliction and Reading" brings to the fore the connection between literacy and trauma, from the *punct*ure marks made in the parchment, to the *punct*uation that guides one's progress through the text, to the *com*punct*io cordis* (anxious care) or solicitude [*sollicitudo*] necessary to remember and learn from the text—a solicitude that as Levinas describes it can end in bleeding feet.[8]

Taken together, calcified texts rubbed and sufflated into meaning and perfumes that are secret illustrate how for Levinas the meaning of the text, however immanent and near-to-hand, is not readily apparent to the reader. At first sight its aloofness seems to accord with an exegetic esotericism dominant also in patristic thought, which eschews the lay and the female. Compare Richard of Bury's insistence on the privilege of rubbing the text: "You [O Books] are truly the most pleasing ears of corn, full of grain, to be rubbed hard only by apostolic hands."[9] The veiling of spiritual meaning both sweetens the rewards for those who have striven to understand,[10] and, to borrow the gospel's metaphor, protects its pearls of meaning from uninitiated swine.[11] There resemblance stops. In biblical hermeneutics, this esoteric strain transforms the nature of knowledge itself by valorizing the abstract over the concrete, the allegorical kernel over the literal chaff.[12] The theoretical arts—and most preeminently, philosophy—have traditionally taken precedence over the practical arts (see the hem of Dame Philosophy's garment in Boethius's *Consolation of Philosophy*). Lowest of all, the mechanical arts, poor cousin to the liberal arts, are adulterate, for thought has been mixed with physical labor.[13]

Levinas, on the other hand, though also valuing the arduous over the easy in talmudic exegesis, describes the text's accessibility in mechanical and material terms that hold the theoretical at bay. The teleological orientation toward abstract meaning of the hermeneutical tradition is absent. Idealist notions of interpretation and understanding associated with the philosophy of the subject are thus out of place when imagining the Levinasian reader as textual *frotteur*. The meaning yielded by the rubbed text is less theoretical, an abstract principle to be stored and used later, as it is a local epiphany, an *energeia* sufficient unto the instant action, as concrete as the work of abrading the text. That is not to call it a practice of reading, for the phrase invites the possibility that the practice exists in distinction from and in want of a theory of reading. Thoughts, coupling with labor, produce not more thoughts but ethical events in which knowledge, far from being an acquired *factum*, is brought into being through performance. The banausic task of reading is at once productive and consumptive, inseparably creative and destructive, enjoying the book even in the act of using it. In giving shape to the knowledge the text yields, it appropriates and consumes the raw material of meaning once and for all. To the ethical economy, theory, as pure knowledge attained through the mind's eye alone and abstracted from the concrete conditions of its production, expresses the alienation of thought from life, cognition from consumption.

What is gained through reading is not information, inert and fungible, which can be stored and retrieved at will, commanded into place and ordered according to the dictates of commodity production and circulation. There is an important point of affinity in this regard with Heidegger's repudiation of the generalized transformation of the world into *Bestand,* generally translated as "standing-reserve."[14] Levinas, however, elaborates on this idea through very different language that continues his gustatory leanings when he comments upon the manna sent daily to the Children of Israel in the wilderness: "Wondrous food: the real miracle lies not in the fact that the manna falls from heaven, but that the manna is exactly sufficient to our needs. To be nourished by manna; not to need to lay anything away; messianic times; not to need to think any longer about the following day, and in this sense also we are at the end of time" (*NT* 65; *QT* 140). While the book as artifact may perdure, reading produces no information surplus to be consumed or enjoyed later; it issues in no commodity; it yields no profit as such.

SOLICITING THE TEXT

By this analogy with manna, one is always reading yet never reading: always reading, because the previous reading must continuously be made present again; never reading, because we are forever in-between readings, because, with no leftover, manna is always absent. Suffering no need, and with neither yesterday nor tomorrow to look to, we are "at the end of time" indeed. Ethical reading occurs at an interstice within the sequential time and logical space of critical reading. Pictured variously as sufflation, abrasion, and mastication, the violent nature of ethical reading is captured in the cataclysmic force of what in his talmudic readings Levinas refers to as *sollicitation,* a word whose Latin etymon is associated with shaking and agitation.[15] Reading violently abrades not only the skin of the text but also that of the reader. With no yesterday or tomorrow in which to seek refuge, the reader is left naked before and answerable to the immediate demands of the text, according to "an eschatology without philosophical teleology."[16] We might equally call the moment apocalyptic, in recognition of the revelatory and violent quality of the ethical encounter.[17] Levinas consistently casts the encounter with the Infinite in terms of the "atomic metaphors" of trauma, in which "the subject is cored as if enucleated" (*GCM* 72; *DVI* 119). How different this is from the "enthusiasm" strenuously eschewed by the critical reader, who must by definition, hold back at least in part in self-appraising reserve, "thinking about responsibility from the standpoint of freedom or in terms of a contract," speculating without commitment, committed only to impartiality (71; 117). The truly critical reader must always be able to take or leave it, even in encountering the Infinite. But without recourse to this standpoint of critical freedom, we find an unbridgeable divide between the god of the rationalist philosopher and the God of Abraham, Isaac, and Jacob.

In that word *sollicitation,* the agitated intentness with which the reader pesters the text, we hear echoes of Heideggerian *Dasein,* whose care for the things in the middle of which it lives Heidegger calls *Besorge,* which Levinas translates as *sollicitude.*[18] Levinas's debt to Heidegger[19] — notoriously fraught with gratitude and anger — registers one point on his intellectual trajectory at which he recognized the possibility of finding the philosophical words to speak of God, the Infinite, transcendence. This is no small recognition, for "it is no mere chance that the history of Western philosophy has been a destruction of transcendence" (*GCM* 56; *DVI* 95). The alterity of transcendence must be by some way other than by negation or privation or lack, which together constitute the traditional categories of logical and ontological difference. Philosophy philosophizes by illuminating reality, by making being present. It also insists that all that is illumined is all that there is. Light, and the movement of the soul, must bend back (which is what "re-flect" means) upon itself. Presence is always returning to itself, and for this reason, Levinas calls the command to "know thyself" the foundation of Western philosophy because the universe lies within, and its journey, or rather odyssey, is patterned as a return (*DF* 10; *DL* 24). Transcendence must then be "without a return to its point of departure" (*TO* 66; *TA* 38). To invoke the advent of transcendence, Levinas refashions the optical metaphor through that of the hypnotic. Insomnia is the state in which the self is disturbed by the other (*GCM* 58–59; *DVI* 98–99). It is the condition of the idea of God or of the Infinite being put into us, and entails a bodily experience of wakeful consciousness that cannot be dissociated from the stinging and aching of the unblinking eyeball; this bodily affliction once more echoes monastic and anchoritic experience of sleepless vigils and loneliness of the soul. We do not choose insomnia; it chooses us. In this strange election, the idea of the Infinite breaks up the thinking "I" or *cogito,* so that the experience of the Infinite is not *thought* so much as it is undergone or suffered: "The idea of the Infinite, *Infinity in me,* can only be a passivity of consciousness" (64; 106).

A strange and paradoxical notion since consciousness has always been deemed an active power. Aristotelian hylomorphic notions of passivity—as in the active-passive relation of form and matter—do not do justice here to the crushing passivity Levinas describes. This passivity is not a "welcoming" or active passivity, but a trauma, a blow. When a talmudist "reads into" [*aller solliciter*] a word, the action carries the same seismic power and violence as does Heidegger's etymological undermining of words until they reveal the foundations of their being (*NT* 78; *QT* 168).[20] This asserts a kinship, however, that Levinas would no doubt dispute—for he was disappointed by the increasing importance of the dead letters [*le dit*] of etymology in Heidegger's work, and its consequent disregard of the human interlocutor in saying [*le dire*].[21]

DEAD LETTERS

The affinity traced thus far between Levinasian and medieval reading is better located in the monastic tradition rather than in high scholasticism. Without implying that the former cannot be intellectual and the latter affective, we nonetheless recognize a tension implicit within *lectio divina* between devotional and intellectual purpose, which culminated in the transformation of the *sacra pagina* during the twelfth century, long before printing, "from a score for pious members into an optically organized text for logical thinkers."[22] Moreover, the metaphors of consumption and incorporation of the book employed by the Church fathers are ultimately rabbinical in provenance.[23] Despite affinities between Christianity and Judaism that Levinas himself recognizes, the latter remains for him a faith distinctly separate and particular (*DF* 12; *DL* 26–27).

The difference between Christian and Jewish hermeneutics—at least in the eyes of medieval exegetes—lies most notoriously in the treatment of the letter. The identification of the Jew with literalism is a commonplace of medieval Christian discourse. Bede speaks of the Jewish way [*Judaico more*] of following only the letter of Scripture.[24] Lambert of Ardres criticizes Count Rainier of Boulogne, because he took the meaning literally, like the Jews.[25] Medieval iconography of Synogoga, depicted with blindfold or with eyes obstinately averted from the truth, similarly attests to Judaic fetishism of dead letters.[26]

This noted, we cannot ignore the loving attention given to the literal, historical, and grammatical meaning by Christian exegetes—thinking especially of the schools of Antioch during the fourth and fifth centuries, of St. Victor during the twelfth, or even of less orthodox thinking of Wycliffe and his followers.[27] Christian exegesis routinely invoked the architectural metaphor to assert the necessity of the literal. In the words of the fourteenth century Wycliffite writer of the preface to the translation of the Bible, the literal is the foundation [*foundement*] upon which the building [of *goostly vndirstondings*] stands: Wherfore as a bylding bowing awey fro the foundement is disposid to falling, so a goostly expociscoun, that discordith fro the literal sense, owith to be arettid vnseemely and vncouenable.[28] But like all commonplaces, it might mean less than it says; after all, it was St. Gregory, whose preference for the spiritual at the cost of the literal was well known, who inaugurated the architectural metaphor.[29]

Rehabilitation of the letter seems to reach its completion with Aquinas's statement of its role as the sum of the author s entire intention;[30] an assertion that derives all meaning from the literal meaning, and renders the spiritual dependent on the literal. Aquinas's return to the literal wholly accords with the Aristotelian marriage of form and matter evident throughout his work, where matter corresponds to the literal and form to the higher, spiritual meaning. His contemporary, Guerric of St. Quentin, explicitly correlates the four typological levels of literal, allegorical, moral, and anagogic meaning with the four becauses or kinds of cause identified by Aristotle: *causa materialis* [*hylē*], *causa formalis* [*eidos*], *causa efficiens* [*kinēsis*], *causa finalis* [*to ou eneka*].[31] The literal constitutes the material cause of a thing; the moral the efficient, for both pertain to agency; allegorical meaning constitutes the formal cause; and anagogic the final. It is true that Aristotelian etiology and hylomorphism raise matter to being an object of serious philosophical knowledge; by analogy, the literal also enjoys increased status as the object of theological knowledge. But etiology and hylomorphism are ultimately metaphysical structures, promoting matter to the poor cousin of aristocratic form. In contrast to the role of the literal in talmudic exegesis, which remains its first and final term, the appreciation of the literal we find in Christian hermeneutics never sheds the whiff of the metaphysical.

Levinas is quick to dissociate talmudic from Greco-Christian exegesis because it continues rather than "fulfills" or completes Old Testament history in the typological sense (*NT* 7; *QT* 18–19). This is a delicate distinction, for the early Christians modeled their typological analysis directly from Jewish interpretation of history, particularly prophesy, and it is hard to claim that the traditions differ in method, however much they may in interpretative content.[32] The difference for Levinas, one suspects, lies in a certain (Christian) impatience to turn systematically Old Testament events into prefigurements of the New; in a flattening out of Hebraic narrative; in a diminishment of the originary event or antitype; all of which prevent, in philosophical terms, any phenomenological relationship with the literal thing, with the *res gesta*. Levinas asks, "In receiving the three visitors, does Abraham receive the Lord because of the Trinity prefigured by the three visitors or because of his hospitality?" (*DF*121; *DL*163). Hospitable deeds need no justification beyond their own performance.

Talmudic exegesis also distinguishes four levels of meaning. Far from denying the literalism of talmudic exegesis, Levinas embraces it fully: But the word *sod* (mystery) signifies in talmudic symbolism the ultimate meaning of Scripture, that at which one arrives after having inquired into the literal sense [*pchate*], after which it raises us to the allusive sense [*Remèz*], and from there to the symbolic sense [*Drache*]. But the real mystery remain within the original simplicity, more simple again than the literal meaning.[33] Elsewhere, Levinas describes them as *pchate* (the obvious sense), *rémèze* (the allusive sense), *drache* (the induced sense), and *sod* (the secret sense).[34] Jewish exegesis never leaves the literal, which *completely* signifies, rendering it in the eyes of the Christian exegetic tradition an "idolatry of the letter" (*NT*7; *QT*19). It represents a refusal to reduce reading to the mere means to knowledge. In the beginning, there was the letter; and then there was the letter. The so-called dead letter of the law is a joyful burden: "The daily fidelity to the ritual gesture demands a courage that is calmer, nobler, and grander than that of the warrior" (*DF*19; *DL*35). The reading of the letter issues in the response: "We shall do and we shall hear," in which neither obedience nor understanding is made subject to the other, yet neither is independent of the other (*NT*42; *QT*92). Levinas is careful to emphasize that the doing is not *in order* to hear, and thereby he marks out the difference between this Judaic insistence upon doing the right thing for its own sake and the patristic dictum *credo ut intelligam* (I believe so that I may understand),[35] which, however much it seems to prioritize active faith, still renders it accountable to reason. Derived from the verb *chakak* (to engrave, to decree), the Jewish obligation of *chok* (statute), which means an unreasonable command that provokes only derision in the rationally minded, leaves the will still free, if now redundant, by virtue of its total heteronomy.[36]

The literal in Jewish exegesis is rooted in law that is engraved in stone, in the recalcitrant untranslatability of its "dead" letters. Such exegesis breaks open the Hebrew words, substituting different vowels or rearranging the letters to spell new words,[37] or computing the letters to tally new meanings. Levinas gives the following example: "A curious coincidence: wine is called *yayin* in Hebrew, and the numerical sum of its three letters adds up to seventy, like the sum of the three letters which form the word *sod* (mystery)" (*DF* 66; *DL* 92–93).

In contrast to such intimate involvement with the letter, dialectic is the self-reflection of reason, progressing, as Plato says, by contradictory steps and springs [*epibaseis te kai ormas*][38] to an ultimate understanding of the unity of thought and being. Plato's Attic dialect is thus glorified as dialectic by its elevation to the status of universal *logos*-script, the synchronic language of pure thought thinking itself, divested of the contingent accretion of material inscription. When reason speaks, it speaks in perspicuous Attic that represses the Semitic genealogy of its script. Only in the act of transcription, the moment of transition from speech to writing, is the phonetic transparency of Attic confronted by the historically saturated Semitic embodiment of its square letters. The purity of Attic is undermined with every stroke of the stylus by the resistance of the Semitic characters to erasure under the light of Greek reason. Plato denigrates writing in favor of speech in the *Phaedrus* precisely because inscription always exposes the historicity and local concreteness of thought, and hence the alienation of mental from manual labor, which is the precondition of philosophical inquiry. What Levinas provides is a conception of reading that enables a connection between Plato's antiliteralism and the Semitic origin of the Greek alphabet, the possibility of making the language of philosophy speak of transcendence. To the people of the Book, for whom the law is inscribed in tablets of stone without mediation, directly from God's hand, the concrete labor of the particular remains free from the tyranny of the abstract labor of the universal. Levinas keeps open the perspective of the ethical from which the hierarchical divisions between spirit and letter, head and hand, and philosophy and religion lose their force and effect.

LECTIO AND CRITIQUE

However much medieval Christian reading holds itself apart from Jewish literalism, the assimilation of food imagery by Christianity into mastication of the Logos (its climax in the eucharistic ritual) is so total that we are led to think that there is less difference between Levinas's Judaism and monastic solicitude for the Book than there is between a scriptural tradition (whether Semitic or Christian) and a critical tradition, and also that the resistance of the religious to the philosophical in Levinas's thought is the resistance of tradition to modernity. "Writing," a word of Germanic origin, and well shorn in English usage of religious association, may well be the clerk of the archive who limps behind speech, nothing more than the repository of what was said; but "Scripture," the more etymologically exact transliteration of *écriture*, is prior to *both* writing and speech. It is in Scripture that we encounter *différance*, to borrow terms from Jacques Derrida. And "reading," also Germanic, and meaning "counsel" or "advice," foregrounds the critical, rational aspect of encountering the text at the expense of the craft-work captured in the base meaning of *lectio*, namely the sheer ability to distinguish and enunciate letters on a page. "Reading" too hastily gathers up square letters into *sententiae* that translate into any language. It does not roll sounds on the tongue.

We can speak of the book in terms of its ontology, according to which the book does not so much inhabit a prior world of *realia* as it comes into being through being read: "I think that for fear of seeming bookish," says Levinas, "one underestimates the 'ontological' reference of the human to the book that is commonly taken for a source of information, or a 'tool' of learning, or a handbook, whereas it is rather a modality of our being" (*EI* 21–22; *EeI* 16). Does not this resonate with the experience of facing the translucent, shining page of an illuminated bible, in which "light is immanent in this world of medieval things, and they reach the eye of the beholder as sources of their own luminosity"?[39] The squareness of the letters and the respect for books that Levinas developed early on in life (his father was a bookseller and a great lover of Russian classics) register the phenomenological encounter with the book in all its opacity and concrete specificity, its belonging to the world into which we are thrown. It is through this intransigent "being-there" of the book that we can speak of the intentionality also of limb and organ. It is because we read that we possess nose, hands, cheeks, and feet. We *are* because we read and *as* we read.

For Levinas, the essence of the ethical reading lies beyond the state of freedom required by the critical faculty—that faculty upon which the philosophical or literary reader's judgment so fundamentally depends. As Kant emphasized, critical reason can never think except under the condition of freedom; it can neither submit to dogma nor be seduced by revelation. Otherwise, reason would find itself in contradiction with itself, at one and the same time thinking itself free to make up its own mind while believing that its judgment is determined. Critical reading is thus duty-bound to be punctual and self-referential, to read in the light of its own legislation, to interpret as it sees fit without appeal to authority or tradition. Once again, it is Kant who provides the topography of the critical as occupying not so much the middle ground between the extremes of dogmatism and skepticism, as the received view would have it, but a second-order, reflexive path that lies on a plane superior to that upon which the dogmatic and skeptical points of view are plotted.[40] Critique is less an accommodation of diametrical opposites than it is a radically distinct position, a fanaticism of reason in its own right, before whose tribunal all must submit for judgment.

By contrast, ethical reading believes before it knows and commits before it chooses: "One accepts the Torah," says Levinas, "before knowing it" (*NT* 42; *QT* 91). The Torah demands from its reader a primal assent free of self-presence and its negation, as well as prior to freedom and nonfreedom (37; 82). Not to be confused with the affirmatory enthusiasm of the patristic *credo quia absurdum*,[41] which is no more than the negation of philosophy (as *doxa* is the negative of *episteme*), "the first word, the one that makes all other words possible, the 'no' of negativity . . . is an unconditional 'yes'" (49; 106). Scripture does not stand in relation to philosophy as either its positive or negative term. *Différance* separates them.

Scripture is, quite simply, the revelation of the Word, the gift of the Torah. Revelation sums up the moment of encounter with the purely other, for we cannot perceive what is revealed until *it* comes to *us*. Choice made in the light of knowledge has nothing to do with receiving of the Torah because revelation comes as a gift that is anterior to any such knowledge. But how does one receive such a gift? Does not all giving or sending ultimately return to itself in a circulatory movement within the domain of the same? How can radical difference even be registered as difference without, in that act of reception, assimilating it? Do not these images of incorporation, of ingesting the manna of the Word, affirm that reading consumes difference? Is it possible to eat the Word and encounter the utter otherness of transcendence? The miracle of manna, as Levinas remarks, is not so much that it comes from heaven but that it brings us to the edge of time, that we gather manna but cannot "own" or acknowledge it, that we are nourished by the gift but cannot circulate or return it. It comes as a blow. In preventing all reciprocity, the gift of Scripture places us in a position of "a passivity more passive still than the passivity of matter itself" (*OB* 113–114; *AE* 145). Always eating and never eating, we are nourished by difference yet perpetually desire it: "Desire for what is beyond satisfaction does not identify, as need does, a term or an end" (*GCM* 67; *DVI* 111).[42]

It has become clear that Judaism, a primary source of inspiration for Levinas, also speaks to philosophy, that all reading of the book is the reading of the Book: "National literatures participate in Holy Scripture — Homer and Plato, Racine and Victor Hugo, also Pushkin, Dostoyevsky and Goethe, and of course, Tolstoy and Agnon" (*EI* 117; *EeI* 126). Speaking of his first encounter in the late 1920s with Husserl's *Logical Investigations,* Levinas describes his own experience of rubbing his feet until they bled: "I embarked upon that reading, which was at first extremely difficult, with great industry but also with great perseverance and without any guide at that. It was little by little that the essential truth of Husserl came into focus for me" (29–30; 25). What we have here is not so much a *difficile liberté* (Levinas's term for the freedom-of-responsibility that constitutes Jewish identity) as it is a *difficile lecture* that refuses the free associations of psychoanalytic and literary reading, the contextualizing of historical reading, the calculating distance of critique, and the abstractions and *reductiones* of philosophical reading. Time and again, Levinas describes epiphanies or intellectual junctures in his life in terms of encounters with books: in his youth, Dostoyevsky's *The Idiot;* in Strasbourg, Bergson's *Time and Free Will;* in Freiberg, Heidegger's *Being and Time.*

Ethical Reading

Although he insists on the working discreteness of the two vocabularies, Levinas brings the language of philosophy and that of religion together in the category of the ethical. He speaks of God as *das ganz Andere,* the entirely other. This is not the metaphysical God of the philosophers, the *summum bonum,* the *ens realissimum,* but a being apprehensible by some faculty other than reason, the partisan God of Abraham, Isaac, and Jacob—the unpronounceable YHWH. In ethics, Levinas brings philosophy, that language that can prattle about every subject under the sun, to the limits of its own lexicon, obliging it to utter a name that cannot be pronounced, to write silence. Ethical experience for Levinas involves the encounter with this unfathomable alterity within and without, an experience of transcendence not limited to being in a synagogue, to praying, or to reading the Torah. From how he describes the long months spent in a German camp as a Jewish prisoner of war (protected, as a member of the French armed forces, under the Geneva Convention), we know how Levinas's humanity was restored to him though the affection of a dog he and his fellow-prisoners named Bobby. Religious obligation is not a matter of ceremony so much as it is an unlooked-for act of kindness, as it is the *après vous* when you hold the door for someone. A book or the trust of an animal can make us human again.

The rubbing of feet to bleeding-point, that is, the abrasion of the text through reading awakens truth from letters that are not dead, but asleep. It is what Levinas describes as the struggle between the living word [*le dire*] and its inert trace [*le dit*]: "The living word struggles against this transferring of thought into trace, and struggles against the letter that appears when there is no one there to listen" (*OS* 149; *HS* 221). The trace of the *dire* requires the work of "rubbing" and *sollicitation* to make it a living word again. This labor is what reading [*lire*] is. The work of ethical reading is a shaking of the text back into the living word, disclosing an inherently performative and transformative nature. Even the act of having written this essay, and now of reading it, partakes of that rubbing, that ethical encounter that, like manna, is sufficient only unto the present day. The book appears on the horizon of consciousness through the act of reading. Reading thus becomes, perhaps paradoxically, an oral rather than written event, partaking of the essentially oral nature of the Talmud. Levinas emphasizes that the script of his talmudic readings is just that—a script of a performance "before a room" full of listeners.[43] When challenged about the absence of a philosophy of history in his work, Levinas recounts a further experience of discussing with some priests the crisis of human rights in Latin America, saying that history happened "at least here . . . in the room in which I found myself" (*GCM* 81–82; *DVI* 132). What he means by this is that ethical events, which by definition always occur in the here and now, are what make history. Returning the concept of genealogy to its biblical home, Levinas forges a connection between the present and the past that evades etiological hierarchies of cause and effect in favor of a direct begetting of one ethical encounter by another.

Since Plato, we have been used to thinking of the oral word as vital, if impermanent, and the written as inert, if durable; the former, leaving no retrievable trace, is expended in its own breath; the latter, the archive of thought, is nothing but trace. Does Levinas, despite his solicitude for square letters, then join the long line of philosophers of mind who place the written second to the primacy of the spoken? In valuing the oral, Levinas reembodies its disembodied thought, naming it the "saying" [*le dire*], endowing it with a human face, thereby emphasizing its localness and contingency, as well as its ethicality. Just as YHWH's name cannot be uttered, so can he not be represented unless he appears face to face with man—as he did with Moses when interdicting his own representation in the Ten Commandments. True love for the Infinite cannot engrave any *imago* of its beloved. Its only image is the face of one's neighbor.

The epiphany of the face in Levinasian "orality" leads us to make a distinction between Socratic *bioteon,* which emphasizes the human encounter within and the performative nature of dialectic, and Platonic mentalism, which abstracts the thought uttered from the face of the one uttering it, rendering the logical content of the interlocution extricable from the narrative form of the dialectic exchange. Undoubtedly, this union of literacy (entailing both reading and writing) and orality belongs also to monastic experience, in which books were read aloud to another and mumbled audibly to oneself, the latter in order both to shut out distraction and to commit to memory.[44] So embedded is the experience of reading in community that reading on one's own, as one sometimes does and did, cannot efface the presence of the other. So imprinted on mind and body was a text that it could be experienced without the book. M. Choucani, who taught the young Levinas, "looked like a tramp, and never taught the Talmud having it in front of him. He knew it off by heart. He could tell, when I used to read in front of him, that I had missed a word in the third line below, in small characters."[45] In such cultures, monastic or Judaic, in which books like bread were broken and shared, one may rightly speak of "the experience of texts with no books involved."[46]

Where religion, for Levinas, is primarily associated with solicitude for the book (*EI* 23; *EeI* 17), philosophy favors the transparency of speech. In the epiphany of the face that constitutes the ethical encounter, philosophical speech acquires the gross materiality of a body, and religious reading becomes the reception of a revelation that "can only be the relation with a person, with the other. The Torah is given in the Light of a face.... A direct optics—without the mediation of any idea—can only be achieved as ethics" (*NT* 47; *QT* 103–04). Ethical reading, which is nothing less than the receiving of revelation, can only occur when the gaze of the face is direct and not oblique. The face, that is, is only a face when it looks full upon one's own. Face to face is the only position to receive the gift of the Torah, requiring a direct optics redeemed from the ancient identification of sight with theory. We have lost this sense of the upturned face from our vocabulary of literacy, a sense still evident in the medieval term *praelectio*—a "reading" [*-lectio*] aloud of the word "before" [*prae-*] the face of another.[47] Where German retains this sense of communion in its word for "lecture"— *Vorlesung,* literally a "before-reading"—English has no counterpart, the popular sense of "lecture" having depreciated to authoritative, even dogmatic, pronouncement. Although "prelection" survived from Latin as an English word, its meaning subtly alters, acquiring, by the seventeenth century, the sense of having read something beforehand.[48]

But how, we might ask, can a book have the ethical presence of a face? How can it be anything other than the tomb of living speech, for, in Levinas's thought, the face is no metaphor; the face is a speaking face. But then neither is the book a metaphor: "The Holy Scriptures do not signify through the dogmatic narration of some supernatural or sacred origin, but through the expression of the face of the other man that they illuminate.... For me they have meaning by reason of all that they have awakened within their readers throughout the course of the centuries and of all that they have received from their exegeses and transmission" (*EI* 117; *EeI* 126). In the Jewish tradition, the Torah has living presence—a point that forcibly impressed itself upon Samuel Pepys, who, despite his high spirits from having been recently eased of a bout of chronic constipation, was deeply dismayed by the spectacle of the festival of *Simhat Torah* ("the Rejoicing of the Law"), during which Jews danced for joy with the Torah as if holding another person.[49] Scripture increases in the authority of its humanity through the accretion of commentary and exegesis, bearing, as it were, the stigmata of past readings and inescapably marked by history. Far from being the tomb of living speech, Scripture is the memory of one's neighbor. Always reading, we remember and meditate upon the past; yet never reading, only the present is in focus.

The beautiful writing of Scripture is what makes tradition possible—not a dead tradition but one that has shaped what we are now. Where critique must break free from tradition, converting the calligraphy into print, reenacting a perpetual modernity, and erasing its own origins in history through the *origin*-ality of reason, ethical reading shoulders the gravity of a past whose very mark is those heavy square letters of the Torah. Levinas does not imply that this ethical encounter is singular to Judaism. Christianity shares the same holy book with Jews, and the cherishing of tradition is central to medieval experiences of the book: "In books I discover the dead as if they were alive," observes Richard of Bury.[50] The ethical remains a universal possibility, not just for Jews, or for Jews and Christians (*EI* 114–17; *EeI* 123–27). But despite this ecumenism, the Judaic tradition speaks particularly to the living contemporaneity of the past. The Holocaust's attempt to erase of the letters of the Torah, already long claimed to be dead print superseded by the good news of the New Law, forcibly demonstrated to Levinas the lateness of the Jew and the impossibility of effacing the script of history: "For the first time, this incorrigible latecomer of Sacred History is on time."[51]

We must revise, then, the flat assertion that ethics entails just an inescapable responsibility for the other—a characterization that does not sufficiently acknowledge the relation between alterity and the past. Levinas's commitment to the epiphany of the face—an event that firmly situates the ethical in the present moment—is one and the same with a commitment to tradition. Is Levinas then covertly positing the past, history, as the ground of alterity and thereby undermining the absoluteness of the face of the other? When he invokes the authority of history, it is not the finished events of antiquity that he seeks, for those heavy square letters of Scripture contain the Tetragrammaton, which, in its interdiction against the erasure of even one of its syllables, figures "the trace of a past prior to any historical past capable of being remembered."[52] Levinasian traditionalism invests ethics with a genealogy; the irremissible immediacy of the present resonates with the past. The received division of the world into the one and the many dissolves before the epiphany of a face that is descended from all other faces.

Levinas understood, despite his differences from Husserl's method, that his work was phenomenological in inspiration (*GCM* 87; *DVI* 139–40), and it is this intuition that "God himself can know a material thing only by turning around it" that combines with the solicitude for the Book he inherited from a Jewish cultural legacy (*EI* 31; *EeI* 27). Alongside his grasp of the material, which comes from both phenomenology and Jewish literalism, stands an awareness of transcendence. In his seeking of the plain meaning and the hidden mystery within the text—apparent opposites that turn out not to be so different from each other—we recognize both how talmudic exegesis has shaped his phenomenology and how deep is its affinity to the medieval.[53]

3

Levinas, Allegory, and Chaucer's *Clerk's Tale*

Susan Yager

> An allegory is not a simple
> auxiliary to thought.
> — Emmanuel Levinas

Although Emmanuel Levinas has seldom (if ever) been called an allegorist, some of his writings share surprising elements with medieval allegory. His work, for example, is rich in figurative language, including such terms as the *face,* the *trace,* the *hostage,* and the *neighbor.* It is also evocative, recursive, radically resistant to closure, and thus itself, in a sense, allegorical. Indeed the radical openness of Levinas's writings, which I here identify with the allegorical mode, explains why practitioners in so many disciplines have found inspiration in his ideas; his thought can be taken in many directions, interpreted multiple ways. The fluidity and fecundity of Levinasian discourse give it its closest affinity with medieval allegory; in reading from either set of Levinasian or medieval texts, we are drawn into a tentative, contingent enterprise.

Examining the parallels between Levinas's writing and medieval allegory is useful, then, not only in the encounter with Levinas but also in experiencing fully the alterity or otherness of medieval literature. On the one hand, thinking about Levinas allegorically helps us to navigate his "notoriously difficult" texts;[1] we can read them as gestures, offerings in a particular direction but nonetheless incomplete, calling for a response from us. On the other hand, thinking through medieval allegory in a Levinasian vein invites us to participate in a process of ethical reading, allowing the radical otherness of medieval texts to rest with us. We read, as it were, gently; we read, as I will explain below, *as if* we could fully understand.[2] Such an ethical reading is akin to conversation, not assertion, and can open anew the process of inter-pretation. I will demonstrate such a Levinasian approach in a treatment of Chaucer's *Clerk's Tale.*

THE LEVINASIAN SUBJECT AS UNDER-STANDING ALLEGORY

It should be clear from the outset that neither the medieval literature I have in mind nor the writings of Levinas participate in what we might call *mere* allegory, that is, in a simplistic correspondence of surface and hidden meanings, which is the legacy of Romanticism. Samuel Coleridge, for example, dismisses allegory as a fossil, distinct from the resonance and dynamism of symbol: "an Allegory is but a translation of abstract notions into a picture-language which is itself nothing but an abstraction from objects of the senses; the principal being more worthless even than its phantom proxy, both alike unsubstantial, and the former shapeless to boot."[3] Against this notion of mere allegory, I wish to foreground Jon Whitman's definition from etymology: alle-gory, from *allos* and *agoreuein,* speaks "otherwise" than in the "official assembly" or "open marketplace."[4] That is, allegory is not part of "official" or authorized discourse — it eludes or circumvents it; and it is not overt, rather being something veiled or undisclosed. According to Whitman, the word also suggests "to 'speak otherwise,' to 'say other things,' to say other than that which is meant."[5]

It is in this sense of allegory that we find a Levinasian resonance. It is important here to keep in mind Ewa Rychter's observation that the *allos* of allegory is not in itself the absolute Other so central to Levinasian thought.[6] However, the *allos* is "otherwise than usual," a difference that takes into account the difficulty of communication. As Maureen Quilligan points out, allegory possesses "the possibility of an otherness, a polysemy, inherent in the very words on the page."[7] The polysemy of medieval allegory, its difference from the reader, and its multiplicity and elusiveness are what give it affinities with Levinasian thinking.

Although, as I will explain below, some of Levinas's works enact or participate in allegory as Whitman defines it, Levinas at times expressed an antipathy toward allegory and indeed toward much of art. As Jill Robbins characterizes Levinas's early position, "Art consists in substituting for the object its image ... it is an obscuring or shadow of reality."[8] In his 1948 essay "Reality and Its Shadow," Levinas describes allegory as "an ambiguous commerce with reality in which reality does not refer to itself but to its reflection" (*LR* 135). This description treats allegory in a Coleridgian sense, as something worthless and sterile. Later in the essay Levinas makes a connection between allegory, in this Coleridgian sense, and truth: "In art allegory is introduced to the world, as truth is accomplished in cognition" (136).

In order to understand the strength of this criticism, we must bear in mind that Levinas's great project—establishing ethics, not ontology, as first philosophy—places "truth" in a subordinate position to the ethical, as it subordinates an individual's assertion or thought to the relationship with the other. Because, for Levinas, the key relationship is the ethical, the face to face relationship that precedes and is beyond being, it cannot be reduced to mere cognition or to what he calls "thematization" (*TI* 96). Thus he opposes the philosophical given that "the veritable thought is a true thought, a knowing, a thought referred to Being" (*EI* 166). Anything concretely known or understood places ontology over ethics and partakes in the process by which the other is always reduced to or subsumed by the same. As Levinas puts it in "Reality and Its Shadow," art participates in this process of subsuming the other in the same because it represents beings by means of their images; there is no ethical, face to face encounter with the represented being. In the "finitude of an artwork," in Rychter's phrase,[9] beings are represented, fixed, frozen; thus, for Levinas, art is associated with being, and as such is a mechanism for the perpetuation of the same. As Gerald L. Bruns explains, "An image is, so to speak, not a piece of consciousness, but a piece of the *il y a:* it is a materialization of being, the way a cadaver is the image of the deceased."[10] Thus, for Levinas, "The whole of reality bears on its face its own allegory, outside of its revelation and its truth. In utilizing images art not only reflects, but brings about this allegory" (*LR* 136). This view, like Coleridge's, considers allegory as static and rigid, corresponding to the totalizing reduction of the other to the same.

However, even though Levinas rejects such a notion of allegory, his writings are themselves highly figurative, and his thought is often expressed in terms of literary allusion and metaphor. Keeping in mind Levinas's stress upon the infinity of ethical obligation over the totality of being, we can understand his writing as allegorical in Whitman's sense of the term, as endeavoring to escape from, or function "otherwise" than in, the totality. This relationship begins in and is carried on through language, through speech, but speech understood as expressive rather than what might be called declarative communication, the conveyance of claims or ideas. A taxonomy of utterance exists in Levinas's work that enables us to distinguish speech or ethical communication from other kinds of utterance. For Levinas, voice or speech is associated with the face, the ethical encounter with the other; language is "produced only in the face-to-face; and in language we have recognized teaching" (*TI* 295). To respond to the call of the other, to enter the ethical face to face relationship, is to engage in *discours* (discourse or conversation); this relationship is distinct from disclosure, or truth, where the other is presented as a theme. According to Levinas, the "welcoming of the face and the work of justice—which condition the birth of truth itself—are not interpretable in terms of disclosure" (*TI* 28). Levinas distinguishes disclosure, which I understand to mean a complete, predicated utterance, from revelation, "a coinciding of the expressed with him who expresses, which is the privileged manifestation of the Other." To disclose, he says, is "already to miss the noumenon" (66–67).

Levinas does not wish to "limit the revealing function of language to its coherence, conveying the coherence of concepts;" such a function of language "would consist in suppressing 'the other,' in making the other agree with the same! But in its expressive function language precisely maintains the other—to whom it is addressed, whom it calls upon or invokes." If, according to Levinas, we are to respect the other, "the relationship of discourse is required; pure 'disclosure,' where he is proposed as a theme, does not respect him enough for that. *We call justice this face to face approach, in conversation.*" We hear the voice of the other as a call or a command, not as a theme, nor as a statement or predication. In contrast, "Reason...conducts a monologue," and not a conversation; that is, it emerges from the first person and claims a universal application (*TI* 71–73). As Levinas puts it, "The presence of the Other, or expression, source of all signification, is not contemplated as an intelligible essence, but is heard as language" (297). Language as expression, then, partakes of the infinity; language as a collection of statements (what Levinas calls, in a delightful phrase, "the anarchy of facts") participates in the totality (70). Ethical communication is therefore discursive, a saying [*dire*] and not the totalizing said [*dit*]. Like the *me voici* ("Here I am," I Sam. 3) which Levinas describes as the ethical response to the call of the Other, such communication is prior to knowledge.

   To sum up, for Levinas the ethical relation appears and is maintained in language, but in expression or discourse rather than truth claims or disclosure. If a claim is true, if it is reasonable, it compels consent—and in so doing, it forces conformity with the realm of the same. Unlike the truth claims of disclosure, proclaimed in the grammatical indicative, expressive language is essentially, according to Levinas, an "interpellation, the vocative," which calls one to presence and to relationship (as opposed to objective knowledge, to history and fact). Here, then, is allegory in its other sense, in Whitman's definition. Levinas's speech is allegorical precisely because it is a matter of expression, a call, not an argument or claim. Allegory is *not* the language of the assembly or of the public marketplace. Such language is public, overt, and as a matter of law, or an assertion of fact, this language participates in the power and totality of the same. We may say that such language is "up for grabs" in the etymological sense, in that it can be *comprehended*. But invocation, Levinas makes clear, is not comprehension: "The invoked is not what I comprehend: *he is not under a category,*" not thematized or made an object (*TI* 69). Allegory, then, is expressed but not disclosed in the Levinasian sense.

And yet how is language—how is philosophy, or any other kind of discourse—possible without cognition? How can thematization be avoided? This problem is central to Levinas: if whatever can be articulated as "known" is already part of the order of the same, then articulation itself is already somehow tainted, is already as Levinas puts it "a thought referred to Being." Whatever one strives to express in itself violates alterity; it necessarily belongs to, or is absorbed into, the same. Levinas's own work is subject to this critique, that "in the course of articulating his claim that ethics is beyond being and so unthematizable, he makes a theme of the unthematizable."[11] Ethical communication is possible, according to Levinas, in the vocative or the call to the other, as a matter of the saying and not the said. Such communication, however, cannot begin with the ego; it begins, as Levinas states in *Otherwise Than Being,* "with subjectivity understood as self, with the exciding and dispossession, in which the ego does not appear, but immolates itself" (*OB* 118). In what Levinas calls "the transcendence involved in language" we find "a relationship that is not an empirical speech, but responsibility." Communication, Levinas continues, involves "uncertainty and sacrifice": "It is only in this way that the absolutely exterior other is near to the point of obsession. Here there is proximity and not truth about proximity, not certainty about the presence of the other, but responsibility for him without deliberation, and without the compulsion of truths in which commitments arise, without certainty. This responsibility commits me, and does so before any truth and any certainty" (120).

For Levinas, the ethical relationship makes communication possible as something prior to, or otherwise than, a constitutive utterance. Here we may begin to perceive more clearly that ethical language in Levinas contains an allegorical dimension. It is otherwise than public—a matter, as Sandor Goodhart has put it, of "the two, not the three."[12] It is a mystery, a language without certainty. Its discursivity is inexhaustible, as the ethical response to the other is not bound by time; yet it is not a dialogue, but a discourse of asymmetry. The element of uncertainty in the ethical communication commits us to the "Here

I am," to listening; this is a matter of responsibility to the other, not one of cognition or truth (*OB* 119).

A similar commitment binds the reader of allegory. Although clarity and univocality are not constitutive of allegory, nonetheless we are obliged not to misconstrue it. The strangeness of allegorical literature, perhaps more than literature in other modes, invites, even demands interpretation; yet allegory, in J. Hillis Miller's expression, "keeps its secrets."[13] As a kind of literature that never reveals all its meaning, allegory is a continuing discourse, a saying rather than a said, "a state of openness to the other."[14] It is possible to come near to—or, in a Levinasian sense, ap-*proximate*—definitive meaning in allegory, but never possible to reach it. In Levinasian terms, we may say that the allegorical resists determinate meaning, resists totalization (and is thus entirely different from Coleridge's idea); there is always more *to* allegory, always a surplus that exceeds any particular take or interpretation. In sum, this otherwise of language can be located only in the moment of invocation. And what the speaking voice, the face that speaks in the ethical relationship, expresses cannot be reduced to mere cognition. It remains open, compels reading but resists closure, approaching clarity but never reaching it.

Composing Allegorically; or, Levinas amidst the Middle English Poets

The discussion so far has concerned theoretical or descriptive parallels between Levinas's thought and medieval allegory. In addition, however, we can find elements in these two bodies of writing, shared features of composition, that facilitate an approximation of meaning but do not determine it. One such feature which we have already witnessed is the use of grammar as a mechanism for expression. Levinas is extremely careful in using grammatical features such as case and mood in his efforts to describe the ethical. The horror of being, for example, is described as the *il y a*, the "there is." In *Totality and Infinity*, the essential aspect of the relation of language is "the interpellation, the vocative" (*TI* 69). Levinas describes the ethical response to the other as the response of one accused, that is, one in the accusative case; the proper response to the other's call is not *je* but *me: Me voici.* Levinas uses grammar as metaphor extensively in *Otherwise Than Being,* notably the discussion of the immediate obligation of one for the other: "it is to be an undeclinable *One,* speaking." Grammatical case is also an important component of Levinas's discussion of responsibility: "Everything is from the start in the accusative. Such is the exceptional condition or unconditionality of the self, the signification of the pronoun *self* for which our Latin grammars themselves know no nominative form" (*OB* 92, 112).

Levinas's use of the grammatical metaphor has antecedents in medieval literature both Latin and vernacular, as John A. Alford has explained in his article "The Grammatical Metaphor: A Survey of Its Use in the Middle Ages."[15] Grammatical case and number, for example, provided medieval writers with opportunities for wordplay, sexual puns, and religious edification, as well as direct application in allegory. In William Langland's *Piers Plowman,* for example, the stages of moral perfection are explained "by analogy with the positive, comparative, and superlative degrees of an adjective or adverb" and defined "by means of the grammatical concept of 'infinites' ": "Dowel and Dobet arn two infinites, / Whiche infinites, with a feith fynden oute Dobest" (B.13.127–28).[16] Making use of grammar as metaphor allows for expression at its most abstract, for openness without thematization.

Another feature of Levinas's writing that parallels elements of medieval allegory is its use of figurative language bordering on personification allegory. Again, this language operates by means of association and resemblance, rather than straightforward assertion. For example, to return to a line, cited above, from *Otherwise Than Being:* "It is with subjectivity understood as self, with the exciding and dispossession, in which the ego does not appear, but immolates itself, that the relationship with the other can be communication and transcendence." The ego "that immolates itself" has agency and movement, and is close to a personification of Ego. Levinas's ideas concerning the body also, it seems to me, have a close affinity with personification allegory, for example: "The seeking of the caress constitutes its essence by the fact that *the caress does not know what it seeks*" (*TO* 89; emphasis mine). The caress possesses desires, movement, potentially knowledge; it would be at home with Beauty and Goods in *Everyman*.

Some of Levinas's work also resembles medieval allegory in its use of terse and minimal language to achieve paradoxical effects. For example, in Levinas's 1966 essay on Maurice Blanchot, "The Servant and her Master," the syntax forestalls assertion by defining a thing as its opposite: "Forgetting against reminiscence, waiting that is not waiting for something" (*LR* 155). This technique is commonly seen in the medieval expression of paradox, notably in Geoffrey Chaucer's *Book of the Duchess:* "In travayle ys myn ydelnesse / And eke my reste; my wele is woo, / My good ys harm" (lines 602ff.).[17] The oxymora of the lover's sufferings describe a rootless, unstable state in language that resists certain understanding.

Sentence fragments also offer Levinas a means of achieving suggestion without assertion, for example in these lines from "The Servant and her Master": "A discontinuous and contradictory language of scintillation. A language which can give sign above and beyond all signification. A sign made from afar, from beyond and in the beyond" (*LR* 156) and in this passage from "Ethics as First Philosophy": "Responsibility for the Other, for the naked face of the first individual to come along. A responsibility that goes beyond what I may or may not have done to the Other or whatever acts I may or may not have committed, as if I were devoted to the other man before being devoted to myself" (*LR* 83). Although these are but a few examples from Levinas's work, such fragments may be understood as gestures, as suggestions. In this respect they share the evocative polysemy of medieval lyric, for example:

> Foweles in þe frith,
> þe fisses in þe flod—
> And I mon waxe wod!
> Mulch sorw I walke with,
> For beste of bon and blod.[18]
> [Birds in the wood, / fish in the sea— / And I must go insane! / I walk with great sorrow, / For the best of bone and blood.]

The lyric begins with two truncated fragments, simple images, before turning to two brief statements. Its deep ambiguity is not simply a riddle or binary, that, upon detection, deconstructs. Rather, read in a Levinasian vein as a call, as invocation rather than assertion, the lyric partakes of multiple meanings, each aspect of which deserves a hearing, even as its declarative meaning remains unobtainable. Is sorrow to be taken as a personification, for example? Are we to read beste as "best," or "beast"? Any interpretive decision would thematize the lyric, render it as not saying but said. The only move to make, therefore—that is, the only ethical reading—is to read gently, contingently.

Levinas's use of sentence fragments allows him to dispense, at least at times, with verbs altogether. Because employment of a verb, in any utterance, articulates the predicate, it thematizes the grammatical subject, forcing it into the ontological realm. Use of "to be," according to Levinas, places us in the realm of the said:

> It is clear that the verb *to be,* or the verb *to consist,* is used in the formulas...that name the hither side of being. It is also clear that being makes its apparition, shows itself, in the said. As soon as saying, on the hither side of being, becomes dictation, it expires, or abdicates, in fables and in writing. If being and manifestation go together in the said, it is in fact natural that if the saying on the hither side of the said can show itself, it be said already in terms of being (OB 43).

Thus, if any outright statement that *A is B* is a totalizing move, then avoiding the verb allows one to avoid the totalizing predication. Jacques Derrida criticized this desire of Levinas: "according to Levinas, non-violent language would be a language which would do without the verb *to be,* that is, without predication....Would such a language still deserve its name?"[19]

Levinas clearly thought so, and he found a means of avoiding the totalizing predicate by use of the phrase *comme si,* or "as if." This phrase does not describe a state of being, per se, but one of possibility; it speaks the language of the infinite other in contrast to the totalizing same. The language of *comme si* is evocative and dreamlike, allowing for possibility while avoiding assertion. For example, Levinas writes in "Ethics as First Philosophy":

It is *as if* that inevitable death...were already 'regarding' me prior to confronting me, and becoming the death that stares me in the face. The other man's death calls me into question, *as if,* by my possible future indifference, I had become the accomplice of the death to which the other...is exposed; and *as if,* even before vowing myself to him, I had to answer for this death of the other, and accompany the Other in his mortal solitude. The Other becomes my neighbour precisely through the way the face summons me, calls for me, begs for me, and in so doing recalls my responsibility, and calls me into question (*LR* 83; emphasis mine).

The passage itself is lucid although its claims are tentative, only partially articulate; the phrase *comme si* carves out possible meanings, as a sculptor carves out the space around his statue, but it also shelters the nominative from the predicate, giving us in Levinas's phrase "not knowing but proximity."

Elsewhere, in a footnote to "From Consciousness to Wakefulness," Levinas comments directly upon his double use of *comme si* in a sentence about an insomnia or wakefulness that rends consciousness "*as if* there could be an idea of the Infinite: that is, *as if* God could abide within me" (*GCM* 26). The "as if" in this sentence, Levinas writes, is not the same as the prudential *als ob* (as if) used by philosophers when they want to convey an uncertainty that remains "attached to the truth-result" (190 n. 30). Instead, it expresses "the equivocation or the enigma of the nonphenomenon, the nonrepresentable: a witnessing" to "enigmatic significance and, only thus, signifying beyond being or God" (190).

Levinas's use of *comme si* reveals perhaps his strongest affinity with the allegorical mode and with medieval thought. Consider, for example, the multiple meanings of "perle wyþouten spot" in the first section of the Middle English *Pearl.* The recursivity of the phrase, and its manifold significance, throughout this section exemplify the Levinasian approximation of meaning:

> Perle, plesaunte to prynces paye
> To clanly clos in golde so clere,
> Oute of oryent, I hardyly saye,

Ne proued I neuer her precios pere.
So rounde, so reken in vche araye,
So smal, so smoþe her sydeȝ were,
Quere-so-euer I jugged gemmeȝ gaye,
I sette hyr sengeley in synglere.
Allas! I leste hyr in on erbere;
Þurȝ gresse to grounde hit fro me yot.
I dewyne, fordolked of luf-daungere
Of þat pryuy perle wyþouten spot.   (I.1–12)[20]

[Pearl, pleasant to a prince's delight, / So chastely set in such bright
gold; / in all the orient, I boldly say, / I never found her peer in value.
/ So round, so lovely in every setting, / So small and smooth her sides
were; / Wherever I assessed lovely jewels, / I placed her alone in her
uniqueness. / Alas! I lost her in a garden; / Through grass to ground
it fell from me. / I languish, wounded by the aloofness of that mysterious pearl without spot.]

In this passage, the *perle* is described *as if* a jewel, a woman, a seed;
spot, likewise, *as if* a literal place, as if a sin or imperfection. The poem is
nearly untranslatable, since to translate necessitates a choice among its
possibilities; is the pearl's "luf-daungere" absence, or standoffishness?
Pryuy, which could be read as "special," "private," or "unknown,"
is similarly difficult. Does the shift of pronoun from "her" to "it" in
line 10 refer to a body, a corpse, rather than to a person? Or is it a
reference to a jewel, or a seed in the garden? The pleasure, and the
problem, of reading a text like *Pearl*, like "Foweles in the Frith," is
that no single reading can suffice. Interpretations may draw near to
(in Levinasian terms, approximate) a definitive take, but to read it in
one exclusive way is to do it (again, in a Levinasian sense) an injustice.
To read these texts gently, without violence, is not to force a specific
approach, whether Robertsonian, historicist, or psychoanalytic. Their
attraction is this lack of closure, this suspension. This is allegory that
is always saying, never said, that has a performative dimension.

This "as if" is even stronger in Chaucer, whose dominant persona
relates everything "so as it semed me" (*CT* I.39).[21] Like Levinas,
Chaucer depends on nuance and possibility rather than plain statement,
as in the *General Prologue,* "Housbondes at chirche dore she hadde

fyve, / Withouten oother compaignye in youthe" (I.460–61). In such instances, determinate meaning (or predication) is partially offered, then withdrawn. We do not know, with certainty, whether the Wife had "oother compaignye" in her younger days—this has not been definitively said—though the suggestion is there. We would not label such passages as allegory, certainly, but in their resistance to definitive readings they operate similarly, creating what Donald Howard calls "a literary idea, whose possibilities [are] inexhaustible."[22]

The openness of the text, and the parallels to Levinas's *comme si*, are strongest in passages where Chaucer's syntax contributes to the reader's uncertainty. In many such passages "as" has been described as pleonastic, or superfluous,[23] but frequently "as" performs the same function as does *comme si* in Levinas. For example, in the *Merchant's Tale* Januarie dreams of his lady-love:

> Many fair shap and many a fair visage
> Ther passeth thurgh his herte nyght by nyght,
> As whoso tooke a mirour, polisshed bryght,
> And sette it in a commune market-place,
> Thanne sholde he se ful many a figure pace
> By his mirour.   (*CT* IV.1580–83)

In this passage all the things that make Januarie's love-search odious— the emphasis on surface beauty, the notion that he can purchase a wife—are tucked within the "as" clause. There is no predication here, strictly speaking; Januarie does not actually do the things which are nonetheless associated with him. Januarie and the "commune market-place" are linked inextricably yet only by suggestion, by proximity.

In the *Troilus*, this sort of ambiguity occurs when Criseyde is described in book II:

> Criseyde, which that wel neigh starf for feere,
> So as she was the ferfulleste wight
> That myght be, and herde ek with her ere
> And saugh the sorwful ernest of the knyght,
> And in his preier ek saugh noon unryght,
> And for the harm that myghte ek fallen moore,
> She gan to rewe and dredde hire wonder soore.   (*TC* II.449–55)

Here everything following "which that" belongs in a subordinate clause; "so as," which could mean "because," introduces a second such clause. Thus her state of mind is suggested or alluded to, but not precisely defined. Many phrases in *Troilus* exhibit this lack of closure. Because "as she that" can be rendered in two ways—as "because" or "like a woman who"—it too resists precise translation. Instead, it behaves like the Levinasian *comme si*, as when Criseyde is "ful sore in drede, / As she that nyste what was best to rede; / For bothe a widewe was she and allone / Of any frend to whom she dorste hir mone" (*TC* I.95–98).

Is Criseyde a woman alone and afraid, or does she merely resemble such a woman?[24] Much about Criseyde is expressed, in Levinasian terms, but nothing is disclosed; we see her fear, as in the quotation above, now as ground, now as figure. The apparently useless "as" tilts the semantic balance of Chaucer's expressions, rendering them, finally, unfathomable.

To bring Levinas's writings into proximity with medieval allegory illumines both sets of difficult texts. These briefly sketched parallels do not indicate a direct influence or correspondence between medieval allegory and Levinasian thought, but do suggest a relationship between them. This relationship, as we have seen, concerns both a resistance to definitive interpretation and some similarities in compositional technique that bring about allegorical open-endedness. But these traits serve, as it were, another, larger connection between Levinas's writings and much medieval literature—whether or not it would be classified as allegory proper. They share a fundamental concern about knowledge and truth, and about the inadequacies of cognition or reason. This shared concern invites cross-readings between Levinas and the medieval, and raises the possibility of allegorizing—that is, reopening —texts in relation to Levinasian thought.

CHAUCER'S CLERK'S TALE AS ETHICAL ALLEGORY; OR, THE MASTER AND HIS SERVANT

In the case of Chaucer's *Clerk's Tale*, the possibilities of cross-reading are especially rich because the story itself has an ethical dimension in the Levinasian sense, and because it has been treated by critics, with varying success, as a species of allegory.[25] Reading this complex story of the imperious Walter, who marries Grisilde only if she promises never to contest him, "Neither by word ne frownyng contenance" (*CT* IV.356), can be, as Derek Pearsall said, "a painful experience."[26] Some of that pain manifests as reader resistance, especially to Grisilde; I have witnessed many students express shock or disdain toward Grisilde's astonishing abnegation. Others would not or *could* not read the story; it was too alien, too embittering. Indeed, to many modern readers both Walter and Grisilde are grotesque, and the story as a whole opaque. Yet the *Clerk's Tale* retains its importance, I think precisely because of this challenge. Charlotte Morse has argued that present-day readers are ill-prepared to read "literary texts that mean to effect a moral or spiritual change in us, as the tale of Grisilde" intends.[27] Morse has also claimed that the *Clerk's Tale* "literally strikes home, challenging our private behavior. The experience of World War II demystified the political dimension of private choices, making Grisilde more difficult than she had ever seemed."[28] Its very intractability, Grisilde's matchless patience and Walter's apparent cruelty, make it necessary that the *Clerk's Tale* continue to be read and taught; and it seems fitting that a philosopher whose thinking was profoundly shaped by his experiences in that war can provide a means of considering the ethical implications of the tale.

Though I will treat both Walter and Grisilde in my reading, I focus primarily on Walter and try to show how his inability to see the face of the other, to hear the other's voice has the potential to distract the reader from the ethical import of this tale. The reader may too quickly understand Grisilde, as Walter does, as simply an extension of Walter's totalizing regime. To read only from this position, however, potentially limits Grisilde's presence in the narrative and inhibits the reader from perceiving Grisilde precisely in a state of Levinasian hyperbolic passivity — standing before unruly Walter as one who commands him through this very passivity. This consideration of Walter's blindness (and even deafness), a condition easily appropriated by the reader, offers not a reading, per se, but rather a tentative attempt at opening possible readings without determining one interpretation. The parallels are such, however, that considering the *Clerk's Tale* in a Levinasian mode, highlighting the open-ended nature of the narrative, we may able to say the failure of previous allegorical interpretations is a mark of Chaucer's success as an ethical allegorist.

To begin, Walter's cruelty can be partially understood if we view him as the epitome of the Levinasian autonomous self, a "citizen of paradise" (*TI* 144). Fair, strong and gently born, a ruler "Biloved and drad" (*CT* IV.69), Walter seems blameworthy only in that "on his lust present was al his thought" (IV.80). Hints of advancing age and inevitable death are the only shadows on Walter's pleasant life: his people, fearing to be left without a ruler, beg him to marry and produce an heir, a state which would surely be a "yok / Of soveraynetee, noght of servyse" (IV.113–14). Although he had "rejoysed" in his liberty (IV.145), Walter declares that "of my free wyl I wole assente / To wedde me," warning only that his choice of wife will not be gainsaid (IV.150–51). This powerful, self-sufficient Walter is, in Levinasian terms, at home in the realm of the same. Even the wording of his promise, "To wedde me," offers no recognition of another person, let alone a relationship, as the phrase may be translated as "To get myself married." We recall that for Levinas the response to the call of the Other, to the speaking face, is that of Samuel to God: "Here I am," or *Me voici;* "speak, for your servant hears." But Walter, the hedonistic "I," *le moi,* can be understood as master as the story begins, not servant; he has not yet been accused (that is, turned into a "me") by encountering the face of the other. Seen in this guise, his pledge to marry, hemmed about by his desire not to be gainsaid, subsumes the will of his people to his own—a reduction of the other, the people, to Walter's same. The story's details give further instances of his relationship with them: the people thank him, humbly, on their knees; Walter gives commands to his officers and "to his privee knyghtes and squieres / Swich charge yaf as hym liste on hem leye; / And they to his comandement obeye" (IV.192–94). At the end of part 1, we can read Walter as simply a totalitarian, exercising power unopposed.

This totalizing drive appears again in part 2, in which Walter takes Grisilde as his bride. While it is true that Walter had looked upon Grisilde "in sad wyse" (*CT* IV.237) and acknowledged her virtue, she is finally just another "creature" (IV.232) on whom his eye falls as he rides hunting; if he must take a wife, he will take her. Walter's will is emphasized throughout the marriage-proposal scene; he declares "Thy doghter wol I take" (IV.307) and Janicula quakes, "My willynge / Is as ye wole," adding, "I wol no thynge, ye be my lord so deere; / Right as yow lust, governeth this mateere" (IV.319–22). Walter exercises his power most famously in his "demandes" of Grisilde:

> "... be ye redy with good herte
> To al my lust, and that I frely may,
> As me best thynketh, do yow laughe or smerte,
> And nevere ye to grucche it, nyght ne day?
> And eek whan I sey 'ye,' ne sey nat 'nay,'
> Neither by word ne frownyng contenance?
> Swere this, and heere I swere oure alliance."   (IV.351–57)

Grisilde, in sharp contrast, may be read as exemplifying the ethical response to the call of the other. She cares for her father "in greet reverence and charitee" (IV.221) and does "everich obeisaunce and diligence" (IV.230) to respect and honor him. In her generous, unselfish behavior toward Janicula and also toward Walter's proposal, Grisilde acknowledges an asymmetrical obligation: "The markys cam and gan hire for to calle ... / And doun upon hir knes she gan to falle, / And with sad contenance kneleth stille, / Til she had herd what was the lordes wille" (IV.289, 292–94). Although she is surprised by Walter's proposal, her response is one of acceptance: "Wondrynge upon this word, quakynge for drede" (IV.358), she acknowledges her obligation, declaring herself "undigne and unworthy" (IV.359).

Grisilde's behavior parallels not the response of the egoistic *moi* but that of the ethical *me* which is called into being by relationship with the other. For Levinas the ethical self kneels before the other, sacrificing its own liberty to the other's call: "Vulnerability, exposure to outrage, passivity more passive than all patience," even "to the point of persecution...all this is the self" (*OB* 15). Grisilde also enacts the Levinasian other for Walter; her steadfast "call" over the course of their marriage is eventually heard. The similarities between Grisilde and the ethical other are numerous. The other is lowly, yet somehow powerful, as is Grisilde. The face—and indeed the body—of the other is naked, as is Grisilde when she is prepared for the wedding and again when she returns to her father's house. For Levinas, "The face in its nakedness as a face presents to me the destitution of the poor one and the stranger" but the "poor one, the stranger, presents himself as an equal" (*TI* 213). And although Grisilde makes no claims to equality, nor even to value, clearly as a judge and a human being she is more than equal to Walter. She is also, though in no way an erotic figure, a manifestation of the Levinasian feminine. Levinas's figuring of the Other as feminine has been, of course, subject to vigorous critique,[29] yet it is important to bear in mind that, in Tina Chanter's phrase, "*The feminine* is a privileged term in Levinas, since in it alterity is accomplished."[30] We may understand Grisilde as both other to Walter, and as the ethical self; her femininity encompasses the mystery, generosity, and hospitality she extends to Walter, and even to his replacement wife in part 6.

In one respect, however, Grisilde seems not to exemplify the Levinasian other.[31] According to Levinas, the *me voici* is immediately accompanied by a command, "Thou shalt not kill." The "first word of the face," according to Levinas, "is the 'Thou shalt not Kill.' It is an order. There is a commandment in the appearance of the face, as if a master spoke to me. However, at the same time, the face of the Other is destitute; it is the poor for whom I can do all and to whom I owe all" (*EI* 89). Grisilde, by contrast, and to the readers' horror, tells Walter to go ahead with his plans, whatever *he chooses:* "My child and I, with hertey obeisaunce, / Been youres al, and may ye mowe save or spille / Youre owene thing" (*CT* IV.502–04); she invites him to do "with youre owene thing / Right as yow list" (IV.652–53). More than anything else, the passages highlight not Grisilde's complicity in the act of murder but rather Walter's potential freedom [*soveraynetee*] in the face of the other's vulnerability—that is, his freedom to preserve life. Through Grisilde's passivity, her utter submission [*obeisaunce*] to Walter's desires (and through her constant explicit reminders of this submission), she is able to confront Walter, by offering to him his own responsibility in this manner. The vulnerable face (as defenseless child and as hyperpassive Grisilde) both tempts to murder and challenges with the commandment "Thou shall not murder" ("to save or to spille"). The command against murder exists in the appearance of the face, so we may imagine Walter at this point as still at home in the totality, in the reign of the same; not once has he heard the speech that accompanies her face. Insofar as Grisilde (and his daughter) is merely a "thyng," he cannot recognize her as other. In one sense, he retains the "yok of soveraynetee" which allows him to see Grisilde only within the reign of the same; yet that true soverayntee, that true freedom, offered to him by Grisilde, will come only when he understands the "yok" as a responsibility for which he is most responsible—the very responsibility with which Grisilde's hyperpassivity confronts him.

In understanding freedom divorced from responsibility, Walter cuts himself off from an ethical relation to Grisilde by refusing to allow her any means of opposition, even through the flicker of an expression. Yet her submission to his desire stands precisely as a scandal. Having ruled out in advance any possibility of difference or otherness, Walter guarantees that *to him* she will always be the same, always subsumed. Yet Grisilde resists. There is an elusiveness to her that drives Walter "hir sadness for to knowe" and produces the "merveillous desire his wyf t'assaye" (*CT* IV.452, 454). This is a point of difficulty for many readers, but if we read from a Levinasian perspective, we may see that Walter's epistemological and empirical drive to know, to test, precludes an ethical openness to the other; if she is always thematized, then naturally "he nevere koude hire fynde / But evere in oon ylike sad and kynde" (IV.601–02). Refusing to treat Grisilde ethically, in the Levinasian sense, Walter ensures that to him she is always the same, always subsumed by the totalizing impulse that so frustrates him.

Grisilde, then, can be seen as a mystery to Walter *precisely* because he works so hard to know all about her. As soon as there is predication, she is gone, as the other always exceeds, eludes; at some level she will not be thematized. Again we see in Grisilde the feminine other, since for Levinas, the feminine is "not merely the unknowable, but a mode of being that consists in slipping away from the light" or "withdrawing elsewhere" (*TO* 50). Walter's epistemological bind, then, is that the more he seeks to know, the less he knows. He orders his firstborn, a daughter, and later his young son to be torn from his wife's arms in order to find out whether "by his wyves cheere he myghte se / Or by hire word aperceyve, that she were changed" (*CT* IV.599–601), but of course in neither case can he "fynde variance. / She was ay oon in herte and in visage" (IV.708–11). The "cheere" or face and the spoken word are means by which the other confronts the self, but Walter's resistance to disruption, his refusal of the encounter with alterity, guarantees that he will find only the tyranny of the same.

A Levinasian insight into Walter is especially attractive because of Chaucer's emphasis on the face in this story, evidenced by his focus on the "cheere" not only of Grisilde, but also of Walter, who "feyne[s]" a "drery...cheere" (*CT* IV.513–14), and of the sergeant who seizes the children (IV.541). Of course Chaucer's "face" is not the same as the Levinasian face; one is an item in a narrative, the other a way of conceiving of relationship. Nonetheless, keeping in mind Levinas's idea of the face as relation rather than physical entity, we can appreciate that Walter's staring *at* the face of Grisilde, that "constant...wal" (IV.1047) that he himself has erected, yields no knowledge of her. By contrast, the people of Saluzzo look *into* the face of Grisilde in an ethical relationship. Bruns makes this distinction between *at* and *in* (or *on*), pointing out that for Levinas the "relation to the face is not one of knowing" or "bringing under conceptual control," since it always exceeds what can be thought or known. One can objectify the face, be a mere observer of it rather than enter into relation with it, only by what Bruns calls "a refusal of the face...say by looking *at* it rather than into it. You cannot look *into* a face from the transcendental standpoint of the *ego cogito*."[32] As long as this remains Walter's standpoint, his examination of Grisilde's "cheere" is unavailing.

In contrast to Walter, for the people of Saluzzo Grisilde is so "benigne and so digne of reverence, / And koude so the peples herte embrace, / That ech hire lovede that looked on hir face" (*CT* IV.412–13). Between Grisilde and the people is a relationship of justice, not of violence, notably in Walter's absence:

> If gentil men or othere of hire contree
> Were wrothe, she wolde bryngen hem aton;
> So wise and rype wordes hadde she,
> And juggementz of so greet equitee,
> That she from hevene sent was, as men wende,
> Peple to save and every wronge t'amende.   (IV.436–41)

Levinas's ideas of openness to the other offer one way of reconciling Grisilde's public popularity and her apparent political skills, on the one hand, with her shocking behavior toward Walter on the other. Her lowliness, and her opacity to her husband, are lifted only in the crucial moment when Walter begins to rue his actions concerning her. At this moment, he "gan his herte dresse / To rewen upon hire wyfly stedfastnesse" (*CT* IV. 1049–50). *Dresse*, an interesting verb, here means to prepare or set oneself to a task. Elsewhere in the *Canterbury Tales,* the Man of Law's Custance, on her way to Syria, "Ful pale arist, and dresseth hire to wende" (II.265); the Second Nun prays for help when "to my werk I wol me dresse" (VIII.77). Walter thus prepares his heart for the task of ruing or regretting what he has done, exposing himself at last to the suffering he has inflicted upon Grisilde. Having responded at last to another, to the other, he can see "Hire glade chiere, and no malice at all" (IV.1045) and with the simple phrase "This is ynogh" (IV.1051) ceases the trials he has inflicted. At last Walter and Grisilde are "met yfeere" (IV.1113), so that for each of them, in Simon Critchley's terms, "The face is not something I see, but something I speak to . . . I am not contemplating, I am conversing."[33]

Treating the *Clerk's Tale* in a Levinasian spirit is not, of course, to "do a Levinasian reading," for we cannot simply "apply" Levinas as though his insights were a tool, or amounted to a method. If we tried to do so, we would not succeed; like Grisilde to our Walter, Levinas evades us if we try to push a predication, to know with certainty. Rather, this exercise has brought Levinas and Chaucer only into proximity. Thus I wish to think of this version as an allegorization, an exercise in *ifs*. We may imagine Grisilde *as if* she were the other who displaces Walter and calls him into ethical being. We might therefore envision Grisilde neither as the monster she is sometimes thought nor as a model, as the Envoy to the *Clerk's Tale* bitingly suggests, but rather as an example of what Levinas calls "the holy" (*BPW* 140). We might also think *as if* we were Walter, that it is indeed Walter's totalizing perspective that creates an opaque and frightening Grisilde. We might imagine — or recognize — that as readers we are in league with Walter, and with the Host who holds "governance" (*CT* IV.23) over the pilgrims, and over the Clerk, whom the Host describes as sitting like a "mayde … newe spoused" (IV.2–3).

In the Levinasian allegorical we find reasons for endless reading, and a caution against assuming that we know what we read. Functioning outside the tradition in which "the veritable thought is a true thought, a knowing,"[34] allegory is the not-knowing, a saying and not said. In this sense allegory itself functions as other, displacing its readers from interpretive certainty and making it impossible for readers to be, in Levinasian terms, fully "at home" with what they read.

4

"In his eyes stood a light, not beautiful"
Levinas, Hospitality, *Beowulf*

Eileen A. Joy

> To approach the Other is to put into question my freedom,
> my spontaneity as a living being, my emprise over the things,
> this freedom of a "moving force," this impetuosity of the current
> to which everything is permitted, even murder.
> — Emmanuel Levinas

AN INFINITE AND UNCONDITIONAL HOSPITALITY

I begin with an ending.[1] In *Adieu to Emmanuel Levinas,* Jacques Derrida argues that Emmanuel Levinas's philosophy, especially in *Totality and Infinity,* has bequeathed to us an "immense treatise of hospitality." According to Derrida, although "the word 'hospitality' occurs relatively seldom in *Totality and Infinity,* the word 'welcome' is unarguably one of the most frequent and determinative words in that text."[2] At the very outset of *Totality and Infinity,* Levinas writes about the Other as the "Stranger [*l'Etranger*]...who disturbs the being at home with oneself [*le chez soi*]."[3] In the wake of this disturbance, the ethical subject "is incapable of approaching the Other with empty hands," and by way of "conversation" she "welcomes" the Other's "expression, in which at each instant he overflows the idea a thought would carry away from it."[4] The welcoming [*accueillance*] of the expression of the stranger-Other is a welcoming of a teaching [*enseignement*] that "comes from the exterior" and in which "the very epiphany of the face is produced" (*TI* 51). This is a "face" that is not a material face, per se — the specific physical visage of a specific person — but is, rather, an "exteriority that is not reducible . . . to the interiority of memory," an expression of being that "overflows images" and "breaks through the envelopings" and facades of material form. This face exceeds any possible preconceptions, and calls into question the subject's "joyous possession of the world" (51, 76, 297). At the same time, because "the body does not happen as an accident to the soul," the physical face *is* the important "*mode* in which a being, neither spatial nor foreign to geometrical or physical extension, exists separately." It is the "*somewhere* of a dwelling" of a being — of its solitary and separated being-with-itself.[5]

While Levinas describes the home, or *dwelling,* as a site of inwardness [*intimité*], from which the subject ventures *outside* herself (and therefore, the real home is always a rootless, wandering mode of being), he also points out that this inwardness "opens up in a home which is situated in that outside — for the home, as a building, belongs to a world of objects" (*TI* 152). The "home" possesses two facades, and thereby, two positions, for it "has a 'street front,' but also its secrecy. . . . Circulating between visibility and invisibility, one is always bound for the interior of which one's home, one's corner, one's tent, one's cave is the vestibule" (156). The home, then, is both the architectural site filled with material furnishings [*Bien-meubles,* or "movable goods"] that, by its very nature, is "hospitable to the proprietor," as well as the site of interiority in which the subject withdraws from the elements and can "recollect" herself (157, cf. 153–54). Recollection [*recueillance*], for Levinas, is a kind of "coming to oneself, a retreat home with oneself as in a land of refuge, which answers to a hospitality, an expectancy, a human welcome." This is a self-possession made possible by the subject possessing a home in which she is able to *be welcomed to herself,* which welcoming constitutes the condition by which a certain affection for herself is "produced as a gentleness that spreads over the face of things" and makes the welcome of the stranger-Other possible (155). As a result, the ethical self is also a "*sub-jectum;* it is under the weight of the universe, responsible for everything. The unity of the universe is not what my gaze embraces in its unity of apperception, but what is incumbent on me from all sides...accuses me, is my affair" (*OB* 116). The "I" is ultimately the "non-interchangeable par excellence" and also "the state of being a hostage," and it is only "through the condition of being hostage that there can be in this world pity, compassion, pardon and proximity."[6]

In Derrida's view, Levinas's ideas regarding the welcoming of the enigmatic face of the stranger-Other is a type of hospitality that is "not simply some region of ethics" or "the name of a problem in law or politics: it is ethicity itself, the whole and the principle of ethics."[7] More importantly, Levinas's "infinite and unconditional hospitality" raises the difficult question of whether or not Levinas's philosophy "would be able to found a law and politics, beyond the familial dwelling, within a society, nation, State, or Nation-State."[8] How would such an ethics be "regulated in a particular or juridical practice? How might it, in turn, regulate a particular politics or law? Might it give rise to—keeping the same names—a politics, a law, or a justice for which none of the concepts we have inherited under these names would be adequate?"[9] How, also, might Levinas's thought be seen as a provocation to "think the passage between the ethical... *and* the political, at a moment in the history of humanity and of the Nation-State when the persecution of all of these hostages—the foreigner, the immigrant (with or without papers), the exile, the refugee, those without a country, or State, the displaced person or population (so many distinctions that call for careful analysis)—seems, on every continent, open to a cruelty without precedent."[10]

We might also ask, as Derrida does, how Levinas's hospitality might mark (or open) an important door [*porte*] into a dwelling that must ultimately be "beyond the State in the State"?[11] Levinas himself touches upon the question in his conclusion to *Totality and Infinity,* where he wrote that, in "the measure that the face of the Other relates us with a third party, the metaphysical relation of the I with the Other moves into the form of a We, aspires to a State, institutions, laws, which are the source of universality. But politics left to itself bears a tyranny within itself; it deforms the I and the other who have given rise to it, for it judges them according to universal rules, and thus as in absentia" (*TI* 300).

Although the individual subject is ultimately made invisible by the State's insistence on universality, and therefore hospitality has to define itself, in certain singular situations, *against* the State, the State nevertheless reserves a framework for it (through various of its institutions, such as citizenship, courts of law, and bills of rights). But although the State, in Levinas's view, can function as a rational political order that ends exile and violence and endows persons with freedom, the world in which the welcoming of the stranger-Other is possible will always be radically different from the State, which, "with its *realpolitik*, comes from another universe, sealed off from sensibility, or protest by 'beautiful souls,' or tears shed by an 'unhappy unconsciousness' " (*LR* 274). And this is why Simon Critchley, following the lead of Levinas's thought, describes politics as "praxis in a situation that articulates an *interstitial* distance from the state and allows for the emergence of new political subjects who exert a universal claim."[12] But we must also understand that "this distance from the state is *within* the state, that is, within and upon the state's territory."[13]

What I offer in this essay is a consideration of Levinas's philosophy of hospitality in relation to the *terroristic* figure of Grendel in the Old English poem *Beowulf*, in order to raise some questions about the vexed connections between ethics, violence, and sovereignty, as well as between ethics and politics, both in the early Middle Ages and in our own time. In the trauma created in the wake of the violent, disturbing, and destructive stranger-Other, how is it possible to welcome this disturbance, to open the door to destruction, to offer hospitality (the very foundation of *ethicity*)? If the home constitutes the site of recollection (a *coming-to-oneself*) which is the condition for welcoming (a *going-out-of-oneself* to the Other), what happens to the ethical project of hospitality when the stranger-Other is actively trying to destroy that home? If, as Levinas argues, the "positive deployment of a pacific relation with the other, without frontier or any negativity, is produced in language" (*TI* 172), how can we make peace with those who refuse to speak, to contact us, across a great (yet also intimately proximate) distance, with language? In what way does terroristic violence (whether the anthropophagy of a Grendel or a suicide bombing) simultaneously summon and accuse us as those who are "irreplaceable"?[14] How does Grendel, as an exorbitantly exterior (read: monstrous) figure of terrorism, signify and enact a type of violence (even, a type of radical evil) that the State (Heorot) itself simultaneously exercises and punishes? And finally, in what ways does terroristic violence enact a politics (or, perhaps, more negatively, an *active* political nihilism)[15] that articulates an interstitial relationship that is both distant from and also within the territory of the state?

Most likely written in a tenth to eleventh century Anglo-Saxon monastic setting,[16] that would have been partially structured by its own Christian ethics of hospitality, *Beowulf* takes as its subject an earlier proto-Christian cultural milieu (Scandinavia in the *geardagum,* "the old days") structured by particular socially-regulated modes of hospitality. Because of this, *Beowulf* reveals many of the fissures that often open up when the moral dictums "welcome the stranger" and "love thy neighbor as (and more than) thyself" run up against the troubling sociopolitical question, "what if my neighbor is also my enemy?" The monstrously disfigured yet still humanized form of Grendel, whom Beowulf describes as an "unknown violence" (*BFF* 276) [*uncuðne nið*], refuses even the possibility of all gestures of welcoming while also calling into question the limits of the ethics (and even, the *law*) of hospitality that were clearly important in both Anglo-Saxon England and in the world of the poem. Grendel's violence, in other words, challenges the code of hospitality that founds Hrothgar's great hall, and by extension, the whole "jural feud" society of Daneland,[17] while it simultaneously expresses a kind of excess of the very same violence that helped build that hall. For Hrothgar's "wide" reputation and the wealth of his court are the chief byproducts of his and his troops' "success in war" and "honor in battle" (64, 65) [*heresped* and *wiges weorðmynd*].

As a figure who bears a supposedly *inscrutable* hatred, Grendel poses a certain challenge to a society that claims not to know or understand his aggression, while at the same time, this society (Daneland, and by extension, the more broadly delineated warrior culture within which Daneland makes its geographic and ideological purchases) is itself caught up in ceaseless cycles of violent reprisal for which it has devised particular justifications. As a figure of supposedly extralegal violence, Grendel frustrates the self-identity of a society that considers itself just and humane, and that sees no remedy under its usual codes (for example, *wergild* or gift exchange) for this terrifyingly foreign, yet genealogically related invader. One might argue that Grendel's ability to terrify rests, to a certain extent, upon the ways in which he brings to vivid life (and death) the obscene rage at the heart of a State that supposedly marks the place of a more ethical community. This ability might also rest upon how his very presence inside the ceremonial dwelling of the great hall of Heorot points to a violent displacement and dispossession that seems intrinsic to the guest-host relationship, especially in the world of a poem where almost all of the violent episodes — between men and monsters, but also between men and men — happen within spaces, whether halls or caves, designated as home. As John Michael has written regarding the current "war on terror" and Derrida's writing, by way of Levinas, on hospitality, "If the guest has power over the host, the power of a dangerous and perhaps impossible ethical demand, no one can ever be at home anywhere."[18]

Because Grendel's almost senseless aggression also encloses a kind of insistence on his own murder as the only possible end to that aggression, Grendel refuses conversation with Hrothgar and his Danes, and with Beowulf and his Geats, in order to forcefully open a way out of his solitude onto the plane of a certain futurity (his own death), but also out of a history beyond the judgment of those who would "translate" him into a battle trophy. For in that moment when Beowulf and his Geats return to Hrothgar's court with Grendel's severed head, which they have to drag by its hair across the floor of the great hall ("be feaxe on flet boren / Grendles heafod"; *BFF* 1647–48), the "terrible" and "splendidly-made spectacle" (1649–50) [*egeslic* and *wliteseon wrætlic*] of that head, upon which everyone gazes, is a marvel (and spoil) of alterity which, as Levinas would say, "gleams like a splendor but does not deliver itself" (*TI* 193). Seth Lerer has argued that Beowulf's killing of Grendel can be viewed as a "rite of purification" or "sacrificial act" by which Heorot is "cleansed" (1176) [*Heorot is gefælsod*], with the return of Grendel's severed head to Heorot serving as the "token" or "sign" (1654) [*tacne*] of that purification.[19] Further, by delivering Grendel *in parts,* the monster's body "may remain as parts, safe in their symbolism and inactivity."[20] But I would argue that there is something not completely benign or inert in the spectacle of Grendel's head being dragged across the floor of Heorot; whether it is tied to the rafter beams or left on its "slaughter-pole" (1638) [*wælstenge*], in the words of Jeffrey Cohen, "it smears the formal structure of the symbolic network with its obscene presence — its pleasures, delights, and destructions."[21] It also marks the space of an "unhappy consciousness" that puts into question, paraphrasing Levinas, the freedom of the Danes *as a moving force, the impetuosity of their current to which everything is permitted, even murder.*[22]

IN ALTERITY WE CAN FIND AN ENEMY: A NOTE BEFORE PROCEEDING

According to Howard Caygill, in his book *Levinas and the Political,* "the question of the political consistently troubles Levinas's thought." I must note here, before proceeding, a somewhat irresolvable yet important tension between Caygill's understanding that, for Levinas, "it is irresponsible to speak of peace without war, or to imagine a peace that is but a cessation of war: war is inextricable from peace, violence is inextricable from ethics,"[23] and Simon Critchley's assessment (which is also a hope) that Levinas's ethical thought offers a route out of the impasse of deconstruction's undecidability (which is, nevertheless, ethical in its "hesitations") to an *"ethics [which] is ethical for the sake of politics*— that is, for the sake of a new conception of the organization of political space." For which, according to Critchley, the "leitmotif...is a verse from Isaiah 57, cited in *Otherwise Than Being:* 'Peace, peace, to the neighbor (*le prochain*) and to the one far off (*le lointain*).'"[24]

It was precisely because of a statement that Levinas made in a 1982 radio interview after the massacres in the Chatila and Sabra camps in Israeli-occupied Lebanon, described by Caygill as revealing "an unsentimental understanding of violence and power,"[25] that compelled me to try to delineate some of the tension between Levinas's insistence on the subjection of the "I," as hostage, to the Other, and the idea, espoused in this radio interview, that sometimes the Other can be the enemy. In short, Levinas was asked by his interlocutor, Shlmo Malka, "you are the philosopher of the 'other.' Isn't history, isn't politics the very site of the encounter with the 'other,' and for the Israeli, isn't the 'other' above all the Palestinian?" Levinas responded that, "in alterity we can find an enemy, or at least then we are faced with the problem of knowing who is right and who is wrong, who is just and who is unjust. There are people who are wrong" (*LR* 294).

In Caygill's view, Levinas's response here "opens a wound in his whole oeuvre," and Levinas's "view of the...problem of 'knowing who is right and who is wrong, who is just and who is unjust' uncharacteristically reduces the problem of ethics to knowledge."[26] At the same time, Levinas's last words in this same interview, that a "person is more holy than a land, even a holy land, since, faced with an affront made to a person, this holy land appears in its nakedness to be but stone and wood" (*LR* 297), indicate, in Caygill's words, that "ethics seems once more to prevail over politics and the state."[27] In Critchley's reading of Levinas, totalizing politics, which would stand in the place of the "holy land" invoked above (as opposed to the singular person) "is always associated with the fact of war," which "means both the empirical fact of war, which, Levinas claims, 'suspends morality'...and the Hobbesian claim that the peaceful order of society is founded on the war of all against all."[28] And therefore, in Levinas's own words, "It is not then without importance to know if an egalitarian and just State in which man is fulfilled...proceeds from a war of all against all, or from the irreducible responsibility of the one for all, and if it can do without friendship and faces" (*OB* 159–60). But for Critchley, Levinasian ethics is ultimately "a reduction of war (which...is not a complete reduction),"[29] primarily because of Levinas's insistence, especially in *Otherwise Than Being*, on the "third party" [*le tiers*] which always "troubles" the ethical relation to the Other, primarily because "the other is from the first the brother of all other men" and the neighbor "that obsesses me is already a face, both comparable and incomparable, a unique face and in relationship with faces, which are visible in the concern for justice" (*OB* 158).

There is a direct "passage," then (as opposed to an impasse) from ethics to politics in Levinas's thought, in Critchley's view, which "is synonymous with the move from responsibility to questioning, from the proximity of the one-for-the-other to a relation with all others whereby I feel myself to be an other like the others and where the question of justice can be raised."[30] In this scenario, social space "is an infinite splintering, or fragmentation, of space into spaces where there is consequently a multiplication of political possibilities," and "the just polity is one that can actively maintain its own interruption or ironiza-tion as that which sustains it."[31] Such a just polity would have great need of a political philosophy, such as Levinas's, of the multiple (of the second and third persons), and, as Critchley writes, "If philosophy begins in wonder, then political philosophy—the reflective activity of *polis*-dwelling beings—begins in wonder at the fact of human plural-ity."[32] The troubling question of violence, of course, always remains.

THE DEFEAT OF SOME AND THE (DUBIOUS) VICTORY OF OTHERS

To Derrida's question regarding how Levinas's ethics of hospitality might be regulated in a juridical practice, or whether or not it could give rise to a law, early English law codes, such as those of Ine, Alfred and Æthelstan, demonstrate some of the ways in which the figure of the foreigner, stranger, or lordless man, held a prominent place in the juridical system of Anglo-Saxon England. In the law codes of Alfred (871–99) drafted after the treaty with Guthrum in 886 (referred to as the Danelaw), and modified by Edward the Elder (Alfred's successor, 899–924), it is stipulated that

> Gif man gehadodne oððe ælðeodigne þurh enig ðing forræde æt féo oððe æt feore, þonne sceal him cyng beon—oððan eorl ðær on lande—7 bisceop ðere þeode for mæg 7 for mundboran, buton he

elles oðerne hæbbe; 7 bete man georne be ðam þe seo dæd sy Criste
7 cyninge, swa hit gebyrige; oððe þa dæde wrece swiðe deope þe cyn-
ing sy on ðeode.[33]

[If any attempt is made to deprive in any wise a man in orders, or a
stranger, of either his goods or his life, the king—or the earl of the
province—and the bishop of the diocese shall act as his kinsmen and
protectors, unless he has some other. And such compensation as is due
shall be promptly paid to Christ and the king according to the nature
of the offence; or the king within whose dominions the deed is done
shall avenge it to the uttermost.]

In the early English law codes in general (beginning with the seventh
century laws of Ine and extending through the eleventh century reign of
Cnut) the stranger is most often referred to as *ælðeodigne* (alien person)
or *feorcumen man* ("man who comes from afar," or "foreigner"), and
occasionally the word *gest* (guest) is also used, with the term *gestliðnesse*
(guestliness) denoting "hospitality." Clearly, the displaced person without specific kinship or local group connections, held a special status
within Anglo-Saxon England, and Alfred's law, cited above, could even
be said to denote a space of legal welcoming of the displaced person
into the domestic kin-dwelling and protection of the State. In the law
codes of Cnut (1020–23) we can even see the codification of a *moral*
concern for the treatment of strangers, where it states that "he who
pronounces a worse judgment on a friendless man or a stranger from
a distance than on his own fellows, injures himself."[34]

But in the law codes of Æthelstan (924–39), we can see how the
legal welcoming and protection of the stranger also belies a fear of the
individual who is too foreign, too displaced, or too unwilling to be
attached to the state through a locally-circumscribed domicile:

Ond we cwædon be þam hlafordleasan mannum, ðe mon nán ryht æt-
begytan ne mæg, þæt mon beode ðære mægþe, ðæt hi hine to folcryhte
gehamette 7 him hlaford finden on folcgemote. 7 gif hi hine ðonne
begytan nyllen oððe ne mægen to þam andagan, ðonne beo he syþþan
flyma, 7 hine lecge for ðeof se þe him tocume.[35]

[And we have declared respecting those lordless men from whom no
law may be obtained, that the kin should be commanded to domicile
him to common law, and find for him a lord in the district meeting.

And if they will not or cannot produce him at the appointed day, then he is afterwards a fugitive outlaw, and let anyone slay him for a thief who can come at him.]

Even earlier, in the law codes of Ine (688–725), we can see that the status of the foreigner was ultimately precarious:

Gif feorcund mon oððe fremde butan wege geond wudu gonge 7 ne hrieme ne horn blawe, for ðeof he bið to profianne, oððe to sleanne oððe to áleisanne.[36]

[If a man from afar, or a stranger, travels through a wood off the highway and neither shouts nor blows a horn, he shall be assumed to be a thief, and as such may be either slain or put to ransom.]

The line separating the sacred foreigner whose body and possessions should be protected from the person who is available to be killed (by anyone, no less) precisely because he either does not signify his presence or refuses the invitation into the State's dwelling, is very tenuous here. One could say that all of the law codes cited above are predicated, in the final analysis, upon the State's desire both to regulate and contain immigrants and disenfranchised persons (as well as eliminate them when they cannot be contained), and also to profit from them through fees of protection and taxation. The "fate of the foreigner in the Middle Ages—and in many respects also today," as Julia Kristeva writes, "depended on a subtle, sometimes brutal, play between *caritas* and the *political jurisdiction.*"[37]

Anglo-Saxon law codes point to a legally-codified ethics of care for the stranger-Other who is both threatened yet also threatening in his singularity, and they likely arise from a society that we know, from its imaginative and other literature, was deeply concerned with the protocols of hospitality. And these protocols—in the absence of the law, or beyond the law's reach—functioned as the important means whereby those who were Other to each other could communicate, without hostility, in spaces of *common dwelling,* whose doors, whether barred or open, marked the threshold between the "inside" of the communal dwelling from the "outside" of the stateless forest. Importantly, the very idea of the extralegal was enclosed within the Anglo-Saxon legal definition of the fugitive as one who was *exlex*, or *utlah* ("outlaw"). According to Michael Moore, "The forest was the proper haunt for such figures, ranging far from the houses and protection of the village. No food or lodging was to be offered to the *utlah*." Further, "These criminals, conceived of as demonic creatures outside the boundaries of humanity, were pushed away from the society, absolutely excluded from the shelter of the community and its legal world and suffering what amounted to 'civil death'."[38] As Moore writes, such "acts of exclusion helped to form the community as a legal subject: the law was made by and for the village or kingdom, at the same time enclosing and defining it" and "the concept of outlawry was fundamental to establishing the inner, safe circle of communal law and royal power."[39] The medieval social community, then, had need of an extralegal outside in order to define itself as *bounded*, while at the same time, because of certain moral imperatives, rooted either in Christian belief or more archaic rituals of hospitality, and also for the purposes of strengthening its numbers (both human and economic), that community had to also leave a door open for the welcome of the stranger-Other.

In the realm of Old English poetry, as Hugh Magennis tells us, a "concern with ideas of community and of the relationship of individuals to communities is widely evident."[40] Further, Old English poetic texts often "raise unsettling questions" about "received notions of community," which are reflected in the antithesis between the corpus's positive images of "warmth and security," especially of feasting and drinking in secular halls, and the reverse images of "dislocation and alienation," as we get in *Seafarer, Wanderer,* and *The Ruin*.[41] The Anglo-Saxon hall—both real and poetic—is an especially conflicted site, as both tribal seat and the *civitas* (or State) itself, for it is not only the place where a community gathers, happily and in supposed concord, around a meal and drink, but is also "the seat of business, of political brokering and conflicts, where power...[is] exercised."[42]

Themes of ordered authority and the betrayal of that authority are, fittingly enough, often played out in the hall, and this is especially so in *Beowulf,* where the poet describes Heorot at one point as "filled with friends within" who do not, "*as yet* practice treachery" (*BFF* 1017–19).

One could argue that the gestures of welcoming in *Beowulf,* which are clearly the primary instrument of the ethicopolitics of the world of the story—from the coast guard's welcome of Beowulf and his men into Daneland (237–57, 287–300, and 316–19), to Hrothgar's servant's welcome of them into Heorot itself (333–39), to Hrothgar's initial welcome of Beowulf (457–90), to Wealhtheow's bearing of the banquet feast cup to Beowulf after he has killed Grendel (1216–31), to Hygelac's rewelcoming of Beowulf into Geatland (1975–98)—are all fraught with the anxiety and tension that always arises when ideas of sovereignty (whether of the individual, the family/tribe, or the larger polis-state) come up against an ethics of hospitality that is supposed to transcend those sovereignties. So, for example, when Beowulf returns after his adventures in Daneland to Hygelac's court, Hygelac commands his hall to be cleared for the "foot-guests" (1976) [*feðegestum*] to whom he offers "earnest words" and "cups of mead" (1980) [*meaglum wordum* and *meoduscencum*], one of which his daughter bears directly to Beowulf (1981–83).

Yet Hygelac also reminds Beowulf that he had "mistrusted" (*BFF* 1994) [*siðe ne truwode*] his adventure all along and had asked Beowulf to "let the South-Danes themselves make war with Grendel" (1996–97) [*lete Suð-Dene sylfe geweorðan / guðe wið Grendel*]. By letting Beowulf know of his *not having faith* in Beowulf, Hygelac opens up a line of tension within his rewelcoming home of the "local hero," who clearly understands the challenge (and possible peril) of not properly receiving Hygelac's hospitality, when he concludes his story of his exploits in Hrothgar's country by telling Hygelac,

> "ac he me (maðma)s geaf,
> sunu Healfdenes on (min)ne sylfes dom;
> ða ic ðe, beorncyning, bringan wylle,
> estum geywan. Gen is eall æt ðe
> lissa gelong; ic lyt hafo
> heafodmaga nefne, Hygelac, ðec."   (2146–51)
> [but he gave treasures to me, / the son of the Half-Danes, according to my own judgment, / that I to you, king of men, wish to bring, / to bestow willingly. On you, still, is all / joy dependent; I have few / near relations, Hygelac [except for] you.]

In other words, Beowulf has to reassure Hygelac, through his hospitable (and loving) language and his gifts, where his loyalties as a warrior (and citizen of Hygelac's Geatland) ultimately lie.

In the case of Wealtheow, as the wife of Hrothgar and hostess of the table of the Danish hall, it is her duty to give to Beowulf, following Grendel's defeat, both wine and gifts and to wish him good health and prosperity, and she does so, but not without also voicing her concern that Beowulf will always be kind in deeds to her sons ("Beo þu suna minum / dædum gedefe," *BFF* 1226b–27a). Wealhtheow's anxiety over her sons' future may very well be predicated upon her fear that her husband has gone too far in *his* hospitality and gratitude by having already spoken of Beowulf as a son [*sunu*] in his mind [*ferþe*] to whom he would give everything he is able to give (946b–50).

Hospitality, therefore, is not just a form of charity in this world, but a form of politics — a politics, moreover, that has its breakable limits, evidenced by the poem's multiple digressions into stories about violence erupting within the very site of reception that makes hospitality possible at all — the hall itself. Therefore, in both the story of the battle at Finnsburg told by Hrothgar's *scop* after Beowulf has defeated Grendel (*BFF* 1071–1159a) and also of the destruction of Heorot itself by the Heathobards, first foretold by the poet (81b–85) and then later predicted by Beowulf with great creative embellishment (2032–69a), we hear about the murder of guests in the halls of their former enemies, who have invited them there to share food, drink, and gifts (including women exchanged as brides), ostensibly to smooth over past enmities — enmities which obviously percolate very closely to the surface of the structures of hospitality designed to ameliorate them.

It is significant, as mentioned above, that when Beowulf first arrives in Daneland, he asks Hrothgar to allow him to "cleanse" or "purify" Heorot (*BFF* 432b) [*Heorot fælsian*]: no hospitality, or politics, is possible while Heorot is polluted with the blood of Hrothgar's subjects, many of whom have also abandoned the hall to sleep (and therefore, to reside) elsewhere (138–43), meaning that not only the hall itself, but also the space of sovereignty it marks, has been deserted. The Danish community, thanks to Grendel's relentless violence, has no viable or pure center, no gleaming building with which to signify its supposedly generous heart.[43] But even without Grendel's desecration of Daneland's chief ceremonial and communal space, the poem makes clear again and again in all of its asides regarding the feuds between Frisians and Danes, Danes and Heathobards, Geats and Swedes, and so forth, that it is the men themselves who stain the floors of their halls with each other's blood and who also burn the structures of their communities down to the ground. As a result, the poem keeps in perpetual motion what Levinas defined as one of the more distressing tasks of alterity: defining "who is right and who is wrong, who is just and who is unjust."

In this scenario, Grendel himself can be seen as someone who literally blows open the doors that separate the domicile of the supposedly peaceful State (Heorot) from everything that it has abjected to the extralegal outside of that domicile (and yet is also interstitial within it), and in his terrifyingly excessive aggression, he is, finally, that isolated (yet also heroic?) figure that Levinas might say was produced by Heorot's "virile virtues," as well as the signifier of a politics that transgresses the State, through terror, in order to *transfix its gaze.*[44] For even when Grendel has been partitioned and then reduced to only his lifeless head, he continues to signify as the material excess of a type of violence the State can never do without and of which it will always have difficulty divesting itself. Grendel's head remains, finally, *inside* the hall where, in Cohen's words, in can continue to function as "the 'little piece of the real' that symbolization excludes: it is everything culturally suppressed in order for 'culture' to come into being."[45] As Carolyn Anderson writes, "the banishment of Grendel and his Mother does not rid the world of Heorot or *Beowulf* of disruptions. The abject (repressed) persistently encroaches on and disrupts the symbolic order, so that the subject is always in process, on trial, and always insecure about the boundaries of identity."[46]

Prior to their violent ends at the hands of Beowulf, Grendel, a "grim ghost" (*BFF* 102) [*grimma gæst*], and his mother, a "mighty mere-wife" and "sea-wolf" (1519, 1599) [*merewif mihtig* and *brim-wylf*], live in a landscape which is wild and supposedly unlivable, yet is also situated at the very margin, or border, of the so-called civilized world—specifically, Daneland, whose chief symbol Heorot is upheld by the poet as the "best of all houses" (146) [*husa selest*]. Because Daneland's primary symbol, the hall, is architectural—it is a thing made and built by human design and therefore articulates human identity—it stands in stark contrast to the fen paths, dark headlands, and burning mere that mark the monsters' territory (1357–72). One could argue that the hall is not just a metonym for Daneland (and for its authority), but is, in fact, Daneland itself, for the poet shares no details regarding any village or cultivated fields or other outlying areas that would surely have attached to such a monumental seat of political and cultural power. There is something peculiar about this glittering and golden world whose light shines over many lands ("lixte se leoma ofer landa fela," 311): the only things that really constitute Daneland are the shore that separates it from the rest of the world, the horn-gabled hall, the paved stone road leading to and away from the hall, the blood and flesh-splattered trail that leads to the monsters' mere, and the outland territories of the monsters who are "out there" somewhere.[47] This calls to mind Cohen's argument that the monster always resides in a place "that is doubly dangerous" because it is simultaneously 'exorbitant' and 'quite close'."[48] And similar to the world evoked in *King Lear*, in which there are really only two places—the inside of the houses of degenerate power and the outside with its "all-shaking Thunder" and "House-less heads"—*Beowulf*'s world is partitioned between a sick and ruined *civitas* and a menacing wilderness.

Grendel is the chief border crosser between these two worlds—a "fiend from hell" [*feond on helle*] who, in 12 winters of crafting crimes [*fyrene fremman*] and making murderous incursions into Heorot, has become not only Daneland's chief terror, but also its chief terrorist (*BFF* 101). Many of the descriptions of Grendel within the poem point to his supposedly inherent unknowability, which both fascinates and frightens. He is a "powerful ghost" (86) [*ellengæst*], a "giant" (761) [*eoten*], a "dark death-shadow" (160) [*deorc deapscua*], a "soul killer" (177) [*gastbona*], a "secret hatemonger" (275) [*deogol dædhata*], a "hell-secret" (164) [*helrunan*], and perhaps most importantly, because it is repeated so often, a "terror," or "one who plays with [or fights] the law" (159, 425, 433, 592, 646, 732, 739, 816, 989, 1000, and 1269) [*aglæca*].[49] Although Grendel is definitively strange and monstrous and evil, the poet also tells us that he and his mother are descended from Cain (104–14, 1260–68), and therefore they share a human kinship with the other characters in the poem, while also bearing the mark of Cain's pathology.[50] As Ruth Melinkoff reminds us,

> Grendel and his mother not only are plainly fleshly creatures but also clearly are more human than beast. Although the poet was sparing with physical descriptions, he provides some vividly revealing details: arms and shoulders (835a, 972a, and 1537a), claw-like hands (746–48a, 983b–90), a light shining from Grendel's eyes (726b–27) and his head dragged by the hair (1647–48a). . . . Evil monsters, yes, but with human forms, flesh and minds.[51]

Although Grendel never speaks within the poem, and therefore could be construed as being bereft of a rational or human consciousness, the poet refers often to his mental states. As Katherine O'Brien O'Keeffe has pointed out, when Grendel first approaches Beowulf after bursting into Heorot in the dead of night, "he is angry (*[ge]bolgen,* 723; *yrremod,* 726), his heart laughs (*mod ahlog,* 730), he shows intent (*mynte,* 731), and he thinks (*þohte,* 739)."[52]

Hrothgar and his Danes, and Beowulf and his Geats, see Grendel and his mother as thoroughly Other than themselves, yet, as Carol Braun Pasternack has pointed out, the language in the poem often belies the lines of difference that supposedly separate men from monsters, and thereby also reveals what might be called the poem's "political unconscious":

> *Aglæca* characterizes Grendel and the dragon and *aglæcwif* Grendel's mother, but *aglæca* also characterizes Sigemund (893a), both Beowulf and the dragon together (2592) and, in two instances, ambiguously either Beowulf or his monstrous opponent, in the first possibly Grendel (739a) and in the second possibly mere-monsters (1512a). Klaeber struggles in his glossary to keep a clear distinction between hero and opponent, identifying the same term as, on the one hand, "wretch, monster, demon, fiend," and on the other, "warrior, hero." But, as George Jack recognizes in his edition, "fierce assailant" indicates the common ground for all the referents.[53]

Further, Pasternack explains that "The *aglæcan* are also *wreccan,* and this word and etymologically related terms point even more clearly to an oral-heroic paradigm in which hero and opponent fall within a single concept, the fierce outsider."[54] O'Keeffe has also remarked that the significance of the term *rinc* ("man" or "warrior") as it is applied to Grendel "is underscored by the number of the times the poet uses the word as a simplex or as part of a compound in the . . . description of Grendel's actions in the hall [when he fights Beowulf]. 'Rinca manige' (728), 'magorinca heap' (730), 'slæpende rinc' (741), and finally of Beowulf himself, 'rinc on ræste' (747) confirm Grendel's connection with the men in the hall."[55]

More to the point of Grendel's troublingly intimate exteriority, or *extimacy,*[56] he is simultaneously the "elsewhere ghost", "elsewhere guest", and "elsewhere host" (*BFF* 807) [*ellorgæst*], as well as the "fierce house-guard" (770) [*repe renweardas*], "angry ghost/guest/host" (2073) [*gæst yrre*], and the "hateful hall-thane" (142) [*healðegnes hete*] who Hrothgar calls "my invader" (1776) [*ingenga min*], pointing to his complicit status with those who lie sleeping in the hall at night, and whom he kills and ingests during his visits there. It would appear that somehow, if even on an unconscious level, Hrothgar recognizes that Grendel is somehow his and the Danes' personal nightmare, and even the poet mentions, at lines 152 and 154–55, that Grendel "had fought for a long time against Hrothgar" and "wanted no peace with any man of the Danish troop." Carolyn Anderson, in her analysis of the word *gæst* in the poem, "which appears initially to binarize a social relationship into one of hosts and guests," has shown how "the word's Sanskrit root **ghas* 'to consume,' highlights its deconstruction as a differentiating marker of the most intimate of social categories." Further, there is in the poem "an apparent opposition between the terms *gæst,* 'ghost, spirit, demon' and *gist,* 'guest, stranger, visitor.' This opposition collapses in some passages, suggesting that Beowulf and Grendel view each other similarly, and are even indistinguishable at times." Finally, since the word *gist* also has "etymological relations" with "fury, anger" and its roots **gheis* and **ghois* "fear and amazement" appear "with cognate sense" in **geisa* "to rage" and Gothic *usgaisjan* "to terrify," there may be some kind of original link between the roots **ghas* "to consume" and **gheis* "fear," where the first term "would note what is expected from a social relationship, the offering and consumption of food, while the second would encompass the possible excesses of the guest who destroys."[57]

So, while on the one hand the Danes can claim not to know or understand Grendel, part of his ability to terrify them might be partly rooted in Hrothgar's recognition that somehow and in some way, Grendel's violence is recognizable as a kind of "death-shadow" of the very same violence that founded his own hall and might also have a more materially palpable cause that attaches to specific persons or specific places. That Grendel's feud with Hrothgar's court is somehow personal, and that its original cause might somehow be rooted in Daneland's ostentatious display of its wealth and power in its most visible articulation—the golden keep of Heorot itself—is further evidenced in the lines, early in the poem, that Grendel "sorrowfully endured his time in the darkness, [and] suffered distress, when he heard each day the loud rejoicing in the hall, the music of the harp, and the clear song of the poet" (*BFF* 86–90) [earfoðlice / þrage geþolode, se þe in þystrum bad, / þæt he dogora gewham dream gehyrde / hludne in healle; þær wæs hearpan sweg, / swutol sand scopes]. One of the reasons Grendel may be particularly angry about this music is the subject matter of the song itself—God's creation of the world (91–98)—for Grendel, as one of the deformed or "harm-shaped" creatures spawned by Cain, likely has a special grievance with God, and also with any men like Hrothgar and his Danes who appear to have been blessed by God. One visible sign of this blessing, aside from the Danes' material wealth, is the fact, as the poet tells us in lines 168–69, that because of God, Grendel could not approach nor touch Hrothgar's "gift-seat," nor could he "know" God's "mind" or "love."[58] Although the poet does not say so directly, we can assume that Grendel assumes that he is not, never was, and never will be welcome in the hall and the field of unwelcoming that the hall radiates might be part of what undergirds his rage against the Danes. Perhaps, too, Grendel simply hates all who are foreign *to him* and recognizes no sovereignty except his

own, which sovereignty, moreover, he asserts through the elimina-
tion of all others whom he perceives to be *in his way.* This raises the
troubling question, too, of how Levinas's unconditional, or peaceful,
hospitality can ever be possible in a world that has need of the idea
(and force) of sovereignty.

When Beowulf first arrives in Daneland and is explaining to the coast
guard why he is there, he reveals, as mentioned above, that he and
his men have heard of the "unknown violence" (*BFF* 276) [*uncuðne
nið*] that threatens the country of the Scyldings, and he wishes to
offer Hrothgar counsel as to how he might vanquish this "I don't
know what kind of ravager" (274) [*sceaðona ic nat hwylc*]. It could
be argued that it is not fair to say that the Danes have not properly
recognized Grendel as belonging, in some fashion, to their world
(if even as a type of structural excess), for Grendel stands in stark
contrast to more identifiable human enemies — the Frisian or Heatho-
bard who has been invited to dinner and is quietly seething over old
grudges, and whose killing sword is always close at hand. These are
enemies whose worst motives are understood and even anticipated.
Yet it is precisely this more familiar enemy that Beowulf identifies as
the ultimate cause of the undoing of Heorot when he returns to
Geatland and explains his adventures in Daneland to Hygelac. In
his speech, lines 2000–2162, which constitutes a second telling of
his exploits (the first having been already given to us by the poet),
Beowulf, either through an amazing prescience or a smart reading of
social cues he witnessed while at Hrothgar's court, explains to Hygelac
that Heorot will eventually be destroyed by a failed alliance with an
old enemy, the Heathobards, through an arranged marriage between
Hrothgar's daughter, Freawaru, and Ingeld, the son of Froda, chief of
the Heathobards. Indicating to Hygelac that these kinds of alliances
rarely hold, Beowulf states, "Often, after the fall of princes, in a short
while the deadly spear flies, even if the bride is good" (2029–31) [Oft
seldan hwær / æfter leodhryre lytle hwile / bongar bugeð, þeah seo
bryd duge].

In a strikingly creative moment, Beowulf then imagines the marriage
dinner itself, still in the future, when the Heathobards will welcome the

Danes into *their* hall to celebrate the wedding and, for all their good intentions, will eventually be galled by the sight of all the Danes in their glittering ring-mail, which the Danes wrested from the dead bodies of the Heathobards on the battlefield (*BFF* 2032–40). Because the desire for vengeance always wins out over the desire for reconciliation (and even, sex), violence naturally erupts, regardless of the protocols of hospitality that have been designed to avoid (or at least smooth over) such violent impulses.[59] The poem speaks often of these seemingly ceaseless cycles of tribal violence and their horrific aftermath; the image of Hildeburh in the Finn and Hengest digression, watching the heads of her son and brother melt as their bodies are being consumed on their funeral pyre, blood bursting from the gashes in their bodies (1120b–22a), is a signature moment in this respect. But many of the characters do possess some prescience about this cycle, and they even have social codes to contain it somewhat.[60] Some might argue, then, that Grendel is somehow worse than these familiar enemies because he represents an obdurately opaque type of mythical or archaic violence that will always be worse than anything the men can do to each other.[61] More terrifying still, he cannot be fought with conventional weapons. When Beowulf requests that Hrothgar allow him to fight Grendel, he mentions that he has heard that Grendel, "in his dark thoughtlessness, does not care for weapons" (434) [for his wonhydum wæpna ne recceð], and therefore Beowulf resolves to fight him without sword and shield (437–40). Further, when Beowulf and Grendel are struggling together in hand-to-hand combat in Heorot, and Beowulf's men rush to defend Beowulf with their "ancestral swords" (795) [*ealde lafe*], the poet tells us that,

> Hie þæt ne wiston, þa hie gewin drugon,
> heardhicgende hildemecgas,
> ond on healfa gehwone heawan þohton,
> sawle secan: þone synscaðan
> ænig ofer eorðan irenna cyst,
> guðbilla nan gretan nolde;
> ac he sigewæpnum forsworen hæfde,
> ecga gehwylcre.   (798–805)

[They did not know, when they began the fight, / hard-minded warriors, / thinking to swing [their swords] in every direction, / to seek his soul, that [not any of] the best of iron blades, / of any over the earth, nor any war-sword, / could greet that sin-shadow, / for he had forsworn battle weapons, / all sword-edges.]

Additionally, when Beowulf cuts off the head of Grendel's already-dead body with the ancient giant sword [*eald sweord eotenisc*], he finds hanging on the wall of Grendel's mother's cave (and with which he has also killed Grendel's mother), the poet tells us that the blade of the sword burned up and melted due to Grendel's "too hot" blood (1558, 1615–17), indicating once again the difficulty of penetrating Grendel's body with conventional weapons. Ultimately, Grendel does not answer to standard forms of combat, which we can imagine contributes to his ability to terrorize. In this respect, Grendel appears to be pure, menacing alterity: he does not talk, walk, or fight "straight."

Early on in the poem, the poet notes that Grendel's feud with the Danes was perpetual, that he would never make peace with any Danish man, he would not consent to settle the feud in any manner or by any payment, and he was not regretful about his murders (*BFF* 136, 152–58), all of which give to Grendel the status of a kind of unknown horror who apparently comes, again, from "I know not where." But I would argue that this reading of Grendel belies what Hrothgar himself tells Beowulf about who Grendel is and where he comes from. Because it is only the poet who tells us that Grendel and his mother are descended from Cain (and this happens in two definitive instances at lines 102–14 and 1260–68), and therefore it is only the poet who acknowledges Grendel's genealogical link to the human world, it is important, I think, to look closely at how Grendel's chief enemy, Hrothgar, describes and perceives him. A key passage for understanding this—perhaps *the* key passage—is the somewhat lengthy speech Hrothgar makes to Beowulf (1322–82) after Grendel's mother has burst into Heorot and killed Æschere, Hrothgar's most beloved warrior, rune counselor, and shoulder companion (1325–26). First and foremost, it is clear that Hrothgar understands that the "hand-slayer"

(1330) [*handbanan*] had a comprehensible motivation for her murder: "She revenged that feud when you [Beowulf], last night, killed Grendel" (1333–34) [*Heo þa fæðe wræc, / þe þu gystran niht Grendel cwealdest*], and further, she "would avenge her kinsman" (1339) [*wolde hyre mæg wrecan*]. At the same time, Hrothgar describes Grendel's mother in somewhat oblique terms as a "wandering slaughter-host" (1331) [*wælgæst wæfre*] who goes "I know not where" (1331) [*ic ne wat hwæder*] with her plundered body.

But then, in a striking reversal, Hrothgar shares with Beowulf some very specific details (albeit, borrowed from the hearsay of "land-holders among my people," but also from counselors; *BFF* 1345–46) about who, exactly, Grendel and his mother are, and where they live. In what could even be called slightly excitable tones, Hrothgar explains that some people have seen "two similarly huge borderers, holding the moors, elsewhere ghosts" (1347–49) [*swylce twegen / micle mearcsta- pan moras healdan, / ellorgæstas*], one of whom could "clearly" (1350) [*gewislicost*] be seen "shaped as a woman" (1351) [*idese onlicnæs*], and the other, "harm-shaped, tread the exile-path in the form of a man, although he was much bigger than any man" (1351–53) [*oðer earmsceapen / on weres wæstmum wræc-lastas træd, / næfne he wæs mara þonne ænig man oðer*]. Most important, I think, is that Hrothgar knows this "ghost" has a name, Grendel (1354–55), and that he has no father—given that this is a world in which patrilineal succession is so important, one could argue that Grendel's fatherlessness adds one more layer to his dimension of frightening and unsettling uncanniness, while at the same time, the assumption that he *should* have a father (and is strangely *lacking* one) denotes that he is believed to be, like the Danes, a kin-defined person. Finally, in this same speech, even though Hrothgar claims that Grendel and his kinswoman "guard a secret land" (1357–58) [*Hie dygel lond / warigeað*], he then goes on, in shades of increasing hysteria, to describe in very precise detail this "wolf country": there are fens, windy cliffs, mountain streams under dark bluffs, a flood under the earth, a lake with overhanging branches and frost-covered trees, and at night, strange fires on the water (1357–76).

In Hrothgar's emotional speech to Beowulf, we see that the margins of the world in which the Grendelkin live are sublimely secret and treacherous, yet also geographically recognizable (and therefore, navigable). Likewise, Grendel and his kinswoman are both dark shadows, but also corporeally material and even humanlike. It is fairly obvious that Hrothgar is afraid of the secret, yet familiar country in which Grendel and his mother live (otherwise, why has he not already launched some kind of counter-offensive there, or traveled there himself to survey the obstacles?), perhaps because he realizes that the difference of this landscape is, as Cohen writes, "arbitrary and potentially free-floating, mutable rather than essential,"[62] just like the bodies of the monsters, or the bodies of the men who sleep within Heorot's high walls. As René Girard has written, "Difference that exists outside the system is terrifying because it reveals the truth of the system, its relativity, its fragility, its mortality."[63] Grendel's and his mother's anthropophagy is very apt in this scenario because it both absorbs the warrior's body "into that big Other seemingly beyond (but actually wholly within, because wholly created by) the symbolic order that it menaces,"[64] and also disperses the warrior's being, like so many pieces of flesh, into the wilderness (a kind of anti-Heorot, the space where no hospitality, no State, and no law is thought to be possible). In fact, one of the most terrifying sights for Beowulf and his men when they seek out Grendel's mother in her underwater den, is the spectacle of Æschere's severed head sitting on a cliff beside the burning and blood-swelled waters of the mere (*BFF* 1417–21), and later, when he returns home, Beowulf tells Hygelac how upset the Danes were that they could not properly burn Æschere's body on a funeral pyre (2124–26). The memory of Æschere's body having been both ingested and also discarded, almost as trash, along the tracks of the stateless forest, serves as a frightening rebuke to the idea that anyone could ever be safe, *at home,* from the enemy.

By leasing Beowulf, as it were, to destroy Grendel and his ilk, Hrothgar is admirably doing everything he can to stop terror from enveloping and decimating his culture, to be sure, although it does raise the difficult question, posed by Derrida, "What difference is there between, *on the one hand,* the force that can be just, or in any case deemed legitimate (not only an instrument in the service of the law but the practice and even the realization, the essence of droit), and *on the other hand* the violence that one always deems just?"[65] Grendel is so terrifying ultimately because, for the hospitable warrior-*polis* of Heorot, as Cohen writes, the "maintenance of order...is achieved only by the repression of those [murderous] impulses Grendel embodies,"[66] but which nevertheless were once necessary for the founding of Heorot, which then becomes the "law" that keeps violence in check through its alliances, man-payments [*wergild*], diplomacy, and when necessary, controlled reprisal. But as Robert Gibbs notes, "the positivity of law depends on a singular [violent] event, a revolution or war," as well as upon the reiteration of that violence through the coercion that preserves the maintenance of the State.[67] And what puts the law in question (or peril) is the stranger-Other, such as a Grendel, for whom conformity is out of the question and whose violence appears to have no restraint.[68]

Grendel reserves for himself the privilege of murder that, typically, only the State (Hrothgar) can authorize, and similar to the suicide bomber who can never be caught or punished because he is already dead (and there will always be another to die again in his place), Grendel holds the place of a sacrificial violence to which the only response is either fear and resignation or the unleashing of a force of the State that operates outside of the usual laws, such as a Beowulf (who is a "special force"). Indeed, it is precisely in Beowulf's "grappling" with Grendel in Heorot (*BFF* 745b–818a), when it is difficult to tell where Beowulf ends and Grendel begins, and when Heorot literally resounds with Grendel's "wailing cry" (785) [*wealle wop*] as Beowulf is ripping Grendel's arm and shoulder from his body (or Grendel is ripping himself away from Beowulf's grip), that we can glimpse the fluctuating structuration of violence that, tragically, has always undergirded this world. This is where we also see, following Levinas, that the Other, "in the hands of forces that break him, exposed to powers, remains unforeseeable" (*TI* 225).

GOING WITHOUT KNOWING WHERE

According to Levinas, "The privileged role of the dwelling does not consist in being the end of human activity but in being its condition, and in this sense its commencement" (*TI* 152). Without the dwelling, what Levinas calls "recollection"—the "coming to oneself...which answers to a hospitality, an expectancy, a human welcome"—is not possible. It is not possible to know, of course, if the underwater mere where Beowulf meets Grendel's mother in combat functioned, in that way, as Grendel's dwelling. But because of what we can imagine to be Grendel's belief that Heorot mocks him, and even denies him welcoming access, and because his home—to which he drags himself to die, leaving blood along the trail, after Beowulf has defeated him—is designated ahead of time by the Danes as everything that is unhomelike, Grendel exists outside the State as the figure of the extralegal and is therefore beyond his own and others' "recollection."

Beowulf's murder and postmortem decapitation of Grendel represents what might have been for Grendel, if he could have been conscious of it, a devastating double-dispossession, especially when we consider that Beowulf first drives Grendel out of the "high hall" that is the home of those who are supposedly blessed by a God whose regard Grendel cannot "know" or "love" and by whose architecture Grendel obviously feels mocked and excluded, and then later, to add insult to injury, Beowulf desecrates Grendel's body by slicing off his head in the "roofed hall" (*BFF* 1515) [*hrofsele*] of his mother.[69] And this is a head that, tellingly, will take four men to haul it along the horse path back to Heorot (1634–39), where, after being dragged across the floor to where the nobles are sitting on the benches, it becomes a spectacle for awe, as well as a trophy (1647–50). The building of Heorot was made possible through the spoils of war, and Grendel's severed head is the most visible marker of the monstrous, outsized rage necessary for founding that hall as well as the signifier of the violent coercion necessary for maintaining the law of the hall that, in the final analysis, is not predicated as much upon an ethics of hospitality as it is upon a force of exclusion that makes hospitality for *some* (as opposed to *all*) possible.

But for the Danes, or even Beowulf and his men, even to pause to consider how they might substitute for or subject themselves to a Grendel, to face him, as it were, without intermediary (Levinas's *face-à-face sans intermediare*), would be to contemplate a justice that literally stands beyond the social totality (Heorot itself) that makes thinking possible. It would be to go "where no clarifying—that is, panoramic—thought precedes, in going without knowing where" in order to a grasp a "pluralism" that can never be totalized and without which peace can never be accomplished, but only when we understand peace as something that "cannot be identified with the end of combats that cease for want of combatants, by the defeat of some and the victory of others, that is, with cemeteries or future universal empires" (*TI* 305–06). It may be, as John Caputo has written of Derrida's reflections on the possible politics that could be founded by Levinas's hospitality, that "Unconditional hospitality requires a politics without sovereignty," and also a "community without community, a city without walls, a nation without borders . . . where the decision procedure for administration is based on a holy undecidability between insider and outsider." And what would result would be a type of "holy hell" that "is the stuff of sacred anarchy."[70] But how to imagine such an anarchic state of affairs into administrative being? Or, to put the question another way: surrounded by so many bad deaths, both in the poem but also in our own troubled times, how to make way, hopefully, for its shining arrival?[71]

Although Grendel can't dine anymore on the beautiful bodies of the Danes, cracking their bones and gulping them down in chunks, nor does the light, which the poet calls "unbeautiful" (*BFF* 727) [*unfæger*], any more shine through his eyes, his head, suspended in the hall in a moment of Anglo-Saxon time, can keep watching them. He can keep gaping and warning as what Levinas would have called, not a face, but a *façade* "whose essence is indifference, cold splendor, and silence."[72] Likewise, Æschere's head, left behind along the cliff beside the burning lake where Grendel's mother discarded it (1421), is also watching and warning. These, finally, are the faces of *Beowulf* that overflow the boundaries of all images and call into question the nature of the proper relationship of violence to justice, and even to the sovereignty of the State. As the expressions of persons "brutally cast forth and forsaken in the world" (*TI* 152), and along with Heorot itself, once it is destroyed, they are also the "somewheres" of dwellings that can no longer open to themselves, but only to those of us—here, in the present—who are willing to behold them with wonder, and even, with trembling. Only then, is justice, and perhaps peace, possible.

5

There Is Horror

The Awntyrs off Arthure, the Face of the Dead, and the Maternal Other

Alexander L. Kaufman

O mother
what have I left out
O mother
what have I forgotten
O mother
farewell
—Allen Ginsberg, *Kaddish*

The Gospel according to St. Luke records Jesus' parable (unique among those in the synoptic Gospels) of the rich man and Lazarus, the poor man, to whose hunger, rags, and sores the wealthy one, living luxuriously, pays no heed. Tormented after his death in the flames of Hades (the Greek term used to translate the Hebrew word *Sheol*), the rich man sees Lazarus at a distance, comforted in the (evocatively maternal) "bosom of Abraham" (Luke 16:22), the great biblical exemplar of hospitality (cf. Gen. 18:1–8).[1] Calling to Abraham, he begs him to send Lazarus, first, to bring him water to cool his tongue, to ease his torment; second, to go to his five brothers, still alive on earth, to warn them to repent. Abraham denies both requests. A chasm, he explains, separates the places of comfort and torment. It would be useless, moreover, to send a ghost to the brothers: "If they do not hear Moses and the prophets, neither will they be convinced if some one should rise from the dead" (Luke 16:31).

Despite this word from Abraham (and Jesus), the medieval imagination, fueled by the developing doctrine of Purgatory,[2] played upon the rich man's requests and produced numerous tales of terrifying visitations by ghosts, who come to warn the living to repent. These suffering souls display their purgatorial or hellish torment and seek the help of those who have not yet undergone death. While such works as *Sir Gawain and the Green Knight, De Tribus Regibus Mortuis,* and the *Trentalle Sancti Gregorii* (*The Trental of Saint Gregory*) all contain elements of horror in spectral form, none matches *The Awntyrs off Arthure* for its combination of horror, pitiful entreaty, and prophetic warning.[3]

At first sight, the traditions—Jewish and philosophical—out of which Emmanuel Levinas writes would seem far removed from such medieval tales. His notion of the horrifying *il y a* (literally, the "there is"), however, owes at least as much from biblical and rabbinic sources, such as the formless chaos [*tohu vavohu*] of Genesis 1:2 and shadowy *Sheol* itself, the scriptural place of the dead, as it does from Martin Heidegger's *es gibt* and Maurice Blanchot's *dis-aster*.[4] Indeed, these ancient sources contributed to the medieval tales in question. Discussing the *il y a,* Levinas himself repeatedly alludes, moreover, to Shakespearean scenes that continue the medieval tradition of purgatorial visitations by ghosts: the appearance of the restless ghost of Hamlet's father; Hamlet's "to be or not to be" speech; the grave-digging scene in which the Dane faces the skull of Yorrick; the appearance of the ghost of Banquo, which is "the shadow of being that horrifies Macbeth."[5]

Such allusions and comparisons suggest that the Lithuanian philosopher's idea of the *il y a* emerges from the very narrative traditions, literary and biblical, that it, in turn, serves to thematize. But how? Tracing Levinas's use of the "there is" from its first appearances in *Existence and Existents* (1947) and *Time and the Other* (1947) to its later occurrences in *Totality and Infinity* (1961), *Otherwise Than Being* (1974), and *Of God Who Comes to Mind* (1986), Colin Davis stresses "the immense difficulties posed by the notion" of the *il y a,*[6] which "names what Levinas calls 'existing without existents (*un exister sans existant*)'... an anonymous, impersonal *existing*... before the constitution of the individual human subject."[7] "Since there is no subject to experience it (the subject is a hypostasis which breaks from the *il y a*) and no language in which to speak of it," Davis remarks, "it must remain incommunicable to subjects whose knowledge is bound to speech and experience."[8] Levinas therefore invokes the imagination in his description of the *il y a*, citing literary examples.[9] "The only available ways of describing the *il y a* seem to be negation," but this too is problematic, because (as Davis notes) "the procedure of negation disqualifies the use of simile by implying that the *il y a* cannot be compared to anything without falsifying it. The text hovers on the edge of nonsense."[10]

Levinas conceives of the *il y a*, however, precisely as a nonsense, an absurdity, that nonetheless signifies.[11] As an impersonal construction, the *il* that occupies the place of the grammatical subject "refers to no identifiable subject,"[12] but rather points to something, someone, that follows it as a futurity or that (in an exclamatory mode) approaches it: "*There is* this void itself. It does not exist by virtue of a play of words" (*TI* 190). Rather than discouraging the reader's discovery of meaning, however, Levinas's difficult language serves to generate it, leading to "very different interpretations and appropriations."[13] Asserting that "what is distinctive about Levinas is his ability to elicit something from his readers," Davis explains: "Like the Talmud, Levinas's manner of writing displaces any fixed meaning, so that the text becomes the site where an event of meaning takes place, rather than where established meanings are communicated. The complexities, repetitions, ellipses and paradoxes ensure that any such event may be infinitely renewable and always different."[14]

Revisiting the concept of the *il y a* in his successive works, Levinas implies a continuing narrative about the genesis of the subject in the face of alterity, each book (in the words of Richard Cohen) in a wave-like sequence "venturing a more radical interpretation."[15] Levinas, in fact, likens his philosophical quest to an Abrahamic journey into a promised land, a journey that—unlike Odysseus'—makes no return to the point of departure.[16] He "denies that his account...should be understood in chronological terms," Davis notes, "yet he continues to use language which suggests that it can and must be understood in precisely such a way."[17] In Levinas's sequential writings, the *il y a* retains its elemental character, but it appears altered in context whenever Levinas's discussion of it stands in proximity to a different term: night, death, language, the maternal feminine, creation, God.[18]

In this essay I map the references to the *il y a* across the course of Levinas's oeuvre against the narrative parts of *The Awntyrs off Arthure*, an alliterative Arthurian/Gawain romance that thematizes the horrors of isolation, of a shadowy existence, of being alone and living in a state where death is near, but will never come to satiate the dying. The *Awntyrs off Arthure* resonates with certain Levinasian concepts. Pairing the ordered parts of that romance with excerpts, chronologically arranged, from Levinas's writings casts his overarching argument about the *il y a* in a narrative light, as a tale beside a tale, each rubbed against the other. Levinas's masculine, Shakespearean examples—Macbeth, Hamlet, and Lear—attempt to stave off the *il y a* by murder, suicide, and idolatry. In this essay I methodologically displace these Shakespearean examples, giving priority to an earlier, medieval work in the same tradition, *The Awntyrs off Arthure*. This displacement, which is not a replacement, allows a different, feminine figure, Gaynour (Guenevere) to highlight other means by which to struggle for existence: the tragic path of covetousness and sensual license, on the one hand, and the righteous way of prayer and almsgiving, the maternal feeding of the poor, on the other. In proximity to this medieval character, the *il y a* Levinas describes is altered again, but in a manner consistent with his own talmudic procedure.

Levinas's concept of "there is" [*il y a*] forms a critical juncture in understanding medieval fascinations with the dead, the process of dying, the afterlife, and of living and being. Whereas Levinas typically stresses the parental responsibility for the child, the *Awntyrs* poet brings to the fore the opposite side of the same relation, the child's for the parent. In this way the *Awntyrs* poet, more directly than Levinas, approaches the issue of the responsibility that the living bear for the dead. A dead mother calls out to her child, Queen Gaynour, and the child must respond. To be motherless in the world at any age is traumatic, but especially so if one was so young at the time of that loss that she has no memory, no recollection of her mother and encounters her for the first time as a horrifying stranger. The poem asks Levinas and us how such a daughter, subject to such a demand, is to respond, and how would this response effect the daughter's subjectivity?

THE *IL Y A* AS THE "DARK BACKGROUND OF EXISTENCE": THE OPENING SCENES OF *THE AWYNTYRS OFF ARTHURE*

In *Existence and Existents,* the first of his major works, Levinas describes the phenomenon of the *il y a* as "an undifferentiated background," the "dark background of existence," a "heavy atmosphere," a "nocturnal space," that approaches in a menacing way to surround and overwhelm the "I": "The things of the day world then do not in the night become the source of the 'horror of darkness' because our look cannot catch them in their 'unforeseeable plots'; on the contrary, they get their fantastic character from this horror. Darkness does not only modify their contours for vision; it reduces them to undetermined, anonymous being, which they exude" (*EE* 53–56; esp. 54). Comparing the *il y a* to an eerie state sometimes experienced at night, Levinas goes on to "speak of different forms of night that occur right in the daytime. Illuminated objects can appear to us as though in twilight shapes. Like the unreal, inverted city we find after an exhausting trip, things and beings strike us as though they no longer composed a world, and were swimming in the chaos of their existence" (54).

The language Levinas uses here works to evoke the *il y a* in dramatic terms as a scene — a space and time — in which something is going to happen, an action to commence, an "unforeseeable plot" to unfold. The poet of *The Awntyrs off Arthure* (*The Adventures of Arthur*) similarly sets an unnerving scene early in the romance, which begins in Inglewood Forest,[19] as Arthur, Gawayn, Dame Gaynour, and other "dukes and dussiperes [companions]" (4) prepare

To hunte at þe herdes þat longe had ben hydde,
On a day þei hem dight to þe depe delles,
To fall of þe femailes in forest were frydde,
Fayre by þe fermyson in frithes and felles.   (5–8)[20]
[To hunt at the herds that had long been hidden, / On a day they
themselves went off to the deep valleys, / To slay the does that were
enclosed in the forest, / And which were thriving because of the close
season in the woods and hills.]

Here is a scene of underlying tension: something is afoot, and some
unknown force approaching. The author is a master not only at building
suspense but also at presenting an atmosphere where the unknown is
all around. The party hunts the does in "holts so hare" (43) [woods so
barren], yet those woods are teeming with a fertile, feminine life, that
is at risk. Within the forest, unseen, the deer are running for their lives.

Þen durken þe dere in þe dymme skuwes
And for drede of þe deth droupes þe do
By þe squyppand watur þat squyperly squoes
Þai werray þe wilde and worchen hem wo.   (53–56)
[Then the deer cower in dark woods, / That for the dread of death
the doe goes to the ground, / And by the quickly moving water that
makes an active rushing sound, / They (the hunters) make war on the
wild and cause them woe.]

Despite the darkness of the forest, the opening scene occurs in the
daytime, and the poet initially plays upon the contrast of dark and
light, nature and art. All the members of the hunting party are clothed
in royal attire. Gaynour especially glides through the forest "Al in
gleterand golde," and with "riche ribaynes... Rayled with rybées of
riall aray" (*AA* 15–17, 27) [All glittering in gold with rich strands of
material... with rubies of royal array]. Her showy visibility stands in
contrast to the hiddenness of the frightened, death-threatened does,
but, like the female deer that are the object of the knights' bows and
arrows, as the hunters shoot at them from their hiding places "under
the bowes" (39) [under the boughs], the queen herself comes to be
menaced by a yet unknown, still approaching presence.

The king and his companions reunite at the sound of the horn "within schaghes schene" (*AA* 67) [within the bright woods], with the exception of Gaynour, who has strayed behind "in greues so grene" (69) [in groves so grene], with Gawain: "By a lauryel ho lay, vndur a lefesale" (70) [She remained by a laurel, under an arbor]. The time of the day is "Fast byfore vndre" (72) [Just before midmorning] when the marvel occurs to the company:

> The day wex als dirke
> As hit were mydniзt myrke;
> Thereof Arthur was irke
> And liзt on his fote.   (75–78)
> [The day became as dark / As if it were as murky as midnight; / Because of this Arthur became distressed and / Alighted on his horse.]

With this advent—literally, a "coming toward"—of night in the midst of day, their adventures (*Awyntyrs*) begin. They enter into some form of a liminal space, reach a threshold, a region of binary constructions (black/white, masculine/feminine, night/day, alive/seemingly dead) that produces, especially for Gawain and Gaynour, a blurring of reality. In the Middle Ages, and in certain societies today, liminal spaces such as this—wild places, ravines, crossroads, and areas where water and land meet in an impassable boundary—are often times associated with the wanderings of the dead into the land of the living.[21] A hail and rain storm drive all the knights but Gawain to the rocks. What happens next is one of the most surreal passages in Middle English Literature, where Gawain and Gaynour encounter the "mother from hell," the ghost of Gaynour's mother.

THE *IL Y A* AS "IMPOSSIBLE NOTHINGNESS": THE APPEARANCE OF THE GHOST

In both *Existence and Existence* and *Time and the Other* (relatively short works published only a year apart, in 1947 and 1948, respectively), the discussion of the impersonal *il y a* is punctuated (with conscious inconsistency) by the appearance of a ghost, a dead-but-living person, who emerges from the "dark background of existence" as an agent who is mysteriously continuous with that background. To illustrate this, Levinas turns to Macbeth, to whom Banquo's ghost appears; to Hamlet, who, having seen his father's ghost, "recoils before the 'not to be' because he has a foreboding of the return of being;" and to Phaedra, who discovers "the impossibility of death, the eternal responsibility of her being."[22] For each of these characters, Levinas observes, "There is horror of immortality, perpetuity of the drama of existence, necessity of forever taking on its burden" (*EE* 58). "A corpse is horrible," according to Levinas, because "it already bears in itself its own phantom, it presages its return. The haunting spectre, the phantom, constitutes the very element of horror" (56).

Despite this commonality between the two works, *Time and the Other* differs from *Existence and Existents* in its diction. In the later work, Levinas prefers to speak of the *il y a* as an impersonal *existing,* rather than *existence,* in order to distinguish his idea more sharply from Heidegger's ontology (the Being of *Being and Time*) and his *Geworfenheit* ("thrownness"), which presuppose an existence into which the existent is thrown (*TO* 44–51). This distinction leads Levinas to back off from describing the *il y a* as a background, a scene, an atmosphere, as he does in *Existence and Existents.* Instead, he tends to characterize it more exclusively in terms of an afterlife of still-existing, a reduction from the personal to the impersonal, general, and anonymous: "Let us imagine all things returning to nothingness. What remains after this imaginary destruction of everything is not something, but the fact that *there is* (*il y a*)" (46). In so doing, of course, Levinas counters Heidegger's anxiety-toward-death with his own view that the real horror is not death, but the impossibility of death.

Like Levinas in *Time and the Other,* the poet of *The Awyntyrs off Arthure* moves away from the description of scenery (the woods and mid-day darkness) to an *effictio* of personal reduction through the sudden, terrible appearance of a ghost: "There come a lowe of the loughe—in lede is not to layne— / In the lyknes of Lucyfere, layetheste in Helle, / And glides to Dame Gaynour þe gates full gayne, / 3auland

ȝamerly, with many loude ȝelle. / Hit ȝaules, hit ȝameres, with wan-
nynges wete" (*AA* 83–87) [There appeared a fire on the lake — not to
conceal a word — / In the likeness of Lucifer, the most hateful in Hell,
/ And it glides towards Dame Gaynour to block her path, / Howl-
ing and wailing with many a loud yell, / It cries out, it wails, with wet
lamentations].[23] Gaynour, frightened and confused, begins to wail
and asks Gawain what they are to do. He quickly tries to explain the
fiery phenomenon in astrological terms: "Hit ar þe clippes of þe son, I
herd a clerk say" (94) [It is an eclipse of the sun, I heard a cleric say].
Gawain then indicates his intention to speak with the spirit: "And of
the wayes I shall wete — / What may þe bales bete / Of þe bodi bare"
(101–04) [And of its pains I shall inquire / What may relieve the torments / Of the bare body.]

This bare body appears as a real horror. It (and the poet often refers
to this being as an impersonal object) does not resemble a human, or
what we often think of as a ghost in human form. Unlike the Green
Knight, or the ghost of Hamlet's father, or Banquo's ghost, this being
that emerges from a lake of fire seems to be beyond the classification
of human:[24]

> Bare was þe body and blak to þe bone,
> Al biclagged in clay vncomly cladde.
> Hit waried, hit waymented, as a woman,
> But nauthyr on hide ne on huwe no heling hit hadde.
> Hit stemered, hit stonayde, hit stode as a stone;
> Hit marred, hit memered, hit mused for madde.
> Agayn þe grisly goost Sir Gawayn is gone;
> He rayked to it on a res, for he was neuer rad.
> Rad was he neuer, ho so right redes.
> On þe chef of þe cholle,
> A pade pikes on the polle,
> With eighen holked ful holle
> That gloed as þe gledes.   (*AA* 105–17)

[The body was bare and black to the bone, / All clotted with foully
covered earth. / It cursed, it wailed, like a woman, / But neither skin, nor
complexion, nor covering did it have. / It stammered, it was stunned,
it stood as a stone, / It grieved, it murmured, it groaned as if it were

mad. / Again the grisly ghost goes towards Gawain; / He moved to
it in a rush, for he was never frightened. / On the top of the neck, /
A toad bites into the skull, / With eyes sunken and very hollow / that
glowed as coals.][25]

The Middle Ages knew, better than Heidegger, that it is impossible simply not to be after one has come into being: not-to-be is not
a possibility for an existent. Inconsolable throughout most of the
encounter with the ghost, Gaynour gets a glimpse into what her own
future existence may be. This is especially true after she and Gawain
realize that the spirit they have encountered is not only a former
queen, but Gaynour's own deceased mother: "Lo, how delful deth
has þi dame diȝt!" (*AA* 160) [Behold, how grievous death has dealt
with thy mother!]. Like Gaynour, her mother was once brighter in
looks than Berell or Brangwayn; she also lived even more luxuriously
than her daughter does:

> Of al gamen or gle þat on grounde growes
> Gretter þen Dame Gaynour—of garson and golde,
> Of palaies, of parkes, of pondes, of plowes,
> Of townes, of toures, of tresour vntolde,
> Of castelles, of contreyes, of cragges, of clowes.   (146–50)
> [Of all the games or merriment that occurs on Earth / I enjoyed more
> than Dame Gaynour—of treasure and gold, / Of palisades, of parks,
> of ponds, / Of towns, of towers, of treasure untold, / Of castles, of
> countries, of mountains, of valleys.]

Gaynour and her mother, when facing each other, are both the
present and the future united in each one: the "living" Gaynour who
must now assume a responsibility for the "dead" mother, and the
"dead" mother whose responsibility for the "living" Gaynour extends
even beyond death. Gaynour's future is forever linked not only with
her mother's future but also with her mother's past (a rupturing of
time potentially opened up by this liminal space); and Arthur's queen
is bound for a similar end should she fail to respond to her mother's
requests.

In *Time and the Other,* Levinas describes the struggle for existence
as the attempt to vanquish death through an ethical relation to an

Other: "The strangeness of the future of death does not leave the subject any initiative. There is an abyss between the present and death, between the ego and the alterity of mystery. It is not the fact that death cuts existence short, that it is end and nothingness, but the fact that the ego is absolutely without initiative in the face of it. Vanquishing death is to maintain, with the alterity of the event, a relationship that must still be personal" (*TO* 81). The appearance of the ghost of her mother, who resembles a vivified corpse, makes possible such a personal relationship with death. Prior to this moment, Gaynour's egoism has afforded her no possibility for initiative. Dethroned (at least for the present) by shock, Gaynour's ego bows before her mother's face, whose horrifying, needy appearance suddenly initiates the possibility of Gaynour's subjectivity.

The *Il y a* as an Absurdity that Signifies: The Face of the Ghost as Commanding Prophet

In *Totality and Infinity*, Levinas has little to say about the *il y a*, mentioning it directly only briefly in the contexts of discussions of the elemental and of signification. Instead, he writes at great length about the face and signification: "The face to face founds language" (*TI* 207). As he explains to Philippe Nemo, "Face and discourse are tied. The face speaks" (*EI* 87). What does the face say? Because "the relation to the face is straightaway ethical," meaning "you are you," the face is, for Levinas, "what one cannot kill, or at least it is that whose *meaning* consists in saying: 'thou shalt not kill'" (86–87).

What is seldom noticed is that the face, thus understood, is closely connected in the train of Levinas's thought to the *il y a* and its signification as a grammatical absurdity that points. Levinas, in fact, explicitly contrasts the advent of the impersonal *il y a* to the face: "This coming forth from nowhere opposes the element to what we describe under the name of face [visage], where precisely an existent presents itself personally" (*TI* 142). Like the *il y a*, the Levinasian face is curiously lacking in particular attributes (for example, eye color), unseen, uncontainable (*EI* 85–87). The *il y a* announces an approach, gestures toward an exteriority, the impossibility of death, even as the face (as signification itself) is the Infinite that prohibits murder. The *il y a* takes the paradoxically formless form of a ghost, who has suffered death, but whose apparition indicates it cannot die; it must continue to exist. The corpse, the ghost, is in Levinas's writings, the nocturnal face of the *il y a*, which speaks against the possibility of the very death it dies. It might be argued that the literary allusions to ghosts in Levinas's discussions of the *il y a* in *Existence and Existents* and in *Time and the Other* actually facilitated Levinas's turn to the face.

As Levinas does in *Totality and Infinity*, the poet of *The Awyntyrs* moves in the argument of his plot from the ghost's appearance to its speech. Confessing her past sins, including the breaking of a solemn vow (*AA* 205), the ghost explains to Gaynour that she continues to suffer in her body in punishment for her "luf paramour, listes and delites" (213) [adulterous love, pleasures, and delights], and that death will treat Gaynour similarly: "Þus deth wil you diȝt, thare you not doute; / Þereon hertly take hede while þou art here" (170–71) [Thus will death treat you, have no doubt about it; Take heed of this heartily while you are here]. The ghost instructs her daughter to repent for her sinful indulgences, to give to the poor, and moreover to commemorate her with "thritty trentales" (218) [thirty trentals].[26] Feeding the poor, the ghost reveals, will lessen not only her torments in Purgatory, but also Gaynour's own: "Þe praier of þe poer may purchase þe pes, / Of þase þat ȝellis at thi ȝete" (178–79) [The prayer of the poor may purchase for you peace, / Of those who yell at your gate].

The ghost speaks prophetically in warning. The worldly flattery Gaynour enjoys will bring her no true comfort, her mother says. When Gaynour asks what displeases God most, the ghost replies: "Pride with þe appurtenaunce, as prophetez han tolde / Bifore the peple, apert in her preching" (*AA* 239–40) [Pride with the showy excess, as prophets have told / Openly before the people in their preaching]. Condemning the covetousness of Arthur and the pride of his court, the ghost also predicts the destruction of the Round Table and the deaths of Gawain and Arthur. Not only her words, but also her body speaks, offering a visual sign of the way in which one's actions on earth will have a direct (and possibly horrifying) impact on the afterlife; her putrid presence is what Jacques Le Goff describes as a metaphor of "ineluctable decay," where the body, as a metaphor for society and the world and for deeds committed on earth, will continue to putrefy and rot.[27]

Addressed directly by the ghost, Gaynour speaks for the first time in the poem. When the ghost tells her, "Be war be my wo!" (*AA* 195) [Be warned by my woe!], Gaynour replies that she is worried for her mother's suffering: "Wo is me for þi wirde!" (196) [Woe is me on account of your fate!]. She uses, again for the first time in the poem, the word "moder" (202) [mother], instead of the word "dame." She questions her mother about her past life, her present sufferings, and her hope for comfort in eternity. Referring to Christ's mother Mary, Gaynour commends her mother's soul to God's mercy. She also asks her mother about what is pleasing to God, beseeches her guidance, and promises her that she will fulfill her mother's requests, in particular, for the offering of Masses and liturgical hours.

The ghost reminds her daughter to perform this sacred act more than once, and before she vanishes, she makes her commandment to her daughter clear:

> "Fede folke for my sake þat fauten þe fode
> And menne me with matens and masse in melle.
> Masses arn medecynes to vs þat bale bides;
> Vs þenke a masse as swete
> As eny spice þat euer ye yete."   (*AA* 319–23)
> [Feed people for my sake who lack food, / and remember me with matins and Masses together. / Masses are medicines to us who endure torment; / it seems to us a Mass is as sweet as any spice that you ever ate.]

Shortly thereafter, the ghost disappears from view:

> With a grisly grete, þe goost awey glides
> And goes with gronyng sore and a grym bere.
> Þe wyndes, þe weders, þe welken vnhides —
> Þen vnclosed þe cloudes; þe son wex clere.   (326–29)

[With a grisly groan, the ghost glides away / And continues with its
grievous groaning and a grim outcry. / The winds, the storms, the sky
lay open— / Then the clouds parted; the sun became clear.]

We as readers (and also Gawain and Gaynour) are returned to daylight,
but the horror of what has just transpired—the manifestation of the
il y a—does not vanish with the parting of the clouds and mist.

The *Il y a* as Womb; or, The Maternal Other

The first page of Levinas's *Otherwise Than Being* invokes "the mute
and anonymous rustling of the *il y a*" as that which signals an alternative response to the question "to be or not to be" by pointing to
the possibility of an ethical transcendence (*OB* 3). What is significant,
Levinas explains, is not each one's own death, but the death of the
other person, for whom one is responsible: "The place left vacant by
the one who died is filled with the murmur of the attendants" (3).

The masterpiece of his mature philosophical expression, *Otherwise
Than Being*, presents the *il y a* from two different sides: sense (associated
with essence, cognition, and the ego) and nonsense (associated with the
an-archic, the ethical, the subject). The two, sense and nonsense, are
imagined as laboring together to give birth to an offspring, a subject:
"The rumbling of the *there is* the non-sense in which essence turns,
and in which thus turns the justice issued out of signification. . . . It
is in its ex-ception and ex-pulsion as a responsible one that a subject
outside of being can be conceived" (*OB* 163). Whereas in *Existence
and Existents* the *il y a* appears primarily as an approaching horror, in
Otherwise Than Being it retains that horror chiefly from the perspective
of an egoic sense, threatened by its own submergence, while from the
point of view of nonsense it signifies an "ethical deliverance of the self
through substitution for the other": "To support [an Other] without
compensation, the excessive or disheartening hubbub and encumber-
ment of the *there is* is needed" (164).

Regarded as a support for the subject, who is in turn a support for
the Other, the rumbling darkness of the *il y a* becomes, for Levinas,

a maternal source, a "pre-birth or pre-nature": "The *there is* is all the weight that alterity weighs supported by a subjectivity that does not found it" (*OB* 75, 164). Translated into a feminine form, the subject supports the life of the Other as a pregnant woman bears the weight of a child still unborn. As Claire Elise Katz has maintained, female subjectivity is formed out of the " 'there is' (*il y a*), the impersonal existence;" that is, "the relation to the feminine, conceived as radical alterity, is the means by which subjectivity is first constituted;"[28] it is, she insists, the "radical alterity housed in the feminine that enables the movement from the *there is* to the hypostasis."[29] Interpreting Levinas's concept of subjectivity through his use of biblical and rabbinic sources, Katz regards this movement out of the *il y a* to the hypostasis as a movement from anonymity to "particular subjectivity," a movement "out of the silence before creation, out of chaos, to a world of separation and individuation."[30]

Elements of gestation and creation are to be found in *The Awyntyrs,* especially in the leafy bower in which Gaynour lingers and where she subsequently encounters her mother, who appears out of the fiery lake during a dark rainfall. Primordial and protean, both the bower and the lake act as a source for life, and yet they are forever changing, as if they yearn for a new and perhaps more fulfilling state of existence. Nature appears almost ill-content and unsatisfied with itself. Interpreted otherwise—that is, from the perspective of the ethical, the end of the narrative—the dark grove, which at first seemed only menacing with the threat of death, now churns and teems with the possibility of new life.

Within this fecund environment, the avenues of time and eternity meet in their relation to death and the beyond. The ghostly mother, who faces Gaynour with her decaying face, is curiously anonymous, never called by name, and at first unrecognized. Motherhood, as Levinas describes it in *Otherwise Than Being,* is equivalent to the accusation of being responsible; it opens one, passive and vulnerable, to the suffering of accusation.[31] One of the poem's more problematic and striking moments occurs when the suffering ghost curses "þe body me bare!" (89). That is, she curses the body that gave birth to her—her own mother, Gaynour's grandmother. Through this curse, the gift of birth and of existence is summarily (but also impossibly) rejected. Her intensely passionate declaration, which severs the biological and spiritual connection with her mother, leaves her lagging behind her own existence submerged in the *il y a*. The ghostly mother's cursing of her mother can be read as an obstacle to her subjectivity *as* mother to Gaynour, who stands on the hither side of her self. At the same time, however, the daughter's curse evokes the possibility of a daughter's blessing; even as the passivity and the horror of the *il y a* entails the potential for both the absolute dissolution or the emergence of a living subjectivity.

The poem leaves Gaynour, like her mother, enigmatic, undefined, telling us nothing explicitly about her past (as an orphan), her present (as an adulteress with Lancelot, a childless wife to Arthur), her future (as a young widow, perhaps a nun).[32] Although the Arthurian tradition may inform readers who draw upon other sources, the poem itself reveals Gaynour's past and present indirectly, through the prophesying ghost, who is the shadow of herself and the sign of her own possible future.

The wretchedness of the ghost as Other and mother allows the poet to explore a doubled ethical relation. In need of Gaynour's motherly prayers and good works as a remedy for her Purgatorial pain, the ghost is an "orphan" to her own childless daughter, whom she calls into a maternity.[33] (Levinas, of course, names the Other precisely as "the weak, the poor, 'the widow and the orphan.'") (*TO* 83). At the same time, the ghost is and remains Gaynour's mother. Her words of warning and moral counsel express her concern and ongoing responsibility for her daughter's life. She calls Gaynour to attention by confessing her sins and describing her woe. Confronted with the face of her mother and thus placed within an ethical framework of responsibility, Gaynour, who has been both motherless and childless, is forced into the role of surrogate mother for her own mother.[34]

In the poem Gaynour speaks, reminding her mother's ghost of her baptism as an infant (*AA* 224–25),[35] of the birth of baby Jesus [*þe blisful barne*] in Bethlehem (227), and of the Virgin Mary's gentleness and might (226):

> "To blisse bring þe þe Barne þat bought þe on Rode,
> Þat was crucifiged on Croys and crowned with þorne.
> As þou was cristened and crisomed with candel and code,
> Folowed in fontestone frely byforne —
> Mary þe miȝti, myldest of mode,
> Of whom þe blisful barne in Bedlem was borne,
> Lene me grace to grete þi soule with gode."   (222–28)
>
> [May the Child that redeemed thee on the tree bring thee to bliss, / Who was crucified on the cross and crowned with thorns. / As you were christened and anointed with candle and chrism cloth, / Baptized freely at the font in public — / Mary the mighty, mildest in spirit, / Of whom the blissful babe was born in Bethlehem, / Grant me grace that I may greet your soul with good.]

In this way Gaynour explicitly portrays her mother as a child and names a maternal role model for herself. The author of *The Awntyrs* presents the familial bond shared between the two women as a powerful, regenerative force.[36] Gaynour is now clearly within the role of the maternal; as a subject to and of an Other,[37] she has the duty and responsibility to act for the betterment of her mother, herself reduced to a helpless, almost childlike state. Pledging her prayers, Gaynour binds herself in service to her dead mother,[38] and is herself, the poem suggests, reborn anew. Helen Philips has demonstrated how *The Awntyrs off Arthure* uses the liturgy and theology of baptism as a central organizing principle.[39] Specifically, Philips argues that it is the memory of the ghost's baptism that imbues the narrative with a "liturgical, almost a sacramental, approach."[40]

The Masses that Gaynour will organize for her departed mother serve as a path toward Gaynour's subjectivity and thus the biblical finding of her life.[41] As Levinas himself writes, "The subject begins, starting from its relation, its obligation with regards to the other" (*IRB* 64). This feminine relationship in *The Awntyrs* is grounded on the ethical decision by Gaynour to honor her mother (her life and her death) through prayer, as she is always already bound to do. "The feminine is the future," observes Levinas.[42] Gaynour's potential subjectivity, her future self, is connected with the Masses offered meritoriously for her mother, who commands her in the present, but also from the past.[43] This ethical journey of Gaynour's, however, is not certain. The mother has declared the parameters by which her daughter's subjectivity is possible, calling for the performance of spiritual and corporal works of mercy, yet it is clearly Gaynour's decision *and* her responsibility to follow through.

The second half of the *Awntyrs off Arthure* begins abruptly after the departure of the ghost, the reunion of Gaynour with Arthur, and the return to the hunting party to the hall. No sooner has the King sat down to his supper when an errant knight and his lady arrive, well armed and richly arrayed. The stranger, who identifies himself as Sir Galleron of Galloway, demands honorable combat with Gawain, to reclaim from him lands to which (Galleron believes) he is not legally entitled. The symmetries between the two halves of the poem suggest a parallel between the demanding stranger and the ghost, both of whom appear unexpectedly. The complaint of Sir Galleron about the lands Arthur has conquered and given to Gawain, moreover, repeats the charge of the ghost that Arthur and his men are "to couetous" (*AA* 265) [too covetous]. The episode evokes anxieties about entitlement, but also (perhaps) about the inheritance from the dead, who continue to claim legal control (via their last wills) over the uses to which their property is put. Demonstrating what Christine Chism has called "the inadequacy of institutional ritual,"[44] the knights fight nearly to the death without a resolution of the question. The battle takes place in broad daylight, but the bloodiness of the fight, the strangeness of the encounter, and the uncertainty of the cause mingle sense with nonsense.

The groaning [*gronyng*] (*AA* 620) of Galleron's lady, who seeks Gaynour's help, finds its second in Gaynour's own plea to Arthur to end the combat: "The grones of Sir Gawayne greuen me sare" (633) [The groans of Sir Gawain grieve me sorely]. The two knights then mutually concede to each other, are enriched by each other and by Arthur, and are ultimately dubbed dukes together on a single day in

Camelot. While Gaynour's compassionate intercession on behalf of the bleeding knights is not exactly the feeding of the poor to which her mother called her, it indicates that she has (perhaps) become attuned to the sound of an Other's suffering, the rustling of the *il y a*. The final stanza finds Gaynour organizing "a mylion of masses to make þe mynnynge" [a million Masses to make the memorial] to be undertaken and administered by "Bokelered burnes, bisshops þe best" (706–707) [men learned in book, the best bishops]. The last words of the poem repeat its opening line, circling back to the beginning, the woods, and the adventure of the ghost, but Gaynour seems altered, changed by her encounter with the dead.

Il y a, Illeity, and Death; or, Undying Responsibility for and to the Dead

In Levinas's last two major works, *Otherwise Than Being* and *Of God Who Comes to Mind,* he coins the word, and develops the notion of, *illeity* to name as God the impersonal quality of otherness in the Other, that which Alphonso Lingis terms "the nonphenomenal force of the other," the "he" (*ille*)—rather than a "Thou"—whose "voice...speaks in the ethical imperative" to demand always more than one can give and whose judgment never ceases to call us "into question."[45] "A neologism formed with *il* (he) or *ille*," Levinas explains, "it [*illeity*] indicates a way of concerning me without entering into conjunction with me;" a "detour at a face," it "cannot be tracked down like game by a hunter," but always eludes our retracing of it (*OB* 12). It is the "He at the root of the You" (*GCM* 69). Named in the third person, God's alterity or *illeity* does not admit, for Levinas, any direct, personal, or intimate relationship to the "I." Indeed, in its impersonality, in its being otherwise than the human other, this *illeity* of God exists "prior to the ethical obligation to the other and different from every neighbor, transcendent to the point of absence, to the point of its possible confusion with the agitation of the *There is* [*il y a*]" (69).

The notion of *illeity* enables Levinas to deal with the question, among others, of the responsibility owed *to* the dead, above and beyond the responsibility one bears *for the death* of the other. Earlier in his work, in *Totality and Infinity,* Levinas raises the issue of "the dead one's refusal to fall into the time of the other, the personal time free from common time" (*TI* 57). He rejects traditional, religious ideas of the afterlife as mythological means for a continued being, even as he rejects both the totalizing end of the historiographer and the Heideggerian anxiety toward death-as-non-being. For Levinas, "to be or not to be" is *not* the question. He seeks a third, transcendent path. His religious concern is with the living, with life itself as it contains a hidden, infinite dimension.[46] This very concern, however, leads him to consider the question of the relation of the living to the departed and, ultimately, to the notion of *illeity*.[47] In the absence of the other through death—an absence that underscores the impossibility of a direct relation, an exteriority—he discovers an *illeity* that continues to command an ethical response, an imperative that issues from an other that is other than the other one simply remembers.

Despite this antitheological, secular bent, which "may seem to many to be irreligiousness itself" (as Annette Aronowicz observes), Levinas is remarkable for his insistence on "the centrality, the importance, of Jewish ritual," which, he says, "conditions [conscience] and permits it to enter into itself and to stay awake."[48] Although Levinas has avoided explicit comment on the Jewish prayers for the dead, in particular, the *kaddish*,[49] the conscience formed by their recital is not unrelated to the notion of *illeity*. Levinas suggests as much when, in reference to the "saying" of the psalms, he writes: "The detachment of the Infinite from the thought that seeks to thematize it and the language that tries to hold it in the said is what we call *illeity*" (*OB* 147). He continues: "One is tempted to call this plot religious" (147). Elsewhere in *Otherwise Than Being* he links *illeity* to God's glory and glorification: "It is glorified . . . in the glorification of its glory by the subject. . . . Glorification is saying, that is, a sign given to the other, peace announced to the other, responsibility for the other, to the extent of substitution" (148).

The *kaddish* is a communal prayer and (like the reading of the Torah) can only be performed when a *Minyan* is present—a quorum of ten.[50] The communal nature of the *kaddish* signifies the wholeness of the congregation, and it also unites the living—those saying the prayer—to those to whom the prayer is directed. In the Jewish tradition, the prayers for the dead (such as the *kaddish*) are to be seen as a testament to the Creator, and thus they symbolize the continued ethical responsibility one must have to the dead. The *kaddish* is a prayer that does not contain any literal proclamations of sadness or loss. Rather, the prayer is a "doxology—a listing of God's holy attributes."[51] Saying *kaddish* is an aural and verbal experience; it is a powerful prayer that transcends the plane of existence.

The *kaddish* affirms the world and God's creation of it, God's sovereignty, and God's greatness. In the *kaddish,* Diamant says, "God is beyond us."[52] The *kaddish,* though, offers no picture of the afterlife. Diamant asserts that Judaism has a relative "indifference to the afterlife," which is apparent in the customs and laws that surround death. A Jewish funeral (as well as the *kaddish*) focuses on the life that is, or was.[53] Maurice Lamm poetically says that the Old Testament is "silent about the world to come" and that this silence is "a tribute to an awesome concept, taken for granted like the biosphere in which we live. No elaborate apologia, no complex abstractions are necessary. The Bible, which records the sacred dialogue between God and man, surely must be founded on the soul's eternal existence."[54] As Samuel Heilman demonstrates, the Hasidim turned the *yahrzeit* (the yearly anniversary of someone's death) into a joyous feast, where cakes and *schnapps* were enjoyed and the traditional toast of *l'chaim* ("a toast to and embrace of eternal life") was made.[55]

If there is a moment in Levinas's writing where he approaches the solemn yet utterly communal sense of the *kaddish,* it can be located within his opening memorial dedication of *Otherwise Than Being* to the victims of the Holocaust. It appears on the page as a double dedication: one in English and one in Hebrew.[56] For his English dedication, Levinas writes: "To the memory of those who were closest among the six million assassinated by the National Socialists, and of the millions on millions of all confessions and all nations, victims of the same hatred of the other man, the same anti-Semitism" (*OB* v). The dedication written in Hebrew is far more personal, for in it Levinas records the names of his six family members who were all victims of the Holocaust, and who all (with the exception of his father-in-law) were murdered.[57] Levinas's dedication memorializes his family, and it also serves as a prayer for the dead and for the living.

While it is not a formal *kaddish,* Levinas's double dedication achieves a similar end: as the living son, it would be his responsibility and obligation to recite the *kaddish;* as a human deeply affected by the suffering of others (those who have passed as well as those who have lived through the horrors of the Holocaust), Levinas remembers their death as well as their life. Death necessarily entails separation for Levinas, but not the loss of relation itself. As he writes elsewhere: "daily death—and the death of every instant—of other persons, as they withdraw into themselves, does not plunge beings into incommunicable solitude: that is precisely what nurtures love" (*PN* 103).

Levinas's dedication, then, to *Otherwise Than Being,* while not as celebratory as the Mass organized by Gaynour, nor as festive as the *yahrzeits* performed by the Hasidim, does achieve a similar end to that of the Masses, announced throughout England with the ringing of bells, with which *The Awntyrs off Arthure* concludes. Both works recall the departed as ones to whom the living remain bound and indebted, and for whom they are called to substitute themselves in works of prayer and serve to the poor, in answer to the command of God. If Levinas's dedication may be seen in retrospect as a dedication of his entire work, beginning with *Existence and Existents,* then his writings, not unfittingly, can be mapped against the unfolding plot of a didactic, medieval romance that moves (in Levinasian terms) from the horror of the *il y a* to the glory of *illeity.*[58]

6

Doing Justice to Isaac
Levinas, the *Akedah,*
and the Brome Play of *Abraham and Isaac*

Daniel T. Kline

> If I am getting ready to speak at length about ghosts,
> inheritance, and generations, generations of ghosts,
> which is to say about certain others who are not present,
> nor presently living, either to us, in us, or outside us,
> it is in the name of justice.
> —Derrida, *Specters of Marx*

> We're one, but we're not the same.
> —U2, "One"

As Eric Auerbach so famously noted, the account of Abraham's near sacrifice of Isaac is spare and enigmatic, but in the fifteenth and sixteenth centuries, Middle English dramatists fleshed out Genesis 22 to suit their own dramatic needs, religious aims, and ideological purposes.[1] Six versions of the Abraham and Isaac episode are preserved in Middle English drama, and while these dramas might appear undifferentiated in their appeal to a common biblical text, each revises the *akedah* to markedly different effect.[2] Medieval Christianity found in the *akedah* the typological prefiguration of the sacrificial death of Christ; however, by giving voice to Isaac, the Brome play of *Abraham and Isaac* raises the specter of resistance to, and a critique of, the sacrificial economy of late medieval Christianity.[3] Specifically, by depicting the sacrificial victim as an articulate subject who speaks from an embodied position, the Brome play of *Abraham and Isaac* calls for a reformulation of the relationship of the ethical to the religious in light of what I call "the afterlife of sacrifice." At the same time, contemporary thinkers have analyzed the *akedah* intensely. One of the most important analyses has been Emmanuel Levinas's engagement with Søren Kierkegaard. While Kierkegaard, via the pseudonymous Johannes de Silentio, lauds Abraham as the father of faith for his "teleological suspension of the ethical," Levinas criticizes Kierkegaard's formulation of subjectivity, his understanding of ethics, and his conception of the *akedah* in *Fear and Trembling*.

This essay will proceed along several trajectories. First, after a brief overview in which I contextualize Silentio's understanding of the *akedah* in *Fear and Trembling*, I bring Levinas's understanding of subjectivity, paternity, and filiation to bear upon Kierkegaard's reading of Genesis 22. Second, I then move to Levinas's explicit critique of the violence of Kierkegaard's account of subjectivity, his separation of the ethical from the religious sphere, and his incomplete view of Abraham. Third, in Levinasian terms, I consider not simply the face of the Other as ethical demand, but the inevitability of the third, the Other of the Other—in this case, Isaac, the marginalized, spectral child—as the basis of sociality and ethics. Fourth, by attending to the voice of Ysaac, the dynamics of age and filiation, the passion of the face, and Abraham and Ysaac's "pluralist existing" in the Brome *Abraham and Isaac*, I reassess both Kierkegaard and Levinas's reading of the *akedah*. To do so, I focus upon Brome's characterization of Ysaac, specifically the ethical demands he makes upon his father and his ongoing reactions to the sacrificial encounter. Finally, I argue that the Brome play is in some ways more Levinasian than Levinas himself. By giving Isaac a voice, by calling Abraham to account, by invoking Sarah as witness, and by dramatizing the human cost of sacrifice against the primacy of the ethical relation, the Brome play offers a remarkable, even midrashic reading of the *akedah* that, rather than sealing the text under a typological *integumentum*, invites renewed engagement with the biblical episode it glosses, dramatizes, extends, and to which it remains inassimilable.

As a result, my focus throughout this essay is upon the child, Isaac, as the unacknowledged center of the *akedah*. I contend that the figure of the child as self-same Otherness, in a Levinasian sense, provides an avenue of resistance against sacrificial ideology. I conclude that readings of the *akedah* concentrating solely upon the relationship between Abraham and God, without facing up to the traumatized Isaac, "the third party [who] listens, wounded, to the amorous dialogue" (*EN* 21), fail to account adequately for the call of ethics in the face of the sacrificial imperative. With apologies to John Lennon, love is *not* all you need. In opposing Kierkegaard's "teleological suspension of the ethical," my reading of the Brome Ysaac yields a corrective formulation, "the ethical suspension of the teleological," that substitutes an ongoing ethical relation with the self-same Other for egological subjectivity tensed upon itself in isolation. The Brome Ysaac, in his voluptuous proximity to his father Abraham, offers an open futuriority, a nonteleological glimpse of the hither side of egological subjectivity and sacrificial deity.

The story of the *akedah* (Gen. 22:1–19) is so well known that I will only convey its outline. After his dispute with Abimelech, "God tempted Abraham," commanded him to take Isaac "into the land of Vision," and "offer him for a holocaust" (or burnt offering) (22:2).[4] Abraham took two young men, Isaac, wood for the sacrifice, and traveled for three days to the appointed place. Leaving the two youths, Abraham laid the wood upon Isaac, and they went together to the mount. There Isaac saw that while they had wood and fire, there was no "victim for the holocaust" (22:7). Abraham responded that God would provide a victim (22:8). Abraham built an altar and placed the wood, and then bound Isaac and laid him upon the altar. Then, taking the sword "to sacrifice his son" (22:11), an angel commanded Abraham to spare Ysaac (22:12), for the angel now knew that Abraham feared God. Lifting his eyes, Abraham saw a ram caught in the briars, which he sacrificed instead of his son (22:13). Abraham named the place, "The Lord seeth" (22:14). The angel called a second time and said that because Abraham did not spare his son, God would then bless Abraham, multiply his descendents, defeat their enemies, and bless "all the nations of the earth" through him (22:18). Abraham then returned with the young men to Bersabee. "Immediately after that," in Shalom Spiegel's words, "all traces of Isaac son of Father Abraham disappear."[5]

The Akedah in Kierkegaard's Fear and Trembling

In traditional sacrificial readings of the *akedah,* Isaac serves as Abraham's Other, and the violence against the child is rationalized as theologically necessary and soteriologically justifiable because it serves a greater good. Kierkegaard's interpretation of the *akedah,* in the voice of the pseudonymous Johannes de Silentio in *Fear and Trembling,* serves as the canonical interpretation with which modern critics must reckon.[6]

In *Fear and Trembling,* Silentio rings the changes upon the key themes of contemporary thought (subjectivity, ethics, faith, sacrifice, the Other). Because of his obedience to God's call to sacrifice Isaac, which opposes the most basic ethical demand against murder (particularly killing a beloved son), Silentio's Abraham becomes "the knight of faith" who transcends mere human moral constraints and enters an absolute relationship to the God that subordinates every other human affinity. Unlike the "tragic hero" who remains within the ethical realm and bound to social relations, Abraham transcends conventional morality, in Kierkegaard's famous formulation, through a "teleological suspension of the ethical."[7] Silentio asks: "How then did Abraham exist? He believed. This is the paradox which keeps him upon the sheer edge and which he cannot make clear to any other man, for the paradox is that he as the individual puts himself in an absolute relation to the absolute. Is he justified in doing this? His justification is once more the paradox; for if he is justified, it is not by virtue of anything universal, but by virtue of being the particular individual."[8]

The defining relationship in Silentio's account of Abraham's uniqueness is the one between Abraham and God,[9] and as a result Isaac is diminished to "a position of relativity" (*FT* 80) rather than a relation of a responsibility: "His relation to Isaac, ethically expressed, is this, that the father should love the son. This ethical relation is reduced to a relative position in contrast to the absolute relation to God" (81). Silentio's account of Abraham's ethical paradox is doubly (and hierarchically) dyadic though the system is triadic: God's demand upon Abraham is absolute, and Abraham's response to God is total, but in both cases, Isaac, as child and son, is individually marginalized yet absolutely necessary in his abnegation. In his critique of Hegel, Silentio claims repeatedly that Abraham exists beyond mediation, and although Isaac is effaced, he also serves an absolutely essential mediatory function: He is sacrificeable. Silentio continues, "But now when the ethical is thus teleologically suspended, how does the individual exist in whom it is suspended? He exists as the particular in opposition to the universal" (72). Significantly, then, only the sovereign subject obtains in Kierkegaard's vision of faith. There is no third party to whom Abraham must answer or the silent child may appeal. There is only the exclusive couple, Abraham and God. All Others must be excluded for that relation to be absolute.

Furthermore, the logic of Christian typology makes Kierkegaard's diminution of Isaac in *Fear and Trembling* theologically, ideologically, and narratively sensible, for Christianity itself veils Isaac as well. The *flesh and blood* son of Abraham is potent only as a *type* of Christ, a prefiguration of the crucified messiah to come, and Isaac's historical reality is important only as it is absorbed into prophetic Christian fulfillment. Kierkegaard substitutes salvation of the *individual* for the redemption of the *nation*, making Isaac and the physical, historical continuation of the nation of Israel necessary only for its fulfillment in Christ. Kierkegaard thus is locked into a teleological determinism, and Abraham reaches the "teleological suspension of the ethical" only because Christianity has always already fulfilled Judaism's insufficiencies. Isaac is therefore the prototype of Christian reification, and his incomplete sacrifice in the *akedah* is meaningful only insofar as it is read in light of the final sacrifice and crucifixion of Christ.

Fear and Trembling's utter effacement of Isaac is not simply the product of Silentio's narrative choices but is a function of Kierkegaard's subordination of childish Judaism and to mature Christian triumphalism.[10] Ultimately, Abraham suffers and Isaac is violently traumatized so that *Christianity* may flourish. This is the essence of theodicy and Holocaustic logic, that another's suffering be rationalized and justified as part of a grand telos.[11] How then is one to do justice to Isaac? By suspending the telos through open, ongoing ethical relation.

LEVINAS'S COLLOQUY WITH KIERKEGAARD

While Levinas's overt critique of Kierkegaard is centered in several well known texts, I find it significant that Levinas never engages in a sustained, explicit interpretation of *Fear and Trembling* or the *akedah*. Instead, Levinas's generalized criticism of Kierkegaard, scattered throughout his *oeuvre*, offers an indirect reading of Genesis 22, and when Levinas does comment on the *akedah* (or, more generally, upon Abraham), I believe it is largely in dialogue with *Fear and Trembling*.

In Levinas's reading of Kierkegaard, the subject harbors an inexpressible secret in secret, like Abraham, and Levinas fears that a "return to a subjectivity that turns away from thought" may itself "lead us to other forms of violence" (*PN* 68). These forms of violence cohere in the scissions evident throughout Silentio's account of the *akedah*. In the first scission, the Kierkegaardian subject is tensed upon itself in what Levinas calls "egotism." Because Kierkegaard's truth cannot be harnessed in exteriority, but only interiorly, the confirmation of belief is found in internal suffering, a self-rending "that does not open man to other men but to God, in solitude" (70). In the second scission, the relationship of the I to any Other is extinguished in Kierkegaard's religious realm, for the "singularity of the *I* would be lost under the rule that is valid for all" (72; emphasis Levinas's). Thus, all Others are reduced to the same in opposition to the "I" in relation to God. These two scissions join in a third, when Kierkegaard severs the ethical sphere from the religious, and "Violence emerges in Kierkegaard at the precise moment when, moving beyond the esthetic stage, existence can no longer limit itself to what it takes to be the ethical stage and enters the religious one, the domain of belief" (72). The autonomous, suffering, egological self is for Kierkegaard the only basis for relationship to God, the absolute, who stands beyond all ethics and sociality. In contrast to Kierkegaard, Levinas argues that the "I" emerges only through sociality: "Sociality [is] not to be confused with some weakness or privation in the unity of the One. From the depths of natural perseverance in the being of a being who is assured of his right to be, from the heart of the original identity of the *I*—and against the perseverance, and against that identity—there arises, awakened before the face of the other, a responsibility for the other to whom I was committed *before* any committing, before being present to myself or coming back to self" (*AT* 30–31; emphasis Levinas). The Kierkegaardian movement from social relations to internal, affective authenticity before God is exactly the opposite of the Levinasian paradigm of ethical relation that gives birth to subjectivity.

At the end of "Kierkegaard: Existence and Ethics," Levinas turns explicitly to *Fear and Trembling,* countermanding these scissions by returning to the demands of sociality (*PN* 74). First, Levinas explicitly criticizes Kierkegaard for separating the ethical from the religious sphere and placing God beyond the ethical order. Levinas wonders aloud, with no little incredulity, how Kierkegaard can possibly separate God from ethics. Second, Levinas notes that Kierkegaard effectively focuses only upon part of God's test of Abraham, the call to sacrifice Isaac, rather than the correlative call to spare Isaac and sacrifice the substitutionary animal. Finally, he notes that Kierkegaard reads the *akedah* in isolation from Abraham's ongoing colloquy with God, particularly Abraham's intervention on behalf of Sodom and Gomorrah "in the name of the just who may be present there."[12] In that remarkable text from Genesis 18, Abraham *opposes* God's judgment on behalf of those unknown Others to whom and for whom Abraham reckons himself responsible before God. Whereas Kierkegaard adroitly fragments Abraham's history into isolated segments, thematically placing the *akedah* above all others, Levinas views Abraham in the context of his total history of relation to God, and this relationship is neither isolated nor egological but is always socially engaged and grounded in human need. God chooses Abraham so that he will teach his household to pursue justice and to obey God, and when Abraham intervenes on behalf of Sodom and Gomorrah, Abraham confronts even God's apparent injustice: Will you destroy an entire city because of the wicked, or will you spare the city if a minority—even ten—are yet righteous? Abraham's relation to God is based upon the pursuit of justice and the demands of sociality in recognition of the Other before whom Abraham is no more than "dust and ashes" (Gen. 18:27). One is compelled to act justly on behalf of Others, and that orientation remains forever open. Thus, Levinas explicitly questions Kierkegaard's obsessive focus upon the "subject tensed upon itself" to the neglect of the social—Kierkegaard's ethical—realm and implicitly rejects the teleological determinism that governs Kierkegaard's logic.

In fact, Levinas famously reads the *akedah* against Kierkegaard by noting that perhaps the most important moment in the *akedah* is when Abraham heeds the angel's second command not to harm Isaac in any way, thus returning Abraham to the ethical order (*PN* 74). Rather than separating Abraham from Isaac and from each other and the *socius*, the *sub-stitution* of the ram for Isaac reestablishes the ethical order and reincorporates God, Abraham, and Isaac within it.[13] In the talmudic tradition, according to Levinas, Abraham as the father of faith is "above all the one who knew how to receive and feed men: the one whose tent was open on all sides" (*NT* 99). Symbolically opposite of Kierkegaard's socially insulated, egological subject, Abraham's open tent signifies his continual openness toward, and responsibility for, the Other, taking as his duty "the form of obligation toward the body, the obligation of feeding and sheltering" (99), as in the moment that he tends to the three mysterious visitors at the oaks of Mamre (Gen. 18). Significantly, after Abraham has received, washed, and fed the three visitors, he is told that Sarah will bear a child. Memorably, she laughed, but the scripture records, "Is anything too hard for God?" (18:14), and Sarah later gives birth to Isaac. At each point in his critique, Levinas directs Kierkegaard back to the complete history of Abraham's relationship to God, for the *akedah*, as supervening as it is, is nonetheless one episode in an ongoing narrative of faith; in each criticism, Levinas points Kierkegaard back to the ethical; in each instance, he points Kierkegaard to Abraham's journey of faith as it concerns the Other(s) to whom he stands in the accusative, and for whom he is responsible.

Above all, Levinas is "disturbed" by Kierkegaard's conception of subjectivity, a self whose absolute singularity severs all connection to Others in pursuit of an absolute relation to the absolute *apart* from the ethical. First of all, Kierkegaard's struggle against being absorbed in Hegel's universalism results in an "exhibitionist, immodest subjectivity." According to Levinas, this sovereign "I" must be challenged in its ipseity, and the Other poses that challenge: "The putting in question of the *I* in the face of the Other is a new tension in the *I*, a tension that is not a tensing on oneself. Instead of destroying the *I*, the putting in question binds it to the other in an incomparable, unique manner" (*PN* 73; emphasis Levinas's). The exteriority of the face challenges the egophilic, isolated subject tensed upon itself. For Levinas, such exteriority puts Kierkegaard's "I" into question and "signifies the responsibility of the I for the Other," for the "uniqueness of the *I* consists in the fact that no one can answer in his or her place" (73; emphasis Levinas's). Being placed thus in the accusative rather than the nominative, the Kierkegaardian "I" is "elected," to use Levinas's pregnant theological term, and "promoted to a privileged place on which all that is not me depends" (73). Second, Kierkegaard's philosophical violence "shocks" him, for Levinas "perceive[s] by anticipation the echoes of certain cases of verbal violence that claimed to be schools of thought, and pure ones at that. I am thinking not only of National Socialism, but of all the sorts of thought it exalted" (76). Levinas's strong condemnation here has itself shocked a number of commentators, but its logic is clear: a single-minded focus upon the one to the neglect of all Others is the source of violence, for "Violence is to be found in any action in which one acts as if one were alone to act: as if the rest of the universe were there only to *receive* the action" (*DF* 6).

Kierkegaard's Abraham acts in precisely such a way, as if there are no Others in his universe, and Abraham's elevation depends upon the denigration of his son, Isaac. It is no accident that Isaac, the silent mediator in Abraham's "absolute relation to the absolute," is a male child within a patriarchal system, for when Silentio invokes Isaac, it is invariably only in relation to the father. Yet, paradoxically, the patriarchal male can become a *father* only if he *fathers* a child, making the father dependent upon the child and mother for his power and position. Thus, in patriarchy, the father's absolute separation of the son's identity from his own allows the father to ignore his son's unique face and see in it only the mirror of his own needs. In contrast, Levinas argues that paternity involves *both* alterity and self-identity: "Paternity is the relationship with a stranger who, entirely while being Other, is me. It is the relationship of the ego with a selfsame ego who is nonetheless a stranger to the ego. The son in fact is not simply my work, like a poem or manufactured object, neither is he my property. Neither the categories of power nor those of having can indicate the relationship with the child. Neither the notion of cause nor the notion of ownership permit grasping the fact of fecundity."[14] Rather than separation and possession, the child represents coexistence and "incommen-surability."

For Levinas, the paternal relationship is uniquely structured in fecundity, for the child is at the same time the stranger, the Other, and the neighbor who is in some sense also myself. Here, the child (the son for Levinas) is this selfsame Other who can neither be reduced to the father's work nor to the father's property, yet who is somehow essentially *of*, and coextensive to, the father. Against the patriarchal tendency to view reproduction as possession, Levinas writes: "The fact of seeing the possibilities of the other as your own possibilities, of being able to escape the closure of your own identity and what is bestowed on you, toward something which is not bestowed on you and which nevertheless is yours — this is paternity" (*EI* 70). Kierkegaard's Abraham sees Isaac only as extension of his own needs rather than an Other who will enable him "to escape the closure of his own identity" into openness and freedom through accountability. It is easy to see how Abraham's (and Silentio's) reduction of Isaac's ontological status to his patriarchal utility facilitates the ancient (or perhaps not so ancient) practice of child sacrifice, particularly the sacrifice of the first born, and the father's absolute right of life and death.[15]

Yet even in the biblical text one may discern Isaac's call to Abraham for recognition and responsibility. In the only verse in which he speaks (Gen. 22:7), Isaac recognizes his filial dependence upon, and mutual coexisting with, Abraham when he says simply, "My father" (22:7). This is the unvarnished ethical relation, the naked *il y a* of the Other. Abraham responds, "What wilt thou, son?" without recognizing that Isaac's statement is both a recognition and demand, for what Isaac *wills* is what he has said: (I want to be recognized by) my father. Isaac indeed sees that two of the three ingredients for sacrifice are present, but the victim is missing: "Behold, saith he, fire and wood: where is the victim for the holocaust?" (22:7). At this moment of recognition, Isaac attempts to call his father back to relationship and responsibility: *I want my father.* Levinas notes that "The one *to* whom I am answerable is the same one *for* whom I am answerable. The 'for whom' and 'to whom' coincide. It is this double movement of responsibility that designates the dimension of height" (*PN* 74; emphasis Levinas's). Transcendence is thus immanent as responsibility. Again, although Levinas never offers a sustained reading of Genesis 22, I think it is no coincidence that Levinas often echoes Abraham's initial response to God's call in the *akedah*—"Here I am" [*heneni*]—but in a way that completely reorients the relationships, possibilities, and demands of the *akedah* away from violent appropriation and toward responsibility to and for the Other: "Thus there emerges, from that fear for the other man, an unlimited responsibility, one that we are never discharged of, one that does not end in the last extremity of the neighbour, even if the responsibility then only amounts to responding, in the powerless confrontation with the death of the other, 'Here I am.'"[16]

From a Levinasian perspective, then, the unacceptable Kierkegaardian paradox of Abraham's faith is that his individual ascension beyond the ethical requires the effacement of Isaac, another particular individual, rather than responsibility to and for that individual.

Isaac's "My father" is counterpoised in Genesis 22 against God's "Abraham, Abraham!," but the "for whom" and "to whom" coincide only in Abraham's relation to God. In contrast, Levinas develops the notion of the paternal relationship:

> I do not have my child, I *am* in some way my child. But the words
> 'I am' here have a significance different from an Eleatic or Platonic
> significance.... Then again, the son is not any event whatsoever that
> happens to me — for example, my sadness, my ordeal, or my suffering.
> The son is an ego, a person. Lastly, the alterity of the son is not that
> of an alter ego. Paternity is not a sympathy through which I can put
> myself in the son's place.... Paternity is not simply the renewal of the
> father in the son and the father's merger with him, it is also the father's
> exteriority in relation to the son, a pluralist existing.[17]

Often critiqued by feminist thinkers, Levinas's meditation here on
fecundity and paternity illuminates the notion of children as ethical subjects and childhood as a privileged nexus at the same time it
obliquely but powerfully comments upon the *akedah* (and thus *Fear
and Trembling*).[18] Levinas dismantles the hierarchy of father over
son, of parent over child, by observing that the father's exteriority,
the most clearly present Other who calls the father to responsibility,
is found in, but is not reducible to, the child. Rather than separated
beings, theirs is a *pluralist existing*. The parent-child relationship subsists not in some transcendental, unchanging Platonic ideal, Hegelian
telos, or Kierkegaardian paradox, but continually reconfigures itself
in freedom toward an ever opening, nonteleological, even *messianic,*
future. Levinas declares that "I am" is not an ontological essence but
a consociation in constant temporal openness and proximal reorientation. Levinas does not denote "I am my son's father" or "I am my
father's son" as shared essences, but renders their affinity in terms of
multiple individual freedoms ("The coexistence of several freedoms is a
multiplicity that leaves the unity of each intact") within and not outside
or at the end of time ("Time constitutes not the fallen form of being,
but its very event") (*LR* 52–53). The plurality of "I am" is found in
continual openness to the future with the self-same Other independent
of a suffocating, isolating, overdetermined telos.[19] Levinas's "my sadness, my ordeal, my suffering" could be aimed directly at Kierkegaard's
Silentio, who has made of Abraham's trial an existential drama of the
passions, entirely without regard for the Other, the child Isaac, who
abides eternally beneath his father's blade.

Three points need to be emphasized here in reading the Levinasian child against Silentio's account of the *akedah*. First, in focusing on the *akedah* as the single defining "event" in the life of Abraham, in contrast to 'Ten Trials' of Judaic tradition,[20] Kierkegaard renders Isaac into Abraham's possession to be sacrificed to God rather than the divine gift Isaac is to Abraham and Sarah. Levinasian "voluptuosity" — the caress of skin upon skin or the open face of the child raised in wonder toward the parent, "in this *trans-substantiation*... beyond every possible project, beyond every meaningful and intelligent power" that "engender[s] the child" — is nowhere present in *Fear and Trembling* (*TI* 266). Instead, Isaac is Abraham's sacrificeable possession. Second, the child is both familiar and strange, an Other yet intimately familiar not simply in ipseity but in expression and gesture. For Kierkegaard, Isaac is bereft of a body except to invoke its immolation, for Silentio never gazes upon Isaac with the same intensity as he fixes upon Abraham. As Claire Elise Katz has persuasively written, perhaps what finally stayed Abraham's blade was that he looked into his son's face and *recognized* him.[21] In Kierkegaard, however, Isaac has no face.

Finally, the Levinasian child in her messianic responsibility must be read in conjunction with other scripture, particularly Isaiah 49. In Levinas's *Totality and Infinity,* the child is the paradigmatic Other who prevents the Kierkegaardian closure of the self in the "tensing of being" and thereby releases the "I" to the openness of the future in the radical *trans-substantiation* of child and parent.[22] Levinas's child presents an Otherness infolded within the paternal self, womb-like and möbian: "Possession of the child by the father does not exhaust the meaning of the relationship that is accomplished in paternity, where the father discovers himself not only in the gestures of his son, but in his substance and his unicity. My child is a stranger (Isaiah 49), but a stranger who is not only mine, for he *is* me. He is me a stranger to myself" (*TI* 267; emphasis Levinas's). Called "the Second Servant Song" by contemporary biblical critics, Isaiah 49:1–6 describes the Lord's servant (regarded as Israel itself or the coming messiah), who calls upon Israel to return to faithfulness, so that Israel might be, in turn, a light to the nations.[23] The Lord calls the servant to responsibility even before his creation and the onset of being, while (in a beautiful image of distinction within unicity) he is still in his mother's womb, and the messianic child-servant calls the world back to openness to, and ethical relation with, God. Thus, Isaiah 49 modulates, even commutes, the child's etiology and teleology prior to any ontology, for the servant's task is the redemption not just of the individual, nor even the community, but of the entire world. "It is a small"—even childish—"thing" (Isaiah 49:1–6). The servant-child of Isaiah 49 is exemplary, for the child is responsible to and for every Other even prior to being. So the servant-child's "small thing," redeeming Israel, is *too* small, too limiting, too restricted, and the Lord calls the servant-child to witness, to be the face of God, to the entire world. The child represents for Levinas the ethical demand *par excellence,* for any child, and every child, is never singular but manifests a "pluralist existing." In her dependence upon many Others, the child calls them to responsibility.

From a Levinasian perspective, Silentio's (and Kierkegaard's) disavowal of Isaac is absurdly impossible, and while Silentio trembles in the face of Abraham's absolute devotion, what of Isaac's horror at the edge of his father's raised blade? In the face of such suffering, in the face of the child, the Brome play of *Abraham and Isaac* dramatizes both Abraham's horror (*a la* Kierkegaard) and Ysaac's demand (*a la* Levinas), but instead of being silenced by Abraham's sacrificial demand, the Brome Ysaac calls his father to responsibility for him and to accountability to the third party, the Other of the Other. At the same time, the Brome play goes beyond Levinas, doing what Levinas fails to do, and that is both to subvert sacrificial readings of the *akedah* and to give the servant-child Ysaac a face, a voice, and a body with which to gesture beyond the sacrificial telos to the hither side of God.

The Voice of Isaac in the Brome Play of Abraham and Isaac

In contrast to Genesis 22's narrative terseness and Silentio's "dialectical lyric," the Brome play dramatizes the familial dynamics latent in the *akedah* and reveals the human cost of the sacrifice. Supplementing the Genesis 22 account at several key points, the Brome *Abraham and*

Isaac follows the biblical outline, with three episodes separated by an Angell's intervention. The play begins with Abraham's opening prayer, Isaac's proclamation of fidelity, and Deus' sacrificial command through the Angell (lines 1–100). The long central segment is composed of Abraham and Ysaac's two intense dialogues (101–315), the interactions divided when Abraham reveals that Ysaac is to be sacrificed. The final episode begins with the Angell staying Abraham's stroke and concludes with a learned Doctor's homily (316–69).[24]

Part One: Feudal Obedience

As the play begins, the noncycle Brome particularizes the nature of God's test and grounds its social environment in a recognizable medieval context. Abraham's prayer opens the play, and he offers thanks to God, who has given him land, rent, and livelihood. He looks back toward Adam and Eve and recognizes how he is part of that blessed lineage to whom God has given "thys lond to lede my lyffe" (*AI* 10). God is thus depicted as a feudal lord who provides Abraham the accoutrements of vassalage (land, rent, and livelihood) and is the one to whom Abraham owes fealty. Above all things, God gives Abraham a young son, Ysaac (12), and the son is figured as part of the feudal behest, the offspring necessary to convey Abraham's inheritance. Throughout the play, the Brome Abraham emphasizes with a kind of Levinasian voluptuousity the unparalleled love Abraham feels for Ysaac, the miracle child of his and Sarah's old age. Abraham loves nothing more than Ysaac "Excepe þin owyn selffe, der Fader of blyss" (13). Like many a parent medieval and modern, Abraham prays for Ysaac's health and happiness, and as Abraham's prayer ends, he beckons Ysaac to return home.

When Abraham and Ysaac turn toward home, the place of rest and security, Deus commands the Angell to "medyll-erth" to test whether Abraham "be stedfast or noo" (*AI* 34–35) and commands Abraham to take Ysaac, the "ȝowng sonne, þat he love so wyll, / And wyth hys blood sacryfyce he make" (38–39). In this test, Deus proposes to ascertain whether Abraham "lovyth better hys chyld or me" (44).

Here the language of feudal relationship melds with divine jealousy and mimetic desire, and the Brome play splits the divine perspective between Deus and an Angell who gives the command to sacrifice (thus relieving God of the sacrificial demand), it enacts Kierkegaard's distinction between the "religious" (the monstrous demand to obey God in the face of moral prohibitions against child sacrifice) and the "ethical" (the requirements of conventional morality not to kill the son). Abraham's opening prayer thus situates the patriarch in conflicting roles: in the genealogy (as a son) of Adam and as father to Ysaac, separating Abraham's past from his future and pitting feudal loyalty against paternal love. Faced by this political as well as personal challenge, Abraham must choose between the contradictory and mutually exclusive demands levied by his feudal overlord and the requirements owning to his beloved son. If he spares Ysaac, Abraham risks losing God's "freynchepe" (40), yet if he fulfill Deus's demand, he must kill his beloved son.

Unlike Silentio's Abraham in *Fear and Trembling* and the biblical Abraham of Genesis 22, the Brome Abraham is anything but silent in his fear and trembling. Instead, Abraham, caught in a maelstrom of conflicting emotions, lays out the terrible emotional cost of God's demand and shows how "Thys chyldys wordys all towond my harte" (*AI* 121). For example, his conscience is "strongly steryd" against the command, yet he is "sorely afered / To groche" against God's will (79–80). He loves none better than Ysaac, even his own life, yet he must "smyth of hys [Ysaac's] hed" (87). He will diligently follow the Lord's command (85) but laments the "hard deth my son schall fell / For to honore" the Lord (89–90). Assessing even Sarah's potential to disrupt the sacrifice, Abraham also declares that no matter what she might do, "ʒet wyll I not spare for child nor wyffe" (84). Abraham's willingness and Sarah's suffering are not necessarily congruent, for Abraham cannot command (or commend) Sarah's suffering for (or to) himself. One cannot take another's suffering upon oneself but must instead suffer the suffering of the Other. For Levinas, one's suffering is wholly one's own and is not commutative, and the ethical demand requires one to take upon oneself the suffering of the Other rather than to inflict that suffering upon the Other. Here, however, Abraham indicates that he will inflict suffering upon Sarah rather than deny Deus's command and risk God's displeasure himself.

Putting the sacrificial command in the mouth of the Angell mitigates against Deus's direct responsibility for the sacrificial command, as does the Angell's reassurance that Abraham should "be nothing dysmayd" (*AI* 93), both of which are unsupported by the biblical account and militate against the absolute terror so clear to Silentio. The Brome Abraham brushes aside the Angell's reassurance and commits "To see the blood of my owyn dere son" (97) despite his sorrow. With these repeated attestations of the father's sorrow and the son's blood, the Brome characters oscillate representationally between historical Old Testament figures and their New Testament fulfillments: Abraham as both patriarch and symbolic of the Christian Father-God and Ysaac as Abraham's son and a type of the crucified Christ. Abraham, the typological Father, is willing to sacrifice his son, and Isaac makes "preyerys to þe Trenyte" (104), stamping this Old Testament episode with a New Testament imprimatur. Indeed, Ysaac later echoes Jesus' words from the cross ("forȝyffe me þat I haue donne" [267, cf. Luke 23:34] and "Lord, reseyve me into thy hand" [296, cf. Luke 23:46]). These references are oddly skewed to the typological import, however, for although Ysaac piously commits his soul to God, as did Jesus, Ysaac also asks God's forgiveness, though innocent, rather than calling upon God to pardon those who "know not what they do." Rather than just "medieval anachronisms," such references stretch typological coherence. At the same time, typology obviates the destructive social and historical consequences of the sacrificial demand by appealing to accomplished soteriological necessities in a teleologically determined, totalitarian theological system. In its relentless dogmatism, typological thinking can be a form of interpretive violence.

Part Two: Abraham and Ysaac in Dialogue

Once the Angell gives Abraham the command, the second part of the Brome play, *Abraham* begins as father and child travel toward the mount of sacrifice. At the outset of their journey, Abraham tells Ysaac that "*we* to [two] child must goo to-geder, / And onto *my* Lord make sacryffyce" (*AI* 107–08; emphasis mine). Such a comment initially indicates age and family position, for Ysaac is not old enough to make his own sacrifice, but is old enough to assist his father. Yet horror lurks between the pronouns, for Ysaac *is* his father's sacrifice: *We* two go to make *my* sacrifice. As they begin, Abraham blesses his son: "A! Ysaac, my owyn son so dere, / *Godys blyssyng I ȝyffe the, and myn*" (115; emphasis mine). This distinctive turn of phrase, as noted by Norman Davis, is an epistolary conclusion common in parents' letters to their children, a *topos* also invoked in the Middle English *Pearl*.[25] Affectively, Abraham's bequest indicates great love for Ysaac. Discursively, however, this phraseology indicates that their journey is concluded at the outset. Here is the crucial point: From the beginning, the telos is already predetermined. The letter is concluded, and Ysaac is already dead. Following the logic of the epistolary attribution, Abraham has already "written off" Ysaac at the beginning of their trek. Ysaac, already discursively sacrificed, now subsists between two deaths, though only his father knows it.

Even though Ysaac has been proleptically condemned to death and teleologically prescribed as a sacrifice, in the Brome play he is very much full of life. He is not an acquiescent victim. One of the most striking aspects of the Brome *Abraham and Isaac* is its representation of the child Ysaac. Internal evidence indicates that Ysaac was likely played by a youngster, a "gentyll barn" (*AI* 106), and other textual clues indicate that he is youthful, fragile, and slightly built. Further, Ysaac's scrupulous attention to his father's every gesture, glance, and emotion also realistically dramatizes the way children learn by watching their parents closely and imitating them. Abraham prays, and Ysaac does so as well, in the same language. Abraham loves his lord, and so does Ysaac in equal measure. Abraham strives to obey his lord, and Ysaac obediently does likewise. As they wend their way to the mount (63), the youthful Ysaac peppers his father matter-of-factly with the kind of banter familiar to anyone on a road trip with kids: What are we doing? Where are we going? What are we going to do when we get there? And, ultimately, "Are we there yet?" As portrayed in the Brome play, Ysaac is indeed the *trans-substantiation* of his father, to use the Levinasian phrase. They are one, but they are not the same.[26]

The uniqueness of the Brome *Abraham and Isaac* play rests in the fact that Ysaac is given a voice and speaks and acts like a child, and not simply as a typological abstraction or theological exemplum. Ysaac is represented on his own behalf and not solely for the benefit of another, yet his childlike imitation of his father indicates his voluptuous paternal connection to, and unadulterated dependence upon, Abraham. During their passage to the mount, Ysaac's insatiable curiosity, coupled with Abraham's evasiveness and disquiet, gradually heighten the son's anxiety, and his recognition of the sacrificial instruments coalesce into entreaty and horror. Ysaac is intently focused upon his father's mood and questions his "heuy chere" (136). Ysaac wonders repeatedly, anxiously, where the sacrificial beast might be, for there is fire and wood but no animal (138–42). As Abraham prepares the site of sacrifice, Ysaac sees his father's drawn sword and reacts, his heart quaking frightfully "To [see] þat scharpe sword in ȝowre hond. / Wy bere ȝe yowre sword drawyn soo? / Off ȝowre contenaunce I haue much wonder" (148–50). Ysaac has watched his father closely. He already knows the material needs of the sacrificial process, and he recognizes his father's behavior in such circumstances. Yet Ysaac also understands that something is amiss. Abraham's regular practice has somehow been disrupted. The sacrificial animal is missing; Abraham's sword is drawn; and Ysaac fears for his life.

A marvel of increasing emotional intensity, this section of the Brome play sees Ysaac's horror rise as Abraham's purpose becomes clearer and his equivocation greater. Thus, another authentic aspect of their interaction is how Ysaac continually searches his father's *face* for clues to his intent and affect, for when an adult is incommunicative and secretive, children must read other, less tangible cues in an attempt to remain in the good graces of the towering adult who has so much power over them. Ysaac apprehends clearly the revelatory dimensions of the face. It speaks even when the mouth is closed. Throughout their dialogue, while Abraham continues to distance himself from Ysaac and turn inward upon himself, like Kierkegaard's Abraham, Ysaac's attention moves constantly from his father's mien to his hands, from his expression to his gestures, so that he can intuit his father's emotional state and ultimate purpose. Ysaac sees "That ȝe morne thus more and more" (158), until he finally asks the fateful question: "I preye ȝow, fader, þat ȝe wyll let me yt wyt, / Wyther schall I haue any harme or noo?" (161–62). When Abraham demurs a second time, Ysaac asks directly, "Dere fader, I prey ȝow, hydygth not from me, / But sum of ȝowr thowt þat ȝe tell me" (165–66). In effect, Ysaac's pestering attempts to elicit an ethical response, an openness, from his father, and a recognition of their unicity. Instead, in that horrible moment, Abraham finally reveals the truth: "A! Ysaac, Ysaac, I must kyll thee" (166) or else "greve God right sore" (182). The verisimilitude of Ysaac's interactions with Abraham set the Brome play apart from the other Middle English accounts of the *akedah,* particularly because Ysaac reveals the sacrificial victim's perspective in the voice of a child (172).

Once Abraham reveals the nature of his task, Ysaac engages his father in another lengthy dialogue, but this time rather than exactly mirroring his father's enthusiasm, intuiting his intent, and searching his face, Ysaac gradually differentiates his perspective from his father's and forces Abraham to clarify his own desire. Having sought out his father's face, Ysaac now attempts to make his own visage again visible to Abraham through their social relations and shared "sensuous lived experience."[27] After learning Abraham's intent to kill him, Ysaac first wonders what he has done to deserve death. If he has trespassed in any way, he indicates that "a ȝard may make me full myld / And with ȝowre scharp sword kyll me nogth" (170–71). Like an abused but innocent child, Ysaac internalizes the intimation of guilt, accepts responsibility for his father's unhappiness, and embraces Abraham's violence in what Levinas calls "absolute passivity."[28] Ysaac places himself in accusative though he has done no wrong, even as he interrogates his father. Ysaac next appeals to paternity, fecundity, and sociality and reminds Abraham that he also has other children, "wyche ȝe schuld love wyll be kynd" (199). Admonishing Abraham that any harm to him would reverberate far beyond the two of them in this moment and at this place, Ysaac's death would distress not only his mother but also the entire extended household. Finally, Ysaac even charges that once he is dead, his father will soon forget him, and because Ysaac fears that not even his memory will remain, he asks his father to pray for him after his death (201–04). Ysaac's impassioned pleas constantly point his father back to their unicity, and giving the sacrificial child a voice and differentiated subjectivity disturbs conventional sacrificial and typologically inflected understandings of the *akedah*. As Ysaac says, "iwys, fader, I am but a chyld" (172).

Most importantly, Ysaac consistently invokes Sarah, the third party to whom Abraham must answer and for whose sake the ethical relationship between Abraham and Ysaac becomes a matter of justice.[29] As mother and wife, Sarah is the Other of the Other, in Levinasian terms, for whose well-being Abraham might reconsider his action. Ysaac initially invokes her presence as a moderating influence upon Abraham's sacrificial intent: "Now I wold to God [my] mother were her on þis hyll! / Sche woold knele for me on both hyre kneys / To save my lyffe" (175–77). Because Abraham knows that Sarah would intercede on her son's behalf, Ysaac asks his father to change his "chere" and spare his life (178)—significantly, "chere" denotes "bearing," "behavior," or "face." If Abraham will not consider Sarah and spare her son, at least he might lie and spare her feelings, so subsequently Ysaac begs Abraham to "Sey þat I am in another cuntré dwelling" (206). Conjuring Sarah before Abraham's eyes, Ysaac summons a logic of proximity and pluralist existing, and by appealing to Sarah, Ysaac invokes his and his father's "pluralist existing" together with Sarah, the mother and wife upon whom they both depend and to whom Ysaac also was given as a divine gift. Isaac's invocation of "the third" into his colloquy with Abraham marks the move from ethics to justice, for the third represents the one to whom I is answerable, in responsibility for the Other, the second (*OB* 150–62). For Abraham, however, the future is foreclosed from the outset and the horizon holds only one destiny.

However, in my view, the most stunning moment in this brief play is when Ysaac raises the haunting possibility that *there might be another option*, for God "might a sent me a better destiny / Yf yt had a be hys placer [pleasure]" (*AI* 192–93). God might have done something else. At that moment, if only for a moment, Ysaac offers Abraham a glimpse of a nonteleological possibility, a future potentiality outside of Abraham's reckoning, and perhaps even outside of God's. It is Ysaac, the sacrificial child, in his openness to his father and his absolute "passivity beyond passivity," who points Abraham to the hither side, to a God otherwise than being and a human selfhood found in infinite responsibility (*OB* 30–31).

In conventional readings of child sacrifice—like traditional readings of Chaucer's *Physician's Tale*, for example—a child's inability to stave off execution or to defend herself physically is seen as her acquiescence to being sacrificed.[30] What these readings ignore is that the naked vulnerability of the face is itself a call to responsibility prior to ipseity, and what these readings discount are the forms of resistance available to a child against the much stronger adult who is bent upon murder theologically rationalized as sacrifice. What these readings do is perpetuate a sacrificial ideology as a theoretical paradigm, and what children do have is their vulnerability, their passivity, their dependency, their voices, and their shared experiences with parents and adults. In Levinasian terms, Ysaac's passivity exposes the nakedness of the face, an exposedness that calls to the Other in responsibility and demands an account. Such "weakness" is generally dismissed simply as "pathos," but Levinas transforms these childlike attributes into the potential for an ethical relation before ontology and or even temporality.

In the Brome play, Ysaac thus utilizes the resources available to him, what James Scott calls "the weapons of the weak," to disrupt Abraham's teleological determinism and to suggest the possibility for new forms of ethical relation.[31] Even though Abraham has already "written off" Ysaac in his epistolary blessing, the son calls the father back to the social grounding and pluralist existing of their voluptuous relation. Ysaac's petitions demonstrate neither the actions nor attitudes of a youngster quietly acquiescing to an unalterable fate.[32] These are the spirited attempts of a desperate, perceptive child to save his own life, and the dramatic brilliance of the Brome *Abraham* is that although the story of the *akedah* is *narratively* determined, Ysaac's tenacious, vigorous, and insistently youthful repartee with Abraham provides a glimpse of that hither side, that *something else* might happen, and so their relationship remains *dramatically* open ended. Ysaac enjoins his father in *the ethical suspension of the teleological.* There is always another possibility, Ysaac dares to suggest. Only definitive, violent action — the reduction of all to the one — forecloses the ethical relationship invoked by continued openness toward and responsibility for the Other.

This continually imminent latency of the "I" in relation to others is Isaac/Ysaac's birthright. He is the unforeseen child of blessing, of Abraham and Sarah's old age, the unexpected gift from God (*AI* 11–15), foretold under the oaks of Mamre. In Isaac/Ysaac's uncalculated forthcoming, then, the sacrificial telos is not fully determined in the same way his *arkhe* was unanticipated and literally laughable. Unlike Abraham's silence in the biblical account and stoicism in Silentio's dialectical lyric, Abraham weeps, sorrows, wavers, and delays in the Brome play to the point that he cannot continue: "Son, thy wordys make me to wepe full sore; / Now, my dere son Ysaac, speke no more" (224–25). Abraham begs for Ysaac's silence because he repeatedly invokes the paternal bonds within which he and his father abide. Contrary to Silentio's selective retelling, neither Abraham nor Ysaac in the Brome play persists in imperious isolation, alone and beyond the call of sociality. Ysaac was born into relationship with Abraham "*be kynd*" (199), according to the *il y a* of their unicity. The fecund Middle English term "kynde" indicates the broad sweep of ethical relation envisioned by Levinas — with kin, as kindred, by kindness, according to nature — and as such Ysaac and Abraham are intimately and unalterably coexistent in paternity, household, and community. Ysaac is the trans-substantiation of Abraham, united with yet distinct from his father, even when God's command attempts to sever their link of *kynde,* the sensuous mutuality of father and son.

By placing himself in the accusative (*AI* 168), by passively accepting Abraham's violence, and by reckoning himself as guilty, Ysaac reveals the substitution at the heart of ethical subjectivity. In Levinas's words, "Obsessed with responsibilities which did not arise in decision taken by a subject 'contemplating freely,' consequently accused in its innocence, subjectivity in itself is being thrown back on oneself. This means concretely: accused of what the others do or suffer, or responsible for what they do or suffer. The uniqueness of the self is the very fact of bearing the fault of another" (*OB* 112). Ysaac accepts and embraces, though innocent, his father's violence, and by implication, the violence of Abraham's God. Levinas very specifically identifies the emergence of this brutality: "Violence emerges in Kierkegaard at the precise moment when, moving beyond the aesthetic stage, existence can no longer limit itself to what it takes to be an ethical stage and enters the religious one, the domain of belief" (*PN* 72, 76). This aggression has two components, one emerging in the scission of the ethical from the religious and the other in the constitution of belief as ontology.

This is a question Silentio never asks in *Fear and Trembling* and Kierkegaard never considers: After having risen above the ethical to an absolute relation to the absolute, why should Abraham return to the ethical order? The Brome play offers an answer: Ysaac appeals to their self-sameness via paternity, his plea concerns their shared sensuous experience and mutual coexisting, his claim invokes their shared sociality and kindred, and his evacuation to the hither side creates the conditions under which Abraham can hear the Angell's second command. It is the ethical suspension of the teleological. As Levinas pointedly comments, "Abraham's attentiveness to the voice that led him back to the ethical order, in forbidding him to perform a human sacrifice, is the highest point in the drama. That he obeyed the first voice is astonishing: that he had sufficient distance with respect to that obedience to hear the second voice—that is essential" (*PN* 77). What Levinas claims about the *akedah* as a corrective of Kierkegaard, the Brome play enacts and problematizes.

As a result, during this long central episode in the Brome *Abraham and Isaac,* the longest stretch of dialogue between Abraham and Isaac in any Middle English Abraham play, the locus of authority shifts subtly from the father to the son, for as Abraham initially situated their relationship as one of power, the feudal lord over his heir, Ysaac reframes their connection as one of unimpeachable mutuality. Throughout the preparations for sacrifice, Ysaac continually encourages his father to do

God's will, to the point that he must tell Abraham how to prepare for and to perform the sacrifice. Ysaac presses forward to the degree that he controls the conditions under which he will die, to the point that one must question to what degree the sacrifice is really Abraham's anymore at all. Ysaac uses the hortatory subjunctive to move the ritual forward ("Let yt pass ouer," [*AI* 211]). Ysaac begs that Abraham give him a quick, clean death (230–31).[33] Ysaac urges Abraham not to botch the execution with too many strokes of the blade (288). Most tellingly, Ysaac asks Abraham to hide his eyes prior to the death blow "That my fleysse schall defile" (221, 285) and to turn his head away from the fearsome blade (291–92). The nakedness of Ysaac's face is too much to bear, but this is the weight to which Abraham must be subjected. I myself wonder what God saw in Isaac's face at Mt. Moriah.

If horror lurked between the pronouns in Abraham's earlier epistolary conclusion, Ysaac's grammatical substitution under the drawn blade offers Abraham the potential to redeem himself and to do justice to his son.[34] Abraham claims that he must bind Ysaac, but the boy refuses, saying "*I* wylle not let *ʒow*" (*AI* 247; emphasis mine), and then *twice* Ysaac uses the imperative voice, the language of command, to direct his father: "Do on for *me ʒowre wyll*" (248) and "Do on *ʒowre lyst* for *me* hardly" (253; emphasis mine). Although Deus gives the sacrificial command through the Angell, Ysaac grants his father permission, "My fayer swere fader, *I* ʒeffe *ʒow* leve" (254). Here Ysaac indicates again both their irreducible alterity and intimate unicity by invoking himself in the first person and his father in the second person. However, Ysaac's language must not be confused with submission. If, following Girard, mimetic desire masks the true violence of sacrificial scapegoating, then the degree to which Abraham mirrors God's desire for Ysaac's sacrifice marks the father's consolidation to the sacrificial demand.[35] By demanding that Abraham do *his own will,* Ysaac charges Abraham to distinguish his own desire—"*ʒowre wyll*" and "*ʒowre lyst*"—from Deus's and to consider the repercussions of that violence. Ysaac demands that his father must do *his own will, and not God's.* In doing so, Ysaac raises the possibility of an antisacrificial alternative, and Abraham is nearly undone by Ysaac's interrogation. Facing "thys ʒowng

innocent" (303) who has placed him in the accusative, Abraham, his
sword drawn, cries at his climactic moment of indecision and despair,
"O, Fader of Heuyn! What schall I doo?" (305), but it is Ysaac who
answers first: "schorte me of my woo" (309). Abraham calls to God,
but *Ysaac* answers, and the Angell intervenes.

Part Three: Ysaac and the Afterlife of Sacrifice

In conventional terms familiar from the biblical account, the Angell
reports that Deus does not require Ysaac's death. The Angell reveals
the sacrificial ram and conveys the divine promise that Abraham's
innumerable progeny will bless the earth because of his obedience
(Gen. 22:15–18). However, Brome *Abraham and Isaac* has not yet
yielded all of its revelatory surprises. Whereas Levinas, Kierkegaard,
and the biblical account end, the Brome play veers into remarkable
and uncharted territory. While Kierkegaard separates Abraham from
the ethical realm (figured as social relations) in order to consolidate
Abraham's absolute relation to the absolute (figured as the religious
domain), the Brome *Abraham* explores what I call the "afterlife of
sacrifice." Brome dramatizes what even Levinas fails to imagine, and
that is to envision the *akedah* from Isaac's perspective and to expose
the insuperable damage inflicted by the sacrificial demand. Again,
Ysaac's childlike reactions to his putative rescue are key.

As in the biblical text, the Angell stays Abraham's stroke (*AI* 315)
and provides a "fayrr ram" (323) for the sacrifice. Relieved, Abraham
calls out, "Arysse vp, Ysaac, my dere sunne, arysse, / Arysse vp, swete
child, and cum to me" (335–36). This typologically appropriate phrase
would seem to complete the Christic pattern of death and resurrection and seal the narrative under a typological carapace, but then the
Brome play takes a most amazing turn: Ysaac does not recognize that
he has been spared. Ysaac understands that the sheep dies both for
him and because of him (360), yet he finds Abraham's explanation of
his rescue a distemperate delay, a kind of extended, torturous agony,
saying, "A, mercy, fader, wy smyght ʒe not ʒyt? / A, smyght on, fader,
onys with ʒowre knyffe!" (337–38).[36] When Abraham explains again

that God has granted his life, Ysaac sputters: "A fader, full glad than wer I, / Iwys, fader, I sey iwys, / Yif thus tall [tale] were trew!" (343–45). Ysaac's profound skepticism is revealed in his use of the subjunctive and the multiple adverbs *iwys* ("indeed" or "truly"): I would be completely relieved if, father, and I say again, only if I could trust that your word was believable! After his trauma, his father's suffering, and God's command, Ysaac simply cannot accept that he has been spared, and he believes that Deus will be angry that Abraham has not completed the task (349). Even as he builds the sacrificial fire with his father, Ysaac remains steadfastly unpersuaded that his life is safe: "But fader, wyll I stowppe down lowe, / ȝe wyll not kyll me with ȝoure sword, I trowe?" (377–78). Whereas he previously searched his father's face for hope, responsibility, and reprieve, Ysaac cannot now ever turn his back on his father; he must now always *face* Abraham not in openness but in suspicion. Even when Abraham reassures him a *fourth* time, Ysaac still fears his father's unsheathed sword (381–82), for once a child is threatened with murder, that child is always threatened with murder. The menace can never be withdrawn, and something irreparable has been forever lost.

Abraham, however, fails to see the violence to which he has subjected Ysaac, and he believes the divine reprieve has reestablished the paternal bond with his son. He assumes that Ysaac shares his perspective once more and that their unicity is intact. The pronouns are again significant, for Abraham appropriates Ysaac's ordeal to his own benefit—"how thynke ȝe / Be thys warke that *we* haue wroght?" (*AI* 403–04)—and glibly states how glad he is that "*we* grucched nott" against God's will (406). Abraham proclaims that "*My* morning is past" (380), but the same cannot be said of Ysaac. At the beginning of the play, Ysaac proclaims that he would do whatever Abraham commanded (111, 119), but Ysaac now exclaims that he will never again go to that place "But yet be aȝens my wyll" (418) and vows, "For by my trowthe, wer I at home / I wold neuer gon owt vnder that form" (430–31). While tradition accounts Mt. Moriah as a place of revelation and redemption, "the Lond of V[y]syon" (63), for Ysaac it is a place of suffering at his father's hands.

Conclusion

In line with the biblical account, Deus renews the covenant with Abraham and his descendents (*AI* 391–402). Although the Brome play moves toward conciliation, with Abraham laughing off Ysaac's fear (411) and Ysaac looking forward to getting home and talking to his mom (423), something irreparable has been lost. Although Abraham has been given a glimpse of a Levinasian hither side, he ultimately tenses back upon himself, and Ysaac endures (in) the ontological rupture brought by the sacrificial command. Against Christian readings that ameliorate the *akedah's* violence into typological fulfillment and soteriological destiny—remember, Christians call it "the *sacrifice* of Isaac"—the Brome play demonstrates that the sacrificial demand, even if left unfinished, is fundamentally violent and irreparable.

Like the Chester pageant (with whom it shares many characteristics) the Brome *Abraham and Isaac* ends with a learned Doctor interpreting the play as a moral exemplum upon how all should keep God's commandments "withowt grochyng" (*AI* 442). The Doctor asks rhetorically whether any in the audience would complain if "God sent an angell / and commawndyd зow to smyght of зowre chyldys hed" (443–45).[37] But rather than turning toward a typological resolution of sacred violence, the Brome Doctor brings the exemplum directly into the harsh realities of medieval childhood and the personal fears of medieval parents, the closing parallel to Abraham's opening prayer for Ysaac's health and safety. What of those women who weep, he asks, "Whan that hyr chyldryn dey them froo, / As nature woll, and kind; / Yt ys but folly" (447–52). The God who commanded Abraham to sacrifice Isaac is the same God who allows children to die, but in the same way God gave Isaac back, the Doctor intones, so too God will "amend" (459). God's command to sacrifice Ysaac is thereby equated to the natural, sometimes fatal, vagaries of childhood, and those who weep are foolish and misguided. In this rather callous, facile moralization, the *akedah* becomes above all an exemplum of obedience and a plea for stoic patience in the face of child death, an all too common event in the medieval (or even contemporary) period.

One of Levinas's overarching concerns was to bring Athens and Jerusalem into conversation, the language of philosophy with the history of faith. At the risk of overgeneralizing, I would argue that the *akedah* is the mount upon which the two traditions converge in Levinas, or, if you prefer, the fount from which Levinas's complementary analyses flow. The paradox within which Levinas struggles is that the philosophy of Greece envisions certainty and closure in pursuit of answers, of a transcendent truth, but the faith of Israel, the source of the great Abrahamic religions, envisages redemption, an ongoing openness toward the world in its imperfection and human brokenness. And so, Levinas wrestles continually with the *akedah,* like Jacob with the angel, but yet without blessing and answer. Like the great rabbis of antiquity who read the *akedah* midrashically, supplementing the spare narrative with insight from the Hebrew scriptures and the opinions of their forbearers, the Brome *Abraham* likewise reads *akedah* midrashically, exploiting fissures in the text and opening it to contrary understandings, but never fully foreclosing the *akedah* in a settled theological finality. The Brome play wrestles with Ysaac/Isaac's place, function, and afterlife under the sacrificial command like the ancient sages who developed a fascinating body of interpretation in which Isaac is sacrificed and immediately resurrected, his ashes laid on the altar and revivified, or his soul fled to the bellweather of Abraham's flock and consumed.[38] It is in this sense that the Brome *Abraham and Isaac* is essentially midrashic.

In the afterlife of sacrifice, Isaac is given back his body though his *soul,* one might say, is forever marred. He is not sacrificed, or at least, his body is not killed, but Isaac understands that he is expendable. In sacrificial readings of the *akedah,* like Kierkegaard's, Isaac is transformed through "the ghost effect" into a Levinasian *concept,* a *theme,* a *said:*

> The production of the ghost, the constitution of the *ghost* effect is not simply a spiritualization or even a autonomization of spirit, idea, or thought, as happens *par excellence* in Hegelian idealism.... For there to be a ghost, there must be a return to the body, but to a body that is more abstract than ever. The spectrogenic process corresponds therefore to a paradoxical *incorporation.* Once ideas or thoughts (*Gedanke*) are

detached from their substratum, one engenders some ghosts by *giving them a body.* Not by returning to the living body from which ideas and thoughts have been torn loose, but by incarnating the latter in *another artifactual body, a prosthetic body.*[39]

A Levinasian ethics demands that one remain ever faithful and open, even to the dead. Like Marx, about whom Derrida comments here, Kierkegaard opposed Hegel, and like Marx, Kierkegaard unleashed a specter whose figure haunts our age. Kierkegaard's Isaac, like the Isaac of too many theologies, too many readings, and too many analyses, is an embodied ghost, an abstraction serving the sacrificial system. He hovers always near Abraham or perhaps just beyond, though he is not often seen, but only half-seen, at a glance, and never surely. He lives only to die, partially, and live again, damaged by the experience. This specter, constituted in the corpus of *Fear and Trembling,* is the phantom of Isaac, the sacrificeable child who persists in the shadow of father Abraham's faith, whose sword is always poised over his head and the blade never falling. Countless Others have taken Isaac's place, sacrificed for another's benefit, those who turn back upon themselves rather than toward the child's naked face and those who dare neither to substitute themselves into that place of traumatic responsibility nor to recognize their own violent culpability.

How can it be that child murder is heinous, but child sacrifice is heroic?

7

The Personificational Face
Piers Plowman Rethought through Levinas and Bronowski

James J. Paxson

Among the ancient rhetorical tropes, *prosopopeia,* or personification, has, along with its superordinate mode allegory, come to enjoy some renewed attention in *Piers Plowman* studies. Most notably (and recently) Mary Carruthers has urged readers of the poem to think of a scale or spectrum concerning Langland's figural language, ranging from allegorical obscurity to physical "picturity" (in my rendering of the concept).[1] Similarly, Larry Scanlon has been rethinking Paul de Man's postmodern theory of allegory also in terms of a revitalized physicality for personification itself, Langland's uniquely deployed poetic device, which (he argues) allows another scale or hierarchy (between the poles of the abstract allegorical and the physically mimetic) to collapse together at certain key moments of Langland's narrative.[2] I have long contended that part of the poem's "semantic complexity [that] is nearly inexhaustible" (Scanlon's phrase), as well as its unending semiosis,[3] is rooted in the concept of *prosopopeia*'s self-reflexive semantic value itself. Complex allegories, from Prudentius's *Psychomachia* through Langland's poem, have thematized, through wordplay and sensuous imagery, the "making (and un-making) of face," manifesting the very significance of the old Hellenic rhetorical expression, *prosopon poiein,* as I shall address below.

In this essay, I shall experiment in rethinking the cryptic depiction of Anima or Soul in passus 15 of the *Piers Plowman* B text using a range of postmodern theories that I shall bracket with two poles which, as well, come to lie together: the philosophical speculation of Emmanuel Levinas and the scientific humanism of an allied Jewish thinker. This ally might at first seem a potentially unlikely one: the mathematician, poet, literary critic, and historian of science, Jacob Bronowski (1908–74). In opening up an understanding of Langland's striking personificational face, I imply that a "prefiguration" of the Levinasian face could be construed not only in Langland's poem but also in Bronowski's thought experiment, and technological demonstration in the 1970s, of the real human face viewed according to a scale or range of electromagnetic radiations. My argument is thus doubly anachronistic. The now somewhat neglected thinking of Bronowski might help us to understand better the key concept of Levinas's *face*. The Levinasian face can serve, in turn, as a means of better grasping the centrality of *prosopopeia* as a device for allegorists of the high Middle Ages such as William Langland.

LANGLAND'S PERSONIFICATIONAL ANIMA

As I have implied so far, I have tried in previously published studies to understand the strange depiction of Anima or Soul in passus 15 of the *Piers Plowman* B text by employing a range of theoretical imperatives and historical principles. The extended dialogue that occurs between Will the dreamer and the spectral presence he meets on the level of the second of the poem's two inner dreams has been set out by Langland to clarify some of the common knowledge available in the fourteenth century about various faculties of human consciousness, designated in a list no doubt drawn from the famous tally in Isidore's *Etymologies,* 11.1.13. And the list seems to privilege, as a root identity or atavistic core, the concept Anima (though one could argue that the ultimately atavistic core is the historical William Langland or his most common proxy, the paranomastically named narrator-dreamer Will). Following Isidore (who was himself following St. Augustine) perfectly, Langland's Anima has it that:

"The whiles I quykne þe cors...called am I *anima*;
And whan I wilne and wolde *animus* ich hatte;
And for þat I kan [and] knowe called am I *mens*;
And whan I make mone to god *memoria* is my name;
And whan I deme domes and do as truþe techeþ
Thanne is *Racio* my riȝte name, reson on englissh;
And whan I feele þat folk telleþ my firste name is *sensus*,
And þat is wit and wisdom, þe welle of alle craftes;
And whan I chalange or chalange noȝt, chepe or refuse,
Thanne am I *conscience* ycalled, goddess clerk and his Notarie;
And whan I loue leelly oure lord and alle oþere
Thanne is lele loue my name, and in latyn *Amor*;
And whan I flee fro þe flesh and forsake þe careyne
Thann am I spirit spechelees; *Spiritus* þanne ich hatte."[4]

Perhaps taking part in an exercise in conceptual nominalism, Langland's endorsement of the Isidorean list resolves a battery of psychic or cognitive entities—Will, Knowledge, Memory, Reason, the human Sensorium, Conscience, Love and Spirit—down to a precursor or more pure form, Soul. Yet Scanlon's claim that Langlandian personification approaches something we modern readers might recognize as "character" formation "in the conventional sense"[5] holds true in this case, wherein a projection or aspect of the dream contains a universe of qualities predicated by human or real characterization. That is to say, Anima is not merely the monodimensional or hollow ontology of the allegorical daemon, as Angus Fletcher once understood the simple personification figure.[6] Some of Langland's personifications approach the ontological density of real humans—for Scanlon, say, the figure Gluttony during his confession; for me, the figure Anima as a semiotically overcharged entity. That density arises, moreover, from both the poet's complex representation of interiority and flesh-and-bone human physicality. The sophisticated spectration or scaling of a being's ontological "interior," as in the Isidorean scene of Anima's construction, taken together with the sheerly vulnerable humanness of the exterior and solid human *face*, will afford me a means to think along with Levinas, Langland, and Bronowski. I link together Levinas's meditation on that human vulnerability, the allegorical range of experience and characterization that runs linearly from passus 1 through passus 20 of *Piers Plowman* B (with special emphasis on the crypticism of Anima in B 15), and some useful insights culled from Bronowki's late-twentieth century model of what constitutes a human being. Central to his elegant and often moving scientific humanism (and central to this essay) is the human face.

In *Piers Plowman,* the appearance of Anima to the dreamer is one indication of the growth or change that Will must be undergoing through his allegorical adventures. Following the initial vision of the field of folk and the subjacent parable of the mice, rats, and the cat that constitute the prologue, the instantiating and defining ontological fact, the experiential starting point designated by Holy Church at the outset of passus 1 as she first addresses Will, seems to presage well the Levinasian understanding of the physical or bodily status of the human other:

> "The tour on þe toft," quod she, "truþe is þerInne,
> And wolde þat ye wrouȝte as his word techeþ.
> For he is fader of feiþ, and formed yow alle
> Boþe with fel and with face, and yaf yow fyue wittes
> For to worshipe hym þerwiþ while ye ben here.
> And þerfore he hiȝte þe erþe to helpe yow echone
> Of wollene, of lynnen, of liflode at need
> In mesurable manere to make yow at ese;
> And comaunded of his curteisie in commune þree þynges;
> Are none nedfulle but þo; and nempne hem I þynke
> And rekene hem by reson: reherce þow hem after.
> That oon [is] vesture from [chele] þee to saue;
> [That oþer is] mete at meel for mysese of þiselue;
> And drynke whan þ[ee] drie[þ]..."   (*PP* 12–25)

The physical, even biological, parameters of human ontology reduce to the most basic *needs:* clothing from the elements, food, and water. The initial reasonable guard against nakedness, the first vulnerability tallied, comes, moreover, on the heels of the designation that a human being is initially a sign constituted by *fel* and *face*—naked skin and that most concentrated sign of human identity (figural or mimetic), human visage, *prosopon*.

Is it a shock that by passus 20, after the enigmatic though linear sequence of allegorical encounters, layered dreams, typologically charged visions, and spare waking moments (of madness), Will comes finally to encounter Need, and, incredibly, not in a dream but as a being existing finally on the outer level of Will's living and waking experience?[7] The poem's arc from initial to final need in over 20 passus depicts the Levinasian body: at first a naked, vulnerable, and scorned body that then, as other, must be embraced and clothed by us, not violated or harmed by us. Citing one of Emmanuel Levinas's talmudic readings, *Judaism and Revolution,* along with a well-known passage from his *Totality and Infinity,* Catherine Chalier expresses the most basic of human ontological qualities according to Levinas (and in the context of the philosopher's investigation into the role of Abraham—typological proxy for Langland's personification Faith, child of Truth—as the assuager or fulfiller of human physical needs): "None the less, [the] equivalence between the physical needs of the other—his hunger and his thirst, his pain as an abandoned man in a world so often indifferent or cruel—and the spiritual needs of the descendant of Abraham is not self-evident. In fact, according to Levinas, needs express the search for a satisfaction or a happiness for oneself."[8] That is, the nakedness, thirst, and hunger of the other marks the initial point at which one identifies with that other, even though the identification marks as well only the *preliminary* point of spiritual journey, of "desire for God," which has to come after. But as we shall see in my sketch of Levinas's humane program as it relates to the sign-systems of allegory in *Piers Plowman,* the icon of the vulnerability of basic need that must unite me with the other before spiritual discovery can take place is the face (though the journey of discovery might circle back to mere need, as it does for Will by passus 20).

A Prelude to Langland: Some Postmodern Theorists of the Face

In the philosophical writings of Emmanuel Levinas, the face enjoys primacy as a central concept or image, while in the vast commentary on Levinas's work it has likewise garnered great attention. These are well-known facts.[9] Instead of attempting an exhaustive recapitulation of Levinas's notion of the face this essay seeks to give a summary account of how the concept can illuminate some aesthetically overdetermined and semiotically intransigent images in the literary allegory of Langland's poem. Using this analysis to approach the key and strange moment regarding Anima in *Piers Plowman,* I will also draw upon some other modern theorizations of the face—specifically, those from what I call "the deManian cult of *prosopopeia,*" including the Deleuzean notion of machinal "facialization"; and, the rationalist employment of the perceived human face in the "scientific humanism" of poet, philosopher, mathematician, and historian of science, Jacob Bronowski.

As the primacy of the face for Levinas has long been known to be linked, if even tangentially and by implication though never quite directly, to the Lithuanian philosopher's apprehension of the Holocaust,[10] my findings regarding Bronowski flash out with particular relevance—so much so that the deManian and Deleuzean machinal images of the rhetorical face and of the semiotic face, respectively, take second place in helping us to understand the ethical and material dimensions of faceness and in aiding us to decode more fully the cryptic images in Langlandian personification allegory. My approach is thus comparative and sparing in terms of the representative materials it draws on; but I believe it achieves a newly illuminating triangulation of what are essentially *allegorical* writers—Langland, Levinas, and Bronowski, the three representing the medieval, the modern rationalist-ethical, and the modern scientific-ethical or scientific-humanist.

That I begin by taking up Paul de Man's theory of personification or *prosopopeia,* the "master trope in poetic discourse,"[11] must seem inevitable, given the deconstructionist's championing of the lexical properties of terms constitutive of critical or rhetorical discourse themselves. The classical trope *prosopopoeia,* as de Man stressed, derived etymologically from the Hellenic expression *prosopon poiein* ("to make a face"). The preponderance of de Man's rhetorical readings of the Romantic poets, of modern philosophers (such as Rousseau and Nietzsche), and of modernist poets (such as Rimbaud, Hugo, and Baudelaire), focus on the thematization of face-making, as well as face-unmaking, in both luridly sensuous or in encoded, encrypted strains.[12]

Construed merely at the rhetorical or tropological level, Levinas's face becomes a gigantic philosopheme built on de Man's master trope *prosopopeia.* The apprehension of the Other in the guise of the face, which commands ethical response in us, feels from the start to have the dynamic command of personification allegory or of the sublime poetics of nature, in the Romanticist conceptual scheme, which hinges on the Other ever personified as a human face or sentience. As the Levinasian face is supposed to elicit compassion and communion (since it is supposed to be the nexus of the avoidance of extreme violence, even though it can often be the catalyst of violence—Levinas's so-designated "violence of the face") (*AT* 144–45), its function as a rhetorical trope constituted by the deconstructive protocols of de Man's enfacement/ defacement paradox motorizes even putatively nonallegorical narratives built around literal defacements of an appallingly violent quality.[13]

Nevertheless, since de Man's rhetorical critique of Western metaphysics, of ontologies of unity or "philosophies of wholeness," as Susan Handelman labels them, "appeals to impersonal and anonymous forces to rupture [such] totalities," it must be recognized that Levinas "worked so intensively" against just such a machinal and impersonal valorization of language in itself and of itself alone.[14] This does not mean I would totally reject deManian rhetorical analysis from my program altogether; it is simply that it needs a fuller complement of modern conceptual schemes that better evoke the Levinasian expression of the face, while helping to decode the fourteenth century English literary precursor I had set out after in the first place. De Man's basic sense that the "enfacement" of *prosopopeia* always embodies its reciprocal "defacement" is indeed a useful place to enter the odd and startling way Levinas explains the face, as I will show in a moment. For now, it is worth remembering that commentary on Levinas centralizes a number of rhetorical master tropes that motorize and enable his hermetic brand of philosophical writing itself.[15]

To begin with, nothing could be more enigmatic than the sensuous apprehension of the Levinasian face, a self-disfiguring figure designed, it would seem, to restrict any ready apprehension and simplification. Summary are his pronouncements in his important essay "Meaning and Sense" [*Signification et le sense*]—among them, the declaration that the face comes starkly from "the beyond" as it "transcend[s] all cognition" (*BPW* 59). It is, as Levinas asserts in "Enigma and Phenomenon," the "absent" ground for the potential of "signifyingness" itself and is "the very essence of an irrecuperable absence" (70), while it "enigmatically comes from the Infinite and its immemorial past" (77). We can pile up such aphorisms about the face, many of them recasting Platonic or Parmenidean thoughts on the beyond, the infinite; many more echoing, as Critchley and others have well catalogued, Derrida's own elliptical statements about philosophical grounds that are, in Levinas's favorite later formulation, "otherwise than being." As such, the face at once *is* and *is not* (in the quotidian order of ontic experience), while it must yet be imminently human, the visage of the one we meet and *must not* do violence against, the forward sign of the human body we must clothe, feed and whose thirst we must slake.

The evanescent, wavering status of the face conforms to a rhetorical idea of defacement, to be sure; it is in evidence to the perceiver, yet it dissolves from his full apprehension: "The face of the Other at each moment destroys and overflows the *plastic image* it leaves me" (*TI* 50; emphasis mine). It is, paradoxically, like rhetorical enfacement/defacement, imminent and infinite, or beyond sensible grasp, *and* bearing requisitely paradoxical ethical or social markers. "Inevitably," Levinas continues, "across my idea of the Infinite the other faces me—hostile, friend, my master, my student" (81). The intensive use of paradox, coupled with the structural or lexical rhetoric of *prosopopeia*, must for some readers invoke deconstruction's rhetorical aporia or state of "hole-ness." The face recapitulates Derrida's notion of the trace, in fact.

And as Handelman summarizes further, "What Levinas is trying to articulate with [the] complex notion of face as trace is the logical paradox of 'personal absence.' What is 'absent' is absent only in *onto-logical* terms, i.e., absent as 'being'; but it is present-absent in the race which passes through the personal other of human beings, and which is the very call to responsibility for the other. *The refusal of presence is converted into my presence as present for-the-other.*"[16]

Yet even in Levinas's own insistence on the imminent, the real and present dimension of the face, do we find a strange imaging of evacuation, of nonpalpability, that I think actually turns us back to prefigurations, as I will show momentarily in medieval allegory. In more practical terms, we might take up those utterances where Levinas reemphasizes the sensuous though compromised humanness, the very materiality, of the face — that is, utterances in which the face does not come off as absolutely "abstract," as he himself admits it often must be in philosophical discourse (*BPW* 59). Most striking among these utterances is his opening remark to interviewer Phillipe Nemo in which he actually delineates what medievalists would call the beginnings of a facial *effictio*. Levinas says, "You turn yourself toward the Other as toward an object when you see a nose, eyes, a forehead, a chin, and you can describe them. The best way of encountering the Other is not even to notice the color of his eyes! When one observes the color of the eyes one is not in social relationship with the Other" (*EI* 85). Suffice it to say that the evacuation of color from the living eye of the perceived fellow human face strikes an odd chord. Is it perhaps the incipient step toward a defacialization, a defacement in its insistent depersonalization or impersonalism?

Taken literally for the moment, the Levinasian colorless eye invokes for me the vacuity of a white or a black hole, a kind of blank disc; it certainly denatures the actual faces of our fellow, living human beings in order to render an abstract and semiotically processed form that perhaps transcends the locus of real and temporally situated faces. This effect, in turn, might require that we push Levinas's reconstitution of the face through at least one radical account of faciality or "facialization" in contemporaneous postmodern thought, though one ultimately made up of the residual vocabulary of high structuralism (and even though it may seem redolent of a ferocious antihumanism). I refer to Deleuze and Guattari's now infamous geometrical topology of the *divine face* in art as presented in their antiaesthetic (and antipsychoanalytical) manifesto, *A Thousand Plateaus*. Writing of the angelic and demonic faces constituting the numinous images of Ethiopian sacred scrolls painted to depict the lives of the prophets, the saints, and of Christ, they summarize: "The face is part of a surface-hole, holey surface system. This system should under no circumstances be confused with the volume-cavity system proper to the body. The head is included in the body; but the face is not. The face is a surface: facial traits, lines, wrinkles; long face, square face, triangular face; the face is a map, even when it is applied to and wraps a volume, even when it surrounds and borders cavities that are now no more than holes."[17] This description constitutes what Deleuze and Guattari call the "white wall/black hole system," a semiotic system, working at the level of deep structure as part of the epigenetic origins of human consciousness and the advent of language (though not, as in the case of Levinas's face, as an onto-logical verity). Rather, the white wall/black hole system is a process of semiosis marked by absentation in presentation, just as the chromic or optical features of white-in-black and black-in-white signify the reciprocity of present-in-absence and absent-in-presence. The system forms a powerful tool in Deleuze and Guattari's regime of so-called "schizoanalysis," a regime that seeks to undo the epistemological and ontological centralization and certainty in Cartesian and neo-Cartesian (that is, Freudian) models of consciousness, language formation, and therapeutization.

Deleuze and Guattari (largely through a rambling stream of end-notes) trace the white wall/black hole machine of faciality through centuries of artistic praxis (asserting even that prehistoric cultures nei-ther used or knew the face *qua* face), imaginative literature, psychotic fantasy, and religious vision. Their combinatory discourse of antipsy-choanalysis, late structuralism, historical materialism, and ethnography yields ultimately to a kind of mathematical or geometrical topology of faciality.[18] They continue, "What accomplishes [all] this is the screen with holes, the white wall/black hole, the abstract machine producing faciality." They ultimately engage in the self-multiplicatory character of holes in the pierced "screen," having initially engaged the system's semiotic pulse to explain the function of painted demons (often poly-ocular) in the Ethiopian religious art once studied exhaustively by ico-nographer Jacques Mercier.[19] Such polyface or polyocular devils parallel iconographically the polyocular divine as witnessed in the *tetrazoon* or *hayothim* of Ezekiel 1 and Revelation 4—the so-called Four Living Creatures, the Seraphs, peppered on their surfaces by living eyes!

I thus insist that Deleuze and Guattari's elaborate systemic descrip-tion could be taken as a maximal semiotization of the optical or visual status of an ethical (and frankly attenuated) conceptual *effictio* only begun by Levinas. We must also note, however, that the ultimate sentiment of Deleuzean schizoanalysis could potentially take us, like deManian deconstruction centered on its master trope *prosopopeia,* in the direction of the "anonymous" and de-person[aliz]ing and polymorphic Machine of Language (rather, in the direction here of "semiosis" in general) feared by Levinas, according to at least one suspicious interpretation made by Susan Handelman.

Yet Deleuze and Guattari's process invokes the craftsmanlike, the technical, the carving up of an object of study to yield further signify-ing functions or practices. Their regime of thought seems to militate against the rationalist enterprise of post-Cartesian ontology and epis-temology; and that has always been the ethicist danger, if we adhere to Handelman's caveat, of deconstructive or schizoanalytical practices. Handelman, incidentally, arrived at that lucid caveat by reminding the student of Levinas that the Lithuanian-Jewish philosopher, though hermetic in polemical pose and style and ever-dedicated in part to the extreme mental calisthenics of Husserlian phenomenology, is nonetheless of a persistently *rationalist* bent. She places Levinas in the contemporary context, following the horrors of World War II and the Holocaust, of other Jewish thinkers, such as Joseph Soloveitchik, who are of likewise rationalist proclivity in their thinking. Such rationalist intention could tend to corral all forms of structural, phenomenological, gestaltist, mystical, and rhetoricalist rumination put in the service of an enduring ethics and to place them under severe scrutiny.[20]

This particular rescue operation would force us to collate the rationalist Jewish Levinas with other Jewish thinkers of the mid-twentieth century who had embraced the rationalist mode of thought even unto the heights of truly scientific principles—perhaps Soloveitchik, but more so a synthetic thinker such as the rationalist Franz Rosenzweig. As is well known, Levinas admired Rosenzweig,[21] whose important *Star of Redemption* stands out as a mediation between the Jewish walked-line of the realized tragic history of one's people and the promise of rationalism to overcome that tragedy, with deference to the mystical in thought.[22]

Might the Levinasian discourse of the face, numinous and hermetic as it overwhelmingly seems, have a strong analog in the modern discourse of the humanist, specifically scientific-humanist, musing of the middle to late twentieth century? I take a lead from John Llewelyn's prescient comments made as he applies Levinasian imagery and ethics to the fiction of Daniel Defoe. In explaining Levinas's other difficult concept, the notion of *illéité* ("illeity" or "He-ness"), Llewelyn insists that illeity's "third-person pronominality...is not to be divorced from the concreteness of a singular 'you' face to face with 'me'."[23] He flatly declares that the imagined ocular status of a trope involving such intensive grammatical wavering is based on "Levinas's non-Newtonian optics of ethics."[24] It would seem that my naked eye must behold the naked face of the Other, a face vulnerable in and as the countenancing of vulnerable nakedness itself.[25] The naked eye, however, primatizes the ocularcentrist and Newtonian physics of "normal" human vision. Though a rationalist who hermetically interrogates and impugns the whole Cartesian infrastructure of human consciousness predicated upon *its* node of primacy, the *cogito* or hierarchically valorized and enthroned *ratio* or *logos*, Levinas impugns the primacy of a tacitly Newtonian optics of vision. Might the scientifically reproducible, rationalistically sanctioned, even technological alternatives to the instrumentality of merely Newtonian optics, therefore, further enable and energize our conceptual grasp of that greatest of Levinasian conceits, the face of the Other beheld by me?

Bronowski's Post-Newtonian Optics of the Face and Levinas's Ethics as Optics

Jacob Bronowski, another prominent Jewish thinker, joins with Levinas and Soloveitchik precisely in questioning Newtonian optics. As a fellow condemner of the Holocaust who had managed to avoid its horrors directly, Jacob Bronowski has in fact provided an astonishing essay on faciality that echoes Deleuze and Guattari's antihumanist, antipsychologistic picture in its very iconography, even as it departs from that picture's antirationalist intention, joining forces instead with the rationalist ethical program of Levinas, of Soloveitchik, or of Rosenzweig. I find that it is more than a coincidence that the technical and rationalist heights of Bronowski's own critique of ethics and knowledge during the hegemony of the Nazis comes as a catalogue of non-Newtonian ways of perceiving the face of the Other. His astonishing essay, "Knowledge and Certainty" (which serves as the eleventh chapter of his monumental history of human culture and science, *The Ascent of Man,* a treatise also rendered as a popular television documentary in the early 1970s),[26] culminates as a narrative about the discovery of quantum physics by various European scientists from the 1910s through the 1940s (Niels Bohr of Denmark, Max Born and Werner Heisenberg of Germany, Louis de Broglie of France, Enrico Fermi of Italy, Leo Szilard of Hungary)—exactly when Europe suffered its catastrophic collapse of reason under the Nazis. Bronowski takes great care defining his operating terms—"knowledge," which is a limited and always "tolerant" form of human mental operation; and "certainty," the imperious, misdirected, avaricious, and dangerous desire for *absolute* knowledge. The essay concludes with a scene in which Bronowski wades into the flushing ponds at Auschwitz that still contain the ashes of thousands of Jews—his countrymen from Poland, some of them actually his own relatives. At this chilling site he emphatically distinguishes knowledge from certainty: "When people believe they have absolute knowledge, with no test in reality, this is how they behave. This is what men do when they aspire to the knowledge of gods...Science is a very human form of knowledge. We are always at the brink of the known, we always feel forward for what is to be hoped. Every judgment in science stands on the edge of error, and is personal. Science is a tribute to what we can know although we are fallible" (*AM* 374).

In order to arrive at his narrative history of the discovery of quantum physics and its sobering aftermath as he ponders the ashes of the dead, Bronowski provides a "parable" of how we "see" the human face according to various kinds of electromagnetic radiation constituting the electromagnetic spectrum first hypothesized by James Clerk Maxwell in the 1860s. The particular face used as parabolic subject for the essay is haunting, portentous: it belongs to one Stephan Borgrajewicz, a Jew who had personally suffered internment at Auschwitz but who survived. The essay and the telefilm documentary alike open with a blind woman using her fingers to probe the face of the actual Borgrajewicz, now very aged in the early 1970s, and to describe it verbally for Bronowski's mike and camera—accurately, poignantly: the subject is elderly; has not a happy face; is Eastern European (*AM* 353). This affords Bronowski the opportunity to consider Borgrajewicz's face as it has been rendered, not as a realistic simulation of what we could *see* with our naked eyes but, first, as a felt surface of naked flesh; and next, as an abstract congeries of geometric shapes, strokes and colors in a series of compositions about Borgrajewicz's face done by the famous Polish surrealist painter, Feliks Topolski.

We are then treated to technologically captured images of Borgrajewicz's face according to the ascending patterns of electromagnetic energy—that is, following the linear and ascending values of *wavelength*—available to current imaging technologies. As Bronowski promises, "The spectrum of visible light [with which we normally see], from red to violet, is only an octave or so in the range of invisible radiations. There is a whole keyboard of information, all the way from the longest wavelengths of radio waves (the low notes) to the shortest wavelengths of X-rays and beyond (the highest notes). We will shine it all, turn by turn, on the human face" (*AM* 353–54). And so he does. First, a radar scanner set up on a broad and isolated tidal flat produces only an outline of the whole man, Borgrajewicz, standing next to a gigantic plaster effigy of his actual face and head. The two juxtaposed images appear each as white, vacant blobs (viewed top-down) with no surface features yet with outlines alone.[27] Second is an infrared image of the face which shows no recognizable detail, rather only the heat distributions, variably and artificially color-marked as yellows and reds, invisible to the normal or naked eye; the breath and the nostrils show pronounced hue (white). Next is the (photographic or cinematographic) face apprehended in quotidian white light, giving us "no longer [any] man," for "it is the man we know: Stephan Borgrajewicz...White light reveals him to the eye visibly, in detail; the small hairs, the pores in the skin, a blemish here, a broken vessel there" (354–55).

And yet, this moment of Newtonian optical certainty—or so it would seem to be a moment of certainty—does not enjoy epistemological privileging for Bronowski. As we continue our trek up the ascending spectrum of increasingly shortening electromagnetic wavelengths and heightening electromagnetic energies, we attain knowledges of the face that are, at each step, both less and more generous regarding information we might or might not expect to glean. In the ultraviolet phase, the face of the man Borgrajewicz, as well as the gigantic effigy of his head, are simply bathed in an eerie glow, a soft fogginess. Enlarged through an optical microscope, the face of our subject reveals its sinuous crevices, its very cells and tissues, though no collective or complete image of *identity* can any longer be proffered. On to the wavelength of the X-ray: we now see under the man's skin, and we learn that his face had concealed a toothless skull (ravaged by the ill nutrition of life in Auschwitz), the soft tissues—the sagging jowls, the watery eyes, the tongue especially—having faded away to an imperceptible tint clouding the dark outlines of bony occiput, temples, eye sockets, maxilla and mandible (*AM* 356).

X-ray Borgrajewicz may just be the most uncanny, certainly the most macabre, of all the facialized Borgrajewiczes: his has become the facial image of the Death's Head—allegory's most persistent personificational countenance (for it is the very countenance of tragic history itself, as Walter Benjamin has ruminated in his dialectical study of baroque aesthetics and allegory),[28] as well as a potential rebus of Deleuze and Guattari's semiotically reductive white wall/black hole machine of facialization. The final step to take, the imaging of Borgrajewicz using the scanning electronic microscope, shows only a constituent atom here or there in the man's sculpted effigy (for we cannot fire electrons at *living* matter...such would be radical violence to the living face). The geometrical simplification produced would be as ineffable and abstract, once again, as the geometrical simples in a Deleuzean machinal com- posite of holes, circles, and rectangles. (Bronowski demonstrates by displaying the geometrical splotch that is the S.E.M. image of a thorium atom, the smallest thing, by 1973, ever imaged.) In any event, these scanning "rays are so concentrated that we no longer know whether to call them waves or particles" (*AM* 356)—the epistemological state of affairs which itself *is* the very definition of quantum physics, a discourse or discipline all about things that are now one thing, now another (just like the personifications who seem to ontologically waver or grow unstable in an allegorical text).[29]

The imaging of Borgrajewicz thus becomes clear as a parable of *seeing*—a veritable "dialectics of seeing" (to borrow the title phrase of an important recent commentary on the theoretical production of Benjamin himself),[30] as we move along a progressively synthetic path of imaging phenomenologies. This parable of seeing may be understood to preface modern science's embracing of quantum physics with its epistemology of the ineffable. In aptly Levinasian language, Bronowski writes: "We are here *face to face* with the crucial paradox of knowledge. Year by year we devise more precise instruments with which to observe nature with more fineness. And when we look at the observations, we are discomfited to see that they are still fuzzy, and we feel that they are as uncertain as ever. We seem to be running after a goal which lurches away from us *to infinity* every time we come within sight of it" (*AM* 356; emphases added). This uncertainty requires that we proceed with humility, and that, to quote the final line of Bronowski's essay as he crouches down in the flushing pool at Auschwitz to stir the waters containing his dead ancestors' very ashes, "We have to touch people" (374). We must not condemn and savage the Other, placing him in the death camp (nor under the fall to earth of an atomic bomb);[31] we must see his vulnerability and touch the nakedness of his face. Borgrajewicz's face is an allegory or parable, recall, of science's climb up the epistemological ladder, through the linear pattern of the electromagnetic spectrum, toward an ever-finer apprehension of matter that must embrace the Infinite. And the Infinite for Levinas stands as that aspect of the Other allegorized as face. The telefilm of "Knowledge or Certainty" aptly ends with a painted version of Borgrajewicz's numbered mug shot, costume of prison stripes and all, when he was taken into Auschwitz. The painted effigy mimics an earlier, photographic gallery of the sorrowful faces of other camp victims.

The foregoing theoretical framework should now begin to elucidate what I have been implying about Langland's Augustinian-Isidorean slate of entities subtended by Anima: the slate marks something of a spectrum, a gradated tally, not unlike the electromagnetically realized spectrum of Borgrajewicz's "identities" that "exist" at different times, different energies, and under differing cognitive circumstances. As Bronowski's spectrum of Borgrajewicz's face teaches us, there may be no epistemologically privileged—and thus no ontologically paramount—form of the face. This might be so regarding Langland's spectrum of Long Will's face with its counterpart in his own soul, his own Anima.

THE PERSONIFICATIONAL FACE OF LANGLAND'S ANIMA

We come now to that most mysterious of imagistically overdetermined moments in Langland's text. The resolution that Anima stands as a cognitively or existentially atavistic root gets compromised, moreover, not by logical faults in Anima's authoritative discourse drawn from Isidore but by the sole and singularly cryptic *effictio* of the creature's face—an *effictio,* as well as an act of nominational labeling (*"Anima"*), which was so fraught with epistemological complexity that Langland had to erase these details in the C text by replacing Anima with *Liberum Arbitrium* or "Free Will," who appears instead to conduct this central dialogue with the dreamer-narrator.[32] Langland's words uncannily presage, I believe, some of the features of analysis I have tendered regarding the Levinasian face and my buttress for that face coming in the form of the scientific spectration of cognitive adjustments—of visions, to be sure—proffered by Bronowski in "Knowledge or Certainty." Prior to the Isidorean slate voiced by Anima, prior to his/its self-proclaimed *notatio,* comes the cryptic *effictio*:

> in þat folie I raued
> Til reson hadde ruþe on me and rokked me aslepe,
> Til I seiȝ, as it sorcerie were, a sotil þyng wiþ alle.
> Oon wiþouten tonge and teeþ tolde me whider I sholde
> And whereof I cam & of what kynde. I coniured hym at þe laste
> If he were cristes creature [for cristes loue] me to tellen. (*PP* 15.10–15)

Like the various facializations of Borgrajewicz, Langland's Anima seems foggyish, faint, merely an outline at times—indeed a "subtle" or "soft" thing "with all." The phantasmagoric quality of Bronowski's spectrations find their primordial representation in so strange an image that it invokes for its narrating witness the sense of sorcery. But most emphatically, X-ray Borgrajewicz, the stripped face of the Other rendered totally vulnerable, indeed subvisible, in Levinas's conceptual scheme, palpably appears as a creature "without tongue or teeth."[33] Old philosophical ideas about Soul might dictate that its poetic rendering as an immaterial, nonfleshly simulacrum, dispense with the carnal apparatus of eating—tongue and teeth; to be sure, the personification of Anima as Spiritus, the posthuman excarnation of Soul as something speechless, would seem to dictate the loss of organs or mouth parts of speech in iconographic terms.

But more powerfully, the association of Anima as a kind of Death's Head underlines the uncanny force of Langland's poetic vision itself.[34] In this scene, Will [*Voluntas*] is speaking to himself—more precisely to the Other ("*Christ's* creature") that is coincident with the willing self. That Other/self takes the form of a Benjaminian Death's Head, yet also the realistic effigy of what Will the Narrator admits to having become physically by passus 20, a sick old man without any teeth left—a man who must look like the tired and aged Stephan Borgrajewicz.[35] No doubt a number of the tallied entities in the Isidorean passage take on a kind of primacy when viewed at this or that moment. Toothless old man or Old Age, as well as Death's Head, match up with X-ray Borgrajewicz. The *Ratio* of line 28 and its coterminous Reason of line 11 prefigure the very thought regime itself that seems the most rightly designated atavistic core of the tally—a poetic counterpart to the analytical mind of Bronowski *himself* perceiving his forlorn countryman. To be sure, both Levinas and Bronowski use reason as the road to compassion—that which the face of the Other is supposed to elicit in the human imagination. And compassion, *rupe* in Langland's Middle English (also line 11), marks precisely where Reason had carried the tormented and aged Will as she rocks him to healing sleep, the precincts of a more hermetically constituted psychic laboratory, a psychomantium par excellence—another inner dream or dream-within-the-dream. And as well, this semiotic complex takes us back to Holy Church's primal ontological designations about Man, about Will the dreamer, in lines 12–25 of passus 1. There Truth, father of Faith, gave us first our five wits or senses (just as Bronowski, uncannily perhaps, has tallied for us five Maxwellian wits or senses—radar, infrared, white-light, ultraviolet, X-ray—with which we actually get to "see" Borgrajewicz's face-head) in order to know our three basic needs (clothing, eating, and drinking) so that we in turn may, in *reason,* seek our origin, Truth.

I think I have made the ethical and spiritual analogies of this essay clearly and strongly enough. But the reading of the phantasmagoric passage presenting Anima in passus 15 of the B text still wavers between de-personing Anima, that atavistically basic entity, and the prospect of de-personing the Other's face — a potentially dangerous effect ethically, as the rationalist-humanist protocols of my Bronowskian-Levinasian model should portend and as the very skeptical Susan Handelman have made clear. Yet that same model or regime of thought cannot at times avoid evacuating the face of its living and sensuous human aspect in its recasting as Death's Head, for the face of the Other does seem to conform to Benjamin's tragic icon of history, while the face that is most centrally characterized by its tongueless, toothless orifice — by a mere hole or graphic, geometric vacuity more compelling than the face's presumed eyes — might be yet another version of the machinally "drilled" holes in the Deleuze-Guattari "white-wall/black-hole system." The rationalism of Bronowski's analytical modeling of the face has the power to evacuate at the same time that rationalism's humane and humanistic source, which wants to call for compassion by showing the many possible faces of that category of being known as the human. Yet *all* the radical ways of re-seeing the face which I have proposed in this essay seem to militate against and potentially undercut the human *look* that is the action of the face — what John Burrow, in rethinking the simply conveyed *effictiones* of *Piers Plowman* and of similar late medieval texts most recently, has taken as the supremely human and humane aspect of Langland's visual poetics.[36]

My triangulation of Langland, Levinas, and Bronowski has shown various representations, each ethical, rational, and allegorical by turns, of the face which is not a face — the face of the Other, of the Infinite, which is my face (and your face) as well. The thought regimes of de Man, as well as Deleuze and Guattari, still serve to help explain Langland's and Levinas's striking poetic facializations; but it is Bronowski's scientific-humanist treatment, born in the context of mid-twentieth century irrationalism and the horrible violence done to the Jew, to the Other, that augments and enriches an analytical regime in which the thought of Emmanuel Levinas still allows a literary scholar such as a medievalist to find freshness and to experience awe in the old genre of personification allegory.[37]

8

The Infinite Desire of *Pearl*

J. A. Jackson

When Abba Zacharias was at the point of death,
Abba Moses asked, "What do you see?"
He said, "Is it not better to hold peace, my Father?"
And Abba Moses said, "Yes, it is better to hold your peace, my child."
— *Sayings of the Desert Fathers*

Theodore Bogdanos's beautiful meditation on *Pearl* begins to define the inexpressibility of the poem's theopoetics: "A fraction of historical time in a man's life is engulfed in eternity; yet it suddenly expands and possesses eternity within itself—if only for a flashing moment of powerful vision."[1] The vision at the heart of the poem cannot be properly expressed because it can only be experienced, lived—in the world to come, of course, but in this one as well. My essay charts *Pearl*'s treatment of desire and its relation to this eschatological vision. I begin by focusing on the act of seeing, of vision. Focusing specifically on the *Pearl*-Maiden's face, the Dreamer's first optical gesture is a narcissistic one, an unconscious collapsing of the distance between the Maiden and himself. The Other who is visible, the poem will show, is precisely the other that can be effaced, absorbed into the same, though one must resist this temptation at all times.

Through various rhetorical and didactic devices, the Maiden attempts to disrupt the Dreamer's totalizing gestures. As a corrective, and as an assertion of her own alterity, the Maiden explicitly chastises the Dreamer for his unshakeable faith in his own vision. The Dreamer relies not only on his vision but also on his past knowledge of *this* Maiden. But this Maiden no longer remains his daughter, at least not the one he knew, and she remains now, as ever before, entirely inassimilable. Thinking about paternity and futurity (perhaps even the eschatologi-cal), Levinas names the obstacle facing the Dreamer: "The fact of seeing the possibilities of the other as your own possibilities, of being able to escape the closure of your identity and what is bestowed on you, toward something which is not bestowed on you and which nevertheless is yours—this is paternity....A future beyond my own being" (*EI* 70). The Dreamer's self-constructed paternity, however, is situated only in his past and thus can offer him no vision of the future.

The problem of vision, then, reveals itself as a problem of desire for the Dreamer, and so to offer him a corrective, the Maiden frames much of the discussion around desire. In the Dreamer one finds an egoic, narcissistic desire. He desires an Other of his own making. His is a desire not for the Other out of a duty to the Other, a loss of one's self to the Other, but a desire *of* the Other only *for* himself. The Maiden, I argue, rather than rejecting desire altogether, attempts to resituate the Dreamer's desire. This new desire is founded upon a structure of infinite substitution, wherein one desires to serve the Other who counts more than oneself. This structure is realized, I argue, in the liturgical procession of the brides of the Lamb, where the Dreamer witnesses each bride offering her place to every Other bride, giving up her own place in the procession for the Other.

This liturgical structure of infinite substitution is the anagogical Church incarnate and acts as a response to the various theological questions throughout the poem—theo-ontological questions, ques-tions of justice, questions of human relations. An explicit appropria-tion of the eschatological, *Pearl* visualizes an *agape* based not solely on undifferentiated love, but on what Levinas will identify as a radical asymmetrical relationship of substitution (*BPW* 90–91). Eschatologi-cal expectation, we come to find out in *Pearl,* is the prophetic naming of an infinite one-for-the-other, a response, a submission, a meeting with my neighbor to which I am always already late. Rather than simply naming divine being as such, the poem depicts an *otherwise than being,* named as the Kingdom of God itself. This is a kingdom composed of individual beings engaged in an infinite substitutionary relationship, a relationship where each individual utters an infinite "after you" to every Other individual. The poem treats the personal (each individual Other) and the communal (The Kingdom of God made of each individual Other) not as separate entities but as ethical extensions of the other. In this way, *Pearl* takes up and stages the very problematics of Being recognized by Levinas by performing for the reader Levinasian excessiveness, infinite desire. The poem quite literally exceeds itself, accomplishes for the reader the very excessiveness of desire which acts as the foundation of the otherwise than being of the Kingdom of Heaven.

Finally, because much of my reading of *Pearl* is concerned with the structural excessiveness of the poem and the way in which this structure comes to perform for the reader the otherwise than beingness of Levinasian ethical onto(theo)logy, I conclude my essay with a meditation on the potential prophetic role of literature. I attempt to create an interchange between Levinas's early thoughts about literature and art, as expounded in "Reality and Its Shadow," with some of his later views regarding the relationship between literature, revelation, and redemption. I hope to make clear that Levinas does indeed amend his earlier views about the nonethical status of literature. Because Levinas both implicitly and explicitly invokes Rosenzweig's categories of creation, revelation, and redemption with regards to literature (both in his earlier and later views about literature), I bring Rosenzweig into the conversation. When one parses Levinas's allusions to the Rosenzweigian categories of revelation and redemption, one finds that Levinas offers us his own understanding of literature as a participant within the realm of ethics.

Optical Elusion

"The first 'vision' of eschatology (hereby distinguished from the revealed opinions of positive religions)," Levinas argues, "reveals the very possibility of eschatology, that is the breach of totality, the

possibility of a *signification without a context*. The experience of morality does not proceed from this vision—it consummates this vision;
ethics is an optics" (*TI* 23). The potential death of the Other, violence
to the Other, and, therefore, responsibility for the Other can only be
my own. Rather than allow him to suffer from paralysis in the face of
death (ironically in the land of eternal life), the presence of the Maiden
calls the Dreamer to responsibility. It is quite literally the death of his
daughter that commands him now—that which was never not commanding him, now only being made explicit—a responsibility that
extends beyond even death.

In the shadow of death, Levinas, writes, the subject "finds itself
enchained, overwhelmed, and in some way passive. Death in this sense is
the limit of idealism. . . . It is not with the nothingness of death, of which
we precisely know nothing, that the analysis must begin, but with the
situation where something absolutely unknowable appears. Absolutely
unknowable means foreign to all light, rendering every assumption of
possibility impossible, but where we ourselves are seized" (*TO* 70–71).
Where we are seized, chained, and enslaved by death is precisely where
we find freedom: in responsibility for the Other.[2] Levinas writes: "The
eschatological, as the 'beyond' of history, draws beings out of the jurisdiction of history and the future; it arouses them and calls them forth
to their full responsibility" (*TI* 23). The mere presence of the Maiden
confronts the Dreamer with his own assumptions about life and death
and will render his assumptions "of possibility impossible." He must
eventually wrestle with this vision of the "impossibility of the possible"
(in the heavenly vision and then back on earth) even as he literally faces
the radical alterity of death (and eternal life). Fittingly, as commentary
on Scripture—indeed, as a participant in the scriptural project—the
poem attempts to envision and to highlight for us a prophetic, ethical
eschatology, to illumine for us a vision of our freedom from our own
history, and our own death.

Yet if ethics is an eschatological optics—a rupturing of totality, an inter-
ruption of the infinite within the finite—then one must look skeptically.
"Þy worde byfore þy wytte con fle," the Maiden says, responding to the
Dreamer's description of her in her new setting, "Þou says þou trawez

me in þis dene / Bycawse þou may with yȝen me se" (*Pearl* 294–96)
[Your words have flown before your understanding. / You say you
believe that I am in this valley, / because you see me with your eyes].³
This seems a very unfair game he is being asked to play. He is afforded
this vision through sight, yet is told that he must not believe what he
sees. If ethics is an optics, then it is an optics that does not see the face
but experiences the face without any prior knowledge—an eschatological vision of the future with no sense of the past.

The Dreamer's initial struggle, we will find, is his refusal to acknowledge that he does not name the Other, but is, in fact, named by the
Other. The use, and overuse, of personal pronouns by the Dreamer
throughout the poem demonstrates, for example, his reliance upon
a worldview framed singularly around autonomy (self-naming) as
opposed to heteronomy (being named by the Other).⁴ Indeed, his
first vision of the Maiden begins a process of naming specifically aimed
at the face:

> On lenghe I loked hyr þere;
> Þe lenger, I knew hyr more and more.
> The more I frayste hyr fayre face,
> Her fygure fyn quen I had fonte,
> Suche gladande glory con to me glace
> As lyttel byfore þerto watz wonte.   (167–72)
>
> [At length I looked at her there; / The longer I looked, I knew her
> more and more. / The more I examined her fair face, / her fair figure
> I had perceived, / a gladdening glory began to glide over me / as little
> as it had been wont to do before].

What the reader notices here is that "face" has now shifted completely
from its context in a euphemism, a turning—"Towarde a foreste I bere
þe face" (67)—to a literalness that explicitly names the face but, in
doing so, excludes *the face* completely. The face of lines 167–72 is not
the face of the Maiden but the face of the Dreamer's own construction,
an obstacle, ultimately, that he creates for himself; in fact, he will refer
again to the Maiden's face twice with increasing detail: "Hyr vysayge
whyt as playn yvore" (178); and "vyse with yȝen graye" (254).⁵ As the
detail of the face (that is, the physicality of the face) becomes more

concrete, however, *the face* of the Maiden (that is, the relationship with the Other, a signification before a context) will become absorbed by the Dreamer's preoccupation with this physicality of her face (relegated to courtly language or to father / daughter dynamics, for example).

The Dreamer describes the Maiden by employing a courtly aesthetic language: "Þy beauté com neuer of nature— / Pymalyon paynted neuer þy vys, / Ne Arystotel nawþer by hys lettrure, / Of carped þe kynde þese propertéz" (*Pearl* 749–52) [Your beauty comes never by nature— / Pygmalion never painted your face, / nor Aristotle, not even with his learning,/spoke of the kind of these properties]. The face of the Maiden, the Dreamer admits, can be captured neither by art nor language; it cannot be represented, thought, or categorized; it has a "nature" of its own. The poem allows the Dreamer to articulate the paradox of the face: the nature of the Maiden's face is the nature of every face, a radical alterity outside of the viewing subject, unable to be captured, ineffable, unique, a signification without context, both universal and radically Other. Yet by allowing the Dreamer to name the Otherness of the Maiden, the poem is also able to highlight the ways in which the Dreamer seems not to pay attention to the Maiden's Otherness.

Rather, in a most Pygmalion-like fashion, the Dreamer's vision disallows the alterity of the Maiden's face. He becomes consumed with its faceness (its whiteness, the grayness of her eyes). At this point, the Dreamer sees the Maiden not as an exterior object which can or cannot be overcome or attained; her face is an obstacle precisely because it is the Dreamer's interior desire manifested as an exterior object. The relationship between the Maiden and the Dreamer is not one of distance, then, but of sameness, where the Dreamer's ego reduces the distance, the radical alterity of the Maiden, to the point where their oppositions will fade away. Levinas describes the dynamics of this type of Pygmalion-like, narcissistic relationship: "The foreign being, instead of maintaining itself in the inexpugnable fortress of its singularity, instead of facing, becomes a theme and an object. It fits under a concept already, or dissolves into relations. It falls into the network of a prior idea, which I bring to bear, so as to capture it" (*CPP* 50). The Dreamer's repeated attempts to efface difference is countered by the Maiden's gestures to reestablish their irreducible distance. Nevertheless, she also must affirm simultaneously his paternal proximity as well. These corrective, assertive, even hyperbolic gestures on her part, I would argue, act not primarily as a sort of "shrill" rhetorical device on the part of the Maiden but as a simple assertion of her absolute Otherness.[6]

The Dreamer, then, must get past the face in order to engage the face. Describing Levinas's treatment of this paradoxical process, Bernhard Waldenfels writes: "We are told that the face is not something we can see or touch, while moving within open horizons, passing through changing perspectives, transforming it into a content we can embrace and manipulate....It has no 'plastic' form to be transformed into images; it has no *eidos*, no 'adequate idea' by which we could represent and grasp it. The face does not fall into the outer world, open the way to the inner world...or take hold in a third world of ideas."[7] The response Levinas provides to this conundrum, Waldenfels observes, is found in the simple truth, "The face speaks."[8] The simplicity of this line underscores the very alterity of the Other and locates precisely the origins of idolatry of the face: there is no "*eidos* by which we could represent and grasp it." The face of the Maiden, then, rather than calling attention to her face (or to her eyes, or to her sides), presents the Dreamer with a radical alterity, a space which his subjectivity can never occupy—a fact that his attempt to cross the river, and his consequent expulsion, will eventually make explicit. The whiteness of her face, the grayness of her eyes (the faceness of her face), however, bear witness to the face's simultaneous effacing of itself as only visible; that is to say, the faceness of the face announces the non-faceness of that very face. The face is the icon of the phenomenon "the face speaks," an icon which marks itself as the presence of a futurity not yet come but already here.

"The disproportion between the Other and the self," Levinas observes, "is precisely moral consciousness. Moral consciousness is not an experience of values, but an access to external being: external being is, *par excellence,* the Other" (*DF* 293). The Dreamer's internalized past—*his* father-daughter relationship, *his* daughter's death—finds its external manifestation in his vision of his daughter, yet she is not treated as "external being;" rather, she functions as an internal *a priori* relationship externalized. There is no presence of the Maiden here, only the Dreamer's idealized past masking itself as the present.

EGOIC DESIRE

Throughout *Pearl* one finds repeated references to a nonstatic, double relationship: the divine-human; the human-human. This double relationship, however, is revealed as a singular diachronic act, where the divine-human relationship is simply an extension of the human-human relationship, and vice-versa. To flesh out the ethical demands of this two-fold relationship, and to tease out the otherwise than beingness of both relationships, *Pearl* involves itself with the question of desire. *Pearl*'s treatment of desire relies primarily on the medieval conception of *imitatio dei,* imitation of the divine, and more specifically, on imitation of the desire of the divine—to desire only what God desires.[9] The Maiden's undertaking of desire throughout her exchange with the Dreamer has a two-fold purpose: 1) to define precisely what divine, nonegoic desire would look like; 2) to stage the way in which the Dreamer participates in a rivalrous, egoic desire of his own narcissistic making. This two-fold movement will then prepare the Dreamer for his final vision of the liturgical procession of brides and the gesture of infinite substitution he will witness.

Upon hearing of the Maiden's exalted position in the heavenly kingdom, the Dreamer asks: "'Blysful,' quoþ I, 'may þys be trwe? — / Dysplesez not if I speke errour'" (*Pearl* 421–22) [Blissful one, I said, can this be true? / Do not be displeased if I speak in error]. The Dreamer's use of "Blysful" here is perhaps more informative of the rest of his theological debate with his daughter than the theological debate itself. He is responding, of course, to her claim that the Lamb of

God, the "rote and grounde" of all *her* bliss, has crowned her queen of heaven. "Blysful" is how he responds to the situation of her queenship and, by extension, to the Maiden herself. In direct opposition to her "bliss," emphasized even more so by the stanzaic concatenation by the rhyme word, the Dreamer locates very precisely the continual location of all of his bliss: on her. Because he misunderstands the relationship she possesses with the "rote and grounde" of her bliss, he necessarily cannot comprehend her bliss. He gives her his understanding of the heavenly hierarchy, and she proceeds to another analogy (the Pauline construction of the Church as Christ's body), and then to another one (the Parable of the Vineyard). Throughout her entire discussion, however, the structures of desire and relationship remain constant. The Maiden assumes the ethical, prophetic position *par excellence,* as she can read everything from both the future and the past, as both bride and daughter, and acts as interlocutor for the Dreamer from this position alone. The Dreamer, on the other hand, reads both the future and the past, *his* daughter as bride and this bride as *his* daughter, only from his past, which is to say, only from his construction of *his* daughter's identity that originates with him and their relationship he once knew.

The Maiden's response to the Dreamer's "Blysful" observation does more than describe the mystical relationship of the many to the one, or the one to the many, unity in diversity, or diversity in unity. She attempts to define for him the structure of desire and *imitatio dei,* both in the Court of Heaven and on earth. She illumines the mechanism of human desire for him in such a way that it reveals the very *possibility* of an ethical, ineffable, mystical relationship. The reason all are kings and queens of heaven is simply because, we are told, the court itself is imitative of God: "The court of þe kyndom of God alyue / Hatz a property in hytself beyng" (*Pearl* 445–46) [The court of the kingdom of the living God / Has a property in its own being]. Line 446 presents a problem with regards to translation. One can render it as I have above. Or one can translate it as, "a property inherent to itself"; or, "a property in being itself." What all three translations affirm, however, is that there is a sort of beingness to the Beingness of God. There is something about the being of the living God, "inherent" even, that names that there is always something more to the being of God. The so-called mysticism of the hierarchical nonhierarchy in *Pearl* can be understood as nothing other than an infinite structure of substitution, where the first becomes the last and, in turn, the last becomes the first, so that the tenth commandment is acted out and all rivalry averted: "And neuer oþter ȝet schal depryue, / Bot vchon fayn of oþerez hafyng" (449–50) [And never shall anyone deprive another, but be pleased with what each other has].

The heavenly court in *Pearl* is nothing other than a structuring of exemplary desire and, only in this way, an appropriation of "God alyue," of Divine living. Nonegoic desire means simply that the Other before me counts more than myself. This asymmetrical relationship, the one-for-the-other, is the foundation for the infinite structure the Maiden describes to the Dreamer. This is precisely what the Maiden refers to on lines 445–46, when she declares that the Kingdom of God, specifically because it is both imitative of God and participatory in the life of "God alyue," has its own being. This "being" described as the heavenly court by the Maiden can only be imagined in terms outside of traditional ontology: the heavenly court's "being" is imitative of God precisely because it is a "being" of a relationship that produces its own surplus (an infinite one-for-the-other), a beyond being, or an otherwise than being, a being alive. Levinas, responding to the Platonic construction of "the Good beyond being," writes: "Goodness consists in taking up a position in being such that the Other counts more than myself" (*TI* 247).

The Dreamer imagines a rivalrous relationship between the Maiden and Mary; for how else could the Maiden become queen if not by displacement, even if it is only by a verbal usurpation? The Maiden quickly reminds the Dreamer that "Bot supplantorez none withinne þys place" (*Pearl* 440) [There are no supplanters in this place]. The imitative desire here is nothing more than the Maiden imitating Mary, Queen of Heaven, who in turn imitates the Lamb of section 19. Mary, in turn, can do nothing other than share the court with every Other king and queen. In calling herself a queen, the Maiden, rather than usurping or even denying the queenship of Mary, only confirms Mary's unique position. The Maiden's use of "supplantorez" both rejects the Dreamer's claim and names in advance the very position the Dreamer himself will appropriate: he will attempt to supplant the Maiden's elevated, though seemingly unwarranted, position in heaven by arguing for an even more regal status for himself.

To acknowledge the absolute alterity and the priority of the Other means in effect that one is always already a hostage to the Other, never a master over the Other, but mastered by the Other. When the Dreamer does not comprehend the relationship between the Maiden and Mary and believes that the Maiden supplants Mary's role as queen, the Maiden responds: "'Cortayse quen,' þenne sayde þat gaye, / Knelande to grounde, folde vp hyr face..." (*Pearl* 433–34) ['Oh courteous queen,' then said the lovely one, / kneeling to the ground, her face upturned / covered...]. The play on "folde vp" reveals a simultaneous turning to Mary and a submission and service to her as well. As the Maiden submits herself to Mary, she does so only out of imitation of Mary, whose disinterestedness in queenship is precisely what defines her queenship. If we take the logic of the kingdom as described in *Pearl* seriously, the Maiden's "submission" to the queen is an appropriation of, and consequently a submission to, Mary's own submission to the every Other king and queen of the kingdom (including the Maiden). This, of course, is imitative of Mary's own actions on earth: "Here I am, the servant of the Lord; let it be to me according to your word" (Luke 1:38). The Annunciation, in this way, becomes yet another extension of one-for-the-Other: Mary's "here I am" to Gabriel is simply her perfect imitation of God's "here I am" to humanity, a synergistic relationship between divine grace and human free will.

The Maiden's bowing down before Mary, face upturned and/or covered, however, exceeds even her relationship to Mary. Her appeal to Mary is not an appeal on her own behalf, nor is it done out of her embarrassment for the Dreamer's theological improprieties, but is taken on as duty to the Dreamer himself. She appeals to Mary on behalf of the Dreamer, in front of the Dreamer, as a model for the Dreamer through her responsibility *for* him. "To be oneself, the state of being hostage," Levinas argues, "is always to have one degree of responsibility more, the responsibility of the responsibility of the other" (*OB* 117). Hers is a pious submission prior to any theological constructions and before any moment of the ego. Rather than a third-party intermediary, her submission to Mary is yet an extension of her being hostage to the Dreamer; her being hostage to the Dreamer can be found in her imitation of and submission to Mary, imitation and submission named as singular responsibility both to Mary and to the Dreamer, and ultimately to the Lamb—a responsibility always already reciprocated. In many ways, our poem has already anticipated and answered, albeit in a most mystical, anagogical fashion, the tension laid out by Levinas in his working through the problematic relationship between the logic of the two and the three—between the ethical and the political.[10]

Rather than negate or compromise the ethical, the introduction of a "third party" in the kingdom (I use scare quotes here because, from the Maiden's perspective, such a Levinasian third party does not actually exist in the kingdom), provides yet another occasion for blissful substitution; every "third party" is an Other for whom I am most responsible and, subsequently, who is now also my king or queen, an Other to whom I am infinitely answerable. The introduction of a "third party" is really only the introduction of an Other. Indeed, the entire ethicopolitical structure in the kingdom is based on a structure a two-party system where there is seemingly never not a "third party" (be it God, the Slain Lamb, Mary, or one of the 144,000 brides). Yet every "third party" acts only in regards to the Other; even in being responsible for an Other, one is always already acting ethically toward the Other of every Other (as we will see later in the procession of the brides). All of the subsequent theological debate between the Maiden and the Dreamer, the parables and the word games, can be seen as extended commentary on this single ethicopolitical act.

The Maiden invokes Saint Paul's image of the body of Christ as the body of the Church to extend the imitative nature of the heavenly court to a human and divine institution, thus making the connection to the Dreamer more exigent.[11] The progression seems natural: first she explains to him *the* model of perfect imitation and desire, and then she applies it to the way in which it manifests itself on earth. She employs courtly language ("Of courtaysye, as saytz Saynt Poule" [458]) to illustrate that the same mechanism of desire is applicable here, especially since the Church is the body of Christ. In this way, through exegesis she attempts to explain for the Dreamer that as a member of the Church, he is always already a potential participant in the mystical union he witnesses at the heavenly court.[12] On the very surface, then, her initial explanation is less about the heavenly realm than it is about the ubiquitous structure of proper desire and substitution, and its potential existence on earth as it is in heaven.

The Dreamer fails to comprehend the Maiden's speech not because they speak different languages—divine (courtly) and earthly (courtly)—but because the Dreamer himself is blind to his own partici-pation in rivalrous desire (divine and earthly). Lines 473–74 are quite telling: "Þyself in heuen ouer hyȝ þou heue, / To make þe quen þat watz so ȝonge" [You elevate yourself too high in heaven, / to make yourself queen who was so young]. Here it is clear that the Dreamer does not question God; he wonders aloud whether the Maiden improp-erly calls herself queen, whether she overreaches in her desire to ascend the heavenly ranks. In lines 475–80, couched in courtly language of course, he describes to her a rival (potentially himself) to her claim of heavenly nobility: one who lives long in the world, undergoes bodily torment, and who does penance. If she is a queen, then this man alone, according to the Dreamer, ought to be crowned king.

The Dreamer at this point becomes consumed with her position and her position alone. He seems to ignore completely what she previously says about the heavenly court: "All þat may Þerinne aryue / Of alle þe reme is quen and oþer kyng" (*Pearl* 447–48) [All who arrive herein / Of all the realm are king and queen]. In no way does she dispute the kingship of the man just described by the Dreamer. Her previous statement—that *all* who arrive are kings and queens (447–48)—would seem to undercut the Dreamer's objection. We see that the Dreamer does not take issue with her construction of the order of heaven and the royal position granted to all. He objects specifically to the position granted to *her*, or at least the one she claims to have, in relation to the position in heaven someone like him would be afforded. In fact, immediately after he characterizes the life of the man who should be crowned king, he defines a more appropriate role for the Maiden: "Of countes, damysel... Oþer ellez a lady of lasse aray" (489, 91). He can only speak of hierarchical, even patriarchal, difference, and even more specifically, the difference between the man who would be crowned a king of heaven and the Maiden. The Dreamer would invert the divine, infinite structure and, in turn, subverting divine commandment, assume the Maiden's exalted position as his own, and *only* his own. Rather than having the last become the first, where, "the Other counts more than myself," (which is the logic of infinite substitution and imitative of the Word), the Dreamer would have the first (the man who *should* be king) remain the first (the king) so that the last (the Maiden) simply would not be the first (maybe she could be the second, or third, or the 143,999th bride[13]—just not the first). His own desire and his attachment to his conception of his former relationship (father-daughter) with the Maiden would lead him to usurp her position in heaven.

Any direct response by the Maiden, however, would simply reciprocate the rivalry the Dreamer sees between the man bound to earth (potentially himself) and the young who die too soon (the Maiden, *his* daughter). Instead, to illumine completely the obstacles his own desire places in front of him, she uses an earthly parable, one to which the Dreamer would be able to relate in strictly earthly terms. The Parable of the Vineyard presents the reader with some interesting alterations to the biblical text[14] and a reversal of the most traditional exegetical readings.[15] The reference to *peny* (*Pearl* 614) in the parable—that is, the contractual reward, the payment for labor—and the Dreamer's horrified reaction to the injustice of its distribution will really bring to the fore the Dreamer's egoic desire. The Maiden's response to his objections will then deconstruct his egoic desire in such a way as to bear witness to the ethical responsibility inherent in this same structure of desire.

I am inclined to agree with the critics who see the *peny* here as a eucharistic symbol,[16] which would then give double meaning to the idea of *mede* (*Pearl* 620) as unwarranted gift.[17] One can see the evolution of the Maiden's continual analysis of desire and witness the divine *pathos* being revealed to the Dreamer:

> "Bot now þou motez, me for to mate,
> Þat I my peny haf wrang tan here;
> Þou sayz þat I þat com to late
> Am not worþy so gret fere.
> Where wystez þou euer any bourne abate
> Euer so holy in hys prayere
> Þat he ne forfeted by sumkyn gate
> Þe mede sumtyme of heuenez clere?"   (613–20)

[But now you argue, to overcome me, / that I my penny have wrongly found here; / you say that I who came too late / am not worthy of so great a reward. / Have you ever known any man who remained / ever so holy in his prayers / that he did not forfeit in some kind of way at some time / the unwarranted gift of heaven clear?]

As a gift, as *the* gift, the *peny* is given freely, asks for nothing in return, and does not await reciprocation.[18] As the model for the Dreamer, and for the reader, the *peny* reminds us (in fact commands us) that through an appropriation of the gift one must be, can never not be, responsible for the Other in community. This responsibility extends to the person even if he rejects this responsibility, or even if he fulfills it. This is a gift that awaits no reciprocation; indeed, it is a gift that continues to wait, utterly passive, a gift held hostage by its very givenness. While scandalized by its earthly implications of injustice, the Dreamer will witness the Maiden's theological explication of the parable in its living incarnation at the liturgy of the brides.

Differentiating between the "righteous" man and the innocent and their entry into the kingdom, the Maiden says: "Þe ryȝtwys man schal se Hys face, / Þe harmlez haþel schal com Hym tylle" (*Pearl* 675–76) [The righteous man shall see His face, / the innocent man shall come to him]. The Maiden catalogues the way in which the righteous can enter the kingdom, and her explanation ultimately grounds itself in God's grace.

But her examples go to great length to describe both deed and grace, action on the part of humans who answer the commandments of God through duty to neighbors and continual repentance. "The Law is the very badgering of love," Levinas writes, "Judaism, woven of commandments, attests the renewal of the instants of God's love for man, without which the commanded love could not have been commanded. The '*mitzvah*,' the commandment that holds the Jew in suspense, is not a moral formalism, but the living *presence* of love" (*OS* 57). Perceiving the seamlessness, the indivisibility of a love for God and neighbor, as commanded throughout Scripture, *Pearl* asserts that the righteous man, "Þat is of hert boþe clene and lyʒt" (682), who through pious action and deed, shall see the face of God.

The Maiden repeatedly demonstrates for the Dreamer that seeing the face of God comes with — proceeds from, is coterminous with — the deconstruction of egoic desire and a simultaneous, diachronic recognition of the responsibility for the Other. Levinas describes the face as a rupturing of the immanent by the transcendent: "The dimension of the divine opens forth from the human face. A relation with the Transcendent free from all captivation by the Transcendent is a social relation. It is here that the Transcendent, infinitely other, solicits us and appeals to us" (*TI* 78). Responsibility reveals an infinite eschatological expectation of the coming of the Kingdom of God, for example, as the poor and the hungry who repeatedly show up at my door): "'When did we see thee a stranger and took thee in? or naked, and covered thee? Or when did we see thee sick or in prison, and came to thee?' And the king answering, shall say to them: 'Amen I say to you, as long as you did it to one of these my least brethren, you did it to me'" (Matt. 25:35–40). Or, from the apocalyptic text *par excellence*, the Revelation to Saint John: "Behold, I stand at the door and knock. If any man shall hear my voice, and open to me the door, I will come in to him, and will sup with him and he with me" (3:20). The transcendent divine presence of the Revelation to Saint John comes to us as the poor and hungry of the Gospel of Matthew. Perhaps even more to the point, the Revelation to Saint John names Revelation as simply "the face speaks" ("if any man shall hear my voice"), a face to be understood as the Other at my door, at the very horizon of my being.

INFINITE SUBSTITUTION

The image of the face in *Pearl* remains unstable, perhaps even playful, throughout the first 800 lines of the poem. The showing up of the face on lines 805–10, however, ruptures human history and stages for the Dreamer, and for the reader, the foundation of the infinite structure of the Kingdom of God. In section 14 of *Pearl*, the Maiden describes for the Dreamer an earthly vision of the heavenly Lamb: "In Jerusalem watz my Lemman slayn / and rent on rode with boyez bolde / ...With boffetez watz Hys face flayn / Þat watz so fayr on to byholde" (805–10) [In Jerusalem was my sweet one slain / and rent on the cross with scoundrels / ...With buffets His face was flayed / That face that was so fair to look upon]. The acknowledgement of the face of Christ here marks a two-fold turning point in the Maiden's narrative: it completes the story of Jesus' time on earth, ending with a description of his face being scourged, "flayn," as if the skin itself were being removed, an attempt to efface the victim on the cross.

This vision of the cross also moves the Dreamer (and reader) from this earthly narrative back to the heavenly realm, where the crucified Christ will become a vision of the Lamb of New Jerusalem.[19] This image of the "face flayn" acts as both a memorial and an eschatological vision of responsibility, a fissure that ruptures both history and transcendence, a fissure that illumines, even if momentarily, the infinite structure of the Kingdom of God on earth as it is in heaven. Levinas writes: "The epiphany of the face brings forth the possibility of gauging the infinity of the temptation to murder, not only as a temptation to total destruction, but also as the purely ethical impossibility of this temptation and attempt" (*TI* 199).

The vision of the heavenly court that both precedes and follows the description of the "face flayn" frames a double reading of the crucifixion scene. We see the beingness of the heavenly court (as described in line

446) as an overflowing of one-for-the-other, an infinite "after you."[20] "In the exposure to wounds and outrages, in the feeling proper to responsibility," Levinas writes, "the oneself is provoked as irreplaceable, as devoted to the others, without being able to resign, and thus incarnated in order to offer itself, to suffer and to give" (*OB* 105). This is precisely the responsibility from which Jonah in *Patience* (another of the *Pearl*-Poet's works in the manuscript) flees. Rather than a turning to the Other, in his case the Ninevites, Jonah turns back to himself (and away from God), literally alone in the hull of the ship, in the belly of the whale, and under the woodbine. The suffering he fears in Nineveh — to be crucified upon a cross (lines 93–96) — is the suffering depicted in lines 800–16 of *Pearl*. Jesus as prophet, the Word of God, Torah itself, performs for humanity not as an Other (though this is part of it), nor only as an I; rather, Jesus is a performance of relationship itself (God's relationship to the world, God's relationship to humanity, and a human's relationship to his fellow humans), a staging of the Law, of commandment on the cross.[21]

Beginning at line 841 (the opening line of section 15), the Maiden's description of the Lamb shifts seamlessly from the earthly lamb of the crucifixion to the Lamb of New Jerusalem, spotless and brilliantly white. The image of the Lamb here has a dual reference, from the Revelation to Saint John and Isaiah 53:7, and acts as a central image for the remainder of the poem. With the exception of the last stanza, the entirety of this section is the Maiden's description of the New Jerusalem. Her description functions as a further elaboration of her previous details about the heavenly court (*Pearl* 445–56), as a response to the Dreamer's argument that her elevation as *the* bride of the Lamb would necessarily mean the rejection of others (769–80), and as a preface to the Dreamer's actual vision of the city.

The Maiden explains again to the Dreamer the infinite structure of the heavenly court. Of those who would enter the City, she says:

> "And þaȝ vch day a store He feche,
> Among vus commez nouþer strot ne stryf,
> Bot vchon enlé we woulde were fyf—

Þe mor þe myryer, so God me blesse!
In compayny gret our luf con þryf,
In honour more and neuer þe lesse."   (*Pearl* 847–52)
[And though each day a great number he brings, / Among us comes
neither quarreling or strife, / But each one separately we wish were
five— / The more the merrier, God bless me! / In a great company
our love thrives, / In more honor and never the less.]

Because there is no egoic desire, there is never an opportunity for strife
or rivalry. Five is better than one because it creates an exponential
increase of the one-for-the-other. If I am responsible even for the Other's responsibility, then five Others would create not only my responsibility for each Other but also for the responsibility of the Other of each
Other, who, of course, is also responsible for the Other of the Other's
Other. In this way, love [*luf*] does not simply grow; it thrives [*þryf*],
constantly reaching out beyond itself, outside of its very grasp. The
Maiden describes an *agape* that exceeds even itself—an *agapeistic* envisioning of *agape*. This *agape* becomes an irreducible, infinite structure
of desire that cascades over itself—a structure upon which everything
else is commentary—so much so that it moves between the always-
wanting (meaning both lacking and desiring) and the always-giving.[22]

   The description of the endless knot of the brides of the Lamb in
section 15, coupled with the stanzaic concatenation of the rhyme words
"neuer þe les," literally performs for the reader the notion of the finite
extending over itself into the infinite. Section 15, of course, has one
more stanza than every other section in the poem. Sandra Pierson
Prior argues: "In section 15, the lesson is that the Lamb's reward for
all his brides is the same perfect and unvarying bliss, literally beyond
comparison, and yet the Pearl Maiden uses comparison when she says
it is 'never any *less*.' Furthermore, the section has 'more' stanzas than
any other, even as it insists on the fullness of sufficiency."[23] Rather than
performing a paradox of totality—that is, a paradox of *both* "more"
and "less," which is precisely what Pierson Prior brings our attention
to—this section, I believe, describes a structure which consummates a
rupture of totality, a logic of "the more *in* the less," "the infinite *within*

the finite." The logic of the infinite within the finite Levinas argues, "is accomplished by the idea of Infinity, is produced as Desire—not a Desire that the possession of the Infinite slakes, but the Desire for the Infinite which the desirable arouses rather than satisfies" (*TI* 50). The always-wanting and the always-giving. Rather than sublimating the totality of the kingdom into a mere verbality—the deferral of meaning between "more" and "less"—the Maiden describes for the Dreamer both a model of proper desire and a model of ethical response. Both models, we come to find out, are diachronic extensions of one another: selfless, nonegoic desire, *imitatio dei*, is responsibility.

After his vision of the New Jerusalem (sections 17 and 18), the Dreamer is allowed, finally, a vision of the heavenly court, the procession of the Lamb's brides.[24] Lines 1095–1104 provide details of the brides' appearance. They match perfectly: "Of such vergynez in þe same gyse" (*Pearl* 1099). They are all adorned in pearls and a white garment—"Depaynt in perlez and wedez qwyte" (1102)—wearing the same crown of pearls, and each one has "Þe blysful perl with gret delyt" fastened to her breast. The Dreamer remarks: "And alle in sute her liurés waase; / Tor to knaw the gladdest chere" (1108–09) [And all their garments were matching; / It was hard to know the happiest face]. Each bride, of course, is a perfect imitation of every other bride, but not in terms of a wall-to-wall bliss. What the Dreamer witnesses in sameness is precisely the logic of the infinite the Maiden described: they are each blissful for the Other's bliss, but as each becomes blissful for the Other's bliss, one's blissfulness overflows and is in turn appropriated exponentially by 143,999 other brides! "The desire is unquenchable," according to Levinas, "not because it answers to an infinite hunger, but because it does not call for food. This desire without satisfaction takes cognizance of the alterity of the other.... The true desire is that which the desired does not satisfy, but hollows out" (*CPP* 56–57). True desire, a *kenotic*, nonegoic desire (the desire for an Other's high position in the kingdom, a position elevated even over my own), hollows out, renders desire both emptied and yet through this emptiness utterly satisfied. In fact, as the Other's bliss is appropriated, one is necessarily experiencing one's own previous bliss for the gift (the *mede*) given to the Other upon entrance into the kingdom, a bliss for the Other's bliss which was appropriated by an additional Other and is now again being appropriated by oneself so that one confronts one's own desire anew (in this case one's original bliss for the Other's bliss), yet one is still outside of one's own grasp of oneself; the subject in this way exceeds oneself, remains inaccessible yet now renders oneself wholly a subject but only through a relationship with the Other. The self becomes emptied of the self (even upon return, as it must venture out again as every new Other blissfully appears) yet even more satisfied, and yearns for even more blissful emptiness.

The procession of the brides in section 19 takes on a liturgical quality, as we are told explicitly: "Bot mylde as maydenez seme at mas, / So droȝ þay forþ with gret delyt (*Pearl* 1115–16) [But mild as maidens seem at Mass, / So they drew forth with great delight].[25] As his brides surround him, as the elders bow, "Grouelyng to Hys fete þay felle" (1120), as the angels cast sweet smelling incense, and as earth and heaven are filled with celebratory song, we are given details about the Lamb: he has seven horns of red and pure gold, is draped in "praysed perlez" (1112), and "So worþly whyt wern wedez Hys" (1133). The Lamb's appearance is described with the same language used to depict the brides, so much so that we must wonder where the Lamb begins and his procession of his brides ends. This is a procession of both submission and service. Quoting Saint Agatha, Geoffrey of Auxerre, writes: "'We find the greatest freedom when our service of Christ is put to the test.' Serving him is not only freedom; it is to reign.[26] All of the kings and queens of heaven are kings and queens precisely because of their imitation of the service of Lamb. In fact, the crown of pearls they wear in this procession is explained earlier by the Maiden in lines (871–72): "On alle her forhedez wryten I fande / Þe Lombez nome, Hys Faderez also" [On all their foreheads I found written / The name of the Lamb and of the Father also]. To wear the name of the Lamb and the Father, this crown, means both to serve (the Lamb, the Father, and each Other) and to reign (by serving the

Lamb and Father and each Other). Theirs is a freedom neither in spite of responsibility, nor despite their service to one another or to the Lamb, but precisely because of this.

The image of the Maidens and the pearls they wear, moreover, is not simply a duplication of the Lamb's garment. Both they and the Lamb are extensions of one another, individual and communal, an infinite appropriative expression of each Other. The Lamb's raiment of pearls and his gloriously white garment is the formation of the brides who surround him. This is the anagogic Church that literally forms the body of Christ, an enactment of the Maiden's previous use of Paul's metaphor of the body of the Church as the allegorical body of Christ (*Pearl* 457–68). The logic of the Maiden's details in lines 842–44 now makes perfect sense: "Of oþer huee bot quyt jolyf / Þat mot ne masklle moȝt on streche, / For wolle quyte so ronk and ryf" [Of no other hue but brilliant white, / that not speck or stain could spread, / for the white wool as thick and abundant]. The distance between the Lamb and the brides, while maintaining a radical distance, becomes negligible here because of the asymmetrical relationship each Other's radical alterity commands in the New Jerusalem. The thickness and abundance of the Lamb's garment is not an image of his beingness (though it is in some sense) but an icon of infinite substitution, non-stasis, otherwise than beingness, where the first becomes the last and the last becomes the first.

The Dreamer sees in the Lamb the wounds of infinite responsibility, the defining eucharistic qualities of the gift *par excellence*: "Anende Hys hert, þurȝ hyde torente. / Of His quyte syde His blod outsprent" (*Pearl* 1136–37) [Near His heart, through torn skin. / From his white side his blood spurted forth].[27] Commenting on Aquinas's treatment of perfect charity and perfect worship, Matthew Levering observes: "Thus, the sacraments have a certain logical priority over the virtues. Moreover, this priority is augmented by the fact that the *telos* of Christian life is perfect charity expressed as perfect worship. The life of virtue (ultimately perfect charity) finds its consummation in perfect worship of God."[28] *Pearl* renders an anagogic reading of the diachronic relationship between charity and worship.[29] Rather than giving the reader an image of *agape* that culminates in the consummation of one individual into an other, all of which would then be joined to the divine, *Pearl* narrates a vision in which perfect charity, infinite substitution, one-for-the-Other, *is* perfect worship. The liturgical procession is an ongoing ecstatic, charitable self-offering of each Other, a recapitulation, in other words, of the triune communion of hypostastic persons—where the diversity of each personhood remains united, though distinct, to the divine otherwise than essence. In fact, perfect charity and perfect worship pour forth from one another, where serving the Other before me literally becomes the wool of the Lamb central to the liturgical procession.

This anagogic liturgical and eucharistic vision finds its counterpart in the final stanza as the Dreamer attempts to reconcile his anagogic vision to his earthly reality, and helps situate the ethical import the poem potentially has for the reader. The reference to the Eucharist at Mass (*Pearl* 1209–10) implies both a service and submission: "He gef vus to be His homly hyne" [He commands us to be His household servants]. The sacrament is both blessing (gift) and commandment. This is a sacrament of charity (the infinite one-for-the-Other) that commands imitation, and through imitation, one performs both deed and worship. To be a household servant is nothing other than to submit to the Other, to serve one's neighbor and, in doing so, to obey commandment.[30] This anagogic vision will potentially move from mystical ineffability and into ethical response only when the Dreamer (and the reader) sees the ethical not separate from the anagogical and the mystical but inherent to its very foundation.

Jim Rhodes writes: "Consolation then will come not only from his vision of the New Jerusalem with the Maiden in it but also from the regeneration of his 'luf-longyng' in his encounter with the other world. If his vision teaches him that his pearl is lost forever to this world . . . it may also teach him that such loss need not result in his surrender of the whole earthly enterprise."[31] In light of our reading here, "luf-longyng"—that is to say, a love that always exceeds itself—allows itself to stay open to the call of the Other, and now names the Dreamer's earthly project. "Luf-longyng" *is* the whole earthly enterprise, and it is that to which one must surrender, to which one must become a hostage—whether or not one chooses to. The Maiden's revelation of the ethical obligation that commands the Dreamer is predicated upon this understanding. Rather than cause him to surrender his whole earthly enterprise, the revelation of obligation, of "luf-longyng," specifically through the understanding of the loss of his daughter, defines precisely for him the whole earthly enterprise. In these terms, a real anagogy emerges, a "practical" earthly anagogy, and is realized in the face of the Other; this is an anagogy beyond contemplation of Scripture, yet inextricable from Scripture's revelation.[32] Responsibility in *Pearl* shows up, then, both as eschatological understanding itself and as a manifestation in the here and now of this eschatological understanding—which is to say, infinite responsibility for the Other, the end to which Scripture moves us. It is to this end, an "unendable" infinite responsibility, toward which our poem quite literally moves us. The last line of the poem, of course, is also the first line of the poem. Yet not quite. The extra stanza in section 15 gives us 101 stanzas for the poem, rupturing the idealized 100, a number representing totality, perfection, and pushing the last stanza over the poem's brim, past perfection and puncturing totality.[33]

LITERATURE AND REDEMPTION

Like Levinas's own talmudic readings, where his exegesis of sacred writings appropriates the ethical tenor he perceives in the rabbinic literature, the *Pearl*-Poet too, I have argued above, stages in many ways the very structure of infinite desire he perceives in imagining what an *imitatio dei* would like in courtly, biblical, and liturgical language. Yes, the poem performs this excessive structure. And, yes, there is an explicit invitation at the end of the poem for the reader to participate in this same, albeit earthly, eucharistic community (a community imagined here in the poem as infinite substitution incarnated) witnessed in the Dreamer's vision. But is that it? Has this poem's hyperbolic, and dare I say beautiful, expression of infinite desire (and the ethical import therein) exhausted itself by simply being performative (even in its pious invitation to eucharistic worship)? Is this the most one can expect from literature with regards to ethics from a Levinasian perspective? Claiming that literature *can be* prophetic, can participate in revelation, Levinas says: "I think across all literature the human face speaks—or stammers, or gives itself a countenance, or struggles with its caricature" (*EI* 117). Fleshing out the parameters of the relationship between literature and ethics, and consequently amending his own position spelled out in "Reality and Its Shadow," Levinas further explains:

> There is participation in Holy Scripture in the national literatures, in Homer and Plato, in Racine and Victor Hugo, as in Pushkin, Dostoevsky or Goethe, as of course in Tolstoy or Agnon. But I am sure of the incomparable prophetic excellence of the Book of Books, which all the Letters of the world awaited or upon which they comment. The Holy Scriptures do not signify through the dogmatic tale of their supernatural or sacred origin, but through the expression of the face of the other man that they illuminate, before he gives himself a countenance or a pose (117).

Characteristically anachronistic, perhaps even polychronistic, Levinas here proposes that even the Greeks participated in a literary tradition not yet known to them—scriptural before Scripture, revelatory before Revelation. This observation is quite medieval of Levinas—to see in prescriptural literature prefigurations of the ethical revelation of Scripture itself. No doubt privileging the prophetic voice within Scripture, as the prophetic voice *par excellence*, Levinas nevertheless, and in unambiguous language, regards *other* literatures as partakers of this same prophetic spirit. This category of prophetic literature finds its genesis not in *a priori* ontological categories—"their supernatural or sacred origin"—but in their existential mode "through the expression of the face of the other man they illuminate." The face of the other man is that which has been there since the foundation of the world, since the moment of creation, and it is this very same face which Scripture, and all prophetic literature, reveals as revelation.

This view of literature no doubt stands in stark contrast to his earlier position spelled out in his essay "Reality and Its Shadow": "Art does not know a particular type of reality; it contrasts with knowledge. It is the very event of obscuring, a descent of the night, and invasion of the shadow. To put it in theological terms, which will enable us to delimit however roughly our ideas by comparison with contemporary notions: art does not belong to the order of revelation. Nor does it belong to that of creation, which moves in just the opposite direction."[34] This passage defines Levinas's skepticism on the ethical role of literature. Yet even here one cannot help but notice that Levinas leaves the door open to a redemptive role for literature. He employs the theological language of Franz Rosenzweig, naming explicitly two of the three categories foundational to all of Rosenzweig's work (creation, revelation, redemption). Perhaps most obvious, however, are not the two categories included but the one category that has been excluded— redemption. Why the curious omission? For Rosenzweig, creation named the relationship between God and the world; revelation the relationship between God and man; and redemption the relationship between human and human. So what is Levinas doing by so obviously excluding redemption from above? Let us for a moment read Levinas here as we ought to as medievalists, trained to regard amplification, juxtaposition, and abridgement of source texts with a critical eye. Does the omission of Rosenzweig's redemption not in some way point to its potential inclusion with regards to literature? Would the possibility of literature's role in redemption help us to define its possible role in revelation (which Levinas here denies)? In what way can literature potentially perform a role in creation, revelation, and redemption, but only participate in the first two by way of the third?

Of primary importance, one must understand these three categories not in terms of a synchronic but a diachronic relationship, in which each serves as an extension of the other. Levinas explains the diachronic relationship between the three:

> The relation between God and the world is accomplished as always past. Creation opens and sustains the dimension of the past; the past does not merely *house* Creation. Revelation is to be understood along the same lines. As the movement of God toward man and human singularity—that is, ipseity—revelation is immediately recognized as love: love opens up that singularity. Not that there is love first and

revelation next: revelation is love from the start. . . . And thus the *present* is the time of the Revelation, just as the past was shown to be the time of Creation. . . . The Revelation, which is love, awaits man's response. This response does not ascend the path opened up by the movement come from God: *the response to the love God bestows on man is the love of man for his neighbor.* To love one's neighbor is to go to Eternity, to redeem the World or prepare the Kingdom of God. Human love is the very work, the efficacy of Redemption. Thus Revelation begins the Redemption that is opened up by the dimension of human love, the work of being absolutely singular—that is, mortal. . . . Redemption lays out the *future* (*OS* 57).

Revelation (the present), then, contains creation (the past), and already names within that revelation the future (redemption). In fact, one can say that redemption (future) is always already present within revelation.

Perhaps literature will only participate in creation-revelation-redemption when we can conceive of the act of reading literature as our own participation within the prophetic tradition itself—that is to say, to treat literature as revelation, as that which is always already pointing to the face of the human, toward redemption. Perhaps the only way in which art can belong to the order of revelation (and bear witness to creation and redemption) is when we allow for the possibility that it may participate in, or at the very least point to, redemption—a commandment for us to "live" its meaning, "were I to die for it" (*EI* 98). Levinas's exclusion of art's role in redemption in his essay "Reality and Its Shadow," I believe, names explicitly why art is not conceived of as belonging to the orders of revelation and creation: there is no creation and revelation, properly speaking, without redemption, and vice versa. Levinas's exclusion of redemption simultaneously names the exclusion of art from creation and revelation. I wish to contend that we take seriously Levinas's later meditations on the potentially redemptive role of literature, an alteration of his previous position.

If we entertain, even for a moment, the order of redemption and its relationship to art (and entertain this relationship not outside of the orders of revelation and creation—for how can we?), we may then find it impossible to exclude art categorically from revelation and creation (as Levinas does in "Reality and Its Shadow"). In this way, we find ourselves taking up a medieval hermeneutical position: reading is a moral and ethical act. Does it not take the category of redemption (responsibility to the face that speaks) to make possible revelation (to bear witness to the face of the human on the other side of the page even before he speaks) and creation? Does not literature in this way, then, stand as an icon of the human—literature pointing beyond itself, effacing its own face, in many ways continually remaining silent about that which it speaks? Just as he likes to point out that his ethics is summed up by the Starets Zosima in Dostoevsky's *The Brothers Karamazov* ("Each of us is responsible for everyone and every thing, but I more so than everyone else"), perhaps Levinas's aesthetic position on literature was likewise always already a Dostoevskyan gesture: "Krasota spasyot mir!"[35] The exquisitely structured *Pearl*, consumed as it is with eschatology, anagogy, infinite desire and substitution, no doubt is an extended meditation on salvation—a salvific vision taken up by the very structure of the poem itself, one of excessive substitution, in which the last line becomes the first, and the first the last. Ultimately, an ethical reading of *Pearl*'s depiction of infinite substitution must take note of the obsessive intricacy of the poem's structure itself, the way in which it too is delighted by its own blissful vision—be it of the *Pearl*-Maiden, the procession, the Lamb, the kingdom itself (if any of these are even to be entirely differentiated). And here I would contend that such an ethical reading based on the poem's aesthetic excessiveness may lead one to believe, at least from a Levinasian perspective, that one may indeed find beauty in the infinite.[36]

◄ ◄ 9 ◄ ◄

Criseyde's Chances
Courtly Love and Ethics About to Come

J. Allan Mitchell

> Chance says,
> come here,
> chance says,
> can you bear
> to part?
> H. D., "Chance"

> Chance is better than choice, it is more lordly.
> Elizabeth Bowen, *The Little Girls*

As is well known *Troilus and Criseyde* stretches the reader's conception of moral and political agency where important constraints on human freedom are concerned, constraints that are repeatedly figured by chance, adventure, and fortune.[1] To take a conspicuous example, Troilus's amorous feeling is generated as a result of a fortuitous glance across the temple, an errant event the narrator merrily refers to as a "right good aventure" (*TC* 1.378).[2] It is an erotic *aventure* (often synonymous with *fortune* in the works of Chaucer) to which Troilus passively submits and "gan fully assent" (1.391), as though he had a choice in the matter. But the lover cannot be understood to have chosen to love outright, for indeed if Troilus's passive assent has any meaning, it is not because he possesses freedom of choice. Rather, he has the good fortune to love, has been given the chance to be so bound and is now embracing the potential risks and rewards involved. On reflection we may safely conclude that an important form of human agency and accomplishment has origins in amatory fortune (instead of prevailing over and against fortune), and in fact love could hardly come about the other way around. Love comes from outside, moves us passively, in other words, passionately and involuntarily.[3]

In mind of such paradoxes as these I want to reconsider the potential moral dimensions of fortune and affect in *Troilus and Criseyde,* and to do so I draw support from Emmanuel Levinas who is particularly sensitive to the way love adumbrates the ethical relation by virtue of its fortuitousness, future contingency, exteriority and anteriority to the active will. Erotic love is for him not just an ethical moment in the life of lovers; it is a prototype of the ethical relation engendering human experience. As we will see, when Levinas speaks of the erotic, he has in mind medieval arts of love and cultivated desire, so it is perhaps not surprising to discover that Chaucerian love as presented in *Troilus and Criseyde* is profoundly ethical in the errant sense articulated by Levinas. That Chaucer treats the ethics of the lovers' case seriously, yet without the solemnity of the ethical theorist, is one difference between the poet and the philosopher to which I must return. Another critical difference to investigate is the large scope Chaucer gives his readers for exploring the *gendering* of the ethical relation. The representation of the tragic fortunes of Criseyde exerts considerable pressure on the passions of *Troilus and Criseyde.* Troilus may reap the rewards of his passive subjection, but what about the woman's erotic adventure? To whose advantage is it to elevate *her* lack of agency to a virtue? Thus I will be concerned with the amatory and political fortunes of Criseyde, for whom undue emphasis on the subtle modulations of agency and passivity can seem beside the point in a narrative of her grim betrayal.[4]

A woman's passivity or susceptibility to fortune (that is, her changeability and weak will) is from an antifeminist viewpoint liable to be considered no good thing. Actually her subjection is a provocation to think ethics anew along the lines of what is possible for the subject. Here a Chaucerian (or "Criseydan")[5] reading of Levinas is in order if we are to appreciate the ethics of her case, and it will become evident that (paradoxically) Levinasian ethics is preliminary to its own critique even as it proves indispensable to our understanding. An important dimension of the Levinasian approach is that it permits us to look again at gender issues that have so far bedeviled modern discussions of "courtly love." It has long been at the center of theoretical debates not only about women's freedoms and fortunes, but also about the very notion of freedom and fortune in the sphere of ethics.[6] That which goes by the name of courtly love has been used to mark out the limits of the *ethical* and the *unethical,* not unlike the way the courtly lady herself seems simultaneously to be idealized and disparaged. What are Criseyde's chances in this context? On the one hand, I will argue that Criseyde's subjection yields a nonappropriative ethical relation, putting her beyond the reach of narcissistic fantasy described by Jacques Lacan. On the other hand, if courtly love does not simply amount to an unethical male fantasy, neither is it a form of the amoral expenditure of desire described by Deleuze and Guattari. What Criseyde's experience as a love object suggests—albeit given the danger of her objectification—is something more than either theoretical model allows for the courtly lady.

On this analysis, Levinasian grounds should emerge on which to think ethical responsibility otherwise as an errant and incommensurable task of being. It is worth pausing here to consider the novelty of this approach to responsibility, upon which Maurice Blanchot has remarked:

> Responsibility: a banal word, a notion moralistically assigned to us as (political) duty. We ought to try to understand the word as it has been opened up and renewed by Levinas so that it has come to signify (beyond the realm of meaning) the responsibility of an other philosophy (which, however, remains in many respects eternal philosophy).... *My* responsibility for the Other presupposes an overturning such that it can only be marked by a change in the status of "me," a change in time and perhaps in language. Responsibility, which withdraws me from my order—perhaps from all orders and from order itself—responsibility, which separates me from myself (from the "me" that is mastery and power, from the free, speaking subject) and reveals the other *in place* of me, requires that I answer for absence, for passivity. It requires, that

is to say, that I answer for the impossibility of being responsible — to which it has always already consigned me by holding me accountable and also discounting me altogether.[7]

If responsibility is not the exclusive domain of the "man of action," does this virtue not properly manifest itself in the passivity and privation of the suffering woman? Once some of the obstacles to this insight are gotten over, I will go on to conclude that it is precisely the ethics of Criseyde's case that puts a strain on any direct "application" of Levinas's ethical theory. By virtue of its difficulty and tragic contingency, the Chaucerian ethical text calls us to respond to its narrative demands in a way that is finally more urgent than Levinas's conceptualization of responsibility can hope to achieve.

A VIRTUE OF NECESSITY

Criseyde is so subject to the chances and changes of events caused by other men that it is necessary to begin by observing her tragic material fortunes before going on to consider the ethical dimensions of her amatory fortunes, since as a matter of course tragedy puts in high relief the problem of agency and passivity. On the face of it the tragic fate of Criseyde may seem to support the narrator's belated revelation that his story is not only for men but "moost for wommen that bitraised be / Thorugh false folk" (*TC* 5.1780–81), a cautionary tale *against* the idealizations of ethical theory. How could her misfortunes be taken as anything but a denial of ethics? Criseyde's objectification, idealization, and betrayal develops into the poem's central crisis, and it is refracted through several specific betrayals: that of her father Calchas, of her uncle Pandarus, of the Trojan "folk," possibly of Hector, certainly of Diomede, and most notably of the literary tradition on which hangs her enduring reputation.[8] "The tresoun that to wommen hath ben do!" (2.793). The episode of the "chaungyng of Criseyde" (4.231) — an apposite phrase, cast in the passive voice, looking forward to questions about whether she is changeable, changed, or simply exchanged — demands close scrutiny here if we are to begin to appreciate the way ethics is even a possibility for Criseyde. Hers may well be the double bind of being held accountable for what was never fully hers to control. The real and relentless power relations impinging on her seem to put the erotic adventure in question just where it touches ethics most nearly. The point to consider is that even if Troilus exemplifies radical passivity in the *amatory* sphere, Criseyde's experience in the *political* sphere may render Levinasian ethics inadequate, even repugnant: she may have no chance but to be "passive," yet not in an ethical sense anyone is willing to accept.

Yet insofar as decisions are not always reducible to a simple willing acceptance, there is more to be said for the ethics of the case—or rather, Criseyde's tragic circumstances. Only in coming to terms with the temporality and contingency of ethics will we begin to see the relevance of Levinasian theory, and proceed to a more accurate historical account of the subject. The problem to consider here is the role of chance, or what medieval writers—allowing the concept a centrality that modern critics have found difficult to accept—routinely call fortune. The Trojan decision to exchange Criseyde for Antenor demonstrates the problem well, revealing just how closely the subject of ethics is related to the fortuitous in *Troilus and Criseyde*. This relationship has not always been acknowledged. Historicist accounts of the exchange of Criseyde end up diminishing the importance of the chancy and contingent, and for reasons that are fairly explicable. Chaucer appears to unmask antecedent political causes of later events that are called fortuitous, as if they were inexplicable, beyond critique. If the narrator begins the book lamenting that Fortune, "traitour comune" (*TC* 4.4), betrayed Troilus, the narrative that follows shows that the real traitor responsible for the tragic reversal is Calchas. Calchas, an individual figure of authority with explicable motives, sets in motion a chain of events which has the Trojan parliamentarians quickly agreeing to the exchange because they need more fighting men. Criseyde they can afford to do without, and so they trade her to the Greeks for Antenor, "oon the grettest of this town" (4.192). Thus a clearly discernable chain of political causation and consequence can be delineated in the way a ruling class of men, Greek and Trojan, arrange the situation in that only seems to the narrator fortuitous.[9]

Pressing further, we may arrive at a powerful sociocultural explanation of the formal cause of the exchange: the changing of Criseyde exemplifies patriarchal culture's usual policy of "trafficking in women," a dire situation to which Hector embarrassingly alludes when he objects, "We usen here no wommen for to selle" (*TC* 4.182), or so he had hoped.[10] Such analyses are now familiar and expose the political and institutional forces of tragedy (or misfortune) and of woman's alienation in particular, suggesting that fortune is really no more than an ideological concealment. A woman's material fortunes—including her literary and ethical fortunes—are subject to very specific and identifiable threats: she represents a mere currency of exchange in the masculine political economy, rather than a moral agent. Criseyde is indeed estranged, seduced, exchanged, isolated, and betrayed by men, ever the "hostage, prize, stereotype."[11] Talk of fortune would only seem to obscure the real issues, as David Aers remarks when he observes that such references are "evasory, pseudo-explanations." Speaking specifically of the exchange of Criseyde, Aers claims that the fourth book "carefully describes the prime importance of social organization and cultural values in determining what happens to Criseyde and the consequences of this in her relationship with Troilus. It too makes addresses to Fortune (and even more metaphysical speculations about destiny) seem an unnecessarily vague and mystifying discourse in which to grasp the events of the last two books, a discourse which can only conceal human practices revealed in the poetic processes Chaucer created."[12]

The substitution of the causal for the casual is a new historicist tenet.[13] But the methodology is not without serious costs to ethics and its eventful histories, since arguably that which is saved through a crude historicization is matched by what is lost to history in the account. Here it would not be difficult to establish that the repudiation of fortune is tantamount to a denial of ethics given in the event before it is neutralized in *ex post facto* histories; nothing less than the future of the subject of history is at stake here, and the new historicism has lately come under critical scrutiny on these very grounds.[14] Moreover, the appeal to social organization and cultural values is arguably just as mystifying as fortune when it comes to explaining causes and consequences. What really "happens to Criseyde" when what occurs is so over-determined? And is she at all subject to the experience? Calchas, or any other force, is no substitute for her in the event. How else but by reference to the vagaries of fortune can one explain her coming-to-be-responsible as a subject?

Certainly, Criseyde may be fungible from the detached "objective" point of view to which much criticism is accustomed, but readers are not restricted to that impersonal viewpoint that tallies costs and benefits. Neither does Criseyde identify herself as an instrumentalized "hostage, prize, stereotype." As Monica McAlpine has recently pointed out, Criseyde acts courageously under duress: "Criseyde's submission to the exchange, her unresisting departure to the camp of the feared Greek enemy, against so many interests of her own, and in the service of Troilus's *trouthe* and her own honor," exhibits an extraordinary patience and passivity which is a peculiar virtue of the unfortunate. Hers is the virtue of "making the involuntary voluntary."[15] Her capacity to make a virtue of necessity despite such depredations should help us understand how fortune may also make virtue possible in the amatory sphere, becoming one among other examples of events to which one is subject but which also activate subjectivization. Levinas will help clarify why it is necessary to keep in play both the causal and contingent elements of personal agency, without which ethics is impoverished.

ROMANCING ETHICS

Sexual love is one arena of human experience in which the utter priority and alterity of the other is deeply felt—and is felt to be fortuitous, perilous, out of control—which is why Levinas recurs to courtly love as a paradigm case of the ethical relation. In his early work he makes direct reference to romance motifs, *chevalerie* and *fin' amor*, to describe the ethical relation—daring to suggest that ethics is like a knightly undertaking.[16] His medievalism is clearly in evidence in *Time and the Other* where he directs his readers "to the great themes of Goethe or Dante, to Beatrice and the *ewig Weibliches,* to the cult of the *Woman* in chivalry" (*TO* 86). Here he finds something exemplary in the "mystery" and "modesty" of the courtly inamorata, on which more below. If the female beloved is central to Levinasian thought, so is the special means whereby the male lover (typically the errant knight) takes the adventure for her. In *Totality and Infinity* Levinas refers to the recognizable "movement by which a being seeks that to which it was bound before even having taken initiative of the search and despite the exteriority in which it finds it." Levinas is describing the erotic as a "supreme adventure" that "is also a predestination, a choice that had not been chosen." Levinas now admits that love can have a narcissistic aspect, satisfying "the most egoist and cruelest of needs," compromising the desire for the total, transcendent other. Still, love "bears witness to an exceptional audacity" and remains an image and impulse of the ethical relation that is never really satisfied (*TI* 254). That Levinas is not always precisely historical is something with which medievalists might quibble; but that the language of chivalry, according to Levinas's major statements, should be morally defensible and even commendable is something worth exploring.

What Levinas seems to be describing is a new allegory of love. In *Troilus and Criseyde* it is easy enough to see how that allegory might be construed for the male lover, and I have already outlined a reading of Troilus as a type of Levinasian knight undertaking the "supreme adventure." Troilus does not choose to love from a position of autonomy or self-sufficiency. His is precisely a "choice that had not been chosen." To elaborate further we can observe that the lover's passivity consists not only in the subjection to the other as sovereign power, but entails a radical passivity before fortune as future time. Because he has no *time* to choose love, the lover undertakes an erotic adventure in an original, temporal sense (L. *ad* + *venire*).[17] It has been said that love is not unlike death in this important respect: "Love and death will strike, come their time; only you have no inkling when that time is. Whenever it comes, it will take you unawares."[18] But unlike death the danger of love is that it will not come soon enough, or at all. Neither might it last. Ethical responsibility, for Chaucer if not Levinas, may originate in just this heroic (Levinas would prefer *un*heroic) orientation: an attitude of passivity, patience, and modesty in the face of the other with no promise of reciprocation.

Yet in drawing such audacious comparisons between courtly love and ethics, Levinas deploys archaic images and ideas that some modern readers may not readily countenance. Other theorists, as we will see, also have recourse to the concepts and conventions of "courtly love." Levinas is indeed not the only ultramodern moral philosopher who regularly uses flamboyant and deliberately provocative images and metaphors to describe ethical responsibility, and there are surely sound reasons for this appropriation and redeployment of traditional language. His distinctively lyric, sometimes rhapsodic mode of writing lends itself to such hyperbole. But there are major liabilities. The sexual politics of Levinasian theory has come under close scrutiny ever since Simone de Beauvoir criticized Levinas, in a footnote to *The Second Sex,* for "deliberately tak[ing] the man's point of view, disregarding the reciprocity of subject and object."[19] While some have attempted eloquent defenses on behalf of Levinas, Luce Irigaray's main objection remains compelling: the female beloved seems consistently to exist merely for the sake of the male lover's transcendence.[20] One only has to attend to the signs of narcissism in so many medieval narratives of male erotic fantasy—the psychoanalytics of which requires elaboration—to reach a similar conclusion about the ethic of courtly love. In the case of *Troilus and Criseyde,* the male lover's fidelity only exists in comparison to her infidelity. Arguably, Troilus's transcendent rewards for having loved and lost Criseyde stem directly from her unfaithfulness in the end.

Courtly love does exhibit its own kind of perversity (though perhaps so does every erotic relationship), for in the history of human sexuality the phenomenon leaves something to be desired. In fact, lingering delectation may be its main function, at least for men, as so many discussions suggest: in the chivalric ethic, as Lacan famously claimed of the troubadour lyric, the female beloved appears to be a prop with which to stage and sustain the play of masculine desire.[21] Feminist scholarship has long been suspicious of the discourse of *fin' amor*, and there seems widespread consensus that the masculine discourse of medieval romance and love lyric idealizes the *domna* at the expense of real *femnas*. Simon Gaunt and Sarah Kay have argued that the image of woman is manipulated in this way as a means of competitive self-advancement among men securing "entry into the feudal hierarchy."[22] Here we come to understand the way in which courtly love is a mediated and appropriative affair, an exchange transacted between men and on their behalf. Such familiar criticisms of mimetic desire are reiterating the Irigarayan critique of Levinas just mentioned: that is, the beloved female figure merely functions to map the coordinates of the male lover's transcendence.

Chaucer's own presentation of an overwrought romantic coupling poses a serious challenge along these very lines, for again *Troilus and Criseyde* can be taken to indicate that empirical women, *femnas,* have less to gain from courtly relationships than their role as lady, *domna,* at first suggests. Is the poet not suggesting that the dated chivalric code is a poor model for a medieval—never mind postmodern—ethical theory? Due to the perversions and power-dynamics inherent in courtly love, how can we say the phenomenon resembles anything like an ethical relation? The answer lies in how these difficult circumstances create a hospitable (Levinas would gladly say *hostile*) context in which the other is encountered from a position of weakness, suffering, and self-sacrifice.

Love, Holy and Profane

What are now commonplace concerns about courtly love should not blind us to the ethical adventure it makes possible for the subject, and here I think Levinas's peculiar orientation toward the psychoanalysis of desire is a powerful corrective. Where does Levinas stand in relation to the libidinal economy of courtly love? To elucidate his theory and distinguish it from others, Levinas advances the following gnomic formulation: "Profanation is not a negation of mystery, but one of the possible relationships with it" (*TO* 86). The easiest way to get a handle on his meaning is by thinking of the ethical relation embodied in the erotic as a form of shared sociality upon which everyday human interaction, good and bad, depends for its intelligibility and normativity.[23] On this reading, ethics is so primordial that it belies every violent exercise of power. No one would know or care about another's exploitation by power if not for some prior sociality; in fact, there would be no power without the presupposition of sociality upon which it is exercised. Levinas describes the phenomenon by using a terminology borrowed from Judeo-Christian theology (in which we can recognize some of the terms of courtly love), claiming that that which is "holy" in human affairs makes any "profanation" of them perceptible and objectionable, for without the one the other is illegible. Holiness is, as he explains, a precondition of profanation: "The influences, complexes and dissimulations that cover over the human do not alter this holiness, but sanction the struggle for exploited man" (*OB* 59). These different but related ways of putting the issue are restatements of Levinas's theory of the ethical as expressed in the erotic—even in the guise of courtly love, despite or rather because of its hazardous sexual politics and the unreasonable suffering and abjection it may entail. On this account of the paradox, erotic desire is one of the forms that the ethical dimension of human experience takes, and may be a *motive force* in struggles for emancipation in the political sphere.

If for Levinas courtly love is not as unethical as some theorists have made out, neither is it just an amoral assemblage of corporeal (subjectless) energies. The image of the body as a love machine is an alternative to the rather dour Lacanian psychoanalysis of desire, and Deleuze and Guattari have given exuberant expression to this body in *A Thousand Plateaus*. In their "anti-psychiatric" account of the phenomenon, courtly love amounts to one among other circuits of carnal energy and pieces of equipment: it is not a means (or barrier) to some other end but a self-perpetuating mechanism through which desire flows promiscuously without ulterior motive, exterior justification, or interdiction. Courtly love is an "immanent" flow of affects not subject to any "transcendent" rationale or regulation, such as is regularly imposed by philosophers or priests. "The most recent figure of the priest," they write, "is the psychoanalyst" with his prim notions of "Pleasure, Death, and Reality." Deleuze and Guattari reject the killjoy attitude of the analyst and of the historicist for that matter (anyone who would attempt to immobilize the body), embracing instead the idea that courtly love is nothing other than itself: a free expenditure of desire, an efficient surge of impersonal forces over the body, a maximization and proliferation of connections, an intensity without interpretation.[24]

Levinas's ethical approach to the erotic contrasts sharply with the discourses of both psychoanalysis and anti-psychiatry, and I think enables a better understanding of medieval amatory experience: since the traumas of Lacanian theory and the decadence of Deleuzeguattarian theory do not do justice to amatory fortune. For Levinas the erotic is not confined within the structure of the psyche, nor is it not just one of many possible "plateaus" of amoral bodily intensities. Unlike Lacan and his disciples, indeed Levinas does not view courtly love as a neurotic detour ("lack") by way of which some other transcendent destination is aimed at and missed. Desire such as is expressed in courtly love constitutes the ethical relation with the other *because* it is never satisfied: privation and errancy of desire is the source of transcendence over cruel and egocentric need.[25] Levinas is also far from simply reveling in the free-play of corporeal energies and intensities; unlike Deleuze and Guattari, he does not treat eroticism as a self-sufficient end, expenditure, or equipmental assemblage ("field of immanence"). Indeed, erotic desire itself points to the fallacy of self-sufficiency or efficiency in any attempts at human assembly, due to the radical contiguity and contingency of self and the other: desire is an affect which, as it were, confesses to the asymmetrical, impossible, and not yet. To locate Levinas vis-à-vis these two rival analyses of courtly love is to say that the immanence or embodiment of erotic desire (explored by Deleuze and Guattari) opens up the self to others; yet the closure of desire (explored by Lacan) is never fully achieved.

Perhaps the most important consequence of this discussion so far is that it permits us to see how cultural phenomena, no matter how artificial or apparently inauthentic, can express the ethical relation without having to be held up as a normative ethical ideal. The ethical relation is immanent, here-and-now, if it is anywhere at all; ethics shows itself in the world. On what other foundation can we base a critique? Lacanians and Deleuzeguattarians would have us look for more solid ground as though ethics were given in another place, separated from the uncertain gift of being (the starting question for Levinas is a twist on the Heideggerian one: Why should there be anything *good* at all, rather than nothing?). Levinas thus shows that it is not necessary to approve of "courtly love" to see how it paradoxically exposes the ethical relation in *Troilus and Criseyde*. For our analysis of Criseyde this means she may remain squarely within the sphere of the ethical (in which she positions herself) without ceasing to motivate strong criticisms of courtly culture to which she is subject; in fact the singular amatory fortunes of the woman give expression to the radical alterities inherent in the love relationship (that is, holiness), if only to enable readers to put in question its particular encryptions and compromised social forms (that is, profanation). How else is it possible for a writer to mobilize his inherited material against tradition in the way that Chaucer does? Chaucer does not on that account repudiate courtly love, and we should not rush too quickly to negative conclusions. If in the end the phenomenon still expresses an ethical relation and remains an indispensable way of speaking ethically (for Chaucer and for Levinas), it is because courtly love is not a negation of mystery, but one of the possible relationships with it.

It helps to recognize that this idea of the originary ethical relation comports well with medieval understandings of the nature of love as expressed, for instance, in the hymn to love in Boethius's *Consolation of Philosophy* and in the derivative verses of Dante's *Purgatorio*.[26] The Boethian notion that love is foundational also informs *Troilus and Criseyde*. The relevant metrum from the *Consolation of Philosophy* is invoked by Troilus to express the transcendence of the erotic. Love,

Troilus sings, creates "an holsom alliaunce" (*TC* 3.1746), harmonizing all things and holding human community together, and by providential design serves "To cerclen hertes alle and faste bynde" (3.1767). As is well known, Troilus is transposing a hymn to metaphysical love into an erotic love song—audaciously assimilating the one to the other. Transcendence is held to be immanent. *Troilus and Criseyde* is, I propose, a *Canticus Troili* writ large.

CRISEYDE'S CHANCES

Against a tradition of criticism that faults Criseyde for her passivity or subjection (for example, making her out to be culpable, complicit, or merely a casualty), at least two critics have already urged that she is no less a moral agent for being susceptible to Fortune.[27] Jill Mann and Monica McAlpine take us up to but not over the threshold of the ethical relation as theorized by Levinas, and I want to press further by showing that Criseyde's susceptibility to fortune (indeed in her very situation as "hostage, prize, stereotype") is the possibility of her being a moral subject. I am not simply restating the idea that moral agency is affected by time and change, but proposing that it is so constituted. Ethics is an event of which medieval eroticism—in its suffering and subjection—is a given instance.

A justly celebrated part of the poem is the expanded *proces* by which Criseyde consents to love Troilus, in light of which Chaucer's particular invention seems to have been to engage and elaborate not just the erotic adventure of men, but also its very conditions of possibility for men and women. Criseyde's finely nuanced cognitive processes are set in motion and carried forward by chance changes in circumstance.[28] Several such external contingencies—interpersonal, political, discursive—are introduced or amplified by Chaucer to create the setting in which Criseyde can encounter the other. After her surprised intoxication in the first window scene ("Who yaf me drynke?" [*TC* 2.651]) Criseyde begins to give serious thought to Troilus, as though she can exercise any real agency. Yet already her love may seem compromised insofar as it conforms to the romantic cliché of love-drunkenness, apparently restricting even as it restructures her relationships to the other. Would it not be more "ethical" to have made a rational choice? Criseyde indeed attempts to line up the pros and cons of consenting to the fortunes of love (2.687–812), as she is seen doing in Boccaccio's *Filostrato*. But perhaps these political considerations hedge in her freedom of choice from another direction, for she soon works out that in prudential terms it would be better not to love at all. Then, just as Criseyde resolves to accept that the negative considerations (that is, the hazards of being betrayed, slandered, and bound to a man) outweigh the positive ones (that is, honor and security), Chaucer invents a set of fortuitous encounters that effectively change her mind. Happening to overhear Antigone's song in the garden allays some of her fears, and the intervention of a nightingale and a weird dream subsequently move her to love (2.813–931). By the time Troilus rides past again in the second window scene, Criseyde discovers she adores Troilus (2.1247–301). But is this yet any kind of agency?

Here falling in love consists of so many inconspicuous modulations of contingency and necessity, chance and destiny, freedom and fortune, so that the precise moment of consent is notoriously difficult to determine.[29] The ambiguity of the situation raises profound questions about the woman's choice and whether and how her consent is given. Does her love develop because of these chance encounters? Or does chance effect a change in her feelings only because she is already disposed to love? The exact ratio of freedom and fortune making up Criseyde's mind is unquantifiable.[30] But if consent is a matter of conforming to external pressures at all, then is not the ethics of the case still put in question? Her love does not arise *ex nihilo* but seems to entail subjection to a dominant discourse of late medieval culture.[31] Granted, Criseyde's amatory intentions are in a paradoxical but powerful way already determined, but this is finally not an argument against ethics. That is rather the gift of ethics.[32] Criseyde's chances illustrate how ethical choices can be as much a matter of passive discovery and acceptance as of positive self-determination. If any decision-making is involved in giving consent to love, to borrow an apt phrase from Simon Critchley, "the decision is not taken by the subject, but rather

the subject...is *taken by the decision.*[33] The *best* decisions of friends
and lovers are made this way and reaffirm the priority of ethics: they
are passive or unconscious, passionate and never dutiful, as if such an
ethics-beyond-freedom were possible.[34] Criseyde therefore finds herself
responding to love without the presumption (which would indeed be
presumptuous) of being able to choose purely and arbitrarily.

Chaucer is presenting not an ethics of mutuality but of disparity and
displacement. Near the climax of the lovers' consummation Troilus
and Criseyde come as close to fusing together as they can, and their
conversation together in bed turns on a significant ambiguity over *who*
consented *when* to *whom.* Troilus cannot believe his good fortune:

> "O swete, as evere mot I gon,
> Now be ye kaught; now is there but we tweyne!
> Now yeldeth yow, for other bote is none!"
> To that Criseyde answerde thus anon,
> "Ne hadde I er now, my swete herte deere,
> Ben yolde, ywis, I were now noughte heere!" (*TC* 3.1206–11)

Mann persuasively argues against the reading that there is a willful
power struggle taking place here: Criseyde's words are not a "coy
revelation that her mind had been consciously made up at some earlier
date: it is rather a realization that her present situation and feelings
imply—and therefore reveal—an earlier unconscious surrender, now
to be made explicit."[35]

Nevertheless, I think there is an unavoidable manner of assertiveness
in her speech that seems to go beyond mere revelation or the making
explicit of the unconscious. Like Troilus earlier, Criseyde is claiming
responsibility at the very moment she confirms her happy surrender
and lack of self-control—saying, archly but decorously, "I would not
be yours *now* if I had not surrendered *already!*" She is not begrudging
Troilus his erotic fantasy, and if anything she is confirming his desire:
he wants her to yield, she says she already has. Except that she does
not say she has yielded exactly, for the past participle construction,
"Ne hadde I er now.../ Ben yolde," indicates something more along
the lines of having been made to submit.[36] We misjudge Criseyde if we

read her speech as a protofeminist assertion of female independence, or a face-saving fiction she is forced to accept against the evidence, or some form of self-deception.[37]

Still, although there may be no willful power struggle taking place, Troilus and Criseyde do not indicate complete agreement in their exchange. Mann's view that we are presented in the consummation with a "vision of sexual mutuality" overstates the case of their intimacy.[38] The emphatic temporal qualification and dislocation of Troilus's speech—"*Now* be ye kaught; *now* is there but we tweyne!/ *Now* yeldeth," set off against the claim to chronological priority in Criseyde's speech about having (been) yielded to her sweet heart already—mark the distance between them *as* lovers even at this most synchronous and harmonious moment in the affair. Just so, in her excited assertion Criseyde is expressing not a desire for autonomy from Troilus, but rather indicating the inescapability of autonomy even when it is *un*desirable. As Levinas puts it, adumbrating the passivity and future contingency of the ethical relation in the erotic adventure, consummation of love never overcomes the "insurmountable duality of beings." Love is ever *à-venire* and resists the synchronicity of being altogether. Against Lacan who would conceive of courtly love as a neurotic defense against the adventure (the other who *n'arrive pas*), Levinas sees it as subjecting the self to the time of the other.[39]

Criseyde's untimely love may be said to instantiate something of the priority of the ethical relation because—whatever else she may become—she takes responsibility for what happens to and remains exterior to her. Her will is unavoidably subordinate to an involuntary affection. While we may agree with Criseyde when she protests, "Ne love a man ne kan I naught ne may / Ayeins my wyl..." (2.478–79), the reverse is not also true: certainly no one can be forced to love against her will, but neither can one love by force of will. Love is a gift of the ethical relation it aims toward, recalling a paradox limned not only in Boethius and later in Dante, as mentioned, but also given eloquent expression by a Middle English writer well acquainted with Chaucer's *Troilus*. Thomas Usk, winding up a discussion of the disposition of the will in his *Testament of Love,* concludes with the following account of the paradoxes of love I have been discussing:

> I saye he maye no love wylne if he no love have, through which thilke love he shuld wylne. But to have this lovyng wyl may no man of him-selfe, but onely through grace toforne-goyng. Consyder nowe every man aright, and let sene if that any wight of himselfe mowe this lovyng wel get, and he therof first nothynge have, for if it shulde of himselfe spring eyther it muste be wyllyng or not wyllyng. Wyllyng by himselfe may he it not have, sythen him fayleth the mater that shulde it forthe bring. The mater him fayleth.[40]

Usk has not fallen prey to circular reasoning but is in effect saying, "Love is presupposed in virtuous action, not produced by it." In this he is reckoning with a primordial ethical phenomenon, apparently prompted by his close reading of Chaucer's *Troilus and Criseyde,* the phenomenology of which he is led to accept against his best attempts to defend free will. That love animates the will is a bold redefinition of volunteerist ethics, and points the way toward understanding what happens to Chaucer's lovers. Like Troilus after all, Criseyde encoun-ters in herself something of the mystery and modesty of erotic desire beyond the active will and strict rational consent. In Levinas's words, the beloved comes around to speak the "welcome" of the other which "expresses a simultaneity of activity and passivity" (*TI* 89), an ethics of heteronomy instead of autonomy.

Love is something she responds to out of her insufficiency and inadequacy. Her love matches Troilus's love by being *un*equal to it and, consequently, the ethical relation serves to radicalize sexual dif-ference beyond the profanity of narcissistic desire. How far all this is from attributing agency or autonomy to women, in the familiar mode of the feminist emancipation of female literary characters, should now be evident. The achievement of the adventure of love lies elsewhere for the poet and the philosopher, for whom the erotic relationship enacts a shared asymmetry of love, an unaccountable surrender of one to the other in the scandal of the event. To put it simply but, I think, without too much distortion: the courtly romance does not liberate the woman by insisting on her independence from men and other women, and if it can be said to do so at all it is only by conferring upon a woman the privilege of subjection to an other. Only then does she have the chance of a real history, one that is both significant enough to recount and worth living in the event. If ethics is a precondition of political history, only this respect for the alterity of the beloved—her secrecy, singularity, and mystery—can inform any ethicopolitical intervention on behalf of women or women's history.

LOVING AGAINST ETHICS

The erotic relationship shows clearly how the duality of subject and object finally breaks down and yields to a higher principle or project, not to form a Platonic spherical unity but to exist in an asymmetrical ethical relation. "The pathos of love," says Levinas, "consists in an insurmountable duality of beings. It is a relationship with what always slips away" (*TO* 86). If the asymmetry of love carries the risk of slipping away (as in fact happens in Chaucer's great tragedy), then that is just the risk of love. But one of the advantages of Chaucer's romance is that it permits him to explore the risks and affects of a phenomenon that remains largely conceptual in Levinas's philosophy; and it is the particular risk of the conceptual in eliding the ethical which is explored in the event rather than in explication. For one thing, the pathos of love slipping away is simply more fully articulated in *Troilus and Criseyde* than *Time and the Other*, and it is my final contention that Chaucer's narrative achieves what is only ever approached in Levinas's lyric mode. On reaching the bitter end of *Troilus and Criseyde* one may reasonably conclude that while Levinas has hit upon a necessary condition of the ethical relation, he has not described sufficient conditions for its survival in the lives of individual moral beings. What is missing from his otherwise astute account is a "thick description" of the contexts in which love flourishes and fails—the adventure of love. One way to state the problem is to say that the eventful character of Chaucer's romance narrative threatens to undo any and all conceptual relations, even the ethical relation conceived as a turn of events. While it has been established that the ethical relation is, on Levinas's own account, subject to the future contingency, perhaps the futurity of ethics is more radically contingent than even Levinas allows. Literary narrative is a form of such contingency.

The epilogue of *Troilus and Criseyde,* in which the narrator seeks escape from narrative via the conceptual and creedal apparatus of religion, expressly acknowledges the fact with its dialectic of pagan and Christian values. The separation of Troilus and Criseyde has already threatened to deflate and perhaps devastate the pretensions of any atheistic ("pagan") ethical reading of the erotic adventure, particularly given the final two reversals of fortune — or to use a Chaucerian coinage, *dysaventures*—marking the tragic end of the love affair. Criseyde apparently reassigns her love to Diomede as a political exigency, and Troilus posthumously relinquishes his love in heaven. If the ethical relation really grounds their love, then why does their relationship not last? Surely their tragedy reveals the fragility of love? A Chaucerian reading of Levinasian ethics presses hard on these questions, exposing the threat of egoistic need. On the one hand, love's vulnerability to external events and involuntary processes, which elucidate the development of Criseyde's love for Troilus, equally enable Criseyde to fall out of love.[41] What then is the advantage of an ethical analysis of the event? One answer is that we may doubt that her new "love" is any more than a rationalization of her infidelity, in which case her original love of Troilus is still (and by contrast) singularly ethical. The story of her infidelity prohibits our making final judgments: not enough is known about what happened (*TC* 5.1050). Judgment is a matter of some interest at the end of *Troilus and Criseyde,* where narrative contingency is subordinated to principle. Chaucer reaches in his epilogue for an eternal and all-encompassing divine love—"Uncircumscript, and al maist circumscrive" (5.1865)—and offers to lift the narrative out of the realm of "payens corsed old rites" and "wrecched worldes appetites" (5.1849–51). What is the effect of his seeking sanctuary in religion? Chaucer seems to acknowledge the risks of love—the adventure of ethics about which he has so eloquently narrated—by showing that contingency goes "all the way down," as it were, even undermining human ethics.

There will always be doubts, too, about whether the erotic model Levinas adopts to figure the ethical relation does not more often reinforce negative heteronormative assumptions than sanction their critique. At least Chaucer situates himself at some ironical distance from the sexual passions he describes. Levinas offers a little relief from the gender fatigue we may feel by clarifying his thinking in respect of empirical men and women: "Perhaps . . . all these allusions to the onto-logical differences between masculine and feminine would appear less archaic if, instead of dividing humanity into two species (or into two genders), they would signify that the participation in the masculine and in the feminine were the attribute of every human being" (*EI* 68). This flexibility would account for the way Levinas occasionally switches the gender of pronouns unexpectedly in speaking of the feminine other or beloved: for example, "Love aims at the Other; it aims at *him* in his frailty" (*TI* 256; emphasis mine). On the other hand, Levinas may simply be perpetuating a medieval eroticism according to which the genders are inverted: on an influential reading of troubadour poetry the *domna* has always been defeminized and attributed a "semi-masculine identity" as an enabling condition of male power.[42] Levinas does not escape such criticisms of his work except perhaps by reasserting that they presuppose a "holy" ethical relation they are trying to do away with in the "profane" phenomenon of courtly love.

There is finally much to recommend the ethical theory so long as a pragmatic, Criseydan sense of the risks and rewards of *l'amour de fortune* qualifies it. Chaucer's portrayal of Troilus and Criseyde presents love for either sex as a preoriginary subjection that is beyond—or as Levinas would rightly say, *better than*—the dichotomies of freedom and fate, contingency and necessity, and so on.[43] But because the ethical relation resides beyond the usual moral categories, in the singularity and alterity of courtly love, there may be a danger of reifying and ideal-izing the subject. Thus we may escape one set of inadequate binaries pertaining to the courtly lady (representing a woman all-powerful or powerless, loved or loathed, idealized or disparaged) only to fall back into another set of generalizations about courtly love. But like the beloved, courtly love may not deliver the ethical relation we seek in it, nor should it be expected to do so if desire is as errant and incommensurable as I am claiming. Chaucer finally does not give us an applied ethics but instead testifies, in so many ways, that the subject is not free to yield to or withdraw from love. It is the fate of amatory fortune that it threatens to undermine the ethical relation conceived along even such primordial lines as desire, even as it dignifies the subject with a promise of a desire it cannot control. Ethics is subject to the mutability of events of which there may be no guarantor besides chance, and perhaps that is the final aptness of the analogy: ethics flourishes and fails no less than does love.

10

The Wound of the Infinite
Rereading Levinas through Rashi's Commentary on the Song of Songs

Cynthia Kraman

According to Hamlet, "there is nothing either good or bad, but thinking makes it so" (II.ii.259). While to the contemporary mind this might suggest moral relativism, a medieval as well as a Renaissance audience (to a large degree) would have rather emphasized the implications of the word *thinking*. The human mind was the instrument with which to read the two books of God, namely, the Creation and the Bible. In order to read them, one of the tools of the medieval critic was the practice of reading any given figure or theme *in bono et in malo*,[1] that is, both as a good thing and a bad one. One striking example is Pierre Bersuire's reading of the goddess Diana in Ovid as either the Virgin Mary or the archetypically wicked woman.[2] This sort of thinking seems odd to the contemporary critical mind. The following essay will demonstrate, however, how the ability of the Jewish medieval exegete Rashi (1040?–1105) to refrain from assigning a settled meaning to any figure or theme in the biblical Song of Songs, and even to accept simultaneous diametrically opposed meanings, enriches the reading of Emmanuel Levinas's philosophical work, which self-consciously situates itself within the Hebraic tradition.

Levinas was, of course, a reader of Rashi and of the Song of Songs. Indeed, much of Levinas's work, as I hope to show, might be regarded as a philosophical extension of Rashi's commentary on the Song, its dialogical mode, its images, and themes—in particular, Eros, death, the name of the beloved, night, sleepiness (indolence), sleeplessness (insomnia, vigilance), and the wound of love. While honoring "a participation of Holy Scripture in the national literatures," Levinas bears witness to "the incomparable prophetic excellence of the Book of Books," which has awakened again and again the conscience of humanity (*EI* 117). Speaking to Philippe Nemo, Levinas observes, "The Holy Scriptures signify to me by all that they awakened in their readers in the course of centuries, and by all they received from exegeses and their transmission" (117). This admission by Levinas—that the Scriptures signify to him "by all they received from exegeses and their transmission"—points us in the direction of Rashi, who was surely one of Levinas's teachers.

One of the greatest Jewish medieval commentators, Rashi opened the Tanakh to his contemporaries and subsequent generations. Commonly regarded as the most explicitly ethical and human of biblical commentators, Rashi understands the Bible to be not only an approach to the divine but, more importantly, a roadmap to human relations, illuminating the human potential for goodness and nurturing the virtues that grow through attention to others. Levinas's project similarly gives primacy to the moral and the ethical.

The ethical turn in the thought of Rashi and Levinas reflects another, terrible similarity. Both men witnessed the unleashing of cultural enmity against the Jews: Rashi lived through the First Crusade, and Levinas the horrors of the World War II. For Jews, these events made scripture, especially Psalms and the prophetic theme of exile and redemption, contemporary to the lived Jewish experience of suffering—not only their own, but also that of others, and in particular the biblical Other: the stranger, the widow, and the orphan. Levinas, of all modern philosophers, reaches out to the stranger, the other, whose face calls forth the self and transforms it. No longer the totalizing "I" who possesses the world and takes its place under the sun with triumphalist glee, declaring (in the words of Rousseau's *Discourse on the Origins of Inequality* [1755]), "Perish if you will, I am safe and secure,"[3] this better self is one who would die for the other, substituting itself if necessary.[4]

The ethical substitution to which Rashi and Levinas call their readers is supported by their verbal practice, which abounds in etymologies, substitutions, word-plays, restatements. Indeed, Levinas does not hesitate to compare our understanding of our neighbor to that of an allegorical figure. In "Enigma and Phenomenon," for example, he observes, "This way the Other has of seeking my recognition while preserving his *incognito*, . . . this way of manifesting himself without manifesting himself, we call enigma."[5] In his commentary on the Song of Songs, Origen explains that the Bride begins to receive the Bridegroom's kisses when she "has begun to discern for herself what was obscure, to unravel what was tangled, to unfold what was involved, to interpret parables and riddles [*aenigmata*], and the sayings of the wise."[6]

The Song of Songs is full of enigmatic sayings that demand attention, seek recognition, without losing their essential mystery. Rashi is concise and clear. Like all Jewish exegetes, he was committed to rendering the *peshat* or literal meaning of a text, but he used his vast knowledge of Midrash to explicate any given verse, to open it to the lay reader, to provide a variety of approaches, while never contradicting the literal meaning. As with Levinas, the concision produces a suggestiveness that allows interpretation to flourish. Rashi often supplies multiple, seemingly contradictory readings, to transform what Levinas would call a *said* into a *saying*—something open. One "goes forth" at each phrase, like the patriarchs who are instructed, *lech lecha*—rather than circling back home like Odysseus to some certainty for which much blood must be spilled.[7]

Among biblical texts, the verses of the Song of Songs have proven especially open to interpretation. A canonical text of great interest to both Jewish and Christian exegetes, the Song confuses the genders of beloved and loved, occupies the Freudian night theater of the erotic, and is itself a love poem and not a story or a history. Although the Song may or may not be, in its historical origins, a collection of nuptial songs, perhaps stemming from Egyptian origins (as German Bible scholars of the nineteenth century thought), it is, like the last revision of Strindberg's *Dream Play*, what it became—the greatest of biblical allegories.[8] Rabbi Akiba declared that the world was never as worthy as on the day that the Song of Songs was given to Israel, for all the Writings are holy, whereas the Song of Songs is the holy of holies.[9]

The rabbis, and Rashi in particular, are persuasive, and most readers are convinced that their allegories unburden the Song from its potentially mundane, totalizing love story. But the Song is not only a striking allegory; it is also, like the problematic categories of Levinas that I address in this essay, *sui generis*. Like the Virgin Mary who is the "garden enclosed" of Song 4:12 in Christian medieval thought, the Song is alone of all its kind.[10] Its initial *shin* is written in large script, unlike any other "S" in the Bible. A Zoharic commentary gives a numerical interpretation that establishes it as the pinnacle of all songs, hence the Song of Songs.[11] Also, Rabbi Akiba comments that while some texts talk of God's love of Israel, and others the reverse, this song is esteemed by the sages because it alone expresses reciprocal praise. This exceptionality might move the Song into the territory "to the side" to which Levinas consigns the other others. But *sui generis* events such as the Song of Songs or the erotic or the night cannot be set aside because of their unique character. It is also in the *rara avis* that the idea of Infinity readies itself for our participation. The singularity of the Song of Songs (in spite—or perhaps because—of the universal experience of love) invites a Levinasian midrash. Everyone loves, yet no one's love is the same, not even unto itself.

What is love? Chaucer's narrator in *The Parliament of Fowls* famously finds it impossible to define, "The lyf so short, the craft so long to lerne."[12] Not unlike Rashi, in his commentary on the Song of Songs, Levinas himself develops love's meaning *in bono* and *in malo*. He very clearly unearths the medieval model of the good and bad Venus in "God and Philosophy," opening section 14 of that essay with a discussion of the goddess (so dear to Boccaccio and Chaucer),[13] by citing one of her main literary sources, Plato's *Symposium:* "Love is possible only through the idea of the Infinite—through the Infinite put in me, the 'more' which devastates and awakens the 'less,' turning away from the teleological, destroying the moment and the happiness of the end.

Plato forces out of Aristophanes an admission which, coming from the lips of the master of comedy is striking indeed: 'These are the people who pass their whole lives together; yet they could not explain what they desire of one another.' "[14] Levinas goes on to develop this sense of love's mystery by invoking its opposites. Love is royally transcendent, and yet "Diotima...will find love to be indigent, needy, and subject to vulgarity. The celestial and vulgar Venus are sisters.... Love is concupiscence, in Pascal's sense of the term.... Is transcendence of the Desirable beyond the inter*estedness* and eroticism in which the Beloved abides possible?"[15] Levinas's answer to this question is, of course, yes. With this answer Levinas places love in its transcendence outside, or beyond, the universal order, as he does elsewhere with such categories of experience as art and poetry, the night, and most problematically, the feminine. But how are we to understand this radical Levinasian exteriority of love, its otherness, beyondness, and transcendence?

In the opening chapter of *Totality and Infinity,* Levinas begins with the Platonic dictum, which he calls the "alibi" of metaphysics: " 'The true life is absent.' But we are in the world." The desire for this "true life," Levinas continues, "is turned toward the 'elsewhere' and the 'otherwise' and the 'other'." Levinas explains how other others — food, one's country, landscape, even "myself for myself" — are alterities on which I feed and satisfy myself, destroying their alterity through my absorption of them. Only that which one approaches without defining it in advance, which one seeks without "the possibility of anticipating the desirable," and which one aims at "aimlessly...as one goes forth unto death," writes Levinas, can evoke transcendental Desire. Only the Desire which "nourishes itself, one might say, with its hunger," that "desires beyond everything that can simply complete it," can grasp the alterity in which the idea of Infinity lies hidden. For such a "Desire, this alterity...has a meaning. It is understood as the alterity of the Other and of the Most-High" (*TI* 33–34).

The "and" is important. A Platonist with respect to his honoring of the "Good beyond being," yet Levinas is far from Platonic in his understanding of earthly realities and of love. "Love as analyzed by

Plato," Levinas declares, "does not coincide with what we have called Desire." For Levinas, the "relationship with the other" that results in "the idea of infinity" lies somewhere "between a philosophy of transcendence...and a philosophy of immanence" (*TI* 52, 63, 103). This between-ness, I argue, expresses itself in Levinas's writings in an exegetical pattern of thought that yokes within a single figure a series of oppositions, this-worldly and other-worldly, visible and invisible, light and dark, past and present, good and bad. Ends and beginnings thus overlap in a figural *infinition*, which is not identical with a *definition*. Medieval commentators like Rashi, who relentlessly allegorize the Song of Songs, teach us to read Levinas as a less exclusionary philosopher than his critics have held him to be.

The *wholly/essentially/absolutely other* as a term for the feminine erotic, for some and sometimes all postclassical (as well as "primitive") art, and for the night as the *il y a*, leaves them all apparently *outside* (or *before* or *after* or *beyond*) the universal order. This is satisfactory for neither Judaism nor Christianity, nor philosophy. Examined alongside Rashi's commentary on the Song of Songs, the Levinasian terms *insomnia, indolence, il y a*, and Eros can be seen to reinvent, to discover anew within the universe, these apparently excluded areas of experience. Levinas himself reinvents them, as I hope to show, using them in different ways at different times. Levinas's reading of them *in bono et in malo* is not, moreover, a matter of his thought changing over time, as the apparent contradictions in his commentaries on Eros were never made into retractions. Neither in the section "Phenomenology of Eros" (*TI* 255–66), nor in the 1979 preface to *Time and the Other,* is there (perhaps regrettably) any real shift in his arguments, his definitions of the feminine. Neither does the night of the stalag become illumined by 20 years of peace. The light, one would say, was always there, but Levinas in *Existence and Existents* was giving us its darkness, which remains present, even when he focuses elsewhere on the light. His presentation of the other, too, is intricately expressed *in malo et in bono.* When he offers us, for example, "the undesirable par excellence, the other (*autrui*)" (*BPW* 140), he is offering us the radiance inside the dark.

Perhaps we can break the container of our own *idées reçues* to confront our forbearers, including Rashi and Levinas, when trying to think along with the Song of Songs, which presents, through its very difficulties, all the hallmarks of Infinity. Then all of creation, even the encounter with Infinity that affirms "the Infinity put in me," must be read both *in bono et in malo*. The hermeneutic tradition of Judaism and its Greek translation, embodied in Levinas's philosophy, allow us to expand, to release, to loosen the said into a saying that includes the world and the more-than-world—in short, to perform the Song of Songs.

READING LEVINAS, READING RASHI, READING THE SONG OF SONGS

In the first spoken verse (1:2) of the Song, the voice of the Beloved cries out:

> **"Let him kiss me with the kisses of his mouth"** — *She recites this song with her mouth in her exile and in her widowhood: "If only King Solomon would kiss me with the kisses of his mouth as of old," because in some places they kiss on the back of the hand or on the shoulder, but I desire and wish that he behave with me as his original behavior, like a bridegroom with a bride, mouth to mouth.* — [Rashi][16]

For Rashi this interaction is the intensity of the face to face *par excellence,* the mouth to mouth of Eros as a prototype for the idea of the Infinite. In Jewish thought, the "kisses of the mouth" names the hearing of the first two commandments at Sinai directly from God,[17] but also, for Rashi, the orality of desire. The bride is the saying face, and she expects the King (to whom Peace belongs in his divine aspect, and in whom the charisma of kingship is apparent in his human aspect) not simply to speak back or to kiss her on the hand, as with an ordinary other human, but to respond to her as the intimate one, with his mouth on hers.

In his commentary on this verse of the Song, Rashi cites Deuteronomy 5:4: "He spoke to us face to face in the mount out of the midst of fire." Levinas, for his part, comments on the parallel passage in Exodus 19, where the Israelites, encamped at the foot of Mount Sinai, hear the voice of the Lord pronouncing his commandments from the smoking, blazing mountaintop above them. Like Rashi, who emphasizes Israel's desire to hear the "innermost secrets" of the Torah (and thus to receive God's kisses), Levinas focuses on Israel's receptiveness to God's commandments: "We will do and we will hear" (Exod. 24:7).[18] Puzzling with the rabbis over the inversion of verbs that places doing before hearing, Levinas (following Rav Hama bar Hanina) glosses Exodus 24:7 with a verse from the Song of Songs 2:3: "Like an apple tree amidst the trees of the forest is my beloved amidst young men." The biblical apple tree, Levinas explains, is probably a citron tree, whose fruit appears to come before its leaves. It thus stands as "the image *par excellence* of the negativity of history and dialectics. The fruit is there from all eternity," even as "the truth of Torah is given without any precursor" (*NT* 45–46). Whereas Rav Hama bar Hanina interprets the apple tree as an allegorical figuration of Israel, Rashi (in his commentary on the Song of Songs) sees it primarily as an image for God, as Israel sees and loves Him.

> **Like an apple (-tree) among the trees of the forest, so is my Beloved among the sons.** *Israel responds: Just as an apple tree among fruitless trees is beloved by virtue of its excellent fruit and fragrance — so is HASHEM superior to all the gods whom the heathen nations foolishly serve, and which are likened to insubstantial trees — simply "wood of the forest."* —[Rashi; *Yalkut Shimoni*][19]

Levinas's interpretation effectively combines that of Rashi and Rav Hama, making the apple (citron) tree an allegory both for God (as the giver and bearer of Torah, emblematized in the tree's fruit) and for Israel (as the one whose acknowledged obligation to do good is already there, prior to her promise to hearken). Because "an undeniable responsibility" exists "before commitments made," prior to the free exercise of choice, Israel responds to Torah like an apple tree whose "fruits come before its leaves," doing before hearing (*NT* 45–46). According to Levinas, "'We will do and we will hear' does not express the purity of a trusting soul, but the structure of a subjectivity clinging to the absolute," possessing "an angel's knowledge" of the good (48–49). One can only hear—really hear and understand—Torah, Levinas argues, if one first (in the order of ethical priority) already consents to it, loves it, does it, performs it, lives it. For Rashi, the desired kisses of the Song convey this enacted way of knowing. For Levinas, the preferred image is that of the foot of the legendary Raba, rubbed sore and bleeding as he poured over the scriptures. Like Israel at the foot of Mount Sinai, Raba held his foot as he read, "rubbing" the text to "arrive at the life it conceals," symbolized in his own rubbed foot and spurted blood (46). Are we wrong to see in this strange rabbinic (and Levinasian) image a glimpse of "the wound of the infinite," the wound of love (4:9), that wounds the Beloved of the Song?[20]

The Song of Songs is enigmatic, requiring the work of an engrossed interpreter like Raba, who struggles to find his or her place in the book. The wildly interactive and occasionally conflated Lover and Beloved meet, repulse, lose, seek, and endlessly chase each other through a landscape which is at once the springtime *topos* and their own bodies. They occur in a temporality that is unequivocal but elusive, in that the order of the poem(s) seems arbitrary. Discontinuities prevail.[21] These "terms of the relationship with mystery" invite the isolation of passages and the rereading of them, with different assignations of Lover and Beloved (*TO* 70). One mystical tradition of Judaism says that in the world to come the scriptures, written without vowels, will assume other vowels and another scripture will be born. With the Song, this multiplicity of texts occurs, moreover, within time and without the necessity of rewriting, revision, or retraction.

Rashi's commentary on the next verse of the Song insists that for Infinity to be poured into the world, it must flow into another vessel, the Beloved, in order to have light *in bono,* "a dazzling, where the eye takes more than it can hold" (*BPW* 139). Responding to the verse, "Because of the fragrance of your goodly oils, your name is 'oil poured forth,'" Rashi comments on the last phrase:

> **your name is 'oil poured forth'** (1:3)—*Your name is* [thus] *called. It is said about you that you are the oil that is constantly being poured forth so*

> *that your fragrant odor wafts forth into a distance, for so it is the nature of fragrant oil. As long as it is in a sealed bottle, its scent does not carry. If one opens it and pours the oil into another vessel, its scent carries.* —[Rashi; *Avodah Zarah* 35b][22]

Julia Kristeva has also made an apt *drash* on 1:3:

> The 'name' that is evoked almost from the very beginning induces intoxication; its precision and uniqueness trigger, it would seem, an overflowing of meaning, a flow of significations and sensations comparable to that produced by caresses, perfumes, and oils. The sensitive and the significant, the body and the name, are thus not only placed on the same level but fused in the same logic of undecidable infinitization, semantic polyvalence brewed by the state of love — seat of imagination, source of allegory.[23]

The saying of the name, unspeakable except as peace, is an event that makes the container burst. The lavalike spread of oil is as good a figure as any for "infinitization," the Levinasian *infinition* that produces the idea of the infinite in us. In the preface to *Totality and Infinity* Levinas has every existent involved in "the astonishing feat of containing more than it is possible to contain" (*TI* 27). The revelation that there is more inside me than what is inside "me" is the revelation that Infinity makes possible. The name of God is fragrance, spreading in all directions. In Gerard Manley Hopkins's irruptive poem, *God's Grandeur,* it is "ooze of oil / Crushed." The superabundance, the plenitude, not only of creation but of what is Uncreated, spills from the Song, from the Name, into the Beloved.

Sadly, the course of true love never does run smooth, and the lovers in the Song soon get into trouble. They have become separated, and when the Lover visits at night, the Beloved is in a state of spiritual conflict. She says in 5:2: "I sleep, but my heart is awake." She then falls into the "positions taken with regard to existence" that Levinas terms indolence and insomnia (*EE* 11). For Levinas, indolence is the refusal to take up existence, the refusal to begin, whereas insomnia, in this first telling in *Existence and Existents,* is the burden of enduring being while confronted by the "there is," the *il y a.*

The Beloved sleeps. What Levinas calls the "slightly *anarchical* ethical individualism taught by Jerusalem" is evident in Rashi's interpretations of 5:2 (*BPW* 24), which do apparent violence to the text, if we are used to a logocentric Western literary critical tradition. Multiplicity of meaning, assignment and reassignment of speakers, etymological leaps, are all stock in trade of the commentary tradition. There were many readings of the Song. For Rashi, the Song is the drama of the love between the Nation of Israel and God. Commenting on 5:2, "I sleep but my heart is awake," Rashi uses a very early compilation of homiletic material, the *Pesikta Rabbathi*:

> **I sleep**— *When I was confident and tranquil in the First Temple, I despaired of worshipping the Holy One, blessed be He, as one who sleeps and slumbers.* — [Rashi]
> **but my heart is awake**— *This is the holy one, blessed be He. So this is explained in the Pesikta. (Rabbathi, ch.15)* — [Rashi]
> **but my heart is awake**— *The Holy One, blessed be He, Who is (Ps.73:26): 'the Rock of my heart and my portion,' is awake to guard me and to benefit me.* — [Rashi; *Pesikta Rabbathi*, ch.15, *Song Rabbah*][24]

One immediately sees that the line has been broken. There seem to be two speakers, the nation and God. The first speaker is Israel, who says that even in the time of the First Temple, before the physical expulsion and exile, it fell into what will later be, in the figure of the Beloved who is too tired to get out of bed and open the door to her Lover, a version of Levinasian indolence. The second speaker, God, is clearly awake,[25] the author of *insomnia*. But, of course, God is within the sleeper, Levinas's "in-finition," which names the possibility to know more than one knows. He is the nation's heart, so that the constant scrutiny of God is called "the rock of my heart" (a phrase from Psalm 73:26). This phrase sends the reader back to reread what he already knows.

Psalm 73 is attributed to Asaph, a figure generally thought of as pre-exilic. This attribution enables Rashi to extrapolate that the "I" speaks in the time of the First Temple, yet knows what is to happen after its destruction, as did Asaph, who, even in the radiance of the time of the First Temple, speaks as one of the future wicked. He was "envious at the arrogant," he confesses, "When [he] saw the prosperity of the wicked" (Ps. 73:3). He was "brutish and ignorant;" he admits: "I was as a beast before Thee" (73:22), but he knows as well that he is continually with God who holds his right hand (73:23). "My flesh and my heart faileth, But God is the rock of my heart and my portion forever" (73:26). So sings Asaph in the phrase quoted by Rashi.

Here the lines of interpretation are so closely knit together as to make it difficult to separate the *in bono* from the *in malo,* but they are embedded into the one stroke of Rashi's brilliance when he separates the line into two phrases. At once it speaks both of Israel's indolence and of God's divine scrutiny, which the nation, poeticized into a single speaker, experiences as insomnia. Israel not only sleeps (is indolent), but also experiences insomnia, because it desires to awaken to Infinity. Later well-known commentaries found other allegorical possibilities. For Rabbi Obadiah Sforno (sixteenth century), the speaker of both phrases is the Jew who admits he was asleep to the Torah's command-ments. The sages, his heart, awoke him, but he rebelled anyway. In the *Mezudath David* (eighteenth century) the speaker is the female soul (of the male Jew) who is not yet asleep; in expectation of her lover, her heart is awake with desire. Whereas these later commentators simplify the interpretation of the verse by choosing between *in malo* and *in bono* readings, Rashi preserves both by dividing the line between two speakers. Rashi's learned, concise reading opens the text to the reader who reads the Song in his or her own exile—whether in France, or in the chamber of a spiritually dead heart. The indolent heart of Asaph is brutish and like a beast, lacking the love that will awaken it to the "rock of the heart," the wakefulness, the insomnia that is continual care from a divine love.

Verse 5:2 continues after what is an endstop in English: "Hark! My beloved is knocking: 'Open for me, my sister, my beloved my dove, my perfect one, for my head is full of dew, my locks with the drops of the night.'" There is copious commentary from Rashi on this verse, but what is of interest here is his *in bono et in malo* reading of night rain.

> **the drops of the night** —*the rains of the night, which represent hardship and weariness…both "dew" and "drops of the night" may also be explained favorably viz. the reward for precepts that are easy to perform, like dew, and the reward for precepts that are difficult as the hardship of the drops of the night.* —[Rashi][26]

He does not break stride, we see, when an exact phrase can mean two contradictory things. Human action will decide whether this will become a night *in bono* (that is, with rewards for the easy or difficult fulfillment of Torah) or *in malo* (that is, filled with suffering).

The Beloved, unfortunately, takes up the position of indolence, defined by Levinas as "a recoil before action…a hesitation before existence" (*EE* 15). In 5:3, she responds to the Lover's knock, saying, "I have taken off my tunic, how can I put it on? I have bathed my feet, how can I soil them?" This is indeed the image of indolence. Israel has even made Rashi weary.

> **I have taken off my tunic** —*i.e., I have already accustomed myself to other ways; I can no longer return to You*…[is] *the language of an adulterous wife, who does not wish to open the door for her husband* —[Rashi][27]

The Beloved has refused to sign on to existence for the good (to evoke Levinas's language). She has let the promise of rest and sleep become the *sloumbe-selepe, and sloberande* of Jonah in the Middle English *Patience,*[28] the same Jonah to whom Levinas refers in *Existence and Existents:* "In the Bible when Jonas, the hero of impossible escapes, invoker of not hingness and death, observes in the midst of the raging elements the failure of his flight and the fatality of his mission, he climbs down into the hold of the ship and goes to sleep" (*EE* 64). The night, once known *in bono,* now becomes a detachment from the call to action that constitutes being, and forgoes the *hineni* (*me voici,* here I am) which calls forth the Infinite. That existence is a burden is true, and here there is no escape from it; indolence converts the drops of night into night itself, reward into punishment, the night into night *in malo*—the *il y a.*

The most striking Levinasian image of nocturnal chaos is the *il y a.* In *Existence and Existents* Levinas links it to Durkheim's "primitive,"

God-less, prerevelation Sacred, which is "impersonal." The *il y a* is horror, which throws consciousness into "*an impersonal vigilance*," Levinas explains. Rather than leading us to a God, the notion of the *there is* leads us to the absence of God, the absence of any being: "Primitive men live before all Revelation, before the light comes." The insomnia associated with the *il y a* "is the night itself that watches," and the watching is hostile. Modern painting and poetry have "the intention to present reality as it is in itself, after the world has come to an end," Levinas observes, "In contemporary painting things no longer count as elements in a universal order" (*EE* 50, 55–56, 63). Artistic representations of the return to chaos, however apocalyptic they may be in conception, fall short of conveying this hostile, impersonal, destructive wakefulness, which is, by definition, inexpressible.

For Levinas, however, insomnia is not always destructive and not essentially opposed to the good. It can evoke apocalyptic destruction, but also the primordial chaos before creation.[29] In "God and Philosophy," Levinas associates it with a kind of passivity that does not resist formation: "Insomnia is wakefulness, but a wakefulness without intentionality—dis-interested. Its indeterminateness does not call for a form, is not a materiality. It is a form that does not *terminate* the drawing out of a form in it, and does not condense its own emptiness into a content. It is uncontained—Infinity" (*BPW* 133). Insomnia, consciousness burdened by the great chaos of the *il y a* in the earlier work, is here given a positive valuation as bulwark against an opaque slumbering consciousness, and it is thus reinvented inside the universe.

This creaturely indolence, imaged in the sleepy Beloved of the Song of Songs, is first met with a passionate advance from the Lover; but when the indolence of the Beloved changes to desire, the Lover has already withdrawn: "I opened for my beloved, but my beloved had hidden and was gone; my soul went out when he spoke; I sought him, but found him not; I called him, but he did not answer me" (5:6). The Infinite has withdrawn. What are the results?

The Beloved, who goes out to seek the Lover, reports, "The watchmen who patrol the city found and smote me and wounded me" (5:7). Rashi identifies the watchmen as those who consciously (like Moses and Aaron) or unconsciously (like Nebuchadnezzar) enact God's will, fulfilling his providential plan. This double identification of the watchmen enables, of course, an *in malo et in bono* interpretation of the wounding, as wreaked by Israel's own shepherds or by her foes. While Rashi frequently uses Old French to bring greater clarity to his commentary, here he refers to expressions for inflicting a wound three times in Hebrew, and once more in Old French. (As Rosenberg notes, the Old French word *navredure* means "a wound.")

> **they smote me and wounded me**— *They inflicted a wound upon me. Every* [instance of] petzah *is an expression of a wound* [inflicted] *by a weapon*—[Rashi][30]

For Levinas, too, the wound is a multivalent image, which he names "the wound of the Infinite." At the close of "The Idea of the Infinite in Us," he suggests that "the proximity of the infinite and the sociality it initiates...may be *better* than coincidence and oneness" (*EN* 222). But instead of this initiating happiness in the human, the idea of the infinite sometimes only leads to a shaky world, a "domain of uncertainty in human finitude" (221). Levinas admits to this mournfully in closing: "But perhaps it is already indicated in the very awakening to the insomnia of the psyche before the finitude of being, *wounded by the infinite,* which is moved to withdraw into a hegemonic and atheistic *I*" (222).

When the idea of the infinite in us and its trace, transcendental desire, is evoked by a meeting of self and other, it is not always a happy moment. The meetings of Moses and the patriarchs with the Ineffable have both *in malo* and *in bono* aspects; the lived human experience is always difficult. The nation of Israel moves into the territory of difficult freedom once it leaves Egypt. There, as in the Song, proximity with the Infinite produces confusion, and each brush with it may well initiate a falling off. Intimacy is always painful, and finitude is wounded by the infinition it desires. The disappointed Jew eating manna after the fish and pickles of Egypt, the religious person praying with a dead heart, the student locked in the classroom completely misunderstood, the poet finding failure in the word she writes—each of us stands close to the Infinite only to feel confused and rebuffed, ordered to return and flee simultaneously, like the Beloved of the Song.

The remedy for Levinas lies in the face to face with the other. But does helping the suffering other offer permanent exit from existence as burden, the *il y a*? Or is it one of many antidotes which are not merely anodynes? Despair can sometimes be sent to its corner by rehearsing the talmudic injunction, "Isn't it enough that you are alive?" Not that you merely are, but that you are alive. Care for the other, an other for whom one bears no love or friendship, may well be the highest and most complete emblem of this being alive. But the *moi-même* that lies in bed alone or with someone, that reads and writes poetry or takes the night as a friend through study or vigilance or righteous action, does not merely substitute the idea of infinity, or the horrific *il y a*, for being which poises itself like a swinging bridge over an abyss. Nor does it merely furnish being with things and events. How these specific others, the *sui generis* before or beyond the domestic and economic adequations of self, might use this wound, will hopefully be the subject of many meditations. The Song is the ancient ur-mediation. (It is not by chance that Luce Irigaray, in a glorious attempt to find in carnal love not an echo but a structure of the divine, uses this text.)[31] Indeed, the Song offers a salve, if not a cure, for the wound so central to human experience.

The indolence that sends the Beloved into the *il y a* is the symptom of a wounding that makes her "lovesick" (Song 5:8). When others ask her, "What is your beloved more than another beloved?" (5:9), the question opens a floodgate of remembrance and praise. Toward the close of the poem, in verse 8:5, she evokes their former intimacy:

> **Under the apple tree I aroused you** — *So she says in request of the affection of the beloved: "Under the apple tree I aroused You." I remember that under Mount Sinai, formed over my head as a sort of apple tree, I aroused You. That is an expression of the affection of the wife of one's youth, who arouses her beloved at night when he is asleep in his bed, and embraces him and kisses him.* — [Rashi][32]

Through the allegorical interpretation of the "apple tree" as referring to Mount Sinai, formed over the head of Israel "as a sort of apple tree,"[33]

Rashi's exegesis links this verse to commentary on Song 2:3. The Beloved remembers that she desired and received the commandments as God's "kisses," or "apples" (Song 2:3), while the tribes watched, trembling, at the foot of Sinai (or, according to a midrashic account, actually under the mountain, which God had suspended above them). Her desire, the manifestation of her adoration, aroused God to speak, to give the love-gift of Torah.

The flawed Beloved, giving voice to the created order, with all of its *in bono et in malo* contradictions, asks in 8:6 "Place me like seal on your heart, like a seal on your arms, for love is as strong as death." In the context of the allegorical interpretation, the request that the Beloved wear a seal over the heart or on the arm suggests the sealing of a covenantal relationship between God and Israel, as at Mount Sinai, even as it depicts that relationship in marital terms.

> **Place me like a seal**—*for the sake of that love, You shall seal me on Your heart, so that you should not forget me, and you will see.* —[Rashi][34]

See what? Perceive what?

> **That love is strong as death**—*i.e., to me the extent of my love for You is as strong as the deaths which I suffered for Your sake [i.e., my love for You is so strong that I endure death for its sake].*—[Rashi][35]

Interpreting the phrase "strong as death" as a synchrony that veils a prior diachrony—"strong [to the point of] death"—Rashi anticipates Levinas. Remembered by God's heart and supported by God's mighty arm, Israel will endure, and its faithfulness will be a revelation to God, who will "see" it. Israel herself will be revealed.

At issue for readers of Levinas is the revelation, the coming-to-light, of the erotic feminine, wounded in the night. Famously in *Time and the Other,* in a passage from "Eros" for which Simone de Beauvoir took him to task in *The Second Sex,*[36] Levinas designates the feminine as "wholly other." "What matters to me in this notion of femininity," writes Levinas, "is not merely the unknowable, but a mode of being that consists in slipping away from the light. The feminine in existence is an event different from that of spatial transcendence or of expression [*sic*] that go toward light. It is a flight before light" (*TO* 87). One strategy for answering the objections of Levinas's feminist critics is to see the feminine as accidentally sexual and gendered and give it the familiar meanings of gentleness,[37] withdrawal, and mystery. This reading might associate the Levinasian feminine with the withdrawal, the hiddenness of God,[38] the endless gentleness of Saint-Exupéry's lamb in *Le Petit Prince* for which Levinas can only imagine the container in his beautiful "Beyond Dialogue" (*AT* 79–90). The terms *wholly/ essentially/absolutely other* as names for the human feminine still seem unacceptable, however, especially when we hear that the feminine is also in the unknowable darkness.[39]

Here we have the opportunity to perform an *in bono et in malo* reading, using a rabbinical hermeneutic instrument that will perform a remedy to bring Levinas's desiring feminine, the erotic female, into a positive valuation, as she possesses for Rashi in the opening speech of the Song.[40] Biblical text is explained through fixed principles of interpretation, "the principles through which the Torah is expounded."[41] Rabbi Yishmael's list of 13 principles is recited daily during morning prayers. The two principles of importance here are the second, "Inference from similarity of phrases in a text," and the twelfth, "An interpretation may be deduced from the context or from subsequent terms of the text."[42] The phrase in the problematic Levinasian passage to be interpreted here is "the light," for which we will find an *in bono et in malo* Levinasian reading, when "light" is attached to Eros.

That this approach is not a distortion of Levinas is hinted at in *Existence and Existents,* where friends and lovers seem able to initiate the idea of infinity. They share a status, Levinas writes, "beyond economic activity and the world. For what characterizes love is an essential and insatiable hunger. To shake hands with a friend is to express one's friendship for him, but it is to convey that friendship as something inexpressible, and indeed unfulfilled, a permanent desire. *The very positivity of love lies in its negativity.* The burning bush that feeds the flame is not consumed" (*EE* 35). If love's "positivity" lies for Levinas in its "negativity," then a simply negative reading of the Levinasian feminine is impossible. Indeed, it is an utter misreading, a wrenching of that term out of the larger context, the diachronic (and anarchic) pattern of thought, in which it participates.

The erotic seems privileged, moreover, when Levinas in *Proper Names* discusses the death of Albertine in *À la recherche du temps perdu:* "Death is the death of other people, contrary to the tendency of contemporary philosophy, which is focused on one's own solitary death . . . But the daily death—and the death of every instant—of other persons, as they withdraw into an incommunicable solitude: that is precisely what nurtures love. That is Eros in all its ontological purity, which does not require participation in a third term (tastes, common interests, a connaturality of souls)—but direct relationship with what gives itself in withholding itself, with the other *qua* other, with mystery" (*PN* 103). Lovers "die" to the world and its concerns, and all the others (except each other) "die" to them. When this solitary Eros between lovers is juxtaposed with the "Love without Eros . . . *The glory of a long desire!*" (celebrated by Levinas in "God and Philosophy," *BPW* 144), one feels that Levinas has embraced some aspect of Christian *agape*. But if, as Levinas has written in that same essay, the celestial and vulgar Venus are sisters, then a sisterhood can also be claimed for Eros and *agape*, concupiscence and charity. There is something libidinal in all love, it would seem.[43]

When Levinas, at the end of the passage in "God and Philosophy," does call to a "Love without Eros," it is not a desexualized *agape* that he would put in its place. The Eros that he excludes is that which only reaffirms the self in its own eyes, the male Western ego of which feminists (among whom I count myself) have despaired. When Irigaray rapturously engages with Eros in her essay on the caress,[44] she too would avoid both ideality and animality. Missing its possibility for transcendence, the lived experience of sexuality can be domesticated or distorted into pornographic sterility. From its domestication come the heavens filled with feminized pastel angels singing for a manly bearded father-husband; from its pornographic distortion come the imagined 10,000 virgins, who will capitulate in paradise to the individual martyred male, his will intact. The endlessly reductive egoism of the ascendant self can remake infinity into merely a lot of this or that, and all of it rather nauseating.

The Song of Songs, as interpreted by Rashi and Levinas alike, escapes the twin dangers associated with the erotic. But how? How would one, having received an ancient text (from a nameless poet? from Solomon? transcribed by Hezekiah?),[45] redolent of physical sexuality, preserve its transcendental nature? By reading the Song of Songs as a transformational text. That is how the rabbis and the monks of the Middle Ages read it, knowing it to be (as Bernard of Clairvaux puts it) "the book of our experience."[46] That it is *sui generis,* unique, puts it into a lived situation of joy and sorrow, purification, growth, and fruitfulness, wherein transcendental eroticism is linked to another *sui generis* experience, death. Levinas writes of death, "We could say it is in relationship with mystery" (*TO* 70). "The erotic relationship furnishes us with a prototype of it," he continues, "*Eros, strong as death, will furnish us with the basis of an analysis of this relationship with mystery — provided it is set forth in terms entirely different from those of the Platonism that is a world of light*" (76; emphasis mine).

Paraphrasing Song 8:6: "for love is as strong as death," Levinas has given us the *in bono* reading of a love that must be "set forth in terms entirely different" than the *in malo* light of Plato's *Republic*. Plato has constructed "a Republic that must imitate the world of Ideas; he makes a philosophy of a world of light, a world without time" (*TO* 93). This is not Levinas's world, nor that of the Song and its medieval exegetes. He closes *Time and the Other* with this declaration of his intent: "I have tried to find the temporal transcendence of the present toward the mystery of the future.... It is the face-to-face without intermediary, and is furnished for us in the eros where, in the other's proximity, distance is integrally maintained, and whose pathos is made of both this proximity and duality" (94).

If the wound is ongoing, so is the revelation.[47]

11

"A Land that Devours Its Inhabitants"

Midrashic Reading, Levinas, and Medieval Literary Exegesis

Sandor Goodhart

So they gave-out a (false) report of the land
that they had scouted out
to the Children of Israel saying:
The land that we crossed through to scout it
it is a land that devours its inhabitants
— *Numbers* 13:32

The Gospel according to St. Luke attributes the historical beginning of Christian exegesis of the Hebrew Scriptures in chapter 24:13–32 to Jesus himself.[1] Two disciples, on their way to Emmaus, encounter (but do not immediately recognize) Jesus after his resurrection from the dead. "Beginning with Moses and with all the prophets," Luke relates, "[Jesus] interpreted to them in all the scriptures the things referring to himself" (24:27).[2] Responding to Paul Claudel's "personal exegesis of the Old Testament" in *Emmaüs*, Emmanuel Levinas comments incisively on the differences between Jewish and Christian exegesis. Levinas acknowledges Claudel's "profound piety" and fascinating "poetic imagination," but recoils from his allegorical (and explicitly Christological) interpretation, which is based on that of the medieval commentator "Raban Maur of Mayence, a ninth century scholar of the Holy Scriptures, the Fathers of the Church and Greek," who "knew no Hebrew" (*DF* 119, 121). What troubles Levinas especially is not Claudel's (and Raban Maur's) neglect of the "exact meaning" of the "original text" and "of Jewish exegesis," nor even their adherence to "the idea of prefiguration" (which Levinas acknowledges to be a continuation of Jewish tradition and "legitimate to the extent that it coincides with that of prophecy"); rather, Levinas takes issue with an approach that reduces "man as a person, as an agent of history" to "a figure," effacing him in the process (121). The "representatives of the Church" have not always been so neglectful of Jewish letters, traditions, and persons, Levinas notes, pointing to "the work of the Franciscan Nicholas of Lyra who, in the thirteenth century, attributed the highest value to them," returning "assiduously" to Rashi's commentary as a basis for his own.[3]

The double movement discernible in Levinas's response to medieval Christian exegesis—both to affirm continuities with traditional Jewish exegesis and to note its departure from it—is one I would continue in this essay, which observes in Levinas's own midrashic performance of rabbinic exegesis of the book of Numbers, chapters 13 and 14, the lively continuation of an ancient tradition of interpretation. Whereas it is commonly said that rabbinic thought orients itself primarily along the horizontal plane of the literal and historical, and Christian monastic thought typically emphasizes the vertical plane of allegorical correspondences, this synchronic opposition of horizontal and vertical dimensions veils what is, in fact, a diachronic extension of the horizontal into the vertical through what one might call a "turning." (The rabbis say of Torah: "Turn it and turn it again, for all is contained within it.")[4] For Levinas, as for the rabbis before him, the Biblical "ascent to the land"—a primarily diachronic movement in biblical time—enacts the "ascent to Heaven," in keeping with the commandment to "love the Lord thy God with thy whole heart, and with thy whole soul, and with thy whole strength" (Deut. 6:5). Levinas's interpretive practice, I will suggest, helps to reveal the Jewish origin of one of the most common images in the monastic Middle Ages, that of the ladder of ascent. Understanding Levinas enables us to understand the commonplace Christian monastic schemata of the *scala perfectionis* ("ladder of perfection") not merely as a static trope for discrete levels of scriptural meaning and ethical advancement, but also as a lived experience, fraught (as the wisest of exegetes knew) with peril. The ladder, like the land, can "devour its inhabitants" (Num. 13:32), if they "go up" wrongly.

In this essay, I first take up the theoretical question of the Christian allegorical interpretation [*allegoresis*] of medieval texts as a "historical criticism" of them.[5] I then turn to a definition of midrashic reading broad enough to include the "allegorical" of medieval Christian exegesis as its possible extension. Third, I turn to two chapters in Numbers that provide, in their literal ("plain sense") narrative of the exploration and (failed) conquest of the land of Canaan, an apt text for reflection on the very meaning of scriptural reading and study. Fourth, I present three different midrashic commentaries on these biblical chapters—that of the Talmud, of Levinas, and my own—that approximate the familiar allegorical levels of medieval exegesis: doctrinal, tropological, and anagogical.[6] Fifth, and finally, I comment on how the monastic Middle Ages may be understood (however paradoxically) to have both paralleled and extended the pattern of ancient Jewish exegesis exemplified in Levinas as its latter-day practitioner.

CRITICIZING ALLEGORY (AND ALLEGORICAL CRITICISM)

What does the work of a contemporary, French-speaking, Jewish teacher and philosopher, or the study of the ancient rabbinic practice of midrashic reading, have to do with the study of medieval literature? Is not the study of medieval literature above all a study of Christian allegory? Did not D. W. Robertson, in his ground-breaking articles in the 1950s and later in his *Preface to Chaucer* open an entirely new era of medieval study?[7] Was his point not that if we were to offset the impact of Hegelian dynamism, and not be unduly swayed by modern conceptions of self (and the approach to literature through irony that such consciousness-based conceptions appeared to foster), we needed to study Augustinian *caritas* and *cupiditas* as a prelude? His use of allegory as a means of reading was not opposed to irony, of course—and he took pains to publish essays in collaboration with his colleague Bernard Huppé to demonstrate their harmony.[8] But the conjunction only begged the question. He wanted to show that without allegory, and in particular without Christian Augustinian approaches to allegory, we were missing a great deal—perhaps the most fundamental portion—of what the Middle Ages had to offer us.

What Robertson undertook for medieval studies was, of course, hardly isolated. Under the influence somewhat later of Michel Foucault's work (and especially the notion of discrete historico-epistemological configurations), a number of scholars at Berkeley and elsewhere began doing similar things for Renaissance studies.[9] If the Middle Ages were separable from the over arching retrospective nineteenth century reading for which Hegel seems to have been the most articulate spokesman, then so was the Renaissance, these scholars argued.[10] It was understandably not long before literary historians of other periods began following suit. Could not the same be said, these scholars argued, for the period in England from the middle of the seventeenth century to the end of the eighteenth?[11] Indeed, it was probably inevitable that the nineteenth century itself would come to be regarded as separable from "Hegelian" conceptualizations. This period could be studied, some argued, as a kind of inverted eighteenth century humanism, as an "analytic of finitude," to use Foucault's phrase, an examination of the limiting capacity of death and desire that delineated in time and space the epistemological figure known as "man."[12] The itinerary had come full circle.

And yet, within the preserve he claimed for medieval studies, Robertson's approach was never entirely successful. Even at its origin, Huppé maintained the relevance of irony in *Canterbury Tales*.[13] Irony was not, it turned out, just an older outdated retrospective approach. If *caritas* worked for reading Augustine, it was not immediately clear that it worked the same way for reading Chaucer. Chaucer's Parson, for example, might very well be considered at polar extremes from his Pardoner, but the road between them was by no means unobstructed. The endless stories of the pilgrims, their inseparability from their storytellers, even the unfinishedness of the *Canterbury Tales* itself, may reflect as much a tension with such allegorical constructions as they do its implementation. And irony functioned similarly for other medieval writers.

Moreover, as the work of such scholars as Jon Whitman, Carolynn Van Dyke, Maureen Quilligan, and Ann W. Astell have shown, the notion of medieval allegory itself turns out much more complicated than it first appeared to nineteenth century critics, notably Samuel Coleridge.[14] Our contemporary understandings of both allegory and irony still derive one-sidedly from the romantics. Paul de Man's famous essay on the origins of these two modes in English and European literary studies suggests that the advent of German idealism occasioned a larger cultural shift than had previously been acknowledged, one that continued to dominate theoretical discussion into the latter half of the twentieth century.[15] But, as Gerald Bruns notes, if we think about allegory in more classical terms — as a condition for interpretation in the ancient world rather than one of its modes — then allegory retains in fact deep affinities with the Jewish tradition in which Philo encountered it in Alexandria (in connection with the Septuagint, for example), and maintains those connections later in other Christian writers.[16] Midrashic reading, and in fact rabbinic reading at large, was already highly developed by the beginning of the modern era ("modern" here understood in the sense in which it is used in studies of the ancient world). With the collapse of the Second Temple, and the formation of the rabbinic academy at Yavneh, it continued through the period of the later rabbis (indeed, some commentators would argue, it continues still).

The introduction of Levinas and, in particular, midrashic approaches to the discussion of the literary within the Middle Ages, is, at bottom, I would like to argue, a way of setting aside both irony and allegory understood as representational, metaphoric, synchronic, in short, Platonic approaches to reading, and a way of taking up in their place prophetic, metonymic, diachronic, Hebraic modes as a foundation not only for reading Hebrew writing, but for reading secular and Christian writing as well. In other words, a Hebrew mode of reading sets aside the kinds of romantic redefinitions of the ancient world (by which the two, allegory and Midrash, may have seemed in opposition) to rediscover the contexts from which medieval literature appears to have come. From this hermeneutical perspective, the reader is able to recognize continuities with the ancient world in which *allegoria* as translation extends what in fact midrashic thought of the rabbis was already practicing, and in which perspective it becomes clear Christian allegorical thinking as a consequence extends Jewish rabbinic thinking at large.

Without abandoning Robertson's admirable efforts to release the Middle Ages from Hegel's retrospection, we may be able to recapture an older sense of allegory (than the representational understanding of it), one closer to Hebraic sources if, as Bruns argues, we recognize that already at the moment of its invention, allegory was a way of continuing Midrash as translation, a diachronic extension of the same thing in another context.[17] Levinas's own definition of Jewish midrashic interpretation reads, in fact, like many a definition of Christian *allegoresis:* "The specifically Jewish exegesis of the Scriptures is punctuated by these concerns: the distinction between the obvious meaning and the one which has to be deciphered, the search for this buried meaning, and for one which lies deeper still, contained within the first.... This exegesis of the Old Testament is called *Midrash,* meaning exposition or research or interrogation.... [The] invitation to seek, to decipher, to the *Midrash,* already marks the reader's participation in the Revelation, in the Scriptures" (*LR* 194).

The Hebraic for Levinas — as for the rabbis — means the midrashic. If I turn, then, to the work of Levinas, as a resource for the study of medieval literature, I do so as an example of the practice of midrashic reading upon a talmudic text that is already itself a commentary upon a series of biblical texts, as a taking up, in other words, after the Holocaust, of a medieval practice upon a medieval interpretative text that may be at the origin of Christian exegetical practices, one that may prove useful for examining both religious and secular texts alike. I will begin by defining more precisely what I mean by Midrash (and midrashic reading), taking an example from within the biblical canon. Next, I will take an extended example from the work of Levinas where he is reading Talmud reading Torah. In my conclusion, I will return to the question with which we have begun this inquiry: what can Levinasian reading (or Hebraic midrashic reading at large) offer to medieval studies — to Jewish texts, to Christian texts, and to secular texts? In that connection, I will return to an idea by which Levinas comes to define the political as the messianic, namely, "the ascent to heaven."

MIDRASHIC READING

What is Midrash? The word, as is well known, comes from the Hebrew word *darash* meaning an "inquiry into" or "seeking out." The story told about the origins of Midrash (which of course is a Midrash itself) is that the ancient rabbis told homiletic stories to supplement places in Scripture where something appears to be missing, where something appears to be left out. Known commonly as simply "Midrash" ("Midrashim" in the plural), these collections added to the more formal interpretative methods employed in Talmud (where stories and interpretations of more legalistic passages were offered), in esoteric interpretations (for example, of the letters of Scripture), in later rabbinic writings (like those of Rashi, Maimonides, or Nachmanides), or in Scripture itself.[18]

In the 1970s in America, under the influence of feminism, a movement began to tell the stories of women whose histories were left out of the biblical texts — the stories of Sarah, Rivka, Rachel, or Leah, for example — in an attempt to answer the question: what might these women have been feeling that the Scripture has declined to tell us?[19] Then in the 1980s, what might be called a third wave of interest in midrashic stories began, to which such scholars as Gerald Bruns, Geoffrey Hartman, Michael Fishbane, Susan Handelman, David Stern, and Daniel Boyarin, among others, contributed important studies.[20] But the project for some reason was stillborn. Over the past ten years, strangely little has been done either in Jewish studies or in literary studies to foster this kind of midrashic reading within the context of the sophisticated techniques of literary reading learned in the sixties and seventies in this country. In a volume introducing the biblical criticism of Martin Buber, Harold Bloom, in his own particularly prescient way, lamented the absence of a critic like Buber who could open the door to a new biblical criticism.[21] Bloom imagined such critical writing would look the way Kafka's commentary on the Bible looked (and it is tempting to imagine that Jacques Derrida in his final writing on Judaism may have considered his essays to be styled in just this way).[22] Perhaps the needed critical mass was the presence on the scene of a philosophical, religiously minded, literary thinker like Emmanuel Levinas.

I return, then, to the question with which this section began: What is Midrash? In critical language, a Midrash, we may say, is a story told in response to a gap or tear in a prior or previous text in such a way that constitutes a material extension of that earlier text. "Midrash is best understood," Daniel Boyarin writes, "as a continuation of the literary activity which engendered the Scriptures themselves."[23] Thus, there are several qualities of a midrashic narrative, the lack of any one of which would diminish the capacity of the narrative to be characterized fairly as "midrashic." In the first place, a Midrash is a story. It is not something other than a story. It is not a piece of expository prose, for example, although there may well be midrashic components to a piece of expository prose. In the second place, a midrashic story itself is necessarily secondary in status; there is a prior text to which it is a response. Midrash is never an original production. In the third place, it is a response to, or supplement to, that prior text, and not a text that has some other kind of connection with it. It is not, for example, a text that just happens to reside nearby or next to that other text. Nor is it even just analogous to that other text. It issues from the primary text in response to it. In the fourth place, that to which it is a response in the prior text is a gap, tear, hole, or discontinuity of some kind; a wound, silence, absence, or lack. The prior text is broken in some fashion; it lacks wholeness or completeness. Something is missing, and Midrash is a response to that hole. In the fifth place, as a response to that tear or hole, it is a particular kind of response to that prior text (and not just any old response to that gap). It is not, for example, a filling in of the missing piece, or a patching over of the missing piece, but it is a response that in some way materially extends that prior text.

Let me offer an example. In Genesis 22, we read: God said to Abraham, "Take your son, whom you love, your only son, your favorite son, Isaac, and bring him up as an offering up" [kach na et binchah, et ahavta, et y'echidchah, et Yitzhak, et va aleihu sham l'olah]. The Midrash asks: Why does God say it four times: *kach na et binchah,* "take your son" (one); *et ahavta,* "whom you love" (two); *et y'echidchah,* "your only son or favorite son" (three); *et Yitzhak,* "Isaac" (four)? Why not just say "take Isaac!"? The Midrash answers in the following way. This biblical sentence, it tells us, is part of a larger conversation between God and Abraham, one in which God says to Abraham "Take your son," and Abraham says "I have two sons." (Remember that he has another son, Ishmael, who is in fact his first born son). So God says, "whom you love," and Abraham replies, "I love them both," lest we think Abraham loves only one of them. So God says, "your favorite son, your only son," and Abraham replies, "well, let's see, to each mother, each child is her 'only' son her 'favorite' son; to Hagar, Ishmael is her only son, and to Sarah, Isaac is her only son." So, God says, "Isaac!" to which Abraham can only respond, "Oh, okay."[24]

What does this Midrash teach us? In the first place, it teaches us what appears to have been excluded in this "filling in" of the story. But something else occurs as well. If we ask what is the first thing we think of when we learn that God says to Abraham "Take your son, your only one, whom you love, and prepare him as an *olah,* or sacrifice," we realize that God's saying it four times may not be the primary issue on our mind. Indeed, our thinking of that repetition may be itself a kind of dislocation of the real issue. Our response might more understandably be closer to something like: "How could God make such an outrageous demand of Abraham? What kind of God would do that?" and, "Why is Abraham so passive about it? Can he not argue with God? Is this the same man who argued with God just a while earlier in the narrative to save complete strangers?"

Midrash, in other words, does more than just respond to a perceived gap in the text; it performs that dislocation itself; it echoes the dislocation that is already a part of the primary narrative to which it is responding. Appearing to fill in a gap, it in fact extends that text, and it does so in a way that is materially present since there it is in front of us in (and as) the Midrash. To show how this midrashic technique works in action, I turn to a talmudic discussion upon which Emmanuel Levinas has commented (or, better, in which he has participated). In doing so, I too respond with Levinas to what he calls the "invitation to seek, to decipher, to the *Midrash*," which "already marks the reader's participation in the Revelation" (*LR* 194). My own performative interpretation thus proceeds through "four levels of meaning or reading": reading biblical passages, reading Talmud, reading Levinas's commentary on Talmud, and formulating a response to Levinas's commentary. The four different levels of meaning I explore in this essay—first, the biblical "plain sense" of Numbers 13 and 14; second, the midrashic meaning of "the fear of God" (as contrasted with the fear of other human beings); third, the ethical or moral meaning of "universal justice" (as Levinas discerns it); and fourth, the prophetic meaning of the ascent to the promised land (as articulated in my commentary on Levinas's). These four levels of meaning approximate those of the four-fold exegesis of the medieval Church: *littera, allegoria, tropologia (or moralia), anagogia.*[25]

BIBLICAL READING I: NUMBERS 13–14, FEAR OF GOD, AND FEAR OF HUMAN BEINGS

Levinas's essay, "Promised Land or Permitted Land," concerns a passage from the talmudic *Tractate Sotah*, 34b–35a (*NT*51–69).[26] The *Sotah* commentary is already itself a commentary on at least two (and possibly three) biblical texts—one from Numbers chapters 13 and 14 (that is reread in the first chapter of Deuteronomy), and a passage from Isaiah that the rabbis link with these two texts. The biblical story from Numbers in chapters 13 and 14 is about fear. I begin with the plain sense of the text. The people have reached the wilderness of Paran, and are ready to enter into the land of Israel, the Promised Land. It is decided that spies should be sent into the land in advance of their move to check it out. The 12 who go are selected from among the leaders of the tribes (and therefore are not some expendable mercenaries), and Moses, Aaron, and even God are thought to accede to the plan.

The 12 go; they are away 40 days; and when they return, they are of two opinions: ten out of the 12 report: "Yes, it is a good land, flowing with milk and honey, as we heard it was going to be, but the forces are just too strong, the people too fierce (and too large of stature), and we are afraid that if we go in and try to possess the land, we will be decimated" (cf. Num. 13:27–29). The other two, Caleb and Joshua, are of the opinion that the ten are wrong, that the land was promised to the Israelites, and that they all need to put aside whatever fears have arisen and proceed with the entry. Caleb calms the people down, ending his speech with the exhortation: "Let us go up, yes, up, and possess it. For we can prevail, yes, prevail against it!"(13:30).[27] At this point the other explorers reiterate their opposition, giving a "false report" about the land, which they describe as "a land that devours its inhabitants," where all the men there are "giants" — so big that, seeing them, the explorers saw themselves as little more than "grasshoppers" (13:32–33).

In the second part of the story (chapter 14), things spiral even more out of control. The people panic and want to return to Egypt for fear of dying in the wilderness (14:2–4). Moses and Aharon fling themselves on the ground (14:5). Caleb and Joshua rip their clothing (14:6), reiterate their position that it is a good land (that God is with them and that they should give up rebelling), and a near stoning of Moses, Aharon, Caleb, and Joshua takes place (14:10). At this point, God complains: "How long will this people scorn me?" (14:11). When God threatens to destroy Israel and to make a new nation of Moses' descendants (14:12), Moses appeals to the patience and long-suffering of YHWH, who relents, decreeing instead that the people shall wander in the wilderness for forty years, one year for each day that the scouts had explored Canaan (14:34). The people (other than the explorers) unexpectedly and curiously reverse themselves and decide to go into the land anyway: "The people mourned, exceedingly, they started-early in the morning and went up to the top of the hill-country, saying: Here we are, let us go up to (attack) the place that YHWH promised, for we have sinned" (14:39–40).

Now they go! Now they say all the right things—"here we are," "we have sinned"—but now they do precisely the wrong things. They are as excessive now as they have been all along. Moses informs them that God is not with them, and that they will fail. But they will not listen now any more than they did before. They are as impetuous in their desire to attack as they were fearful a moment ago and nostalgic for good old Egypt. And so they go up and, of course, are utterly routed: "But they went up recklessly to the top of the hill country...And the Amalekite and the Canaanite who were settled in that hill-country came down. They struck them and crushed them, near Horma" (14:44–45).

If ever there were a story dominated by fear, this seems to be it. The first group of explorers, the ten who lie about the land, fear other men more than they fear God. (Here the maxim, "everything is given to God except the fear of God," ascribed to rabbinic tradition, applies.)[28] The smaller group of two trusts God completely and is ready to take possession of the land, but when, later in the story, the community at large tries to do that, they fail utterly. If the first group fears God insufficiently, this second group in some weird way appears to fear God too much, or to fear God inappropriately. What are we to make of this curious text?

BIBLICAL READING II: DEUTERONOMY 1:22–2:1 AND INTERPRETATION

Or rather, and more importantly, what do the rabbis make of it? The biblical account requires interpretation (the rabbis', Levinas's, and our own). According to the rabbis, (1) both groups of explorers are wrong; (2) they are wrong because in both cases their actions are linked to shame; and (3) that shame entails an inappropriate "fear of God." By extension, if we have misunderstood that view and tried to make a political decision about which group was right, it is because we have lodged ourselves interpretatively in the same place as the explorers.

The Rabbinic passage quoted by Levinas opens with the phrase from Deuteronomy from which all else in the *Sotah* passage may be derived:

> "That they may explore the land for us" (Deuteronomy 1:22). Rav Hiyya bar Abba said: The explorers sought only the shame of the land, for about this it has been said, "That they may explore (*veyashperu*) the land." And elsewhere it has been said (Isaiah 24:23): "The moon will be ashamed (*veshapra*) and the sun will be confounded."[29]

The initial reference to Deuteronomy is critical, first, because a different Hebrew word is used there for "explore" than is used in Numbers. In Numbers we read *vayitrou,* which is commonly translated as "spy" or "scout" (for example in the standard JPS 1985 translation) or "spy out" or "scout out" (as in Everett Fox), while in Deuteronomy the word used is *veyachperu,* which is similar but which really means "to dig" or "probe more deeply into." This second word, *veyachperu,* is sometimes translated as "reconnoiter" (as, for example, in the 1985 JPS) or "explore" (as, for example, in the Everett Fox translation and our English version of Levinas).[30] The sense of *vayitrou* is that of surveying the surface in the way a tourist might do, where the sense of *veyachperu* is more like digging holes into the ground, a distinction that will become particularly important for the rabbis later in the passage. The root of the word in Deuteronomy, *HPR,* pronounced as *chet pey reish,* means "dig a hole," which of course is an action not unlike the action of a Midrash itself, which means to "seek into" or "inquire into," or even to "draw out of."

The rabbis also turn to Deuteronomy rather than Numbers in opening their discussion for a second reason that concerns the special status of Deuteronomy as a text. In Deuteronomy, the earlier history of Numbers is retold by Moses in the first person as a kind of Mosaic autobiography. Moses talks about expounding upon Torah. The words of Deuteronomy, we learn in the first line, "are the words that Moshe [Moses] spoke to all Israel in (the country) across the Jordan" (1:1) in the fortieth year. Just before they go into Canaan, in other words, Moshe speaks "to explain this Instruction" (1:5).

In other words, Deuteronomy is in some sense the first interpretation of Torah. It is an internal interpretation, of course, because it takes place within *Chumash*, which is to say, within the first five books of Moses, but it is an interpretation nonetheless, and therefore in some sense also outside of the material it reads. Michael Fishbane rightly observes, "The foundation document of Judaism, the Hebrew Bible, not only sponsored a monumental culture of textual exegesis, but was itself its own first product."[31] If other biblical texts (perhaps even all of them) function similarly to Deuteronomy, rabbinic thinking itself may be imagined as a way of negotiating this double status of midrashic interpretation, as a way of continuing it, at once inside and outside of the text that it reads, not unlike a möbius strip (a mathematical figure in which one side is separated at every point by a nontraversable boundary from a surface that turns out, through an unexpected twist, to be the same side).

In any event, the rabbis draw upon the first internal interpretation of the passage rather than the passage itself; they talk about a reading of the passage, in place of (or perhaps as a way of) talking about the passage. But in their use of midrashic method, the rabbis often do one thing in order to do another. So perhaps it is also a way of saying this text too is about the people and their behavior, and not about God. Recall one other moment in Numbers that is reread in Deuteronomy where the distinction between what was God's choice and what was the people's choice is more explicit: "Then you came-near to me, all of you, and said: Let us send men before us that they may explore the land for us and return us word about the route that we should (use to) go up against it and about the towns that we will come to" (Deut. 1:22).

In Numbers 13:1 we read: "YHWH spoke to Moshe, saying: "Send for yourself men, that they may scout out the land of Canaan that I am giving to the Children of Israel." In other words, in this second version of the Numbers story told in Deuteronomy, it is not God but the people who requested the sending of spies. The rabbis focus upon this important shift from divine to human responsibility, for no sooner have they cited Deuteronomy's account, than they link it with a word in Isaiah, which is translated "be ashamed": "About this it has been said, 'That they may explore [*veyashperu*] the land.'" And elsewhere it has been said (Isa. 24:23): "The moon will be ashamed [*veshapra*] and the sun will be confounded."

Why do the rabbis make the comparison of exploring to shaming? The Hebrew word translated "explore" in Deuteronomy and the Hebrew word translated as "be ashamed" in Isaiah do not actually have the same Hebrew root,[32] but the similarity in sound between the two words allows the rabbis to create a pun that suggests that shaming is a matter of shedding blood. Textuality is all-important to the midrashic point of view, whatever the relation to historical fact (and the rabbis do not exclude there being a historical link). Their reference allows us to understand that feeling shame is a matter of "digging a hole" for oneself (so to speak), and that turning pale, experiencing the loss of color, as a consequence of being shamed, is a visual pun; it means for the rabbis, literally, that the one doing the shaming is shedding blood (as the shedding of color).[33] Saying that shaming, for the rabbis, is a matter of shedding of blood makes it clear that it is very bad for them. It is a capital offense, identified by the rabbis elsewhere as one of the unforgivable offenses. After you have committed it, after you have shamed someone, how do you repair the injury? In some of the texts, they suggest that the one who shames another in public risks the danger of becoming subject to the same punishment for which the shaming of the other has been undertaken. Shaming, verbal slander, verbal *ona'ah* or injury, kills three people, the rabbis say: the slanderer, the one who is slandered, and the one (or ones) who hear or receive the slander.[34]

In the discussion of the passage from Numbers, Rav Hiyya bar Abba links shame specifically with exploring because "the explorers sought only the shame of the land." Speaking in the name of R. Simon bar Yohai, Rabbi Johanan asserts that the explorers had "bad intentions" already when they arrived in Canaan (*NT* 52). They were not really open to exploring; they came to confirm, deny, condemn, or judge, but not openly to examine, not to explore. Their goal was to shame others in public, and choosing to do so was shameful with regard to themselves (since to shame others is a capital offense from the rabbis' point of view), whether the story they are giving out has any basis in fact or not. They concealed the object of the action of shaming, moreover, behind other concerns, namely, "the land" rather than the people. They are in fact shaming the people of Canaan, although they say that they are shaming the ground. Shame is undeniably a theme in the story: the explorers shame the others in slandering the others, in lying about the others, in saying, for example, it is "a land that devours its inhabitants" (Num. 13:32). In the rabbis' view, the shaming of others entails a denial of God. In this way the theme of shame allows us to understand the rabbis' interpretive strategy in this talmudic passage. Shaming the other is a midrashic dislocation of another crime that the explorers are committing, one that speaks more directly to the biblical passage upon which they are commenting; shaming is a midrashic way of thinking out the "fear of God."

What is the "fear of God"? The rabbis understand by it a profound respect, awe, or reverence, or radical appreciation for God, an attitude that they call *yirat shamayim* (literally, the fear or awe of heaven, that is, of God). Without it, they assert, the Torah is of no use to an individual, because "it [*yirat shamayim*] is the very peg upon which everything hangs."[35] Fear of God, in other words, is a way of thinking prophetically; it is a version, we may say, of the law itself, of the Judaic law of anti-idolatry. Akin to what René Girard defines as the anti-sacrificial and perhaps to what Levinas identifies with the holy [*le saint*]—for example, in the title "From the Sacred to the Holy" [*Du sacré au saint*]—fear of God is respect for what will happen if God is not respected.[36] "For Judaism," Byron Sherwin writes, "*yirat shamayim* is almost a synonym for *religion*. . . . While Scripture considers love as the primary attitude of God vis-à-vis human beings, *yirah* is Scripture's primary attitudinal requirement for human beings in their relationship with God. The obligation for one to have *yirah* of God is stated many more times in Hebrew Scripture than is the requirement for one to love God."[37]

The choices are few. "Everything is given to God except the fear of God," the rabbis are fond of saying. If we take that phrase seriously (and it seems to me that the rabbis intend for us to do that) then the fear of God and the fear of human beings are thus mutually exclusive. Where there is the fear of God, there is no fear of human beings. Where there is the fear of human beings, there is no fear of God. The fear on the part of the explorers, both their mindless embrace of the divine promise, and their mindless rejection of the divine promise, are equally "versions" in the rabbis' view of the lack of the fear of God, which is to say, an indication of the denial of God. In this context, then, it becomes clear that all the explorers without exception are wrong from the rabbis' point of view. All the explorers are identified by the rabbis as shameful; the majority report is not singled out for condemnation.

The fear of God means giving up the fear of other human beings. The majority report given by the ten explorers fears other human beings in place of fearing God. And the minority report? Do they not fear God? Their difficulty is the same, the rabbis say, for Caleb and Joshua enact a negative imitation of the ten's rejection of fear of God. The midrashim included in Tractate *Sotah* include two stories that describe their fearfully breaking away from the group. Caleb "separated himself," the rabbis relate, and went to the rock of the ancestors, where he prayed to be delivered from the wicked group and their "plot" (*NT* 51). Joshua seems to have been protected by the special blessing of Moses, which had already singled him out as different from those around him, but he is strangely silent in the biblical passage, when the explorers first return to camp, and the ten tell their shameful tale (51). So they too fear other men; it is just different men that they fear. The majority reporters fear the giants of the other land; the minority reporters fear the other members of the company of explorers and the tribes they represent. If this smaller group really felt right was on their side, could they not simply have gathered their forces and marched into the land on their own? Instead they marched off with the others, with no further discussion of the matter. And when of course the group decides to go on in they are slaughtered, decimated utterly.

Both positions are wrong from the rabbinical point of view. One is idealistic and prizes right independent of might. The other is hyper *realpolitik* and prizes might independent of right. And both are identified as borrowing the perspectives of others, as mimetic, as grasshopperlike, or insectlike, to use the biblical language. The one assumes (from a perspective like that of a child) that "promised land" means it is mine no matter what the others think. And this group has a childish sense of the world. Promised for them means guaranteed; ownership has fallen to me. The other group thinks what has been promised is unrealistic and that God is not in control on his own land. These are the atheists. So there are atheists (the majority report) and deists (the minority report). It is not simply that the idealists are unrealistic and that realism needs to be added to idealism but that the idealists are doing so in negative imitation of what the others are doing and so are just as mimetic as they are. With the exception of Joshua and Caleb, who live to learn from their mistake, none of the first generation is able to cross into the land.

So what, then, would the right answer have been? To embrace God through embracing other men, to enter the land as if one is entering heaven, to do what Abraham did in sojourning in the land and become acclimated to it, or what Jacob did in learning its ways before claiming what he feels is rightfully his, in growing a part of the land, rather than going in with a childish sense of entitlement or a nihilist assessment of *realpolitik*. But that leads us to the door of Levinas's view, to which we must now turn.

LEVINASIAN READING: JUSTICE, ISRAEL, AND THE ASCENT TO HEAVEN

Recognizing that both interpretations (that of the ten explorers and that of the two) are shameful, Levinas poses for himself the question: what should they have done? What would going up to the land be like if done properly from the rabbinical perspective? And he answers: to enter as if entering heaven, as if ascending the ladder to heaven, universal justice, messianic politics. Moreover, and secondly, in addressing the positive side of the rabbinic view, Levinas will also show us precisely how that can be done, namely, by reading; by understanding talmudic passage itself as Israel and its study as the performative of the text of anti-idolatry, a gesture of talmudic reading by which we may come to understand in a new way his view of justice and the political.

Because the biblical text relates that Caleb "calmed the people" (Num. 13:30),[38] but does not explain how he did so, the rabbis offer as a Midrash the following speech, which they attribute to Caleb: "'Has the son of Amram [Moses] done nothing but this?'" Hearing these words, the Midrash continues: "They [the people] then thought he [Caleb] was going to attack Moses and became quiet."

Here is the key moment of Levinas's commentary, the point at which he enters into the rabbinic discussion as a participant:

> [Levinas]: Did he not call him the son of Amram? Has he done noth-
> ing but this?
> [Caleb, continuing his midrashic speech]: He brought us out of Egypt,
> split the sea for us and fed us manna. Shouldn't we listen to him, even
> if he were to tell us to build ladders and ascend to heaven?
> [Levinas]: Where does the idea of a ladder and of heaven, which are
> missing in the biblical text, come from? Does the text say: "We shall
> go up and gain possession of it" (Numbers 13:30)? It is this "we
> shall go up" which the Midrash uses as a pretext to introduce the
> idea of a "ladder to ascend to heaven" (*NT* 65).

Seizing upon the midrashic construction of the "ladder to ascend to heaven," Levinas finds in it an indication of the proper way to "go up" and possess the land—indeed, a way of defining the difference between "messianic politics and all other politics" (65). He projects himself into the part of Caleb and imaginatively continues the speech that the rabbis of old attributed to him:

> [Levinas]: If Moses brought us out of Egypt, split the sea, and fed us
> manna, do you think then that under his leadership we are going
> to conquer a country the way one conquers a colony? Do you think

that our act of conquest can be an imperialistic act? Do you think
that we will appropriate a plot of land for ourselves so that we can
use and abuse it? We are going—and here the text is extraordinar-
ily explicit—we are going toward this land in order to experience
celestial life (*NT* 65).

Here Levinas offers a positive way out of the problem: go into the
land as if one would ascend to heaven; as if one had the proper fear of
heaven or fear of God. Treat the land of Israel, Levinas proposes, as
if to enter Israel was to climb Jacob's ladder to heaven (Gen. 28:12),
indeed, to take on Jacob's very name, which is, of course, appropriately
enough, "Israel" (Gen. 32:29). Commenting upon each line, Levinas
follows Talmud, turning the "even if" of Caleb's midrashic ascent to
heaven into a moral imperative, a means of tropological revelation for
the present time.

> [Levinas]: "We are going into this land in order to ascend to heaven." We
> will not possess the land as it is usually possessed; we will found a just
> community in this land....A society in which man is not exploited,
> a society in which men are equal, a society such as the first founders
> of the kibutzes wanted it—because they too built ladders to ascend
> to heaven despite the repugnance most of them felt for heaven—is
> the very contestation of moral relativism. What we call the Torah
> provides norms for human justice. And it is in the name of this uni-
> versal justice, and not in the name of some national justice or other
> that the Israelites lay claim to the land of Israel (*NT* 65–66).

Justice for him, in other words, is Torah itself! The messianic, universal
justice as an ascent to heaven! From the rabbis' perspective, in other
words, the only proper relationship to God would be neither theodicy nor atheism, but entrance into the land of the future Israel as an
entrance into heaven. Levinas makes clear that this is what the rabbis
have added to the discussion. He also makes clear that his own method
is midrashic by renewing our capacity to read Talmud, by reading it as
a continuation of theirs, which is to say, performatively.

PROPHETIC READING

Levinas's midrashic reading of rabbis in context of Israel, extends the rabbinic reading, and answers question of politics in his own work: the good political, justice, is the messianic, the ascent to heaven, the entrance into Israel. The good politics is always therefore a redemptive politics of the future, as Franz Rosenzweig defines it in *The Star of Redemption* (not a Derridean "promise of a promise").[39] Rosenzweig's schema spells it out. Justice coincides with the moment of the redemptive. The good political is always the future political, is always a politics of the future, of the anagogic.

If we align the ethical with creation, and the good political with redemption, we are always between the ethical and the good political. And it would seem we have avoided facing that fact in one of two ways: displacing either the ethical or the political; acting as if either the ethical or the political is out of place; treating ethics as if it is after the law, and the political as if it is already determinable. Politics is commonly engaged too early, in other words, and the ethical commonly engaged too late. We are in fact, in Levinas's view, always *in medias res*, in the middle of things. The good political is coextant with justice, and the messianic, for Levinas, is Judaism itself; if we misread it, if we read it from our fears, then it becomes a land that uses up its inhabitants. We become grasshoppers and we do nothing but hop from one perspective of moral relativism to another, from atheism to theodicy, or theodicy to atheism.

The good political is what will have turned out to be the case after the ethical is spread everywhere. The first principle must be that the political is always after ethics. But now we understand that there is a second principle, and that the second principle is that politics is always "to come," *à-venir*, to use Maurice Blanchot's words, messianic. Judaism itself is nothing else than the working out of the details of this interim condition. The true politics, the politics answerable to the ethical, is always the politics to come, messianic politics, redemptive politics.[40] Or, in other language, the political is the sacrificial. Any position on the political is premature. The only viable politics is messianic politics; if you act ethically, then everything takes care of itself; if you do not act ethically, then nothing takes care of itself, no matter what you do. Both naive hopefulness and despairing cynicism are equally unacceptable because both assume that the good political has already happened! Naïveté about the sacrificial leads to murder. But cynicism about the sacrificial leads equally to murder.

If we read from God's perspective, Levinas tells us, then suddenly it all makes sense. The Torah is the norm of universal justice. Antisemitism is antihumanism. Judaism is the invention of the human, the responsibility for the other individual, as Levinas told us in the dedication to *Otherwise than Being*. How we shall get from the creation to redemption, from responsibility to justice, from the ethical to the messianic, remains of course to be seen. The promised land only means permitted land. We still have to do something to gain it. But the means are clear: rejection of idolatry, the rejection of the idolatry of anti-idolatry, the adoption of the methods of prophetic reading and midrashic reading, midrashic reading for what has already begun, prophetic reading for what has not yet been completed.

READING THE LAND AS THE TEXT: THE BUILDING OF LADDERS

Here Levinas's renewal points us to the importance of talmudic study. With the rabbis, Levinas sees the proper "ascent to the land" as a profound approach to Torah as read through Talmud. The Scripture itself, with the accompanying talmudic, midrashic, and other rabbinic commentaries, becomes in this instance the land of Israel. On the one hand, this land becomes "the land that devours its inhabitants" if we enter it improperly by thinking we are about to conquer it (since it is rightfully ours), or by thinking it is simply too powerful for us and likely to defeat our efforts (and therefore abandoning completely)—in other words, theodicy or atheism in interpretation. On the other hand, it becomes the land that enacts for us the ascent to heaven about which Levinas speaks (if we read it in the spirit of Jewish renewal that Levinas recommends).

Levinas's reading, which associates the "ascent to the land" of Israel with the study of Torah in context of rabbinic commentary, calls to mind an ancient Midrash from the mystical tradition, recounted in *The Babylonian Talmud* (sometimes called "the core" of the 'Pardes' Tradition). The following translation is from *Tosefta Hagigah* 2:3–4:

> Four entered the Orchard (Pardes): Ben Azzai, Ben Zoma, Akher and Rabbi Aqiva. One peeked and died; one peeked and was smitten; one peeked and cut down the shoots; one ascended safely and descended safely.
>
> Ben Azzai peeked and died. Concerning him Scripture says: "Precious in the eyes of the Lord is the death of His loyal ones" (Ps. 16:15).
>
> Ben Zoma peeked and was smitten. Concerning him Scripture says: "If you have found honey, eat only your fill lest you become filled with it and vomit" (Prov. 25:16).
>
> Akher peeked and cut down the shoots. Concerning him Scripture says: "Do not let your mouth bring your flesh to sin, and do not say before the angel that it is an error; why should God become angry at your voice, and ruin your handiwork" (Eccl. 5:5).
>
> Rabbi Aqiva ascended safely and descended safely. Concerning him Scripture says: "Draw me, let us run after you, the King has brought me into His chambers" (Song 1:4).[41]

In this famous tale of four sages, their exploratory entry into the garden or orchard (*PaRDeS* in Hebrew, sometimes identified with paradise) signals an enactment of scriptural interpretation at four different levels: *Peshat* (literal or plain sense), *Ramez* (allegorical or midrashic), *Drash* (moral or ethical) and *Sod* (mystical or prophetic).[42] The different fates of the individual sages point to exegetical and spiritual dangers at each level. One looks ("peeks") but does nothing. He simply dies. More precious than seeing or looking is loyalty to the Holy One. Another looks and what he does causes him to be killed. Desire replaces respect for alterity. A third (identified simply as "the Stranger" or "Other") looks and acts (speaks?) in judgment. He substitutes human reality for divine. Rabbi Aquiba alone returns, alive and in peace from the perilous land, alone avoiding the sins committed by the explorers in Numbers 13. He does not mistake an idolatrous glimpse for the reality; he does not desire what he sees; he does not speak or act judgmentally in context of what he sees. As a result, Scripture speaks to him; draws him; runs after him; gains, in short, for him access to the Holy One.

Surveying the land and reading the Scriptures are perilous. In the passage we have been discussing from Tractate *Sotah,* one of the rabbis observes that the terrible fates suffered by the Israelites at the entrance to the land resulted from their misinterpretation of it, their misreading of the customs they observed, and their misconstruing of God's intention: " 'It is a land which uses up its inhabitants' (Num. 13:32). Raba taught: The Holy One, Blessed be He, said: I had a good intention but they interpreted it for the worst. My intention was good: wherever they went, the leading citizens died so that, in the confusion, they could not be noticed. Some say: It is Job who died and all the inhabitants were in mourning. But they interpreted it in a bad sense: it is a land which uses up its inhabitants" (*NT* 53). Clearly, the issue in the passage is interpretation itself. Inventing a speech for God, Raba says: "Here is what God says: 'I, God, had a good intention but they did a bad job at understanding it. They misread it. They read it as if I were doing something negative. But in fact my intention was a good one.' " As a result of the explorers' fundamental misreading of God's intention, confusion ensued; what should have been noticed was not noticed. Was Job involved? Were the inhabitants in the land misread?[43] In this way, through a shameful interpretation, the text devours or "uses up" its inhabitants.

Perhaps, Raba suggests, we should give up a reading out of fear and start taking possession of the text, of the land, differently. Perhaps, in other words, taking possession of the text is like taking possession of the land. Maybe the talmudic text is performing in the text by (or through) the text the very drama being described outside of the text. In that case, the way we enter Israel, the way we ascend to heaven, is by reading talmudically, by building ladders.

When the rabbis attribute to Caleb the speech in which he calls for the Israelites to ascend to the land through the building of ladders, they are, no doubt, alluding to other biblical passages related to the ladder to heaven. The first is the tower of Bavel, an edifice reflective of the destruction of the relation to God of prepatriarchal generations, the top of which would "reach to heaven" (Gen. 11:4). The second is Jacob's ladder (Gen. 28:10–12):

> Yaakov went out from Be-er-Sheva and went toward Haran, and encoun-
> tered a certain place. He had to spend the night there, for the sun had
> come in. And he took one of the stones of the place and set it at his
> head and lay down at that place. And he dreamt: Here, a ladder was set
> up on the earth, its top reaching the heavens. And here: messengers of
> God were going up and down on it.

In this passage, the ladder is a site that literally inspires "the fear of God." Jacob experiences the presence of YHWH. He is "awestruck" and exclaims: "How awe-inspiring is this place! This is none other than a house of God, and that is the gate of heaven!" (Gen. 28:17).

The rabbis are not content to let Jacob be merely a literal model of the positive "fear of God," however. The midrashim on this passage, through a process of dislocation, also see Jacob as exemplifying a nega-tive "fear of men," from which he is converted. The rabbis imagine that the vision awakened a fear in Jacob, who saw the rulers of this world upon the rungs of the ladder: "the prince of Babylon going up and coming down, the prince of Media going up and coming down, the prince of Edom [Rome] going up and coming down."[44] When Jacob interpreted the dream as a portent of his own impending fall from prosperity into earthly misfortune, the Lord responded to him in the words of Isaiah 44:2: "But fear not, O Jacob My servant."[45] Only the servant of God, the truly humble one, can climb without fear.

The ladder itself, then, like the land to which one ascends, can be perilous. Using the image of Jacob's ladder, medieval Christian exegetes similarly saw the ascent to heaven as a ladder-climbing. The literature is vast. One thinks immediately of Saint John Climacus's *Ladder of Divine Ascent;* the *Rule* of Saint Benedict, which uses the "scala Jacobis" in chapter 7 to name the 12 degrees of humility; Saint Bernard of Clair-vaux's *The Steps of Humility and Pride,* which answers to Benedict's

Rule by using the same image; Hildegard of Bingen's vision of a pillar, in which "there was an ascent like a ladder from bottom to top";[46] Saint Catherine of Siena's image of the ladder-like tiers of Christ's body — his feet, his pierced side, his mouth — that mark the soul's advance from a penitential compunction to fearless, apostolic preaching;[47] Hugh of St. Victor's image of ladders — labeled with the names of biblical books, the modes of their reading, and the virtues associated with their proper reception — on the different stories of the mystical Ark of Noah;[48] Saint Bonaventure's *Itinerarium mentis in Deum,* which names "six stages of illumination," wherein the soul passes "to peace through ecstatic elevations of Christian wisdom";[49] and Walter Hilton's Middle English *Ladder of Perfection* [*Scala perfectionis*].

One cannot account for this rich medieval tradition without acknowledging its roots in midrashic reading. The Christian reading practice of the *lectio divina* is, Ivan Illich writes, "of Jewish, rabbinical origin, like the plainchant which anchors the lines in the heart. Gregorian chant takes its inspiration from that of the synagogue. The desire to live with the book is also a part of Jewish mysticism."[50] "The process by which the written text of Scripture becomes part of each monk's biography," he concludes, "is typically Jewish rather than Greek."[51]

Midrashic reading, as Levinas practices it, performs the ascent he describes. Midrashic reading understood as the heart of Hebraic rabbinic reading, constitutes a return to the oldest versions of reading we have, readings at one with divine worship, and readings from which Christian understandings as well, from its beginnings until at least the twelfth century, derive. After the collapse of the Temple, and the end of sacrifice, we pray and read. The moral life in this context (in both the Jewish and at least the monastic Christian tradition) is the product of reading itself, reading understood as the practice of anti-idolatry. *Allegoria* was the means by which Hellenizing Jews translated their moral life, the law of anti-idolatry, to a new context, the means by which midrashic assumed a new life in new clothing. The misreadings of allegory to which we have become accustomed since romanticism, as a mode of representation rather than as a continuation of Midrash, perform at the level of critical reading the transgressions described within the Scripture they read: when allegory is thus misread, it constructs for us the idols that remove us anew from proximity to the divine within and without. The act of substituting synchronic reading (whether literal or metaphoric), for diachronic reading of the text (which is to say, for its prophetic metonymic reading), performs the very gesture Midrash enables us to read. Midrashic reading serves to remind us of the traps of reading, the idolatries into which we are prone to tumble, even as we recognize such behavior as our very subject matter.

12

When Pardon Is Impossible
Two Talmudic Tales,
Chaucer's *Pardoner's Tale*, and Levinas

Ann W. Astell

> The pardoned being is not the innocent being.
> — Emmanuel Levinas

> There is only forgiveness...where there is the unforgiveable....
> Forgiveness must announce itself as impossibility itself.
> — Jacques Derrida, "On Forgiveness"

In the long history of thought about pardon, questions about the impossibility of forgiveness have traditionally arisen at one of two poles in the affected relationship: that of the injured party and its capacity to forgive or that of the offender, who must first beg and then accept forgiveness. Emphasizing the first of these, Emmanuel Levinas sees the problem of the unpardonable writ large over the Holocaust; he shares what Derrida calls "the immense and painful experience of the survivor: who would have the right to forgive in the name of the disappeared victims," the dead, who alone "could legitimately consider forgiveness."[1] In "Toward the Other," his commentary on a talmudic text about the refusal of forgiveness, Levinas alludes to the Holocaust and declares, "It is difficult to forgive Heidegger" (*NT* 25). Another survivor (albeit not of the Holocaust, but of the horrors of the Black Death), Geoffrey Chaucer explores in his *Pardoner's Tale* the impossibility of forgiveness from the opposite side of the relation, that of the offender who is guilty of the "unforgivable sin" of despair (cf. Matt. 12:32; Mark 3:28–29), the sin that cuts off the possibility of ever receiving forgiveness.

Rubbing Levinas's talmudic tales and commentary against Chaucer's *Pardoner's Tale,* I argue that the tales do not contradict but complement one other in uncanny ways, each bringing out the hither side, the *unsaid* (and thus the vital saying) of the other. They each uphold (albeit from opposite directions) the firm conditions attendant upon forgiveness, conditions that can make forgiveness an impossibility in the present, while yet referring to an obligatory charity, a responsibility to and for the other, that exists prior to all offense and all pardon, that cannot be annulled, and that maintains the offended and the offender in an inescapable relationship to one another. The impossibility of pardon at a given moment in time demonstrates, in fact, the strength of the bond, the commandment to love and not to kill, that deforms time through its moral priority. The fundamental relationship to the neighbor, also and especially the persecuting neighbor, is unbreakable. Whether one focuses on the offended (as Levinas does, in his talmudic commentary) or on the offender (as Chaucer does, in *Pardoner's Tale*), the character in question becomes a bridge to the other, due to this inexorable relatedness. This holds true both within the tales themselves and in their midrashic function as commentaries on other affected relationships, such as that between Levinas and Heidegger.

The Talmud puts the two tales of Rab next to each other as exempla concerning the seeking of human forgiveness in the face of its refusal. In so doing, it employs what Levinas calls a "paradigmatic method," wherein "ideas are never separated from the example which both suggests and delimits them" (*NT* 21). Such a method works to unsay the said, to make it a saying (again). The concreteness of the example protects and enlivens the principle it illustrates by keeping it from becoming a disembodied concept. Similarly, the multiplication of exempla, which transfer the idea being illustrated from one narrative "climate" to another "wrests new possibilities from it," with the result that "ideas do not become fixed by a process of conceptualization" (23).

If we add Chaucer's *Pardoner's Tale* to the two tales of Rab as a third, belated exemplum and a new narrative "climate" in which to explore principles concerning the impossibility of forgiveness, we see the tale bearing out the possibility of wrongful confession. Like the prophetic dream of Rabbi Hanina, which reveals the unsaid in Rab's confession, the Pardoner's tale is the Pardoner's autobiographical confession told *otherwise*. Whereas the figure of Rab exposes in Levinas's reading the inescapable intersubjectivity between Levinas and his teacher, Heidegger (and that between Heidegger and his teacher, Husserl), foregrounding the disciple's relationship to and responsibility for his paternal master, the figure of the Pardoner can be seen to presage that same relationship from the other side—that of the impotent, despairing father who holds the otherness of the child as a sheer impossibility within himself. For such an old man, there can be no "beginning over again," no child, and no forgiveness. Chaucer figures this despair in a hypocritical sermon and a tale of violent death, but he refuses to end with this ending, reserving that place in his Canterbury collection to the *Parson's Tale* of penitence and futurity. Similarly, Levinas signals an ending—"He never forgave. This is the end of the story"—only to make that ending open-ended, the start of his commentary (*NT* 23). The pilgrim "ways" of Chaucer's Parson, who quotes the prophet Jeremiah, powerfully connect with Levinas's "straight and sure way," the biblical phrase with which he concludes his essay, "Toward the Other."[2]

Pardon Refused: Levinas's Rabbinic Exempla

In October 1963, in the context of a Parisian colloquium dedicated to the topic of forgiveness, Levinas chose to comment on a Mishna and Gemara in the *Tractate Yoma* of the Talmud. He selected these texts of the Oral Law, as he says, because they are not "without immediate relation to the question posed by German guilt" and, in particular, by "new attempts to clear Heidegger, to take away his responsibility —unceasing attempts which, it must be admitted, are at the origin of this colloquium" (*NT* 20, 25).

The Mishna concerns the Day of Atonement, Yom Kippur: "The transgressions of man toward God are forgiven him by the Day of Atonement; the transgressions against other people are not forgiven him by the Day of Atonement if he has not first appeased the other person" (*NT* 12). The Gemara records rabbinic discussions of this Mishna. Levinas comments on these discussions, emphasizing the qualitative difference between offenses against God and one's neighbor. To obtain forgiveness from God, one need only—in the sense of a great aloneness, a "most severe isolation" of conscience—practice *Teshuvah,* the return of one's heart and mind to God in "repentance and good deeds" (17, 19). Since God is always ready to forgive the penitent, the sinner's reconciliation with God is—in a certain sense—dependent upon the sinner alone, whose return to God, fueled by a turning away from sin, is also a return to himself, and whose transgression against God is *ipso facto* an utter self-destruction and thereby a crime against all of one's neighbors. "That an evil requires a healing of the self by the self measures the depth of the injury," observes Levinas (17).

God and neighbor are others to oneself in different ways. God is radically Other in that God is always ready to forgive, whereas the neighbor is, Levinas writes, "in a certain way more other than God: to obtain his forgiveness on the Day of Atonement I must first succeed in appeasing him. What if he refuses?...The other can refuse forgiveness and leave me forever unpardoned" (*NT* 16). Recognizing this possibility, Levinas concludes: "It is thus a very serious matter to offend another man. Forgiveness depends on him. One finds oneself in his hands. There can be no forgiveness that the guilty party has not sought! The guilty party must recognize his fault. The offended party must want to receive the entreaties of the offending party. Further, no party can forgive if forgiveness has not been asked him by the offender, if the guilty party has not tried to appease the offended" (19). What Levinas emphasizes in this list of conditions are the risks involved in the process of human reconciliation. To illustrate these dangers, Levinas focuses in the second half of his remarks on two anecdotes in the Gemara concerned a character named "Rab," who seeks reconciliation with two different neighbors, each time without success.

In the first of these tales, Rab initially plays the part of the offended party, waiting for the supposed offender, a "slaughterer of livestock," to come to him on the eve of Yom Kippur to seek forgiveness. When he fails to appear, Rab decides to seek him out. The Gemara does not state who was really at fault, only that there was "an altercation" between them, so it may be that Rab was at least partly to blame. At any rate, in what Levinas calls a "reversal of obligation," Rab switches roles and assumes the part of the guilty offender who must seek forgiveness, saying, "I will go to him myself to appease him" (*NT* 13). Rab thus seems to be fulfilling the counsel of Rabbi Isaac, given earlier in the Mishnah, that one should be bold in seeking reconciliation: "Go, insist energetically, and mount an assault on your neighbor" (12). Following the commentary tradition, Levinas suggests that Rab in this story is truly an innocent, a just man, who feels so responsible for the bad conscience of the butcher that he goes to him to elicit his request for pardon, to "provoke a crisis of conscience in the slaughterer of livestock" (22) The language of "assault" and "provocation" suggests an underlying aggression, however. Rab is warned on the way that he is about to "commit a murder," a warning that he fails to heed (13). In a bizarre turn of events, Rab speaks no word to the butcher. His mere appearance provokes another offense. The butcher looks up from his work and insults Rab: "Go away, Abba. I have nothing in common with you" (13) At that very moment a bone in the ox head he was hammering breaks loose, strikes the butcher in the throat, and kills him. The butcher's accidental self-destruction is, at the same time, Rab's "murder" of him, as angry words translate into a hammer blow, an upturned head into an exposed neck.

Levinas's commentary on this strange story is brief, but it could easily be expanded, using his writings elsewhere, where he speaks of each one's responsibility for the death of the other as a guilt for a murder. What Levinas does emphasize is that Rab's timing was off. Rab sought a reconciliation that was premature, that did not take into account the time of the Other—the butcher who was not ready to admit wrongdoing or to ask pardon—and that impatience aggravated the Other's self-destructive guilt, a guilt for which Rab was—willy-nilly—responsible.

The tale, writes Levinas, speaks to us "of the purity which can kill in a mankind as yet unequally evolved, and of the enormity of the responsibility which Rab took upon himself in his premature confidence in the humanity of the Other" (*NT* 23).

The second rabbinic tale in the Gemara also concerns a refusal of forgiveness to Rab. This time Rab's offense appears to be clear. Rab was commenting on a text before the famous Rabbi Judah Hanassi, the editor of the Mishnah, in that rabbi's school, when one rabbi after another came in late. Three times in a row, Rab went back to the beginning, starting over for the sake of the late-comer. Then, at the entry of a fourth, Rab did something that was unpardonable: "Rab Hanina bar Hama came in and Rab said, 'How many times am I to repeat myself?' He did not go back to the beginning. Rav Hanina was wounded by it. For thirteen years, on Yom Kippur eve, Rab went to seek forgiveness, and Rav Hanina refused to be appeased" (*NT* 23).

Levinas confesses puzzlement at this story. What is unpardonable about Rab's offense? Was it his impatience, after his patience had been sorely tried? Was it that he singled out Rabbi Hanina bar Hama, who was his teacher, for a discourteous treatment? An "offense between intellectuals" can be "irreparable," Levinas observes (*NT* 23). The Talmud itself asks further questions about this episode. Why did Rab ask forgiveness 13 times, when the teaching of Rabbi Jose bar Hanina is that one should not solicit forgiveness for a transgression more than three times? Is not this excess improper—an annual repetition of himself that more than atones for the single repetition "from the beginning" that he initially refused? The answer given in the Gemara is that Rab is exceptional: "Rab, that is altogether different" (13). But how is he different? As in his remarks on the first story, Levinas interprets Rab as a figure of the just man who recognizes that he has offended his master. In this, Rab is for Levinas a model to be followed: "For has anyone, in any case, ever finished asking for forgiveness? Our wrongs appear to us as we humble ourselves. The seeking for forgiveness never comes to an end. Nothing is ever completed" (24).

Still further questions surround Rabbi Hanina's unbending refusal to forgive—a refusal in obvious violation of the rabbinic principle:

"One forgives all sins of whoever cedes his right" (*NT* 13). The Gemara explains that "Rabbi Hanina had a dream in which Rab was hanging from a palm tree" (23). Concluding from this dream that Rab was "destined for sovereignty," Hanina was determined to keep his student in a position of moral bondage, unforgiven, so that he would leave and exercise his "sovereignty" elsewhere, in Babylon.

Levinas is "ill at ease" with the Gemara's explanation of Rabbi Hanina's refusal to forgive—a refusal that seems to stem not from the gravity of Rab's offense but from Hanina's own wounded pride, his fear of being surpassed and succeeded as head of the school by his gifted student, perhaps even his fear of his own death, if Rab's assumption of leadership presupposes that (*NT* 24). These are all egotistical reasons for refusing forgiveness to Rab when he asks sincerely for pardon. Could it be, Levinas wonders, that the dream reveals to Hanina something in Rab, a prideful ambition, of which Rab himself is unaware and for which he has not asked the forgiveness of his teacher? Did Rab on the day of his interrupted lecture unconsciously entertain "secret ambitions...to take his master's place?" (25). Is he asking Hanina's forgiveness in a prideful spirit, thus aggravating the original offense? "The aggressiveness of the offender is perhaps his very unconsciousness," Levinas concludes (25).

These two exempla of refused forgiveness are Levinas's way of saying *a fortiori* "It is difficult to forgive Heidegger" (*NT* 25). The lines between these ancient stories and the history of Martin Heidegger are far from straight, but Levinas in 1963 cannot reflect on the Talmud without thinking of his former teacher, the philosopher he had idolized in his youth. Unlike the just and brilliant Rab in the Talmud, Heidegger never asked for forgiveness, neither from his master, Edmund Husserl, nor from his students, Levinas among them. Heidegger's offenses are well known. "On May 1, 1933, less than six weeks after Hitler assumed dictatorial powers, Heidegger joined the Nazi party in a public ceremony," relates historian Samuel Moyn. "He assumed the rectorship of the university in Freiburg shortly after the Nazi takeover, colluding in the expulsion of Jews from their positions, rejecting his former Jewish students, even allowing the removal of Husserl's name from the dedication page of his book *Being and Time* because of his honored teacher's Jewish background."[3]

Heidegger's Nazi commitment in 1933 was, in fact, so traumatic for Levinas that it precipitated a great soul-searching and guilt concerning his own previous blindness to what was evil in Heidegger's philosophy. The sound of "Hitler on the radio" reminded Levinas of Heidegger's "firm and categorical voice" in the lecture hall,[4] and Levinas recoiled from it. Whereas Heidegger never asked forgiveness, Levinas did, seeking out the widow of Ernst Cassirer many years later to beg her pardon for having sided with Heidegger against her husband in the Spring of 1929, when the two great philosophers had held a celebrated public disputation in Davos, Switzerland.[5] Perhaps Levinas also worried about a refusal of forgiveness—all the more so because he had once so closely identified with Heidegger, whose philosophy he never ceased to admire, but which he came after 1933 to associate closely with "the philosophy of Hitlerism." For the rest of his life, Levinas was to oppose Heidegger's ontology with an ethics, and by the very strength of that opposition to keep himself held hostage to his teacher, Heidegger, responsible for his failed responsibility.

Levinas's commentary on the two rabbinic tales about a refusal of forgiveness hints at this ambivalence. Levinas interprets Rab *in malo et in bono*.[6] On the one hand, Levinas interprets Rab as a hyperbolic, Levinasian hero: forever guilty because he is humble, never ceasing to beg for forgiveness, and living "as if he had only obligations" to his neighbor and "no rights" of his own (*NT* 24). On the other hand, Levinas sees Rab as a Heideggerian figure, "brilliant," ambitious, hard to forgive, unaware and unrepentant of his own unpardonable offense. In Levinas's reading, Rab is, therefore, at once Levinas and Heidegger and a figural bridge between the two, a subterranean confession of Levinas's own otherness, his heteronomy. Heidegger remains joined to Levinas as the one he does not want to be, but who has become inexorably a part of his life and his responsibility, the other side of his very self.

PARDON UNASKED: CHAUCER'S *PARDONER'S TALE*

The Pardoner is the most Heideggerian of Chaucer's characters and therefore the most susceptible to a Levinasian reading by Chaucer himself. If the Pardoner, like Rab in the Talmud, can be read as a figure of Heidegger (and why not?), then Chaucer's tale may be added to Levinas's talmudic commentary as a midrashic extension of it. The Pardoner, like the exceptional Rab, confesses his offense, but he does so with boasting, omitting any request for forgiveness, and he fails to mention the one thing about which he is ashamed. The seeming totality of the Pardoner's confession in the prologue to his tale is ruptured by the tale itself, which speaks otherwise. The Pardoner's tale—like Rabbi Hanina's dream—expresses in images what is unsaid in his confession. When these images of impotence, despair, and mortality bring the Pardoner's face—his vulnerability—before the pilgrims, a reconciliation takes place among them. Harry Bailly kisses the Pardoner, and the pilgrimage with its tale-telling continues. The reconciliation at the tale's end is not, strictly speaking, a forgiveness, but it offers hope that pardon may yet come. "The will . . . on the way to death but a death ever future, exposed to death but not *immediately*," writes Levinas, "has time to be for the Other, and thus to recover meaning, despite death" (*TI* 236).

The diachronic unfolding of the Canterbury collection leads, in one direction, toward the Pardoner's tale; in another, from the Pardoner's tale to the Parson's. These two directions are nonetheless one, as if Chaucer would agree with Levinas, first, that the homeward path to God ("A Dieu") is an Abrahamic path of dramatic leave-taking ("adieu")[7] and of no return, rather than a circling Odyssey, back to London or Ithaca; and second, that such a nomadic path must first go away from God, through a purifying a-theism,[8] a desertion of God, before it can turn toward him and find him precisely there in the desert, on pilgrimage, in the condition of naked, human wretchedness. Levinas opposes this Judaic wandering to the pagan rootedness of Heidegger's universe,[9] but he also carries Heidegger with him, uprooting Heidegger, willy-nilly, by thinking the ethical, the unthought in Heidegger's philosophy. The pilgrims similarly carry the Pardoner with them, despite his wanting to stop for cakes and ale, his readiness to supply his own makeshift shrine as a substitute for that of St. Thomas. Chaucer himself does not supply that shrine. He ends the fictive journey to Canterbury before its arrival there, as if to underscore a simple truth: in this world of wayfarers there can only be the approach to one's goal, never the reaching of it. Indeed, *The Canterbury Tales* ends, not with an end, but with a new beginning, as the Parson charts the penitential path that is the very way of life toward life and pardon.

This new path, however, is also an old path, inclusive of everything that has preceded it. "The paradox of pardon," Levinas explains, "lies in its retroaction; from the point of view of common time, it represents . . . the reversibility of time," because "Pardon acts upon the past, somehow repeats the events, purifying it. . . . The paradox of pardon refers to pardon as constitutive of time itself" (*TI* 283). The link between pardon and temporality in the thought of Levinas provides an interpretive key for the understanding of Chaucer's *Pardoner's Tale*, whose narrative argument provides a unique, irreplaceable scaffolding for a Levinasian dialectic that moves from the alterity of death to the alterity of the Other, and thus from age to the possibility of youth, pardon, and recommencement. Pardoning the past in the present (but not quite yet), Chaucer's tale has a futurity inclusive of Heidegger and Levinas, for it names in advance the quandary of difficult, perhaps impossible, forgiveness.

As a name for the pilgrim, "the Pardoner" is (more than the name of any other pilgrim) a misnomer, an improper name, a heteronomy. Fearful of being charged with defamation, the Pardoner accuses others indirectly, "By signes, and by othere circumstances" (*CT* VI.419), without naming names: "I telle noght his propre name" (VI.417).[10] Similarly, he tells not his own proper name, but reveals his true identity through circumlocution in the tale he tells. The Pardoner is not a priest who can, in sacramental confession, speak *in persona Christi* the words of absolution. The Pardoner cannot forgive sins, nor is he (it seems) actually authorized to remit the temporal punishment due to sin through the offering of indulgences.[11] People may actually receive God's pardon through their own faith, contribution, and almsgiving on the occasion of the Pardoner's preaching, but that effect is not the Pardoner's intent. The Pardoner does not pardon. That is not an action he performs.

Improperly named, the Pardoner cannot give pardon to others, because he has not first received it in what Levinas calls a "passivity," which is prior to a conscious receptivity and prior, too, to compassion. Far from being responsible for the poor (because lagging far behind his own inescapable responsibility), the Pardoner is ready to take "moneie, wolle, chese, and whete" from "the povereste wydwe in a village," even if her children starve as a result: "Al sholde hir children sterve for famyne" (*CT* VI.448, 450–51). He cares nothing for the souls of others and is unconcerned if they be damned forever after the death of their bodies (VI.405–06).

The Pardoner's hypocrisy in relation to others is symptomatic of a refusal to admit a duality, a *hypostasis,* within himself as an existent.[12] His tale, like Rabbi Hanina's dream about Rab, bears witness to the insincerity and incompleteness of his confession. Although he acknowledges a plethora of sins—hypocrisy, fraud, deception, avarice, covetousness, gluttony, lechery—the Pardoner is unrepentant, utterly lacking in contrition, and unwilling to reform his ways. The vehemence with which his confession claims to be a total disclosure—"myself be a ful vicious man" (*CT* VI.459)—suggests that its seeming totality serves as a distracting lure, to cover up what the Pardoner does not and cannot say about himself, the very thing that would disclose his vulnerability and culpability, unveiling his face, and thus, the Levinasian Infinite.

The tale ruptures that confessional totality. Intended as an exemplum to mirror the avarice in his auditors, the Pardoner's tale is necessarily also a self-portrait, since the Pardoner admits to being avaricious himself: "Thus kan I preche agayn that same vice / Which that I use, and that is avarice" (*CT* VI.427–28). After drinking ale, eating cake, and boasting of his own wenching, he describes the young rioters in the tale as eating, drinking, and yielding to "lecherye / That is annexed unto glotonye" (VI.481–82). Expecting "ribaudye" from the Pardoner, the pilgrims would surely see in the avaricious "yonge folke" of the tale an image of the "yonge" Pardoner (VI.324, 464; III.187).

The rioters at the start of the tale are living what is manifestly an inauthentic existence, in Heideggerian terms. They haunt the Flemish taverns and while away their days playing dice, dancing, drinking, eating, and whoring. At first oblivious to the outbreak of the pestilence and the dying all around them, they suddenly awake to the imminent threat of death at the sound of a bell in a funeral procession. In answer to the question, "What cors is this that passeth heer forby," a "boy," a "child" replies that it is an "old felawe" of theirs who has died only a few hours ago in the night, while sitting "fordronke" on his bench (*CT* VI.668, 670, 686, 672, 674).

Significantly, Chaucer places this announcement and its accompanying explanation on the lips of a child, the favorite persona of the poet, who was himself a child of eight at the first terrible onslaught of the Black Death in 1348. Asked by Philippe Nemo, "How does one begin thinking?" Levinas replied, "It probably begins with traumatisms, a separation, a violent scene" (*EI* 21). In that same interview, Levinas goes on to date the start of his own thinking about the "there is" (*il y a*) to his childhood: "My reflection on this subject starts with childhood memories. One sleeps alone, the adults continue life; the child feels the silence of his bedroom as 'rumbling'" (48).

The child in the *Pardoner's Tale* observes with horror the funeral procession that passes by the window and speaks a truth that the young men inside the tavern are reluctant to hear. Their fellow, he says, has been killed by the same Death who has slain thousands in the pestilence: "Ther cam a privee theef men clepeth Deeth / That in this contree al the peple sleeth" (*CT* VI.675–76). To his iconic description of Death as a thief carrying a spear (VI.677), the child adds a word of warning: "Me thynketh that it were necessarie / For to be war of swich an adversarie. / Beth redy for to meete hym everemoore" (VI.681–83).

Unlike Heidegger, who imagines death as an interiority (indeed, as one's in-most and own-most possibility),[13] Chaucer's "child," like

Levinas after him, presents death as a radical exteriority, as something, as someone, who comes when one least expects "to meete hym" (*CT* VI.683). The child, testifies the tavern-keeper, "seith sooth" (VI.686). In the physical suffering that afflicts a person, leaving him or her "no refuge," no possibility "of retreat," one senses the advent of death.[14] Citing the witness of Shakespeare's *Macbeth* and *Hamlet* (and I would add, Chaucer's *Pardoner's Tale*), Levinas affirms: "Death is...never assumed, it comes" (*TO* 73).

Although the rioter asks his "knave" (*CT* VI.666) specifically to find out the name of the dead man—"and looke that thou reporte his name weel" (VI.669)—the child does not actually name Death's victim, except to say that he is an "old felawe" (VI.672) of the rioter. Instead the child names the killer: "a privee theef men clepeth Deeth" (VI.675). This slippage subtly associates the death of the other, of the neighbor, with Death itself. The speech of the tavern-keeper similarly collocates the "habitacioun" of Death with a neighboring village, where "Bothe man and woman, child, and hyne, and page" (VI.688) have perished in the plague. Death dwells in and with the mortal other. The poet's logic, which moves in a fluid line from a single dead man to Death, from Death to the many dead, is similar to the dialectic apparent in the thought of Levinas, who links the "alterity of death," its exteriority and irreducible otherness, to the "alterity of the other person"—the feminine, the child, and the neighbor, especially the widow, the orphan, the stranger (*TO* 75, 92).

Shaken by the sudden death of their drinking companion, the young rioters decide to meet with Death, to seek Death, and to slay the slayer: "Deeth shal be deed" (*CT* VI.710). In the dark drama of the *Pardoner's Tale*, dead metaphors, especially those associated with death itself, come alive, are personified. Anxious about dying, the young men become beings who are inexorably and literally "toward death" in their quest for Death. The Pardoner describes the quest of the young rioters as a solitary, virile action. Challenged by the peril itself and by the apparent strength of Death, the first rioter swears, "I shal hym seke by wey and eek by strete" (VI.694). Only afterward do the other two, at his invitation, join him in his vow. Theirs is a Heideggerian project that unites them not in a face to face, ethical relationship, but in a side-by-side sociality, a *Mitseinandersein,* which does not disrupt, but rather compounds, the solitude of the "I" in its relation to a "we": "We thre been al ones," declares the first rioter (VI.696). As Levinas explains, "*Mitseinandersein,* too, remains the collectivity of the 'with'... sociality in Heidegger is found in the subject alone" (*TO* 93). The virility of their collective assault on Death is underscored by their sworn blood-pact, each to be the "otheres brother" (*CT*VI.698), but that putative brotherhood is quickly and brutally belied by their murdering of one other. United against the Death they seek, they are divided by the florins they find.

"Death is the impossibility of having a project," Levinas observes (*TO* 74). Like Chaucer, whose narrative argument exposes the folly of the rioters' death-defying bravado, Levinas criticizes Heidegger for the virility with which he proposes to master death. "Being toward death, in Heidegger's authentic existence, is a supreme lucidity and hence a supreme virility. It is *Dasein*'s assumption of the uttermost possibility of existence... Death in Heidegger is an event of freedom," Levinas explains, but he goes on to insist, contra Heidegger, "My mastery, my virility, my heroism as a subject can be neither virility nor heroism in relation to death" (72). Like Chaucer and Heidegger, Levinas is concerned with the question: how is death to be vanquished? "Before a pure event, a pure future, which is death," he writes, "I seek a situation... [which I have called] 'victory over death'" (90–91). The "situation" that Levinas calls "the attempt to vanquish death," to make the ego "other" to itself, is an ethical relationship to the other person, an intersubjectivity, a love that is "strong as death" (Song of Songs 8:6): "The other is the future. The very relationship with the other is the relationship with the future" (77).

This relationship with the other, like the relationship with death, is, for Levinas, passive before it is active. It begins with a call or (more perfectly) an accusation. The man must suffer love at the advent of the feminine other if his subjectivity is to become fecund, if he is through paternity to encounter the otherness of himself in the child, who is, as Levinas puts it, "a stranger (Isa. 49), but a stranger who is... me a stranger to myself" (*TI 267*). This biological and psychological scenario is a scaffolding for Levinas's transcendental philosophy, but a scaffolding that cannot be discarded, because it leads him through the child, who is a stranger to father and mother alike, to grasp the ethical bond that connects and binds each one to all the others. "The continuity of development is that of a dialectic," Levinas explains, "starting with the identity of the hypostasis" (*TO* 92). The very structure of the human subject is a duality, a *hypostasis,* for the subject is subject to another, responsible for another: "Fecundity encloses a duality of the Identical" (*TI 268*).

As Levinas sees it, fecundity is a "triumph over death": "This triumph is not a new *possibility* offered after the end of every possibility—but a resurrection in the son in whom the rupture of death is embodied" (*TI 56–57*). A discontinuous continuity that is "a possibility of myself but also a possibility of the other, the Beloved," fecundity is "the relation with a future" that has been altered, a future that somehow remains "my future," but which is "not a future of the same" (267–68). Through a phenomenological reduction, Levinas is able to conclude: "A being capable of another fate than its own is a fecund being... In paternity,... time triumphs over age and fate by its discontinuity" (286).

In the *Pardoner's Tale,* the young rioters' anxious, virile quest constitutes an attempt to conquer death not by paternity, but by killing. The mysterious Old Man, about whom so much has been written, crosses their path as an expression, means, and guarantee for the fate, the adventure, that is decidedly their own. The very embodiment of sterility, impotence, and despair, the Old Man can neither die nor regain his youth. He can only be forever "toward death." His future is the "future of the same" (*TI* 286). The phallic walking-stick with which he knocks on the ground, calling out to mother earth, opens to him neither womb nor tomb.

His is, it seems, a living death, a grim proof of the scriptural word: "He who does not love remains in death" (1 John 3:14). The Old Man seeks not to substitute himself for another by supporting the other, by bearing the weight of the other, who is also burdened with responsibility, by caring for another—the ethical attitude that is, for Levinas, the only way to vanquish death. Instead, the Old Man looks restlessly instead for someone who will take his place, "chaunge his youthe for myn age" (*CT* VI.724).[15] Levinas objects pointedly to this sort of exchange as a perversion of ethical substitution: "The ego involved in responsibility is me and no one else, me with whom one would have liked to pair up a sister soul, from whom one would require substitution and sacrifice. But to say that the other has to sacrifice himself to the others would be to preach human sacrifice!" (*OB* 126). The Old Man, however, lives in accord with exactly this sacrificial logic. When the young men threaten him, he directs them to go to the grove from which he has just come, to the oak tree where they will indeed find Death (*CT* VI.760–63).

Pivotal to the plot, the Old Man appears as if from nowhere and disappears again. Because he yields his place under the oak tree to the three rioters, the logic of the narrative casts the Old Man as the alter ego of the youths, the manifestation of their spiritual condition. More particularly, the Old Man, at the symbolic center of the *Pardoner's Tale*, appears as a symbol of the Pardoner himself, disclosing the despair that motivates his bravado, the ennui beneath his hedonism, the sexual impotence masked by his fictional womanizing, the restless insecurity beneath his superficial rootedness, the lack of any hope for physical or spiritual paternity, the wrenching alienation from his own mother, father, and Creator. In the dream-like image of the Old Man, the Pardoner confesses himself to be who he is, names himself vulnerable, and associates that vulnerability with a commandment, a version of the Golden Rule: "Ne dooth unto an oold man noon harm now, / Namoore than that ye wolde men did to you / In age" (*CT* VI.745–47).

The Old Man is strangely dressed, "al forwrapped save [his] face" (*CT* VI.718). This poignant, Chaucerian detail—the exposure of the Old Man's face—hints at the ethical truth about which Levinas has reflected so deeply. In the face of the other—that is to say, in the embodied expression of the other's vulnerability, the other's naked exposure to menace, Levinas finds the commandment that grounds all ethical relation: "The face is what one cannot kill, or at least it is that whose *meaning* consists in saying: 'Thou shalt not kill'" (*EI* 87).

The face of the Pardoner's poor, Old Man is vulnerable, subject to the verbal abuse of the young rioters, who insult him. That same face, however, is also threatening, accusing. The Old Man does not simply chastise the youths for their rudeness, but he also points them on their way to Death. The young men are aggressive, yet also anxiously defensive. They see the Old Man as Death's "espye" (*CT* VI.755) and accomplice, and they call him by Death's own epithet, "false theef" (VI.759). Chaucer's poetry thus captures in the face of the Old Man the unnerving combination of vulnerability and threat that Levinas, too, finds in the other. To be exposed to the vulnerability of the other, the neighbor, is like being hit, Levinas writes, by "a shot 'at point blank range'" (*LR* 83). Because "mortality lies in the Other," long before the other dies, "The other man's death calls me into question, as if, by my possible future indifference, I had become the accomplice of the death to which the other, who cannot see it, is exposed" (83). The vulnerable neighbor is also the one who persecutes, who accuses, who would make the unresponsive ego a murderer, liable to death.

The rioters in the tale do, of course, murder each other, enacting the "homicide" (*CT* VI.657) that the Pardoner had presented earlier in his sermon as the endpoint of a concatenation of sins: gluttony, gambling, swearing, cheating, and wrath. The Pardoner abridges the account of their horrible deaths, narrating the murders with chilling brevity—a brevity that is part of the Pardoner's message. In the deaths of the rioters, the Pardoner imagines his own and that of the avaricious in his audience, conjuring up a prophetic, warning death in order to push his listeners to convert, to die (before it is too late) to their sins, and to hasten to seek both his pardon and Christ's in the time that is left.

Levinas associates pardon not only with time, but also with fecundity. Most obviously concerned with "the moral phenomenon of fault," committed in the past, pardon exerts a "retroaction" (*TI* 283). Unlike forgetting (a fault to which the Pardoner is prone),[16] which "nullifies the relations with the past," pardon "conserves the past pardoned in the purifed present," in such a way that pardon is "constitutive of time itself" (*TI* 283). Because it breaks the continuity of common time by making a new beginning, it disallows a "future of the same" (286). In this, pardon is analogous to fecundity, is indeed a kind of fecundity, even as fecundity is a kind of pardon: "The discontinuous time of fecundity makes possible an absolute youth and recommencement, . . . in an existence as entirely pardoned" (282). To forgive another is thus a paternity, a maternity. To be forgiven is to be born anew. "The pardoned being is not the innocent being," Levinas observes, but one who knows "a surplus of happiness" in the possibility of making a fresh start (283).

The very evocation of "pardoun"—a word pronounced six times in the space of 28 lines (*CT* VI.906, 917, 920, 926, 927, 932), alongside synonyms of forgiveness (VI.904), absolution (VI.913, 924, 933, 939), and cleansing—weirdly deformalizes the time of the Pardoner at the end of his tale. The words "And lo, sires, thus I preche" (VI.915) apparently end the Pardoner's dramatic reenactment of his customary preaching in churches, but the Pardoner cannot be contained by his own mark of narrative closure. The past has become so vividly present that he goes on to offer to the pilgrims pardon and forgiveness in exchange for their offerings of money and goods, the outward signs of their repentance. He forgets (VI.919) that he has already mentioned his "relikes and pardoun" (VI.920) and revealed them to be fake.

What are we to make of this crux? Before the Pardoner tells his tale, he asserts his sins, hypocrisy, and fraud. At the end of it, he lays claim to marvelous powers of pardon, of spiritual fecundity. These contradictory speeches serve, however, an identical function, which explains their preposterous exchange. Like the apparent totality of his confession of sin and deceit, the excessively "heigh power" (*CT* VI.913) the Pardoner claims to possess—a power to increase the fertility of beasts and of crops, to "multiplie" them (VI.365, 374), and to regenerate the pilgrims, making them "Al newe and fressh" (VI.928), "clene and . . . cleer" as newborns (VI.914–15)—is a cover-up for what he has not confessed, namely his sexual impotence, his status as "a geldyng or a mare" (I.691), and his despair. Impotent, the Pardoner lives "toward death," which, according to Levinas, marks an extreme passivity, the absolute limit of potency and virility, when "we are no longer *able to be able* [*nous ne 'pouvons plus pouvoir'*]" (*TO* 74).

The remedy for such a passivity *in malo* can only be a passivity *in bono*, the passivity of an accusation that summons one to responsibility. The turn to the hither side of passivity is necessarily a suffering. What else can passivity be but a suffering? Provoked by the Pardoner's description of him as "envoluped in synne" (*CT* VI.942) and perhaps by the Pardoner's double-meaning invitation to him to "unbokele anon [his] purs" (VI.945), Harry Bailly turns on his fellow pilgrim and symbolically castrates him, calling attention to the "coillons" (VI.952) he lacks. Only then does the Pardoner know what the pilgrims know about him. Utterly divested, naked, exposed to the ridicule of the pilgrims—"al the peple lough" (VI.961)—the Pardoner falls silent and answers "nat a word" (VI.956). In this silence, his face alone speaks, as Levinas would say.

Wounded and mute, the Pardoner expresses something that is prior to all language, all sincerity and insincerity—his vulnerability, his mortality. In so doing, he draws out from the other pilgrims what Levinas terms "the idea of responsibility,...which is awakened in the face of the death of the other and which is in the consciousness of guilt that colors all compassion."[17] The Host backs off. The Knight intervenes. Two pilgrims kiss and make up. The pilgrimage continues. The "kiss" is, of course, an "ambiguous sign."[18] The reconciliation between the Host and the Pardoner is not a pardon for the Pardoner, who has not fulfilled the conditions for one. The Pardoner is not contrite; he does not ask for forgiveness. He does not offer restitution to those he has defrauded. He does not resolve to reform his ways. Pardon is as yet impossible, but the relationship of mutual responsibility nonetheless obtains between the pilgrims and offers hope for the eventuality of pardon, the time of forgiveness and fecundity. Death comes—so too may grace.

SUFFERING FORGIVENESS: THE "PARSON'S TALE" AND CHAUCER'S
RETRACTION

Chaucer's *Parson's Tale* may be said to rub against his *Pardoner's Tale* (and, indeed, against all the preceding tales) in a manner similar to the way the sayings of the rabbis in the *Tractate Yoma* of the Talmud rub against both the passage from the Mishna about the Day of Atonement (which is the formal object of their commentary) and (more closely) the two tales about Rab's offenses, first against the butcher and then against Rabbi Hanina. The Pardoner, like Rab, remains unpardoned at the end of his tale. Chaucer's Parson, like the rabbis of the Gemara, seeks to solve the problem of the unpardonable. The tale he tells about the "wey...cleped Penitence" (*CT* X.80) is not, in the end, so very different from the rabbinic discussions concerning the observance of Yom Kippur, with which this essay began.

In the general prologue and in the prologue to the *Pardoner's Tale,* Chaucer points to a relationship of special tension between the Pardoner and the Parson. The Pardoner regularly usurps the pulpits of parish priests; he fallaciously appropriates sacramental authority; he apes the Parson in his preaching. When the Parson, therefore, faithfully stands his ground to fulfill his pastoral office, telling "Moralitee and virtuous mateere" (*CT* X.38) and practicing what he preaches, he stands precisely in a subject position, below the Pardoner who has wrongly taken his place, burdened (like a Levinasian Atlas) with the Pardoner's weight, responsible for the responsibility of the Pardoner. A model of responsibility for others, the Parson is charitable, not avaricious. A holy and humble man, daily penitent for his own sins, he is "to sinful men nat despitous" (I.516), but rather, compassionate.

The "Parson's Tale" is a prose treatise on the tripartite, penitential path of contrition, confession, and satisfaction, the second part of which contains an exposition of the seven deadly sins, their various species, and the remedies for each. Whereas the Pardoner's prologue focuses exclusively on avarice (taking 1 Timothy 6:10 as his theme), the *Parson's Tale* offers a *summa* of the sins, through which the Parson engages the assembled pilgrims in a twilight examination of conscience shortly prior to their anticipated arrival at the Shrine of Saint Thomas, a site that symbolizes the heavenly Jerusalem, the end of life's journey.

The Parson's tale-telling is framed by silences. First, there is the singular, potential silence of the Parson himself, whose truthful tale-telling is conditional upon the pilgrim's assent. In answer to the Host's request for a tale, the Parson replies, "Thou getest fable noon ytoold for me" (*CT* X.31). He will speak, he says, only if the pilgrims "list to heere" his moral message and are willing to listen: "And thane that ye wol yeve me audience, / I wol ful fayn, at Cristes reverence, / Do yow plesaunce, leefful, as I kan" (X.39–41). Then, there is the equally singular, hushed silence of the assembled pilgrims who attend to the words of the Parson and who freely and consciously beg him to speak before he speaks, knowing in advance what he is going to say. The pilgrims unanimously agree that they wish their tale-telling "To enden in som virtuous sentence," and they ask Harry Bailly to tell the Parson that "alle we to telle his tale hym preye" (X.63, 66). As the twisted syntax suggests, through Harry Bailly's word, the "Parson's Tale" becomes their own. At the start of the Parson's "myrie tale in prose" (X.46), the pilgrim narrator avers: "Oure Hoost hadde the wordes for us alle" (X.67); at the end of the Parson's tale, Chaucer alone speaks, not on behalf of a group, but as an individual who is guilty, indebted to each and for each. The profoundly responsive silence of the pilgrims, in which the responsible Pardoner also participates, is the hither side of the silence, the passivity, to which the Pardoner (alone among the pilgrims) is reduced at the end of his tale.

Critics have noted several obviously intended structural parallels between the tales of the Parson and the Pardoner.[19] What is seldom observed about the "Parson's Tale" is that it concludes with a discussion of "whiche thinges destourben penaunce" and thus render pardon, the receiving of forgiveness, impossible—namely, dread, shame, (false) hope, and "wanhope, that is desperacion" (*CT* X.1056), the very condition that afflicts the Pardoner's Old Man and the Pardoner himself. The Parson leaves virtually the last word to "wanhope," to despair—a topic he has treated previously in the middle of his tale, where it appears as a species of *accidie,* the Augustinian anguish of heart that constitutes a depressive and self-destructive sloth. The fourth of seven sins in the Parson's ordering of them, the passivity of sloth is central to the array of vices (even as the impotent Pardoner and his tale are central to *The Canterbury* Tales).[20] Acedia appears next to avarice, the sin that immediately follows it, and with which it is concatenated in a chain leading back to pride.[21] The Parson describes slothfulness as a hellish passivity or indolence, a state (vividly described as a phenomenon by Levinas in *Existence and Existents*) in which one is so paralyzed, so bound by inertia, "that they ne may neither wel do ne wel thynke" (X.686) and find themselves incapable of beginning any good work, including repentance. Burdened with past sins, the slothful person fears to commit even more and therefore persists in an unchanged condition, hoping neither for mercy for the past nor for strength for the future.

Whereas the Parson names the virtue of fortitude the remedy for sloth in part two of his tale, prescribing courage and action as a contrary cure, in part three he urges a stronger medicine, namely, passivity as the remedy for passivity: "Certes, agayns that cursed wanhope sholde he thynke that the passion of Jhesu Crist is moore strong for to unbynde than synne is strong for to bynde" (*CT* X.1072). A passion, a suffering, that is strong! Pushed back to the point of utter helplessness and hopelessness, the one who identifies his impotence as a participation in Christ's on the cross — as a compassion — may find a strength to begin anew on the Levinasian hither side of that very passivity, "wanhope" turning into hope and joy.

The *Pardoner's Tale* ends with a reference to his lacking body, his severed testicles, his impotent relics. The *Parson's Tale,* by way of contrast and as a belated response, speaks in its last lines of the glorified body — radiant, strong, and whole — that is promised to those who perform their penance to the end: "Ther as the body, that whilom was syk, freele, and fieble, and mortal, is immortal, and so strong and so hool that ther may no thing apeyren it" (*CT* X.1078). Referring to "lyf" gained through "deeth" and the "mortificacion of sin," the Parson concludes.

The Parson's words of hope immediately inspire the pilgrim Chaucer's own authorial confession of guilt—the retraction with which he takes leave of his book and prepares for his own death, his "lyves ende" (*CT* X.1090). Asking forgiveness of his listeners and readers for any way in which his writings may have offended, seduced, or scandalized them, Chaucer literally "prays" to them (from within the full meaning of the Middle English word, which discloses a Levinasian transcendence): "Now preye I to hem alle that herkne this litel tretys or rede." He does not (and this is a striking feature of the text) ask God's forgiveness directly, apart from that of his readers; instead, he asks his fellow human beings to forgive him, to pray for him, that is, to substitute themselves for him in prayer: "Wherfore I beseke yow meekly, for the mercy of God, that ye preye for me that Crist have mercy on me and foryeve me my giltes" (X.1084). "It is well understood," Levinas notes, "that faults toward one's neighbor are *ipso facto* offenses toward God" (*NT* 16).

Through his retraction, Chaucer performs the very penitence to which his own Parson has imaginatively called him.[22] In so doing, he substitutes himself for all the tale-tellers in the Canterbury collection in the act of seeking pardon, even as he initially substituted himself for them as the (re)teller, the rehearser, the echoic relater of their tales, which are, in the end, his own. The ending of the Parson's "meditacioun" (*CT* X.55) blurs into the ending of the "litel tretys" (X.1081) that is, at the same time, the ending of *The Canterbury Tales*. Chaucer's language signals the "substitutionary" (to echo J. A. Jackson) series: Chaucer stands at the Parson's place, supporting him, even as the Parson stands at the Pardoner's place as his ethical support. Whereas in the first story-block of the *Tales*, Chaucer (as pilgrim narrator) disavows responsibility for both the other pilgrims' tales—"for I moot reherce / Hir tales alle, be they better or werse" (I.3173–74)—and for his readers' choices—"Blameth nat me if that ye chese amys" (I.3181)—in the retraction with which the collection concludes, he (as author and as fellow-traveler) shoulders his responsibility for all the tales and for their possible moral influence, good and bad, upon others.

Chaucer asks, in particular, for forgiveness from his readers and listeners for "the tales of Caunterbury, thilke that sownen into synne" (X.1086). While the Pardoner's is a self-proclaimed "moral tale" (VI.460), it too has the potential to tempt its readers, sow the seeds of scandal. Chaucer, as the historical author and fictive rehearser of the tale, thus asks, as it were, on the Pardoner's behalf for forgiveness; he pleads for a pardon for which the Pardoner himself has not yet, from within the frozen time of the literary work, explicitly asked. He does precisely what the Pardoner cannot do. He does so, moreover, through a meditative participation in the same passivity that seems to trigger the Pardoner's own memory lapse, causing him to forget himself, to be literally beside himself, detached (at least momentarily) from the burden of his own hypocritical past: "I wol yow nat deceyve" (VII.918). In his retraction, Chaucer names the "precious blood" of Jesus' heart, shed on Calvary, even as the Pardoner calls upon the "precious herte-blood" of "Jhesu Crist, that is oure soules leche" (X.1091, VII.902, 916). Perhaps Chaucer echoes the Pardoner at the end of the *Canterbury Tales* to name with his own guilt and as his own the guilt of another for which he is responsible and thus to seek forgiveness from the one who has borne the guilt of all.

"To rub in such a way that blood spurts out," Levinas writes, "is perhaps the way one must 'rub' the text to arrive at the life it conceals" (*NT* 46). It may be easier for us to forgive Chaucer (and Chaucer's Pardoner) than it was for Levinas (and is for us) to forgive Heidegger, but it would be a grave mistake for twenty-first century readers to ignore the petitions for forgiveness with which *The Canterbury Tales* concludes. Some critics have regarded those petitions as characteristically ironic, as simply providing an excuse for Chaucer to list the literary works upon which his claim to fame as a poet rests. If such is the case, we must deny Chaucer pardon, even as Rabbi Hanina refused to forgive Rab, who asked, but who asked (perhaps without even knowing that he did so) wrongly.

Other critics, citing especially Chaucer's life-long engagement with Dante (among other evidence), are more inclined to read the retraction as expressive of a sincere concern on the part of Chaucer, a

Christian poet nearing the time of his death, to judge himself and his works apocalyptically, to separate the chaff from the wheat.[23] If such is the case, each reader is called to bear witness before the tribunal of Chaucer's own face regarding the singular effect of his writings upon him or her; to render a verdict for or against the accused poet that necessarily involves a self-accusation, a self-judgment; and, finally, to enter a plea, perhaps (but not necessarily) for a pardon of the guilty Other that is also, and at the same time, a request for one's own forgiveness. Still other readers, also taking Chaucer's concern of conscience for his readers seriously, regard the retraction as a purgatorial spiritual exercise, an active participation in a redemptive process, whereby all things, even sin, can be worked to the good (cf. Rom. 8:28) through the power of a higher, divine intentionality that is already operative in the good "entente" (*CT* X.1083) of the poet and the reader alike.[24] For such readers, the forgiveness of Chaucer and of themselves may be an "always already" that is, nonetheless, a "not yet." In each of these three possible scenarios (and there may be more), ethical reading demands that Chaucer's plea for forgiveness, heard across time — "I biseke yow meekly, for the mercy of God" (X.1084) — receives a response, one that only the responsible "I" (and no one else) can give.[25]

13

Those Evil Goslings, Those Evil Stories
Letting the Boys Out of Their Cave

Moshe Gold

A Hyperbolic Levinasian Encounter between Boccaccio and the Talmud

How can stories of allegorical caves help demonstrate the value of ethical criticism summoned and scrutinized by Levinas? Unlike narratives in which, according to Levinas, "image[s] neutralize [the] real relationship" between a concept and an object,[1] Boccaccio's introduction to the fourth day of *The Decameron* and the Talmud's story of Rabbi Shimon bar Yochai in a cave, with their exposure of human bodies and fatherhood, with their complicated attitudes toward the women in their respective narratives, and with their frank attempt to expose the horror of being, reevaluate the Platonic good beyond being. In both stories, fathers must confront the other's finitude, frailty, and mortality. Both retellings of the allegory of the cave (from Plato's *Republic*) stress the Other's interruption of self-possession. In each narrative, the proximity between self and other ruptures the retreat from Being to a safe domicile, one, I should add, that conspicuously provides a domestic space without any women.

"TOWARD APPERCEIVING A NON-ALLERGIC RELATION" WITH SHADOWS OF
THE CAVE:[2] ON MY INABILITY TO WRITE A PROPER CRITICAL PAPER ON
LEVINAS AND LITERATURE

However, before spelunking what I will call interruptive stories of caves—Platonic and otherwise—I feel a need to acknowledge my rhetorical situation. On the one hand, after creating the main essay title printed above, I know I should maintain my professional demeanor as a professor of literature engaged in a rhetorical act; hence, you, my readers, probably expect me to write clearly about ethics or about Levinas. If so, you might expect me to proceed by adducing textual and historical evidence that explicitly states Levinas's knowledge of, for example, Rabbi Shimon bar Yochai (henceforth sometimes called in shortened form, Rashbi). Here, I might have to quote from Levinas's essay "Judaism and Revolution": "Rabbi Simeon . . . is the famous Rabbi Simeon bar Yochai, who has a special place among the *Tanaim*. He and his son spend thirteen years in a cave hiding from the Romans. Jewish mystical tradition attributes the Zohar to him. These facts are important."[3] A large portion of my essay would then attempt to develop "the importance of these facts." In addition, I would need to support my selection of Rashbi as part of my essay's focus by finding evidence of his supreme vigilance, since I will claim that a critic's attitude toward an ethics of interruptive cave narratives should manifest extreme vigilance. For example, I might need to refer to the Talmud's claim that Rashbi's sole occupation was the study of Torah (Shabbas 11a), an occupation taken to an extreme. In addition, you would probably expect me to provide equal attention to both Boccaccio and the Talmud, possibly even supplying what I might call a reciprocal reading of all the texts discussed herein (same technique applied, same motivation expressed, same amount of significance interpreted, and so on). This kind of clear exposition, it would seem, is my responsibility to you.

However, on the other hand, I sense that Levinas's prophetic prose, at times reaching beyond my comprehension, actually lends ethical cadence to his reading of rabbinic texts and his critique of art; hence, to engage in ethical criticism, should I not speak hyperbolically, performatively, in excess of propositional clarity? Might not this be my responsibility to you? Would it then be too hyperbolic to say, right away, that my professed dilemma comes from not knowing what or how to write (or how to utter and undo my "said" in a Levinasian timbre)? After all, in the very last sentence of the preface to *Totality and Infinity*, does Levinas not declare that "the very essence of language . . . consists in continually undoing its phrase by the foreword or the exegesis, in unsaying the said" (*TI* 30)? Hyperbolic vigilance in unsaying, in fact, establishes the critical attitude at stake here. Rashbi's love of Torah was beyond vigilant. His was a Torah existence of constant hyperbolic obsession and elevation. In other words, instead of applying the same Levinasian terms yet again to different texts — only to have Levinas returned to us in the exact same state — I write this essay as an attempt to explore what a performance of hyperbolic ethical criticism might entail.[4]

Hyperbolic performativity, though, does not necessitate writing without clarity. Rather, it demands constant unsettling of one's knowledge of ethical responsibility. When Levinas himself speaks of his own method as hyperbolic, he even speaks of emphasis and exasperation as a philosophical method: "Emphasis signifies at the same time a figure of rhetoric, an excess of expression, a manner of overstating oneself, and a manner of showing oneself. The word is very good, like the word 'hyperbole': there are hyperboles whereby notions are transmuted. To describe this mutation is also to do phenomenology. Exasperation as a method of philosophy" (*GCM* 89)!

What kind of critical work does such exasperation, excess, and hyperbolic vigilance involve? For the purposes of this essay, I will provide what may seem like more analysis of the Talmud than of Boccaccio (thus I will not provide a reciprocal reading); however, there has still not been enough critical attention to the importance of talmudic narrative in Levinas's strong claims about art. Boccaccio, though, is not a secondary thinker or writer here; his own authorial interruptions to critics (as expressed in his introduction to the fourth day) will, in fact, alter the dynamics of the entire "excess of expression." Boccaccio's own criticism displays a different "manner of showing oneself" (*GCM*

89) by addressing his audience directly and by proclaiming his own attempt to please others. Boccaccio's interruptive cave tale enacts a rewriting of Plato's allegory of the cave in order to provide a defense of literature! The irony cuts deeply: when read with Plato's allegory of the cave from *The Republic*—the very work that (according to conventional interpretations) exiles most poetic mimesis—Boccaccio's cave story radically alters Plato's philosophical creation into a (narrative) defense of Boccaccio's literary writing.

The Talmud's use of narrative also provides a defense of stories in the midst of another (more technical and legal) discourse, which a cave story interrupts. If the work of hyperbolic ethical criticism demands extreme vigilance, then I must ask, what does the story of Rashbi—a critic of mediation and nonintensity—living in a (Platonic) cave mean for ethical criticism? In the Talmud, Rashbi is often depicted as a man of extremes. For example, he is quoted as saying "If a man plows in the plowing season, and sows in the sowing season, and reaps in the reaping season, and threshes in the threshing season, and winnows in the season of wind, what is to become of Torah? No; but when Israel performs the will of the Omnipotent, their work is performed by others" (Berakhot 35b). One must submit entirely to the will of the Infinite. In other versions, Rashbi expresses an even starker position: "Only to those who have manna to eat is it given to study the Torah. For behold, how can a man be sitting and studying when he does not know where his food and drink will come from, nor where he can get his clothes and coverings? Hence, only to those who have manna to eat is given to study the Torah" (Mekhilta de-Rabbi Yishmael, Va-Yassa 3). According to this sage, the location for rigorous study is the desert or a utopian messianic era when, under (ostensibly) supernatural conditions, there is no need for human beings themselves to deal with natural, earthly, agricultural work.[5] Sustenance will be provided by divine grace. One gets the impression that Rashbi wants nothing to do with grains or this earthly world. How can I suggest an "unsaying of the said" here? Can I really attend to much significance here beyond the said?

To make matters more problematic, my desire to grasp and enjoy my critical labor here tends to distance myself from you, my reading audience. I still want to hear and echo the solicitous sound of Levinas's ethical critique of stories, but the jarring voices of good storytellers fight against Levinas's own voice. Perhaps if I were to pose my problems as a theoretical question, I might ask: In a world of disease, plague, deception, and idolatry, how can we read an allegorical story of the Good without being contaminated by Being? Or, how can I direct my effort "toward apperceiving in discourse a non-allergic relation with alterity" (*TI* 47)? If many critics are correct, then for Levinas—especially in "Reality and Its Shadow"—stories behave without propriety by creating disorder and by causing us to evade our responsibilities; if so, then critical interpretations of stories might reset our responses back to their proper position. Art, it would seem, removes us from the real historical world of the other's needs and demands, but critique can make us acknowledge the other who utters a story.[6] In fact, Levinas himself supports such an understanding when he claims that criticism should move "the inhuman work of the artist into the human world" (*LR* 142). In this essay, however, I suggest that we must, with utmost vigilance, continue to question this standard understanding of Levinas's position. The very last sentence of "Reality and Its Shadow" demands that we critics "have to introduce the perspective of the relation with the other without which being could not be told in its reality, that is, in its time" (143). So many of Levinas's own lectures on talmudic stories accentuate, in fact, the holiness of "the perspective of the relation with the other." Moreover, unlike one traditional acceptance of Plato's claims in *The Republic*—namely, if you want to tell stories make sure you tell nice stories that praise God—Levinas does not necessarily remove stories from what he names "religion," namely "the bond that is established between the same and the other without constituting a totality" (*TI* 40).

Moreover, Levinas's own voice, however compelling or dissonant, constantly interrupts my sense that I have heard his story. Perhaps Levinas suffers to create these interruptive moments because he wants his audience to rub abrasively against his language. At those moments when an author interrupts the narrative's sense of totality, when the author acknowledges the ruse, the rhetorical exploitation, the corruption involved in the story, then the proximity between art and criticism shifts.[7] Instead of applying a Levinasian method to stories—and I am not even sure what such a method would look like—I would rather personally heed the summons of Levinas's talmudic exegesis: "to rub in such a way that blood spurts out is perhaps the way one must 'rub' the text to arrive at the life it conceals...to make it spurt blood—I rise to the challenge!...One must, by rubbing, remove this layer which corrodes [the words of] the text" (*NT* 47). By rubbing Levinas's texts, do I not cause the life of his words to spurt blood, and, by doing so, do I not respond to the obligation Levinas has summoned me to—the height of the good? This critical sensation, I should add, usually does not lead to pleasure. It, so to speak, rubs me the wrong way. It is discomforting. However hard I try to soothe or join Levinas's texts together, his blood keeps spurting out. Moreover, good ethical criticism demands something better than the onanistic enjoyment of more traditional critical strategies. A critical rub should not sacrifice stories as reductive examples of philosophy, the love of wisdom. Rather, by rubbing Levinas's reading of the good, I sacrifice my own understanding of Levinas to the higher wisdom of the love of the good. In other words, my inability to address you, my audience, properly and ethically, might just signify a trace of that which Plato's allegorical cave could never entirely reveal to us: the good. Indeed, the hyperbolic and holy vigilance of Rashbi's experience in and out of the Platonic cave will reveal what Levinas might even consider calling "an extreme vigilance of the messianic consciousness" (*TI* 285).

Up to the Neck and Against the Grain: Natural Living and a Special Diet

As it turns out, Plato's well-known allegorical story of life in and out of a cave is itself allegorized, I argue, in Boccaccio's *Decameron*, and can be read against its grain in the Talmud's famous story of

Rashbi, who literally lives up to his neck in grains of sand when he lives in a cave. Unlike the latter tale, Boccaccio's interruptive tale (in his introduction to the fourth day) is much more familiar to Boccaccio scholars and Medievalists in general.[8] A perusal of the story reminds us that Boccaccio's narrative takes us to an author's incomplete story of Filipo Balducci, whose wife dies, and who withdraws to "a tiny little cave with his son, fasting and praying and living on alms."[9] With great resolve, the father takes "great care not to let [the son] see any worldly things, or even to mention their existence, lest they should distract him from his devotion" (*TD* 286). The boy never leaves the cave, nor does he see any living thing other than his father. Boccaccio then tells us that after many years, upon the son's first visit to Florence, Filippo's boy sees all sorts of objects that fill him with amazement. After receiving answers from his father that satiate the son's curiosity about these objects, Filippo and son "chance" upon "a party of elegantly dressed and beautiful young ladies," whom the father calls evil goslings ("papere") whose "bills are not where you think, and require a special sort of diet" (287). The father, though, realizes that "his wits were no match for Nature" (287); his son is now "captivated" (288) by these ladies. At this point, Boccaccio stops his narrative, claiming to "have no desire to carry this tale any further" (287), and proceeds to address his audience and his critics.[10]

The rabbinic narrative, I imagine, is not nearly as well known. Even though the text is relatively long, this talmudic digression, a critical interruption of sorts, might captivate you, my readers, enough to challenge traditional reading of Plato's cave and Levinas:

> R. Yehuda, R. Yose, and R. Shimon [bar Yochai] were sitting, and Yehuda ben Gerim was sitting next to them. R. Yehuda opened and said, "How pleasant are the deeds of this nation [Rome]. They established markets; they established bridges; they established bathhouses."
>
> R. Yose kept silent. R. Shimon bar Yochai answered and said, "All that they established, they established only for their own needs. **They established markets to house *harlots* there**, bathhouses to make their bodies beautiful, bridges to get tolls."
>
> Yehuda ben Gerim went and told over their words, and [the words] were heard by those in power. The governing authorities said, "Yehuda

who elevated [Rome], he shall be elevated. Yose, who kept silent, he shall be exiled to Tzipori. Shimon [bar Yochai] who disparaged [Rome], he shall be executed."

He [R. Shimon bar Yochai] and his son [R. Elazar] hid in the house of [Torah] study. Every day his wife would bring them bread and a pitcher of water, and they would eat. When the [Roman] proclamation became worse, he said to his son, **"Women are simple-minded [the minds of women are light on them ('nashim daitan kalah alahen')]; perhaps they [the Romans] will torture her ['metza-ari'/cause her to SUFFER] and she will reveal our [location]."**

They went and hid in a cave. A miracle happened; a carob tree and a spring of water were created for them. They removed their clothes, and would sit in sand up to their necks. All day they would study. When prayer-time arrived, they would put on their clothes, cover, and pray. Then they would go back and remove their clothes so they would not wear out.

They dwelled in the cave for twelve years. Elijah came and stood at the mouth of the cave. He said, "Who will inform the son of Yochai the ruler has died and the proclamation has been annulled?"

They came out [of the cave]. They saw men plowing and sowing. They said "[These men] forsake the life of the World-to-Come and busy themselves with the transitory life!" **Every place they turned their gaze would be burned immediately. A heavenly voice went out and declared to them, "Have you come out to destroy *my world*? Return to your cave!"**

So they returned and dwelled [in the cave] twelve months, a year. They said, "The sentence of the evil ones in Gehinnom [Hell] is twelve months." A heavenly voice went out and declared "Go out from your cave!"

They went out. Every place R. Elazar destroyed, R. Shimon would heal. He said, "My son, *the world* has enough with you and me."

As night began to arrive on Friday [twilight before the Sabbath], they saw a certain old man who was grasping two bunches of myrtles, running as twilight came. They said to him, "Why do you need these?" He answered them, "to honor the Sabbath." "But isn't one bundle enough for you?" "One is for 'zachor' [remember the Sabbath (Exodus 20:8)]; one is for 'shamor' [observe the Sabbath (Deuteronomy 5:12)]." He said to his son, "Look how dear the mitzvot [commandments] are to Israel." They were appeased.

R. Pinchas ben Yair, the son-in-law, heard and went out to greet him. He took him into the bathhouse, and was massaging his flesh; he saw that there were cracks in his [R. Shimon's] skin [body/flesh]. He started crying, and tears fell from his eyes and **caused him [R. Shimon] to cry out in SUFFERING ["metzavkha"].** He [R. Pinchas ben Yair] said to him, "Woe is me that I see you like this." He [R. Shimon] said to him, "Fortunate are you for seeing me like this, since if you had not seen me like this, you would not have found in me so [much knowledge of Torah]." For at the start, when R. Shimon ben Yochai would ask a question, R. Pinchas ben Yair would answer with twelve solutions. However, in the end, when R. Pinchas ben Yair would ask a question, R. Shimon ben Yochai would answer with twenty four solutions.

He [R. Shimon bar Yochai] said, "Since a miracle transpired, I will go and improve [establish] something." Since it states, "And Jacob arrived whole ['shalem'/intact (Genesis 33:18)]." And Rav said, "whole in his body, whole in his money, whole in his Torah." "And he encamped ['vayikhan'—from 'khayn'/gracious] before the city [was gracious to the city]" (Genesis 33:18). Rav said, "He [Jacob] established a coin for [the city]." Shamuel said, "He established markets for them." And R. Yochanan said, "He established bathhouses for them."

He [R. Shimon bar Yochai] said, "Is there something to improve [fix]?" They said to him, **"There is a place that has unclear status of impurity, and it is difficult ['tza'arah'/causes SUFFERING] for Kohanim [priests] to go around."** He said, "Is there anyone who knows if there was a presumption of purity established here?" A certain old man responded to him, "Here, ben Zakkai would cut lupines of teruma [so a location of purity]." He also did the same. Everywhere [the ground] was hard, he proclaimed tahor [pure]; everywhere [the ground] was soft, he marked [as impure].

A certain old man [or the same certain old man] said, "Ben Yochai has made a cemetery pure." He [Rashbi] said to him, "If you had not been with us, or even if you had been with us, but had not been counted with us, then what you say would be fine. Now that you were with us, and you were counted with us, [others] will say '*Harlots* **braid each other's hair [paint/dye each other], should not Torah scholars certainly?!**'" R. Shimon turned his eyes on him and his soul left [he died].

He [R. Shimon] went out to the market; he saw Yehuda ben Gerim. He [R. Shimon] said, "Is this one still *in the world?*" He put his eyes on him and made him into a heap of bones. (Shabbat 33b–34a, my translation and emphasis)[11]

The immediate similarities to Boccaccio's story are striking: Filippo's resolve "to withdraw from the world and devote his life to the service of God" (*TD* 286), and Filippo's time in the cave with his son—taking "great very great care not to let him see any worldly things...never permitting the boy to leave the cave or to see any living thing except his father" (286). Indeed, like Boccaccio's tale, the story of Rashbi presents us with another father and son who live in a cave glorifying "the life eternal" (286). Yet, there are important differences. For example, unlike the death of Filippo's wife, what motivates Rashbi's entry into the cave? The Talmud informs us of Rabbi Shimon bar Yochai's denouncement of Roman establishments. Someone tells over the Rabbi's derogatory remarks and the Romans overhear the remarks. A death sentence is immediately decreed on the Rabbi, who proceeds to leave his wife, since she might reveal his location under torture—a departure which intensifies the tale's challenges to human responses to suffering—and together with his son hides in a cave for many years.

When they first leave the cave, they scorch the earth when they see quotidian life seemingly not devoted to eternal pursuits. Commanded by a voice from heaven to return to their cave, they spend another year in exile. When they finally exit again, they see someone preparing for the holy time of the Sabbath, one of God's commandments, and the father rehabilitates his earlier sense of social justice, establishing and fixing social spaces for proper use. The wife, though, does not reappear in the narrative. However, women are not completely absent from the tale since the figure of harlots, for some reason, frames and interrupts the narrative structure. At the start, harlots—dare I say "evil goslings"?—are Rashbi's stated reason Rome established markets; at the end, harlots are better than the individual who critiques the Rabbi's purification of the earth, a decree that stops priests from their small suffering of unnecessary walking around impure ground. Moreover, as we move from the potential suffering of the wife to the actual suffering of the priests, we witness the Rabbi's own suffering body as his son-in-law rubs the wounds in his flesh, wounds caused by living naked in the sand of a cave. How might a Levinasian rubbing of these stories call out to these cave dwelling fathers and sons? What act of saying is a critic to attempt—either to vocalize, write, hear, or read—when faced with Balducci's goslings, or for that matter, with R. Shimon bar Yochai's wife? Can ethical criticism only address fathers and sons in the light of goodness? Are we left with boys who seek control of the dwelling space and even seek to expand their power beyond the confines of the cave?

Now, my responsibility to you, my readers, is once again, I feel, an impossible duty to fulfill; I cannot possibly provide an effective reading of all these texts in the allotted space of an academically published essay. With the hope that beyond the confines of the space here, you will critique these shadowy allegorical caves yourselves, I will just suggest a few ways these texts irritate and rub each other in order to convey the degree to which I feel something is amiss in the more calming readings of Levinas's ethics (including his own reading of art). These seemingly easy-to-read stories enact what is at stake: the interruptive dimension of the stories heightens the critical imperative to address the living time of the Other.

Is it not curious that both Boccaccio's story and the Talmud's story deal with a father and son who leave society to spend years in a cave before encountering human others? Plato's cave has been revamped. No longer is there a Platonic wise man who must leave the shadowy cave to experience the Sun, only to return with, pun intended, en*light*enment to others. The question is now what relation, if any, exists between these Platonic retellings and Levinas's seemingly Platonic denunciation of art and elevation of the good beyond being? After all, does not Levinas want to guard us against that deceitful idol of false forms and images, that thing known as art? And yet, if Levinas proclaims that meaning in the irreducible nakedness of the other's face "is to return to Platonism in a new way" (*CPP* 101), might we not acknowledge "a new way" in Boccaccio and the Talmud, one that still realizes the risks of art's deceptions? Might "a new way" also entail what Levinas calls an experience? According to Levinas, genuine "experience must even lead us beyond the nature that surrounds us...Truth would thus designate the outcome of a movement that leaves a world that is intimate and familiar, even if we have not yet explored it completely, and goes toward the stranger, toward a *beyond*, as Plato puts it" (48). But how might interruptive cave stories (in Boccaccio and the Talmud) signify attempts to trace "a new way" toward a "beyond" as Plato might put it — yet a transcendent beyond embodied in specific human others, not abstract conceptions? Even an author, such as Boccaccio, must, after hundreds of pages, leave his comfort, his brigata, his by now intimate and familiar world to proclaim the fact that he is still here for his readers, giving himself to others. True, his art soon engulfs his interruption, but is he completely removed from any "new way"?

The possibility that Levinas is well aware that art can imitate imitation, thereby providing a critique of imitation in artistic form, needs to be faced if art is to be experienced as anything other than idolatrous mimesis. As Pierre Hayat suggests, "it can also be supposed that aesthetic experience, by its resemblance — even deceptive — to ethics, teaches the language of 'otherwise than being.'"[12] Levinas's critique of artistic shadowing does not simply repeat Plato's diatribe against mimetic ignorance. Epistemology is not Levinas's main issue. Rather, Levinas's writing attempts to confront the good emanating from the Platonic allegory of the cave itself. Does not Levinas himself say that it "matters little that Plato made of it [the good] an idea and a light source" (*OB* 19)? If I were to use what critics might call Levinasian language, I would probably say that the allegory might passively be waiting to be read as ethical, not just mythic; critical, not just artistic; rupturing, not just totalizing; and most surprisingly, as holy, not just sacred.[13] Perhaps the cave in Plato, Boccaccio, and the Talmud takes us to a space wherein we can sense an ethical height, one Levinas calls a "curvature of intersubjective space [that] inflects distance into elevation" (*TI* 291). Perhaps this curvature and inflection might even help us deal with the fact that Boccaccio's cave does not appear in the midst of thematic conversation between members of the brigata, but surprises us when the author talks to us, in first person, interrupting his ordered design. Boccaccio's cave story, it turns out, is his unanticipated gift to his audience. His personal interruption at the start of the fourth day introduces ethical criticism in a form of narrative discourse.

"THE NAKEDNESS OF THE FACE" INTERRUPTING TALES — [14] OR, HOW CAN NARRATIVE TRUTH BE FOUNDED ON THE CALL TO JUSTICE?

There is something deeply unsettling about the way these stories abruptly break off from narrative closure. After all, to return to Rashbi, the last image we have of Rabbi Shimon bar Yochai in our talmudic narrative is the Rabbi's gaze upon another which kills the other person, turning him into "a heap of bones." This haunting image from the talmudic narrative, then, at least on an initial reading, appears to validate the violence of the self's vision.

Both the opening and the closing talmudic scenes reveal the intensity, the extreme, the excessive, the hyperbolic character of Rashbi. He must evaluate the Roman institutions as only abusive and horrid—period, without qualification. Either one embraces Roman idolatry or Jewish Torah; there is no possible passage from one to the other. Yet, Rashbi's wife interrupts this opposition. She silently passes sustenance from the outside world to her husband and son as they hide out in their house of study; Rashbi's response is to leave her since her future time contains the possibility of her "tza'ar"/her suffering, her torture and rape by Romans.[15] In other words, R. Shimon's response to an other's projected suffering is to flee. The woman, in between the Roman world and the masculine world of Torah study, leaves the narrative discourse as well. Yet, whose body suffers violently? The masculine body of Rashbi, out of which hyperbolic denunciation comes forth, scorching the earth and harming others! Even a cry from on high, from the highest good, orders R. Shimon to get back to his cave before he commits more violence!

Prior to cave existence and experience, Rashbi cannot attune his mood to the embodied goodness in women. After all, besides his comment that "the minds of women are light on them," he has also stated that the Romans established markets "to house harlots there." The figure of harlots obviously has nothing whatsoever to do with extreme Torah sages. Is this not what is said in the static narrative form? Yet, R. Shimon's adjusted attunement to embodied post-cave existence and suffering asserts a connection between scholars and harlots! Even though harlots were the reason for markets (in pre-cave discourse), harlots become better than the man who critiques R. Shimon's purification of the earth, a decree that stops priests from their small suffering of unnecessary walking around impure ground: "Harlots braid each other's hair [paint/dye each other], should not Torah scholars certainly?!" This analogical saying acknowledges a possible passage from the market (which is the exact location R. Shimon "went out to" at the end of the story) to the hyperbolic existence of the male Torah scholar. Indeed, as Levinas says, to "explain the notion of [ethical] substitution, it is necessary that I say more, that I use hyperbole" (*GCM* 91).

If we look retrospectively at the moments of suffering in the text, we move from the priests' suffering, pass through R. Shimon's own bodily suffering (as his son-in-law rubs the flesh wounds caused by naked existence in the cave sands of the earth), and pass back to the futural, nonexistent suffering/rape of the unnamed wife. What transpires in this passage? Hyperbolic nature, supernatural transcendence in a cave: no baked bread, no society, no markets, no human others. The image captures the brute naked existence of bodies buried in the sand, only clothed to pray. Miraculously sustained, son and father study Torah. Would it be too much to say that Rashbi has found his messianic desert of miraculous manna (as the said would have seemed to indicate from our earlier sources)? No harlots; no wife. Torah itself with a male companion is taken here to the ultimate extreme. The story challenges us with hyperbolic existence and method par excellence. Indeed, the rebirth of father and son from the cave is, in a strong sense, autochthonous, without need for a woman's reproductive body. Yet Rashbi's wife turns out not to be a danger to humans; Rashbi is the danger! He leaves the cave to eliminate fecundity and life. The transcendence of height, the heavenly voice demands that father and son return to their exile.

After another year of cave existence, the men leave not really changed until they encounter a human other who engages in preparations for holy time. As Levinas would point out, the larger subject matter of this specific talmudic discourse is, in fact, the need to prepare for the holy time of the Sabbath. Indeed, our story is framed by (or better, interrupts legal discourses on) women's obligations to prepare for this holy time. The mishnah[16] before our cave claims that one reason women die in childbirth is that they were not careful regarding the kindling of Sabbath candles (Shabbas 31b). The mishnah after our cave claims that when a man comes home on Sabbath eve, he must ask his wife if she has properly prepared for the holy time—including kindling the Sabbath lights (Shabbas 34a). What is the significance of this frame and what is its relevance to the narrative of Rashbi?

This aside of mine, this move to the technical (halakhic) portions of the Talmud, turns out to be essential to any reading of Levinas. The Halakah, that is, the walking in life following Torah and rabbinic law, does not appear to provide justice here; for Levinas, justice should exceed any specific law. Why should a woman die for not properly kindling Sabbath candles? There is no biblical commandment that decrees any such law. Our cave narrative interrupts the more technically legal sections of the Talmud to respond with the ethical force of an interruptive cave that goes beyond previous Platonic versions. Preparation for holy time goes beyond the letter of the law. The human other who carries myrtles runs to bring pleasantness into his home.[17] This old man's very life is saved, and, one could argue, saves father and son from more exile, by the particular act that demonstrates a move, a running, beyond the letter of the law. Rashbi confronts an other's finitude, frailty, and mortality, but he also encounters human labor for the height of the good. The fecundity of the earth, the labors of plenitude, can create awareness of proximity between husband and wife, between self and other. At this point, Rashbi will not flee from corporeal suffering (real or futural) to a masculine-only space. He experiences the vulnerability to others that exists at the most extreme realm of the self.

However, the story interrupts any sense of security, safety, comfort, and ease of vigilance. We do not leave the story with a nice moral said. Rashbi kills. We are left with a haunting image, a grotesque image of flesh leaving a human corpse's bones. The violence of Rashbi's totalizing vision radically transforms a human being into "a heap of bones." Perhaps the Talmud's overall representation of Rashbi presents us with an ultimate example of Levinas's contention (in *Totality and Infinity*) that a separated self has the potential to be a tyrant and has the potential to welcome the other.

What, we must wonder, can sanction such violent murder? Unlike many children's stories of goodness, in which readers end with a feel-good sense of "be good and kind and nice to others"—a morality we can too easily think we understand—this story demands adult acknowledgement of ongoing power over others. In a completely unexpected manner, does the story not suggest the holiness of infinite goodness? Rashbi's burning of the very earth in which we labor and enjoy, echoes, in fact, the violence of Levinas's goodness (albeit the trace of the good in *Otherwise Than Being*). The good that is other than being, says Levinas, "destroys without leaving souvenirs, without transporting into museums the altars raised to idols of the past for blood sacrifices, it burns the sacred groves in which the echoes of the past reverberate" (*OB* 18). The irreducible signification of the good violently burns sacred accounts of being, especially a being (Yehuda ben Gerim) whose account heard by oppressive political authorities casts more than aspersions on someone's ethos.[18] Rabbi Shimon's violent irruption reacts to more than a breach in courtesy. Rubbed critically, until we suffer to understand, the violence tears us away from easy and clear notions of religion and ethics; it demands that we counter slander, that we oppose those who would easily dismiss the life of those in this world and the life of this world itself. As the heavenly voice of the infinite Other proclaims to father and son when they first scorch the earth, "Have you emerged from your isolated existence with Torah study in your miracle-filled cave in order to destroy My world? Return to your cave!" We must learn from the miracle of nature, from the sensuousness of our naked bodies and our burial in the earth, from the power of the shadowy cave to help those in the sun who suffer to cultivate their gardens. Only by "taking up a position in being such that the Other counts more than myself" can we confront those who oppose others (*TI* 247).

My own writing cannot take up such a position consistently or constantly. So I ask a basic question: why am I horrified at the end of this story? In part, I feel either my inability to comprehend death, or feel my desire to provide a clear resolution to murder (perhaps by saying, "well, the individual must have been an evil person or intended evil"). The Talmud demands nearly unbearable vigilance. There is no real total solace for others. This narrative keeps interrupting my complacency. But more than any interruption, this "new way" out of Plato's cave traces, or marks, or signifies something and some time that can never be represented fully, namely a messianic time and perspective in this world—"an extreme vigilance of the messianic consciousness" (*TI* 285). It addresses the obligation for unending, hyperbolic vigilance to others. Indeed, it challenges notions of utterly mutually exclusive realms between Torah and non-Torah realms. Where is Rasbhi at the end? In the market, the exact location that Rashbi first said was despicable and inhabited by harlots! Before encountering the old man with myrtles who prepares for holy time, the hyperbolic lover of ideal existence (an ancient version of Platonism) can still contrast his self with all inferior forms. Once encountering the pleasantness beyond the letter of the law, once in the bathhouse suffering from rubbed wounds, once purifying ground that caused suffering for priests, the figure of Rashbi, beyond the said, signifies a trace of true transcendence in this world, a trace of goodness and ultimate responsibility.

The story—that which risks being totalizing, idolatrous, corrosive, and corruptive—makes literal and particular what one experiences as complex and difficult to comprehend. The Rabbi needs the holy connection to divine transcendence in the cave to gain Torah wisdom (indeed, as the bathhouse discourse clarifies, Rashbi's analytic skills have multiplied dramatically; he is now a master Teacher). This Sophia, this wisdom, this techne, is absolutely valuable, crucial, and necessary, but insufficient for ethics. A philosophy, a love of wisdom that evades (and even does violence to) proper responsibility to others, a philosophical attunement to wisdom without acknowledgment of the good in the gift of the physical, material, labored-over world and embodied in human production and reproduction (including storytelling)—such wisdom will not suffice to help the suffering of others, nor will it heed the demands and commands of the infinite goodness of the ultimate height of supreme elevation (as the voice from heaven enunciates). As Levinas declares elsewhere, "in rabbinical thought, to obtain grace it is absolutely necessary that there be a first gesture coming from man. Even in Maimonides" (*GCM* 94). The revised Platonism demands a messianic vigilance of acknowledging this-worldly suffering, doing deeds for others (no matter how small and insignificant their suffering might seem), not speaking slander to others, preparing for the time of holiness, creating pleasantness for others, and giving even bread and water for mouths without food or drink, all to counter impurity and suffering, all to acknowledge a passing from Torah brilliance to marketplaces and harlots.[19] To braid an other's hair, to paint an other's countenance, to prettify an other's body, to acknowledge eros without concupiscence (as Levinas might put it)—should critics not engage in such activities? Is it too much beneath our own self assumed height?

And what soul-serarching resounds from Boccaccio's frame-tale and critical reply to his critics, which Boccaccio narrates in the form of an interruptive cave tale? Let us remember that before any of his 100 stories, Boccaccio describes mass death, which describes, as Levinas might say, an "anxiety over Being—horror of Being—[that is] just as primal as anxiety over death" (*EE* 5). Part of the horror here is my inability to comprehend death, but, as importantly, might we sense this affect in art as well as in a corpse? Levinas himself writes, "A corpse is horrible; it already bears in itself its own phantom . . . [In fact] this impossibility of escaping from an anonymous and uncorruptible existence constitutes the final depths of Shakespearean tragedy" (56–57). During the plague of the Black Death (as depicted in the start of *The Decameron*) there are humans who desire to escape from existence while acknowledging that they cannot take possession of their own being. They have not yet come to be ethical subjects for others, taking on the obligations of the others' suffering.[20] They must leave; they cannot dare breathe the air around them; there is simply too much brute existence and too much brute death. The question becomes: will they leave to acknowledge the stranger who knocks on their door or the servants who interrupt their storytelling, or will they build a stronger, safer, home? Will their stories mobilize or immobilize; or, is the real issue here one of radical passivity?

In a sense, prior to portraying ten humans who say stories, ten awake states of consciousness, Boccaccio narrates an inescapable persistence of bodies that are acted upon. By removing themselves from this horror of existence, the brigata attempts to become a group of individual existents. All of their storytelling away from the horror attempts to create a private, safe home where they can pretend that the horror of brute existence does not, in fact, stand at their front door. The entire *Decameron* contains this trace of mass death, of injustice, so that when interruptions happen, Boccaccio makes us aware that stories do not offer real total solace, but stories can both point to a past that can never be represented, and address the need for unending compassion. Whereas a direct representation of the Levinasian *il y a* is impossible, narrative allegory that performs interruptive ethical criticism, can inflect a curvature of space in which a trace of that which cannot be represented echoes in the shadows.

Stated otherwise, Boccaccio rubs against the human desire to be removed from horror. Each story in *The Decameron* tries to help the escape from existence, but those moments that interrupt the comprehension of a full story, mark Boccaccio's awareness that stories inevitably draw consciousness out of its retreat. When Boccaccio interrupts his *Decameron* with his allegorical cave, he seems to be saying, "I know as a storyteller I cannot portray true transcendence," but by doing so, he leaves us with a trace of responsibility. How? A story cannot exist as an anonymous moment; it is fated to stay in its state continuously. However, by interrupting this state at unexpected instances, Boccaccio critiques his own narrative's fate. In other words, an interruptive narrative shows us an author responding to those critics of art who complain that the "eternal duration of the interval in which a statue is immobilized differs radically from the eternity of a concept; it is the meanwhile, never finished, still enduring—something inhuman and monstrous" (*LR* 141). Boccaccio dramatizes for us how often humans try to use monstrous stories to escape the horror of being. Without the interruptive narrative in the fourth day, we might be right to distrust stories; do not stories cover over the murder of the Other's immediacy with an idolatrous layer? However, when we remember Boccaccio's earlier depiction of the plague, we indirectly recall our own coming forth from "the irremissibility of pure existing," from the *il y a*. Boccaccio himself, in other words, tries to rub that idolatrous narrative layer away by interrupting our contemplation of and participation in the 100 stories.

The brigata might wish, and the bulky volume of *The Decameron* might seem (to some readers) to indicate that storytelling in this safe environment away from the plague-ridden others, might somehow be salubrious. But if this is so, why does Boccaccio not attempt to portray what happens upon the brigata's return to the openness of mass death? Can it be that Boccaccio enacts a Levinasian obsession? According to Levinas, "the openness of space as an openness of self without a world, without a place, utopia, the not being walled in, inspiration to the end, even to expiration, is proximity of the other which is possible only as responsibility for the other . . . what took place humanly has never been able to remain closed up in its site" (*OB* 182–84). This new sense of utopian justice, acknowledged in my responsibility for the other, cannot remain closed up or walled in. The other breaks open my illusory invulnerability and sense of neat completeness.

In addition to our mini cave story, one that upsets the ordered 100—titular—stories, the mini story of the servants' own Decameron (which erupts at the start of day six), and the literary criticism Boccaccio performs in his own frame tale (his preface and epilogue), all upset the neat ordering of criticism and literature. These disorderly events expose the impossibility of fully telling what Levinas calls the *said*, not just the *saying* (as, again, a more standard reading of Levinas would have us believe).[21] The said of Boccaccio's interruptive stories of critique actually shows and tells us about those stories' untellability. Like the boy in the introduction to the fourth day, we need to do what Boccaccio calls "natural": we need to exit the (Platonic) cave of isolation and encounter the disorderly interruptions of our own self-narratives, what Boccaccio calls "not a complete story," "a part of one," a "digression" (all words used to tell us the critique-story of the fourth day's introduction). Nature, here, must include the ins and outs (from the cave), the elevations and degradations, the breaks in language (for example, the misnaming that names ladies "goslings," not women) the distress at the loss of the thing one loves.[22] It is even in the nature of ethical criticism to ask how to suffer need. After all, once the incomplete cave story is said, Boccaccio says, "All that remains to be said, then, is that [my critics] are perfectly free to turn me away if I should ever come asking them for anything. Thank God, I am not yet starving in any case; and even if I were, I know, in the words of the Apostle [Paul], both how to abound and to suffer need" (*TD* 289). Is it really so surprising that this particular journey out of the cave turns into an experience with sexual difference? The boy only expresses desire for women after the father hides the literal word for women and names them "goslings." The boy desires what his father says "evil looks like"; the boy desires "goslings"; we desire narrative closure. Boccaccio's sense of nature and criticism connects the "tiny little cave" to language used by those who lie. In a word, the alterations of language and erotic desire might be no match for the father's wits, but such movement is exposed by the author in his interruptive saying.[23] The very first sentence after the unfinished tale is said resounds with Boccaccio's own natural wit: "But I have no desire to carry this tale any further." Boccaccio's own desire is for his own immediate audience.

Through interruptive stories of critique, we can move beyond the image of the cave as a caricature. By doing so, we go beyond Levinas's own call to his audience: "to introduce the perspective of the relation with the other" to criticism. I read the cave stories with a sense of the good here in this world, in this earth, in sexed bodies, yet somehow charging us beyond being. Those who stand in the way of even the smallest acts of kindness to others threaten to remove the good from society, the embodied good rooted in bodies and nature. Who truly interrupts Rashbi's constant estrangement from and endangerment of human others? Not the supreme deity in whose light Rashbi learns wisdom from when in the cave. The interruptive other is the human other who prepares for holy time and the human who suffers, the human who, despite horrid conditions, circumstances, and setting, provides basic human pleasantness to others.

Like Rashbi's wife, we must act responsibly for others and acknowledge the proximity between the cultural institutions of knowledge, knowledge without cultural institutions, and the marketplace. If we are not vigilant in preparing for an other, for shortening distances others must walk, if we do not silence ourselves from words—even unintentional ones—said that can harm, might not we (critics and readers, myself and you, my audience) hear someone say of us, as we walk out in the market one fine day, "Is this one still in the world?" Torah is the supreme value for Rashbi (who endeavors as Levinas says, "To Love the Torah more than God"), but Torah learning must not be disembodied from this worldly existence with others. Empirically and ethically, Rashbi uses his imagination to enact messianic time in the here and now. A hyperbolic methodology and attitude are maintained, but brought down to this earth so that an elevated height can be attained here and now. Even agricultural work (collecting myrtle branches or farming) for the sake of ethical living for others and the commandments of the Infinite can be preparations for the time of holiness. Rashbi is still obsessively hyperbolic, but, in a sense, it is exactly excessiveness—in going beyond the letter of the law, in myrtles, in food and water, in braiding an other's hair, in the death that can happen if a self does not prepare candles—that breaks Rashbi out of his own being.

And from Boccaccio's perspective, those fathers who try to negate sexual difference in their sons soon learn that the metaphysical desire for the other can, in reality, become manifest in a plot to desire real women. When speaking of his ability "to suffer need," Boccaccio rubs harshly against Saint Paul's words: "I know both how to be abased, and

I know how to abound: every where and in all things I am instructed both to be full and to be hungry, both to abound and *to suffer need*" (Phil. 4:12). The other who interrupts Boccaccio's father and son is not Christ, but women; the other who interrupts Rabbi Shimon bar Yochai is not the supreme deity in whose light the Rabbi learns wisdom when in the cave; the interruptive other is the suffering other. Rashbi's wife is given no words to utter, but her face speaks, perhaps in a way not that much unlike the speaking described by Levinas: "The face speaks. The manifestation of the face is already discourse" (*TI* 66). Harlots, better than uncivil men, introduce the perspective of the relation with the other. The silent wife, the unseen harlots, the evil goslings, each, in her own way beyond the self's previous capacity to understand, forces the male self to question what it means to be an ethical subject. To suffer interruptive cave narratives ethically, signifies a metaphysical desire, in hyperbolic vigilance, that exceeds self-enjoyment and even totalizing critiques of art. The self is never finished with the possibility of violence; vigilance means being for others beyond all frames of self-conception or reference.

Notes

NOTES TO ASTELL AND JACKSON, "BEFORE THE FACE OF THE BOOK"

1. Riddle 26, *The Exeter Book,* ed. George Philip Krapp and Elliott Van Kirk Dobbie, Anglo-Saxon Poetic Records III (New York: Columbia University Press, 1936), 194: "Frige hwæt ic hatte,/...Nama min is mære."

2. William Langland, *Piers Plowman: An Edition of the C-text,* ed. Derek Pearsall (Berkeley and Los Angeles: University of California Press, 1979), 239, passus 20, lines 239–40: "Thenne was ther a wihte with two brode yes;/Bock hihte þat beau-pere, a bolde man of speche." Translation ours. The "two broad eyes" are commonly understood to represent the two Testaments.

3. *The Divine Comedy of Dante Alighieri: Purgatorio, A Verse Translation by Allen Mandelbaum* (Toronto: Bantam Books, 1984), 213, canto XXIII, lines 31–33.

4. *The Divine Comedy of Dante Alighieri: The Inferno, A Verse Translation by Allen Mandelbaum* (Toronto: Bantam Books, 1981), 4–5, canto 1, line 67.

5. For other studies linking Levinas to the writings of earlier periods, see Oona Aizenstatt [Eisenstadt], *Driven Back to the Text: The Premodern Sources of Levinas's Postmodernism* (Pittsburgh: Duquesne University Press, 2001); Melvyn New ed., with Robert Bernasconi and Richard A. Cohen, *In Proximity: Emmanuel Levinas and the Eighteenth Century* (Lubbock: Texas Tech University Press, 2001).

6. On this Levinasian translation of "Hebrew" into "Greek," see Annette Aronowicz, "Translator's Introduction," *NT* ix–xxxix.

7. See "The Nun's Priest's Tale" (*Canterbury Tales* VII.3441–42) and "The Parson's Tale" (*Canturbery Tales* X.1083).

8. See "Introductions to the Authors," *Medieval Literary Theory and Criticism c.1100–c.1375: The Commentary Tradition,* ed. A. J. Minnis and A. B. Scott, with the assistance of David Wallace (Oxford: Clarendon Press, 1988); Judson Boyce Allen, *The Ethical Poetic of the Later Middle Ages: A Decorum of Convenient Distinction* (Toronto: University of Toronto Press, 1982).

9. See especially Emmanuel Levinas, "Ethics as First Philosophy," *LR* 75–87.

10. William Franke, "The Ethical Vision of Dante's *Paradiso* in Light of Levinas," *Comparative Literature* 59, no. 3 (2007): 209.

11. See, for example, Joseph Libertson, *Proximity: Levinas, Blanchot, Bataille, and Communication* (The Hague: M. Nijhoff, 1982); Steve McCaffery, "The Scandal of Sincerity: Towards a Levinasian Poetics," *Prior to Meaning: Protosemantics and Poetics* (Evanston: Northwestern University Press, 2001), 204–30; Gabriel Riera, "The Possibility of the Poetic Said," *Angelaki: Journal of Theoretical Humanities* 9, no. 3 (2004): 121–35.

12. Gerald Bruns, "The Concept of Art and Poetry in Emmanuel Levinas's Writings," *The Cambridge Companion to Levinas,* ed. Simon Critchley and Robert Bernasconi (Cambridge: Cambridge University Press, 2002), 206.

13. Jill Robbins, *Altered Reading: Levinas and Literature* (Chicago: University of Chicago Press, 1999), xx.

14. See Joyce Coleman, *Public Reading and the Reading Public in Late Medieval England and France* (Cambridge: Cambridge University Press, 1996).

15. Bruns, "The Concept of Art and Poetry," 229.

16. Emmanuel Levinas, *DF*, 52; quoted in Robbins, *Altered Reading*, xxii.

17. Robbins, *Altered Reading*, xvi.

18. *DF* 53; quoted by Robbins, *Altered Reading*, xxi.

19. Emmanuel Levinas, "On Maurice Blanchot," *PN* 301.

20. On the complexity of the medieval reading process as a *lectio divina*, see Mary Carruthers, *The Book of Memory: A Study of Memory in Medieval Culture* (Cambridge: Cambridge University Press, 1990) and *The Craft of Thought: Meditation, Rhetoric, and the Making of Images, 400–1200* (Cambridge: Cambridge University Press, 2000). See also Jesse M. Gellrich, *The Idea of the Book in the Middle Ages: Language Theory, Mythology, and Fiction* (Ithaca: Cornell University Press, 1985).

21. Emmanuel Levinas, "Reality and Its Shadow," *LR* 129–43.

NOTES TO ALLEN, "DIFFICULT READING"

1. All translations are by the author from the French, but corresponding published translations are cited first, followed by the French original.

2. "Interview with Myriam Anissimov," *IRB*, 87; "Emmanuel Levinas se souvient...," *Les Nouveaux Cahiers: Emmanuel Levinas* 82 (1985): 32.

3. Emmanuel Levinas, *Beyond the Verse: Talmudic Readings and Lectures* [*BV*], trans. Gary D. Mole (London: Athlone, 1994), 210, n. 8; *L'Au-delà du verset: Lectures et discours talmudiques* [*AV*] (Paris: Les Éditions de Minuit, 1982), 135–36.

4. Bernard of Clairvaux, *On the Song of Songs IV*, trans. Irene Edmonds (Kalamazoo, Mich.: Cistercian Publications, 1980), 3–16, Sermon 67.

5. *De Miraculis*, in *Patrologiae Latinae*, ed. Jacques-Paul Migne (Paris: Garnier, 1844–55, 1862–65), Electronic Database (Chadwyck, 1996–2006), 189:0887A. Cited in Ivan Illich, *In the Vineyard of the Text: A Commentary to Hugh's Didascalicon* (Chicago: University of Chicago Press, 1993), 56–57.

6. Richard of Bury, *Philobiblon*, trans. E. C. Thomas, ed. Michael Maclagan (Oxford: Blackwell, 1960), 40: "Primum oportet volumen cum Ezechiele comedere, quo venter memoriae dulcescat intrinsecus."

7. Mary Carruthers, "Reading with Attitude, Remembering the Book," in *The Book and the Body*, ed. Dolores Warwick Frese and Katherine O'Brien O'Keeffe (Notre Dame: University of Notre Dame Press, 1997), 16, 18. Catherine Brown, "In the Middle," *Journal of Medieval and Early Modern Studies* 30 (2000): 559–64.

8. Carruthers, "Reading with Attitude," 6–7, 21, 24. I am indebted to Carruthers' essay throughout for her attention to the violence, both literal and figurative, of monastic reading and meditation.

9. Richard of Bury, *Philobiblon*, 20: "Vos estis revera spicae gratissimae, plenae granis, solis apostolicis manibus confricandae."

10. Augustine, *On Christian Doctrine*, trans. D. W. Robertson, Jr. (New York: Macmillan, 1958), II.vi.8.

11. Matt. 7.6. Henry Knighton uses the same metaphor to lament Wycliffe's 1382 translation of the Bible; *Knighton's Chronicle 1337–1396*, ed. and trans. G. H. Martin (Oxford: Clarendon, 1995), 243–45.

12. Augustine, *On Christian Doctrine*, III.xii.18.

13. Hugh of St Victor, *Didascalicon*, trans. Jerome Taylor, 2nd ed. (New York: Columbia University Press, 1991), I.ix.

14. Martin Heidegger, "The Question Concerning Technology," in *The Question Concerning Technology and Other Essays,* trans. William Lovitt (New York: Harper & Row, 1977), 17.

15. In particular, Levinas, "On the Jewish Reading of the Scriptures," *BV* 110, 136.

16. Jacques Derrida, "At This Very Moment in This Work Here I Am," trans. Ruben Berezdivin, *Re-Reading Levinas,* ed. Robert Bernasconi and Simon Critchley (London: Athlone, 1991), 37.

17. For the connection between the word "apocalypse" and Hebrew *gola,* and hence for the "apocalyptic" laying bare of, for example, the glans in circumscision, see Jacques Derrida, "Of an Apocalyptic Tone Recently Adopted in Philosophy," *Semeia* 23 (1982): 63–65. See also Derrida's use of the word solicitation in *Writing and Difference,* trans. Alan Bass (Chicago: University of Chicago Press, 1978), xvi.

18. Emmanuel Levinas, "Martin Heidegger and Ontology," trans. Committee of Public Safety, *Diacritics* 26 (1996): 19, 30, n. 26.

19. "Martin Heidegger and Ontology" is Levinas's sole pre-war essay about Heidegger. See also the accompanying translators' introduction: Committee of Public Safety, " 'My Place in the Sun:' Reflections on the Thought of Emmanuel Levinas," *Diacritics* 26 (1996): 3–10.

20. For example, Martin Heidegger, *Introduction to Metaphysics,* trans. Gregory Fried and Richard Polt (New Haven: Yale University Press, 2000), 103–22.

21. *EI* 41–42; *EeI* 39–40. Yet note elsewhere his admiration of etymology in talmudic exegesis for the way in which it forces (*solliciter*) the text. See the essay, "Promised Land" *NT* 56; *QT* 122.

22. Illich, *In the Vineyard,* 2. Also Beryl Smalley, *The Study of the Bible in the Middle Ages,* 2nd ed. (Notre Dame: University of Notre Dame, 1964), xvii, 264–355.

23. Illich, *In the Vineyard,* 58–60.

24. *Patrologia Latina,* 91:499B. Quoted in Smalley, *Study of the Bible,* 36.

25. Lambert of Ardres, *The History of the Counts of Guines and Lords of Ardres,* trans. Leah Shopkow (Philadelphia: University of Pennsylvania Press, 2000), 68.

26. See Ruth Mellinkoff, *Outcasts: Signs of Otherness in Northern European Art of the Late Middle Ages* (Berkeley and Los Angeles: University of California Press, 1993), 2.II.36. Also, Christine M. Rose, "The Jewish Mother-in-Law: Synogoga and the *Man of Law's Tale,*" in *Chaucer and the Jews,* ed. Sheila Delany (New York: Routledge, 2002), 8.

27. Smalley, *Study of the Bible,* 14–20 for the Antiochenes; 83–195 for the Victorines. Levinas himself notes how medieval Christians such as Nicholas of Lyra consulted Jews for an exposition of the letter. See the essay, "Persons or Figures," *DF* 119–20; *DL* 161. See Michael A: Signer, "Vision and History: Nicholas of Lyra on the Prophet Ezekiel," *Nicholas of Lyra: The Senses of Scripture,* ed. Philip D. W. Krey and Lesley Smith (Leiden: Brill, 2000), 147–71.

28. John Wycliffe, *The Holy Bible, containing the Old and New Testaments, with the Apocryphal books, in the earliest English versions made from the Latin Vulgate by John Wycliffe and his followers,* ed. Josiah Forshall and Frederic Madden, 4 vols. (Oxford: Oxford University Press, 1850), *Prologue,* 1:53. Also Illich, *In the Vineyard,* 49.

29. Smalley, *Study of the Bible,* 33, 108–09.

30. St. Thomas Aquinas, *Summa Theologiae,* ed. and trans. Thomas Gilby (Oxford: Blackfriars, 1964–75), 1a1.10.corp: "sensus litteralis est quem auctor intendit, auctor autem sacrae Scripturae Deus est" (The literal sense is that which the author intends, and the author of Holy Scripture is God).

31. Smalley, *Study of the Bible,* 296–97. Aristotle, *The Physics, Books I–IV,* ed. and trans. Philip H. Wicksteed and Francis M. Cornford (Cambridge, Mass.: Harvard University Press, 1957), 198a24–25.

32. The holocaust of Sodom and Gomorrah, for example, was a common antitype for the prophesied punishment of an apostate Israel (Isa. 1:9–10; Jer. 23:14; Ezek. 16.44–59; Amos, 4:11). See Leonhard Goppelt, *Typos: The Typological Interpretation of the Old Testament in the New,* trans. Donald H. Madvig (Grand Rapids, Mich.: Eerdmans, 1982), 32–41, 56–58. Also Michael A. Signer, "Searching the Scriptures: Jews, Christians, and the Book," in *Christianity in Jewish Terms,* ed. Tivka Frymer-Kensky et al. (Boulder, Colo.: Westview, 2000), 85–98.

33. *DF* 66–67; *DL* 93. See also Levinas, "On the Jewish Reading of Scriptures," *BV* 101; *AV* 125.

34. Levinas, "The Jewish Understanding of Scripture," *Cross Currents* 44 (1994/1995): 488; "De la lecture juive des Ecritures," *Lumière et Vie* 144 (1977): 5.

35. Anselm, *Proslogion,* chap. 1 in *Patrologia Latina,* 158:0227C. Also Augustine, Sermon 43 in *Patrologia Latina,* 38:0255.

36. Levinas, "On Religious Language and the Fear of God," *BV* 93–94, 206 (n. 10); *AV* 117.

37. Something of this word play is evident in Christian exegesis, but it persists more in grammatical etymologies and in lyrics. For example, while the Christian

fathers had long regarded Mary as the second Eve, the Eva-Ave palindrome (*Ave* heralding Mary by means of Gabriel's greeting) is not known until the ninth century with the lyric "Ave maris stella." Andrew Breeze, "Two Bardic Themes: The Virgin and Child, and 'Ave-Eva,'" *Medium Ævum* 63 (1994): 24.

38. Plato, *The Republic Books 6–10*, ed. and trans. Paul Shorey (Cambridge, Mass.: Harvard University Press, 1935), 511B.

39. Illich, *In the Vineyard*, 19.

40. Immanuel Kant, *Critique of Pure Reason*, trans. Norman Kemp Smith (New York: St. Martin's Press, 1929), A856/B884.

41. Although the tag came to epitomize the spirit of fideism, it appears that Tertullian, from whom the words are misquoted, was making a subtler point, namely, that because the incarnation story is so improbable (*absurdus*) it was reasonable to believe it. Robert D. Sider, "*Credo Quia Absurdum?*," *Classical World* 73 (1980): 417–19.

42. Compare Jacques Derrida, *Given Time: I. Counterfeit Money,* trans. Peggy Kamuf (Chicago: University of Chicago Press, 1992), 17: "For there to be gift event (we say event not act), something must come about or happen...in an instant that no doubt does not belong to the economy of time,...in such a way that the forgetting forgets, that it forgets *itself,* but also in such a way that this forgetting, without being something present, presentable, determinable, sensible or meaningful, is not nothing. What this...forgetting of forgetting would therefore give us to think is something other than a philosophical, psychological, or psychoanalytic category."

43. Levinas, "Model of the West," *BV* 15; *AV* 31.

44. Illich, *In the Vineyard*, 42–43, 54–58. The literature on the complex relationship between the written and the oral is vast. Presenting the two as conceptual opposites, Walter J. Ong, in *Orality and Literacy: The Technologizing of the Word* (London: Methuen, 1982), shows how "pure" orality, in eschewing all forms of record external to the human memory, depends entirely upon face-to-face communication and human relationships. Writing ruptures that immediacy by introducing a third element to the transmission of thought. See also Eric Alfred Havelock, *The Muse Leans to Write: Reflections on Orality and Literacy from Antiquity to the Present* (New Haven: Yale University Press, 1986); Jack Goody, *The Interface between the Written and the Oral* (Cambridge: Cambridge University Press, 1987).

45. Levinas, "Interview with Myriam Anissimov," 87; "Emmanuel Levinas se souvient...," 32.

46. See Joyce Coleman, *Public Reading and the Reading Public in Late Medieval England and France* (Cambridge: Cambridge University Press, 1996), 40. Coleman considers the prevalence of communal reading among secular audiences.

47. John of Salisbury, *The Metalogicon: A Twelfth-Century Defense of the Verbal and Logical Arts of the Trivium*, trans. Daniel D. McGarry (Berkeley and Los Angeles: University of California Press, 1955), I.xxiv. Salisbury distinguishes between the teacher's reading aloud to the students, *praelectio,* and the students'

reading to themselves, *lectio*, whether that "private" reading is done either silently or aloud, *sotto voce*. He borrows the term from Quintilian, whose conception of audience differs somewhat. See Coleman, *Public Reading*, 35.

48. *Oxford English Dictionary*, s.v. "prelection."

49. Samuel Pepys, *Works*, ed. Robert Latham and William Matthews, 8 vols. (Berkeley and Los Angeles: University of California Press, 1970–74), Oct. 14, 1663. For a more contemporary description, see Signer, "Searching the Scriptures," 85.

50. Richard of Bury, *Philobiblon*, 16: "in libris mortuos quasi vivos invenio."

51. *DF* 131; *DL* 175; Committee of Public Safety, "My Place in the Sun," 6–7.

52. Levinas, "The Name of God According to Some Talmudic Texts," *BV* 120; *AV* 149.

53. With particular thanks to Ares Axiotis for his input throughout the essay, and to editors Ann Astell and Justin Jackson for their helpful comments.

NOTES TO YAGER, "LEVINAS, ALLEGORY, AND CHAUCER'S CLERK'S TALE"

1. Colin Davis, *Levinas: An Introduction* (Notre Dame: University of Notre Dame Press, 1996), 5.

2. This is not to argue, however, that reading is impossible, or that the attempt to read is deconstructive. With a single exception, I am attempting here to read Levinas without Derrida, and to trace the possibilities of multiple meaning, rather than the impossibility of a stable reading.

3. Samuel Taylor Coleridge, *Stateman's Manual*, in *The Collected Works of Samuel Taylor Coleridge*, vol. 6, ed. R. J. White (Princeton: Princeton University Press, 1972), 30.

4. Jon Whitman, *Allegory: The Dynamics of an Ancient and Medieval Technique* (Cambridge, Mass.: Harvard University Press, 1987), 263.

5. Ibid., 264.

6. Ewa Rychter, *(Un)Saying the Other: Allegory and Irony in Emmanuel Levinas's Ethical Language* (Frankfurt: Peter Lang, 2004), 33.

7. Maureen Quilligan, *The Language of Allegory: Defining the Genre* (Ithaca: Cornell University Press, 1979), 26.

8. Jill Robbins, *Altered Reading: Levinas and Literature* (Chicago: University of Chicago Press, 1999), 51.

9. Rychter, *(Un)saying the Other*, 44.

10. Gerald L. Bruns, "The Concepts of Art and Poetry in Emmanuel Levinas's Writings," in *The Cambridge Companion to Levinas*, ed. Simon Critchley and Robert Bernasconi (Cambridge: Cambridge University Press, 2002), 215.

11. Robert Bernasconi, quoted in Davis, *Levinas*, 69.

12. Sandor Goodhart, Introductory remarks, Levinas and Medieval Literature I, Thirty-Ninth International Congress on Medieval Studies, Western Michigan University, Kalamazoo, Mich., May 5, 2004.

13. J. Hillis Miller, *On Literature* (New York: Routledge, 2002), 39.

14. Séan Hand, "Introduction," *LR* 6.

15. John A. Alford, "The Grammatical Metaphor: A Survey of Its Use in the Middle Ages," *Speculum* 57, no. 4 (1982): 728–60.

16. Quoted by Alford in William Langland, *The Vision of Piers Plowman: A Complete Edition of the B-Text*, A. V. C. Schmidt, ed. (New York: E. P. Dutton, 1978), 755.

17. Geoffrey Chaucer, *Book of the Duchess*, in *The Riverside Chaucer*, ed. L. Benson, 3rd ed. (Boston: Houghton Mifflin, 1987), 337. All future references to Chaucer, including *Canterbury Tales* [*CT*] *and Troilus and Criseyde* [*TC*] are from this edition. Individual *Canterbury Tales* are cited by fragment and line numbers.

18. Maxwell S. Luria and Richard L. Hoffman, eds., *Middle English Lyrics* (New York: W. W. Norton, 1974), 7.

19. Jacques Derrida, "Violence and Metaphysics," in *Writing and Difference*, trans. Alan Bass (Chicago: University of Chicago Press, 1978), 147.

20. E. V. Gordon, ed., *Pearl* (Oxford: Oxford University Press, 1953), 1.

21. The particular resistance to definitive meaning in Chaucer is ably described by Rosemarie P. McGerr in *Chaucer's Open Books* (Gainesville: University Press of Florida, 1998), esp. 154–55.

22. Donald Howard, *The Idea of* The Canterbury Tales (Berkeley and Los Angeles: University of California Press, 1976), 385.

23. J. Kerkhof, *Studies in the Language of Geoffrey Chaucer* (Leiden: E. J. Brill and Leiden University Press, 1982), 36.

24. See my "'As She That': Syntactical Ambiguity in Chaucer's *Troilus and Criseyde*," *Philological Quarterly* 73, no. 2 (1994): 151–68. See also E. T. Donaldson, "Gallic Flies in Chaucer's English Word Web," in *New Perspectives in Chaucer Criticism*, ed. Donald M. Rose (Norman, OK: Pilgrim Books, 1981), 193–202.

25. See, for example, Alfred L. Kellogg, "The Evolution of the 'Clerk's Tale': A Study in Connotation," in his *Chaucer, Langland, Arthur: Essays in Middle English Literature* (New Brunswick: Rutgers University Press, 1972), 276–329.

26. Derek Pearsall, *The Canterbury Tales* (London: George Allen & Unwin, 1985), 276.

27. Charlotte C. Morse, "The Exemplary Griselda," *Studies in the Age of Chaucer* 7 (1985): 54.

28. Charlotte C. Morse, "Critical Approaches to the *Clerk's Tale*," in *Chaucer's Religious Tales*, ed. C. David Benson and Elizabeth Robertson (Cambridge: Boydell and Brewer, 1990), 80.

29. Levinas's thought has been subject to feminist critique since Simone de Beauvoir's publication of *The Second Sex*. See Tina Chanter, ed., *Feminist Interpretations of Emmanuel Levinas* (University Park: Pennsylvania State University Press, 2001).

30. Tina Chanter, "Introduction," *Feminist Interpretations of Emmanuel Levinas*, 3.

31. Claire Elise Katz explores the case of a contemporary matricide, Rusty Ryan and her insensitive husband, from a Levinasian perspective in her article "Raising Cain: The Problem of Evil and the Question of Responsibility," *Crosscurrents* 55, no. 2 (2005): 215–33.

32. Gerald L. Bruns, "Dialogue and the Truth of Skepticism," *Religion and Literature* 22, nos. 2–3 (Summer-Autumn 1990): 88.

33. Simon Critchley, "Introduction," *The Cambridge Companion to Levinas,* 12.

34. Philippe Nemo, *Job and the Excess of Evil,* trans. Michael Kigel (Pittsburgh: Duquesne University Press, 1998), 166.

NOTES TO JOY, "LEVINAS, HOSPITALITY, *BEOWULF*"

1. This essay has been with me, troubling my thoughts and study, for over three years now, and many have been the readers and friends involved in its evolution. I want to thank, especially, Roy Liuzza, Bruce Gilchrist, and James Earl for their invaluable comments on early drafts. I want to also thank Ann Astell and Justin Jackson for giving me the opportunity to present a protoversion of this essay at Kalamazoo in 2004, for their generous invitation to be a part of this volume, and for their helpful comments for revision through several redraftings. Finally, I thank the external reviewers for their helpful suggestions, especially for the references to the work of Howard Caygill and Simon Critchley. Any remaining errors are entirely my own. The title of this essay is taken from the description of Grendel, in *Beowulf,* as he is striding from the fens toward Hrothgar's hall, Heorot, bearing "God's anger" (711) [*Godes yrre*]. All citations of the poem are from Fr. Klaeber, *Beowulf and the Fight at Finnsburg* [*BFF*], 3rd ed., with supplements (Lexington, Mass.: D. C. Heath, 1950). All translations are mine and are cited parenthetically by line number.

2. Jacques Derrida, *Adieu to Emmanuel Levinas,* trans. Pascale-Anne Brault and Michael Naas (Stanford: Stanford University Press, 1999), 21, 25. Derrida's "adieu" to Levinas forms a major commentary on Levinas's ethics of hospitality. For Derrida's further development of the subject of hospitality, see *Of Hospitality: Anne Dufourmantelle Invites Jacques Derrida to Respond,* trans. Rachel Bowlby (Stanford: Stanford University Press, 2000).

3. *TI* 39. Levinas uses both *autrui* and *autre* in his writings, the first to denote "the personal other," and the second to denote, "otherness in general, or alterity." It has been the habit of Levinas's translators to use the uppercase "O" for the first ("Other") and the lowercase "o" for the second ("other" or "otherness"). On this point, see *TO* 30n3.

4. *TI* 50–51. For Levinas, the role of language in the relationship whereby the subject *opens* to (or *reaches* for) the Other is extremely critical, for the "positive deployment of the pacific relation with the other, without frontier or any negativity, is produced in language. Language does not belong among the relations that could appear through the structures of formal logic; it is contact across a distance, relation with the non-touchable, across a void" (172).

5. *TI* 168, 172–73. For Levinas, hospitality is literally the "home open to the Other," and it is the first condition, as it were, for the encounter with the Other who calls the subject into question *in her own home*. See *TI* 168–74.

6. *OB* 117. To those who would criticize Levinas's ethics as too abstract or even impossible (how, for example, can one person really be expected to submit themselves to a kind of hostagelike "sub-jectum" to the entire universe?), we must keep in mind, I would argue, that this *"sub-jectum"* is type of posture (a type of *leaning toward*) that a singular individual can adopt in a particular time and place, and Levinas was well aware of how it is "the little act of goodness [*la petite bonté*] from one person to his neighbor" that is "the sole refuge of the good in being" (*IRB* 206–07). Goodness, then, is not accomplished all at once in the world when everyone is all of sudden completely and unreservedly for-the-Other-before-them-selves, but in those smaller singular moments when "the human interrupts the pure obstinacy of beings and its wars." This goodness, which is "little" and passes from one person to another, as in that moment when a soldier gives comfort to the enemy by a small gesture, such as bringing him water or touching him gently, is ultimately "fragile before the power of evil," and yet is the only means available for ethical attention since goodness can never be "a regime, an organized system, a social institution" (*IRB* 207, 217–18).

7. Derrida, *Adieu to Emmanuel Levinas,* 50.

8. Ibid., 20. It has to be admitted that, on one level, Levinas's philosophy may be inherently apolitical. As Richard Wolin writes, "Levinas's quasi-mystical veneration of Otherness...resembles an 'ephiphany.' But it is nearly impossible to translate an epiphany into meaningful political action. As an experience of tran-scendence, an epiphany cannot be made into an object of legislation" ("Heidegger Made Kosher," *The Nation,* Feb. 20, 2006. Available at http://www.thenation. com/doc/20060220/wolin/). But I would also argue that the question of whether or not Levinas's ethics of hospitality could ever found a law, or a state, is best left as an open question, and furthermore, if the question is not left open, certain political discourses, such as those centering upon international human rights, would have a much more narrow field of play.

9. Derrida, *Adieu to Emmanuel Levinas,* 48.

10. Ibid., 64.

11. Ibid., 75–76.

12. Simon Critchley, *Infinitely Demanding: Ethics of Commitment, Politics of Resistance* (London: Verso, 2007), 92.

13. Ibid., 113.

14. In *Otherwise Than Being,* Levinas writes that, in substituting oneself for the other, "I am summoned as someone irreplaceable" (114).

15. In his book *Infinitely Demanding,* Critchley distinguishes two types of nihilism: "active" and "passive." Whereas both see the world as meaningless, the passive nihilist "simply focuses on himself and his particular pleasures and projects for perfecting himself," and "in a world that is all too rapidly blowing itself to pieces," he "closes his eyes and makes himself into an island," while the active nihilist "tries to destroy the world and bring another into being" (4–5).

16. The dating of *Beowulf*, as a work of either oral or textual art, or as some hybrid between the two, has a long and contentious history that I do not wish to address here. For the purposes of this essay, I assume a composition date congruent with the most probable date of the unique extant manuscript itself, which everyone agrees is circa 1000 CE. For those more interested in the debates over the dating question, see *The Dating of Beowulf*, ed. Colin Chase (Toronto: University of Toronto Press, 1981); Kevin Kiernan, *Beowulf and the Beowulf Manuscript*, rev. ed. (Ann Arbor: University of Michigan Press, 1996), 13–63; and Roy Michael Liuzza, "On the Dating of *Beowulf*," in *Beowulf: Basic Readings,* ed. Peter Baker (New York: Garland Press, 1995), 281–302.

17. Much of John Hill's work with the poem has been aimed at establishing how the episodes of blood feud, which are seemingly so endemic in *Beowulf*'s world, are not necessarily "dismaying" evidence of a society that cannot control (or legislate) violence, but are rather "socially acute meditations on the prospects for settlement, for accomplished and extended community," as well as "meditations on the dynamic of group reformation...once lethal violence undercuts a prior accommodation" (John M. Hill, "The Ethnopsychology of In-Law Feud and the Remaking of Group Identity in *Beowulf*: The Cases of Hengest and Ingeld," *Philological Quarterly* 78 [1999]: 97). In Hill's view, revenge for past or current injuries in *Beowulf* is often "juridical" and feud is therefore "jural." On this point, see also John M. Hill, *The Cultural World of Beowulf* (Toronto: University of Toronto Press, 1995), and *The Anglo-Saxon Warrior Ethic: Reconstructing Lordship in Early English Literature* (Gainesville: University of Florida Press, 2000). Similarly, in their essay "Civilized Rage in *Beowulf*," Thomas L. Wymer and Erin F. Labbie argue that "controlled" or "highly ritualized" rage "is useful to the development of social relations and the nation" (*Heroic Age* 7 [Spring 2004]. Available at http://www.heroicage.org/issues/7/labbie%26wymer.html).

18. John Michael, "Identity, Masochism, and the Democratic Intellectual in the War on Terror," *The Hedgehog Review* 9, no. 1 (2007): 80.

19. Seth Lerer, "Grendel's Glove," *English Literary History* 61 (1994): 738–39.

20. Ibid., 740.

21. Jeffrey Jerome Cohen, "The Body in Pieces: Identity and the Monstrous in Romance," in *Of Giants: Sex, Monsters, and the Middle Ages* (Minneapolis: University of Minnesota Press, 1999), 94.

22. In *Totality and Infinity*, Levinas writes that, to "approach the Other is to put into question my freedom, my spontaneity as a living being, my emprise over the things, this freedom of a 'moving force,' this impetuosity of the current to which everything is permitted, even murder" (303).

23. Howard Caygill, *Levinas and the Political* (London: Routledge, 2002), 3–4.

24. Simon Critchley, *The Ethics of Deconstruction: Derrida and Levinas*, 2nd ed. (West Lafayette: Purdue University Press, 1999), 223. It is important to note here that, for Critchley (and also for myself), political space needs to be under-

stood as a "factical, ontic, or empirical terrain, on which politics is conceived as an activity of questioning, critique, judgment, and decision; in short, as the creation of antagonism, contestation, and struggle—what one might call the battle over *doxa*" (236).

25. Caygill, *Levinas and the Political,* 1.

26. Ibid., 192–93.

27. Ibid., 194. Such a triumph in Caygill's view of Levinas's thought always involves violent *struggle.*

28. Critchley, *The Ethics of Deconstruction,* 221.

29. Ibid., 221.

30. Ibid., 220.

31. Ibid., 238.

32. Ibid., 239.

33. *The Laws of the Earliest English Kings,* ed. and trans. F. L. Attenborough (Cambridge: Cambridge University Press, 1922), 108–09.

34. Quoted in *English Historical Documents, c. 500–1042,* ed. Dorothy Whitelock, 2nd ed. (London: Methuen, 1979), 460.

35. The Old English is here cited from *The Laws of the Earliest English Kings,* 129; the translation is mine.

36. *The Laws of the Earliest English Kings,* 42–43. Ine's law echoes very closely the earlier law of the Kentish king Wihtred (c. 690–725) that stipulates, "If a man from afar, or a stranger, quits the road, and neither shouts, nor blows a horn, he shall be assumed to be a thief, [and as such] may be either slain or put to ransom" (*The Laws of the Earliest English Kings,* 31).

37. Julia Kristeva, *Strangers to Ourselves,* trans. Leon S. Roudiez (New York: Columbia University Press), 85.

38. Michael E. Moore, "Wolves, Outlaws, and Enemy Combatants," in *Cultural Studies of the Modern Middle Ages,* ed. Eileen Joy, Myra Seaman, Kimberly Bell, and Mary Ramsey (New York: Palgrave Macmillan, 2007). Giorgio Agamben also reminds us that "ancient Germanic law was founded on the concept of peace (*Fried*) and the corresponding exclusion from the community of the wrongdoer, who therefore became *friedlos,* without peace, and whom anyone was permitted to kill without committing homicide" (*Homo Sacer: Sovereign Power and Bare Life,* trans. Daniel Heller-Roazen [Stanford: Stanford University Press, 1998], 104).

39. Moore, "Wolves, Outlaws, and Enemy Combatants."

40. Hugh Magennis, *Images of Community in Old English Poetry* (Cambridge: Cambridge University Press, 1996), 1.

41. Ibid., 3.

42. Ibid., 13.

43. Early on in the poem the poet notes that Hrothgar commanded the building of Heorot as a place where he would "give to all, young and old, such as God gave to him" (71b–72) [*eall gedælan/geongum on ealdum, swylc him God sealed*].

44. In his conclusion to *Totality and Infinity*, Levinas writes: "Situated at the antipodes of the subject living in the infinite time of fecundity is the isolated and heroic being that the State produces by its virile virtues. Such a being confronts death out of pure courage and whatever be the cause for which he dies. He assumes finite time, the death-end or death-transition, which do not arrest the continuation of a being without discontinuity" (306–07). On the psychological operations of terror in association with the figure of Grendel in the poem, see Michael Lapidge, "*Beowulf* and the Psychology of Terror," in *Heroic Poetry in the Anglo-Saxon Period: Studies in Honor of Jess B. Bessinger, Jr.*, ed. Helen Damico and John Leyerle (Kalamazoo, Mich.: Medieval Institute, 1993), 373–402.

45. Cohen, "The Body in Pieces: Identity and the Monstrous in Romance," 94.

46. Carolyn B. Anderson, "*Gæst*, gender, and kin in *Beowulf*: Consumption of the Boundaries," *Heroic Age* 5 (2001). Available at http://www.heroicage.org/issues/5/Anderson1.html.

47. I want to thank Bruce Gilchrist for initially pointing out to me the sparseness of the landscape and architectural features with which Daneland is described in the poem. As Gilchrist himself puts it, "Daneland is only the hall and two narrow horse-path strips of land—one to the ocean, one to the mere. There are some descriptions of celebratory horse riding, but nothing outside the paths. Aristocratic reality ends here and so do viable targets for Grendel's violence" (Bruce Gilchrist to Eileen Joy, April 5, 2004, email communication). Additionally, James Earl has written that the "peculiarity of the world of *Beowulf*...lies in what is not there. Except for the *burs* where men go to sleep, we hear nothing of the village or the people outside the hall.... The poem shows us the world of the hall from the inside and seems totally indifferent to the rest of the world outside" (James W. Earl, *Thinking About Beowulf* [Stanford: Stanford University Press, 1994], 116).

48. Jeffrey Jerome Cohen, "Monster Culture (Seven Theses)," in *Monster Theory: Reading Culture*, ed. Jeffrey Jerome Cohen (Minneapolis: University of Minnesota Press, 1996), 20.

49. The meaning of the word *aglæca* has stirred controversy among Old English scholars, and has been taken to mean, variously, a monster, a warrior, a devil, God, and a force of nature. Most translations of *Beowulf*, following Klaeber, have posited "monster" or "demon" when the word denotes Grendel. Roy M. Liuzza, in his recent verse translation, has used, alternatively, "ravager," "evil beast," "loathsome creature," "monster," "horrible creature," and "awful warrior," among others, but Liuzza also points out that the OE *aglæca* literally means "awesome one" or "terror," and that its translation in his edition is "admittedly tendentious" (R. M. Liuzza, *Beowulf: A New Verse Translation* [Ontario: Broadview Press, 2000], 75, n. 1). Alexandra Hennessey Olsen has suggested that an *aglæca* is one who violates a natural or moral law ("The Aglæca and the Law," *American Notes & Queries* 20 [1982]: 66–68).

50. It should be noted here that although descendancy from Cain does lend to Grendel and his mother a human genealogy, according to the poet, it also means that they are what has been "awakened" and born as a result of Cain's exile: "giants

and elves and bearers of distress, and likewise the gigantic ones" (111–13) [*Þanon untydras ealle onwocon, / eotenas ond ylfe ond orcneas, / swylce gigantas*].

51. Ruth Mellinkoff, "Cain's Monstrous Progeny in *Beowulf*: Part I, Nochaic Tradition," *Anglo-Saxon England* 8 (1979): 151.

52. Katherine O'Brien O'Keeffe, "*Beowulf*, Lines 702b–836: Transformations and the Limits of the Human," *Texas Studies in Literature and Language* 23 (1981): 488.

53. Carol Braun Pasternack, "Post-Structuralist Theories: The Subject and the Text," in *Reading Old English Texts*, ed. Katherine O'Brien O'Keeffe (Cambridge: Cambridge University Press, 1997), 186.

54. Ibid., 186.

55. O'Keeffe, "*Beowulf*," 488.

56. In his writing on the figure of the monster in Old English literature, Jeffrey Cohen uses the term *extimité*, or extimacy, to describe the "intimate alterity" of human identity: "its inescapable self-estrangement, the restless presence as its center of everything it abjects in order to materialize and maintain its borders. To be fully human is to disavow the strange space that the inhuman, the monstrous, occupies within every speaking subject" (Cohen, "The Ruins of Identity," *Of Giants*, 4). *Extimité* is a term borrowed from Lacan, explained by Jacques Alain Miller as designating "in a problematic manner the real in the symbolic." More simply put, *extimité* names the state of affairs whereby the exterior is always present in the interior, and further, extimacy "is not the contrary of intimacy [but]...the intimate is Other—like a foreign body" (Jacques Alain Miller, "Extimité," in *Lacanian Theory of Discourse: Subject, Structure, and Society*, ed. Mark Bracher et al. [New York: New York University Press], 75).

57. Anderson, "*Gæst*, gender, and kin in *Beowulf*."

58. The translation of these lines has been much disputed; my reading follows the lead of Roy Liuzza who takes up in his translation a suggestion made by Fred C. Robinson in "Why is Grendel's Not Greeting the *gifstol* a *wræc micel?*" in *Words, Texts, and Manuscripts*, ed. Michael Korhammer (Cambridge: D. S. Brewer, 1992), 257–62. See Liuzza, *Beowulf: A New Verse Translation*, 58, n. 2.

59. It is worth noting here that almost all of the so-called "digressions" in the poem, such as the Finn and Hengest story (1070–159), as well as Beowulf's account, just prior to fighting the dragon, of the seemingly perpetual hostilities between the Geats and Swedes (2426–89), concern themselves with feuds that can never be settled, except by vengeance, which in turn begets more vengeance, and so on and so forth. While I am mindful of John Hill's cogent and often compelling arguments that, in the social world of *Beowulf*, revenge is not always extralegal or something that can always be better replaced with some other form of nonlethal settlement, but rather, can be "jurally definitive," I am also persuaded by Clare A. Lees's reading of the poem as being about a heroic world whose ethos requires bloodshed and whose chief production is death. See "Men and *Beowulf*," in *Medieval Masculinities: Regarding Men in the Middle Ages*, ed. Clare A. Lees (Minneapolis: University of Minnesota Press, 1994), 129–48.

60. See, again, John Hill, "Ethnopsychology in *Beowulf*."

61. Much critical energy has been expended on Grendel's possible meanings on allegorical, symbolic and "deep structural" levels (in other words, on his role as sign and signifier, as opposed to "creature" or "animal"), and more recently, explanations that take a psychoanalytic approach (and even, an ethnopsychoanalytic approach) are prevalent. According to Hill, Grendel's lawless murders and acts of cannibalism have "savage roots [that]...go deeper than early Oedipal hostility toward siblings, working into an earlier psychological stage of anger: oral aggression organized out of the primal rage that follows the first loss (the breast)" (*The Cultural World of Beowulf*, 124). In "The Ruins of Identity," Jeffrey Cohen offers a Lacanian and Kristevan reading in which Grendel is a type of giant who represents a dangerous return to *jouissance*, and who also haunts the periphery of the warriors' identity, or "architecture of selfhood," from which he has been abjected. Further, Grendel's and his mother's dwelling, often swollen and swirling with blood, represents an "extimate trauma" that "lurks at the center of subjectivity, ensuing that the process of becoming human is also the process of becoming monstrous" (1–28).

62. Cohen, "Monster Culture (Seven Theses)," 12.

63. René Girard, *The Scapegoat*, trans. Yvonne Freccero (Baltimore: Johns Hopkins University Press, 1986), 21.

64. Cohen, "The Ruins of Identity," 8.

65. Jacques Derrida, "Force of Law: The 'Mystical Foundation of Authority,'" trans. Mary Quaintance, in *Deconstruction and the Possibility of Justice*, ed. Drucilla Cornell, Michel Rosenfeld, and David Gray Carlson (London: Routledge, 1992), 6. On the question of whether or violence can ever be "a moral means even to just ends," see also Walter Benjamin, "Critique of Violence," trans. Edmund Jephcott, in *Walter Benjamin: Selected Writings, 1913–1926*, ed. Marcus Bullock and Michael W. Jennings (Cambridge, Mass.: Harvard University Press, 1996), 236–52. Derrida responds to Benjamin's essay in great detail in "Force of Law."

66. Cohen, "The Ruins of Identity," 26.

67. Robert Gibbs, "Philosophy and Law: Questioning Justice," in *The Ethical*, ed. Edith Wyschogrod and Gerald P. McKenny (Oxford: Blackwell, 2003), 105. Gibbs's essay is an extended meditation upon the relations of ethics, law, justice, and violence in the philosophy of Hermann Cohen, Levinas, Benjamin, and Derrida.

68. Levinas's hospitality, of course, would not be able to succeed within any model of conformity; indeed, it depends on the appearance and welcoming of the nonconformist.

69. Andy Orchard has pointed out that Grendel's mother's mere is described in "human, almost homey terms" (*Pride and Prodigies: Studies in the Monsters of the 'Beowulf'-Manuscript* [Cambridge: D. S. Brewer, 1995], 30), and Cohen has written that her underwater cave is "just another version of Heorot" ("The Ruins of Identity," 27).

70. John Caputo, *The Weakness of God: A Theology of the Event* (Bloomington: Indiana University Press, 2006), 278.

71. Simon Critchley provides one possible answer with the Levinasian "anarchic meta-politics" delineated in his book *Infinitely Demanding*.

72. *TI* 193. In book 11 of his *Libri Etymologiarum*, Isidore of Seville wrote that "monstrosities, *monstra*, are named from an admonition, *monitus*, because they point out something by signaling...what may immediately appear" (quoted in John Block Friedman, *The Monstrous Races in Medieval Art and Thought* [Cambridge, Mass.: Harvard University Press, 1981], 112).

NOTES TO KAUFMAN, "THERE IS HORROR"

1. Drawing inspiration primarily from the Old Testament, where Moses likens himself to a mother carrying an infant at her breast (Num. 11:12) and God similarly describes himself as a mother, bearing the Israelites in his bosom, conceiving them in his womb (e.g., Isa. 49:1, 15, and 66:11–13), Christian exegetes, teachers, and preachers of the Middle Ages pictured Jesus as a nursing mother and themselves either as suckling infants or as mothers feeding at their breasts the babes entrusted by God to their instruction. Medieval commentators on the Lukan phrase "the bosom of Abraham" understood it as unabashedly feminine and maternal in its origins, traceable back to the feeding of the unborn in the womb, the nursing of the infant at the breast, and what Francis Gigot terms "the universal custom of parents to take up into their arms, or place upon their knees, their children when they are fatigued, or return home, and to make them rest by their side during the night (cf. 2 Kings [1 Sam.] 12:2; 3 Kings [1 Kings] 3:20; 3 Kings [1 Kings] 17:19; Luke 11:7)." See Francis E. Gigot, "Abraham, the Bosom of," *The Catholic Encyclopedia*, 15 vols. (New York: Encyclopedia Press, 1913), I:55–56. I thank Ann Astell and Justin Jackson for noting this Lukan passage.

2. See Jacques Le Goff, *The Birth of Purgatory*, trans. Arthur Goldhammer (Chicago: University of Chicago Press, 1984), 1–12. For a fruitful examination of Purgatory in Dante's *The Divine Comedy* and Bonvesin da la Riva's *Book of the Three Scriptures* (written a few decades before Dante's work), see Manuele Gragnolati, *Experiencing the Afterlife: Soul and Body in Dante and Medieval Culture* (Notre Dame: University of Notre Dame Press, 2005), esp. 89–137. Gragnolati's analysis, in particular his comparison of Bonvesin's emphasis on Christ's Passion and Mary's compassion and Dante's emphasis on the physical pain of Purgatory, complements Le Goff's perspective. For another engaging study of Purgatory, see Stephen Greenblatt: *Hamlet in Purgatory* (Princeton: Princeton University Press, 2001). Greenblatt focuses his analysis primarily on aspects of cultural memory, religion, and spectral apparitions. The entry for "Purgatory" in the *New Catholic Encyclopedia* cites the following passages which imply a space we identify as Purgatory: 2 Macc. 12:39–45, Matt. 12:32, and 2 Tim. 1:18. J. F. X. Cevetello, "Purgatory:

In The Bible," in *New Catholic Encyclopedia,* 18 vols. (New York: McGraw Hill; Washington, D. C.: The Catholic University of America, 1967), 11:1034.

3. For an edition of *De Tribus Regibus Mortuis,* see Thorlac Turville-Petre, ed., *Alliterative Poetry of the Later Middle Ages: An Anthology* (Washington, D. C.: The Catholic University of America Press, 1989), 148–57. For an edition of *Trentalle Sancti Gregorii,* see Albert Kaufmann, ed., *Trentalle Sancti Gregorii, eine Mittelenglische Legende* (Erlangen and Leipzig, 1889; repr., Amsterdam: Rodopi, 1970).

4. For a partial account of the origins of this idea, see *EI* 47–52.

5. *EE* 57. For other references to Shakespeare's tragedies, see *TO* 50, 72–73, 78; *TI* 146, 231; *OB* 3, 117. For a Levinasian reading of *Macbeth* that pays attention to the special diction of the play, see Jeremy Tambling, "Levinas and *Macbeth*'s 'Strange Images of Death'," *Essays in Criticism* 54, no. 4 (2004): 351–75.

6. Colin Davis, *Levinas: An Introduction* (Notre Dame: University of Notre Dame Press, 1996), 130.

7. Ibid., 23.

8. Ibid., 130.

9. See Jill Robbins, *Altered Reading: Levinas and Literature* (Chicago: University of Chicago Press, 1999), 93–97.

10. Davis, *Levinas,* 131.

11. Levinas consciously echoes Shakespeare's *Macbeth* V.v: "Out, out, brief candle! Life's but a walking shadow. . . . it is a tale told by an idiot, full of sound and fury, signifying nothing."

12. Davis, *Levinas,* 23.

13. Ibid., 136.

14. Ibid., 136.

15. Richard A. Cohen, "Introduction," *TO* 3.

16. Emmanuel Levinas, "The Trace of the Other," trans. Alphonso Lingis, in *Deconstruction in Context,* ed. Mark C. Taylor (Chicago: University of Chicago Press, 1986), 349. On Levinas's use of this Abrahamic comparison, see Robbins, *Altered Reading,* 7, 9, 21, 91, 101, 104, 113, 114.

17. Davis, *Levinas,* 58.

18. This observation extends and develops a suggestion made by Ann W. Astell, "Mater-Natality: Augustine, Arendt, and Levinas," *Analecta Husserliana* 89 (2006): 382.

19. For discussions of the various place-names in the *Awntyrs,* see the following articles: Rosamund Allen, "Place Names in *The Awntyrs Off Arthure*: Corruption, Conjecture, Coincidence," in *Arthurian Studies in Honour of P. J. C. Field,* Arthurian Studies LVII, ed. Bonnie Wheeler (Cambridge: D. S. Brewer, 2004), 181–98; Andrew Breeze, "*The Awntyrs off Arthure,* Caerphilly, Oysterlow, and Wexford," *Arthuriana* 9, no. 4 (1999): 63–68; and Andrew Breeze, "*The Awntyrs off Arthure,* Cywryd of Kent, and Lavery Burn," *Notes and Queries* 45, no. 4 (1998): 431–32.

20. All quotations from *The Awntyrs off Arthure* [*AA*], with corresponding line numbers given in parentheses, are taken from Ralph Hanna III, ed., *The Awntyrs*

off Arthure at the Terne Wathelyn, An Edition Based on Bodleian Library MS. Douce 324 (New York: Barnes & Noble Books, 1974). Hanna dates the poem as roughly 1400–1430 (52). Other editions consulted include *The Awntyrs off Arthur* in Thomas Hahn, ed., *Sir Gawain: Eleven Romances and Tales,* TEAMS Middle English Texts Series (Kalamazoo, Mich.: Medieval Institute Publications, 1995), 169–226; Helen Phillips, ed., *The Awntyrs of Arthure,* Lancaster Modern Spelling Texts 1 (Lancaster: Lancaster University Department of English, 1988); and Robert J. Gates, ed., *The Awntyrs off Arthure at the Terne Wathelyne: A Critical Edition* (Philadelphia: University of Pennsylvania Press, 1969). All subsequent translations of *The Awntyrs* are my own. The "close-season" was a time where it was illegal to hunt male deer. The first hunt in *Sir Gawain and the Green Knight* also occurs during "fermysoun tyme" (1156) in *Sir Gawain and the Green Knight,* ed. J. R. R. Tolkien and E. V. Gordon. 2nd rev. ed., ed. Norman Davis (Oxford: Clarendon Press, 1967).

21. Jean-Claude Schmitt, *Ghosts in the Middle Ages: The Living and the Dead in Medieval Society,* trans. Teresa Lavender Fagan (Chicago: University of Chicago Press, 1998), 184.

22. *EE* 57–58; see also *TO* 50–51, 72–73. In a way, this nonsubjectivity of Levinas's "there is" is similar to what Julia Kristeva identifies in *Powers of Horror* as "Not Me": "A massive and sudden emergence of uncanniness, which, familiar as it might have been in an opaque and forgotten life, now harries me as radically separate, loathsome. Not me. Not that. But not nothing, either. A 'something' that I do not recognize as a thing. A weight of meaninglessness, about which there is nothing insignificant, and which crushes me. On the edge of non-existence and hallucination, of a reality that, if I acknowledge it annihilates me" (*Powers of Horror: An Essay on Abjection,* trans. Leon S. Roudiez [New York: Columbia University Press, 1982], 2).

23. This liminal space upon which Gawain and Gaynour stumble, and its description in the *Awntyrs,* bears close resemblance to two other episodes in medieval English literature, both of which are well-known. The immediate, and most closely connected in terms of the literary similarities of character, is the alliterative late-fourteenth century poem *Sir Gawain and the Green Knight.* On All Saints' Day, Gawain leaves Arthur's court at Camelot to embark on a long journey to the Green Knight's Castle. Gawain suddenly finds himself outside of the realm of civilization and into the clod, bleak terrain of Northern Wales, the "wyldrenesse of Wyrale," (l. 701) where he and his horse Gringolet encounter many strange and marvelous sights (dragons, intense sleet, marshes, bulls and bears, ogres and other wild men). See *Sir Gawain and the Green Knight,* 20–22. For a discussion of the landscape of *Sir Gawain and the Green Knight,* see Ralph Elliot, "Landscape and Geography," in *A Companion to the Gawain Poet,* Arthurian Studies 38, ed. Derek Brewer and Jonathan Gibson (Cambridge: D. S. Brewer, 1997), 105–17.

24. The epic Anglo-Saxon poem *Beowulf* contains a comparative scene. All of the troubles Hrothgar has been having with Grendel are due is large part to the Danish king's carelessness when erecting Heorot, the great hall. Heorot is built

upon what appears to be sacred ground; this upsets Grendel (and we assume his mother), for the killings take place soon after the hall is completed. The Danes, trespassing within the wilderness area, encroaching upon this liminal space, will thus pay for their mistake(s). Even more interesting, though, is Beowulf's journey to the underwater mere where he will battle and kill Grendel's mother as well as behead a virtually lifeless Grendel. This underwater dwelling where the two beings live (one of which is part woman/mother and part creature, similar to Gaynour's Mother) is described thusly: "Þær mæg nihta gehwæm nīðwundor sēon,/fyr on flōde" (1365–66) [There every night a fearful wonder is seen,/fire on the water], in *Beowulf and The Fight at Finnsburg*, ed. Fr. Klaeber, 3rd ed. (Boston: D. C. Heath, 1968). Klaeber notes that the burning lake is a common feature of hell in Western and Eastern religions, 183–84. See also Mary Dockray-Miller, *Motherhood and Mothering in Anglo-Saxon England* (New York: St. Martin's Press, 2000), 77–78; and, William Witherie Lawrence, "The Haunted Mere in *Beowulf*," *PMLA* 27, no. 2 (1912): 208–45.

25. These glowing eyes are the toad's and not the ghost's.

26. As Le Goff explains, Purgatory is essentially an intermediary zone between this life and Heaven, where holy souls are subjected to one or more trials, and where the living, through their intercessory prayers, may lessen or cause to cease the pains that the souls endure. See Le Goff, *The Birth of Purgatory*, 1–12. While in Purgatory, the soul must be freed from certain defects: (1) the guilt of venial sin, (2) the desire to sin, and (3) temporal punishment due to sin. Prayers for the dead, as well as other works of piety (such as fasting, alms, and sacrifices), are maintained to be the ways the faithful on earth can merit indulgences and help those in Purgatory. R. J. Bastian describes this purification as a gradual process ("Purgatory: In Theology," *New Catholic Encyclopedia*, 11:1036.).

27. Jacques Le Goff, *The Medieval Imagination*, trans. by Arthur Goldhammer (Chicago: University of Chicago Press, 1988), 84.

28. Claire Elise Katz, *Levinas, Judaism, and the Feminine: The Silent Footsteps of Rebecca* (Bloomington: Indiana University Press, 2003), 23.

29. Ibid., 50.

30. Ibid., 24–25.

31. *OB* 75–76.

32. Within the Arthurian tradition lies the constant theme of Guenevere as barren. However, the Welsh tradition maintains that she was able to bear Arthur sons. In the *Alliterative Morte Arthur* there is the unique narrative thread that claims that Guenevere bore Mordred's sons.

33. One is tempted to analyze Gaynour's childless state and lack of concern for others as a partial effect of being orphaned. When her mother died, something apparently happened to Gaynour: she lost whatever motherly instincts she had.

34. For an examination of the roles that surrogate parents (godmothers and godfathers) played in medieval England, especially when the birth parent(s) died, see Barbara A. Hanawalt, *The Ties That Bound: Peasant Families in Medieval England* (Oxford: Oxford University Press, 1986), 245–56.

35. The sacrament of baptism was taken so seriously in medieval England — for fear that the child would die in a state of original sin — that children were rapidly baptized. See Hanawalt, *The Ties That Bound,* 172–73.

36. Katz argues quite forcefully that "Levinas's philosophy is life-affirming, and the feminine, as both empirical figure and metaphorical attribute, plays a key role in achieving that end. See her *Levinas, Judaism, and the Feminine,* 155. For an examination of Levinas's approach towards the feminine (and the role it has played in feminist theory—such works by Luce Irigaray and Simone de Beauvoir), see Stella Sandford, "Levinas, feminism, and the feminine," in *The Cambridge Companion to Levinas,* ed. Simon Critchley and Robert Bernasconi (Cambridge: Cambridge University Press, 2002), 139–60.

37. I borrow this expression from Regenia Gagnier, *Subjectivities: A History of Self-Representation in Britain, 1832–1920* (Oxford: Oxford University Press, 1991), 8.

38. The responsibility that children in the Middle Ages bore for their parents was multi-faceted. Parents saw to it that their children received vocational training, in part as a means for their own support in old age. On this topic, see Christopher Dyer, *Making a Living in the Middle Ages: The People of Britain 850–1520* (New Haven: Yale University Press, 2002), 159–60. Anticipating a "good death," parents wrote last wills that bound their children and heirs to care properly for the possessions bequeathed to them. They also instructed and expected their children to provide for the needs of their departed souls through prayers and alms offered on their behalf. See Paul Binski, *Medieval Death: Ritual and Representation* (London: The British Museum Press, 2001), 33.

39. Helen Philips, "The Ghost's Baptism in *The Awntyrs off Arthure,*" *Medium Ævum* 58, no. 1 (1989): 48–58.

40. Ibid., 56.

41. Cf. Matt. 16:25. On the corporal and spiritual powers of the Holy Communion, see: F. W. Dewan, "Eucharist (As Sacrament)," *New Catholic Encyclopedia,* 5:599–608.

42. Emmanuel Levinas, *"'Que dirait Eurydice?'" Emmanuel Levinas en conversation avec Bracha Lichtenberg-Ettinger* (Paris: BLE Atelier, 1977), 27, quoted in Katz, *Levinas, Judaism, and the Feminine,* 52.

43. For a discussion of Christian merit, see C. S. Sullivan, "Merit," in the *New Catholic Encyclopedia,* 9:683–86.

44. Christine Chism, *Alliterative Revivals* (Philadelphia: University of Pennsylvania Press, 2002), 255.

45. Alphonso Lingis, "Translator's Introduction," *OB* xxxix.

46. On this point, see Annette Aronowicz, "Introduction," *NT* xxviii.

47. I do not mean to imply, of course, that the question of the relation of the living to the dead is the only question driving Levinas's formulation of the notion of *illeity.*

48. Aronowicz, *NT* xxviii–xxix.

49. On the *kaddish* prayer and of Jewish practices of death, mourning, and

burial, see Anita Diamant, *Saying Kaddish: How to Comfort the Dying, Bury the Dead, and Mourn as a Jew* (New York: Schocken Books, 1998); Maurice Lamm, *The Jewish Way in Death and Mourning,* revised and expanded (Middle Village, N.Y.: Jonathan David, 2000); Rachel S. Hallote, *Death Burial, and Afterlife in the Biblical World* (Chicago: Ivan R. Dee, 2001); Rochelle L. Millen, *Women, Birth, and Death in Jewish Law and Practice* (Hanover: Brandeis University Press, 2004), esp. 111–59; Samuel C. Heilman, *When a Jew Dies: The Ethnography of a Bereaved Son* (Berkeley and Los Angeles: University of California Press, 2001).

50. Adin Steinsaltz, *A Guide to Jewish Prayer* (New York: Schocken Books), 18–19.

51. Diamant, *Saying Kaddish,* 13. Diamant's study includes several translations of the *Kaddish;* see esp. 202–12.

52. Diamant, *Saying Kaddish,* 16.

53. Ibid., 21.

54. Lamm, *The Jewish Way in Death and Mourning,* 231–32. Maimonides, believed that a person cannot have a clear sense as to what the afterlife is like; see Maimonides, *Mishneh Torah,* vol. 1, ed. and trans. Moses Hymanson (Jerusalem: Boys Town, 1965), 91a.

55. Heilman, *When a Jew Dies,* 198.

56. *The Awntyrs off Arthure* is a poem that is, in many ways, also grounded and driven by doubles. As you recall, we have two central women who are, in a certain sense, mirror images of one another; there is also the ghost/Sir Galleron parallel.

57. For a translation of the names of Levinas's family members into English, see Michael Purcell, *Levinas and Theology* (Cambridge: Cambridge University Press, 2006), 4. The names are Levinas's father, Yekhiel ben Rabbi Avraham Halevi; his mother, Dvora bat Rabbi Moshe Halevi; his brothers, Dov ben Rabbi Yehiel and Aminadav ben Rabbi Yekhiel Halevi; his father-in-law, Shmuel ben Rabbi Guershon Halevi; and his mother-in-law, Malki bat Rabbi Haim.

58. An early version of this paper was presented at The 40th International Congress on Medieval Studies, Western Michigan University, May 5–8, 2005. I would like to thank Ann Astell and Justin Jackson for their insightful comments and our rewarding discussions throughout the writing of this essay, and Ann, in particular, for "hands on" editing in the final revision of this essay.

NOTES TO KLINE, "DOING JUSTICE TO ISAAC"

1. Erich Auerbach, *Mimesis: The Representation of Reality in Western Literature,* trans. Willard Trask (Princeton: Princeton University Press, 1953), 3–24.

2. The six preserved episodes are "The Brome Play of Abraham and Isaac" and "The Northampton Play of Abraham and Isaac," in *Non-Cycle Plays and Fragments,* ed. Norman Davis, EETS s.s. 1 (New York: Oxford University Press, 1970), 43–57, and 33–42; "The Barbers Playe" (Play IV), *The Chester Mystery Cycle,* ed.

R. M. Lumiansky and David Mills, 2 vols., EETS s.s. 3 and 9 (London: Oxford University Press, 1974, 1986); "Abraham and Isaac," *The N-Town Play: Cotton MS Vespasian D.8,* ed. Stephen Spector, 2 vols., EETS s.s. 11 and 12 (Oxford: Oxford University Press, 1991), 1:50–58; "Abraham," *The Towneley Plays,* ed. Martin Stevens and A. C. Cawley, 2 vols., EETS s.s. 13 and 14 (Oxford: Oxford University Press, 1994), 1:48–59; "Abraham and Isaac" (York X, The Parchmentmakers and Bookbinders), in *The York Plays,* ed. Richard Beadle (London: Edward Arnold, 1982), 91–100. A seventh only briefly mentions the incident: "The Beginning of the World" [*Origo Mundi*], *The Ancient Cornish Drama,* ed. Edwin Norris, 2 vols. (Oxford, 1859), 1:97–103.

3. For an analysis using this approach, which we worked out over three years of conversation, see Allen J. Frantzen, "Tears for Abraham: The Chester Play of Abraham and Isaac and Antisacrifice in Works by Wilfred Owen, Benjamin Britten, and Derek Jarman," *Journal of Medieval and Early Modern Studies* 31, no. 3 (Fall 2001): 445–76.

4. From the Douay-Rheims translation of the Vulgate. Available online at http://www.latinvulgate.com. All biblical citations will be from the Douay-Rheims.

5. Shalom Spiegel, *The Last Trial* [*Me-agadot ha-akedah*] (Woodstock, Vt.: Jewish Lights Publishing, 1993), 3.

6. The function of Kierkegaard's pseudonyms and the manner in which the pseudonymous works distance or reveal Kierkegaard's personal view is complex. Two standard works are John W. Elrod, *Being and Existence in Kierkegaard's Pseudonymous Works* (Princeton: Princeton University Press, 1975) and Mark C. Taylor, *Kierkegaard's Pseudonymous Authorship: A Study of Time and the Self* (Princeton: Princeton University Press, 1975). Alastair Hannay's recent *Kierkegaard and Philosophy: Selected Essays* (London: Routledge, 2003) foregrounds the issue of Kierkegaard's pseudonyms in relation to his veronymous writings. Critical views run the gamut, usually influenced by a critic's rhetorical and theoretical purposes. Amy Laura-Hall, in *Kierkegaard and the Treachery of Love* (Cambridge: Cambridge University Press, 2002), argues that Silentio is to be taken as an unreliable narrator (52). M. Holmes Hartshorne, in *Kierkegaard, Godly Deceiver: The Nature and Meaning of His Pseudonymous Writings* (New York: Columbia University Press, 1990), argues that *Fear and Trembling* does not reflect Kierkegaard's views (though it is concerned with his break with Regine) and should be read ironically (75). In a third, perhaps consensus, view, Michael R. Michau argues that Kierkegaard himself moves away from suspending the ethical in the later veronymous *Works of Love* ("The Ethical and Religious Revelation of the Akedah," *Minerva: An Internet Journal of Philosophy* 9 [2005]: 134–52). Historically speaking, Michael Strawser, in *Both/And: Reading Kierkegaard from Irony to Edification* (New York: Fordham University Press, 1997), argues that Kierkegaard's pseudonymity was a strategy for engaging Copenhagen readers and deflecting their criticism (92). Strawser approvingly cites C. Stephen Evans's *Kierkegaard's "Fragments" and "Postscript": The Religious Philosophy of Johannes Climacus* (Atlantic Highlands, N.J.: Humanities Press, 1983) (95). Evans states that "it really does not matter

very much whether Kierkegaard personally held these views. For from the fact that he held a view, nothing follows as to the truth, profundity, or value of the view" (8–9). However, Levinas clearly sees Kierkegaard as the author of *Fear and Trembling*, and *Fear and Trembling* to be indicative of Kierkegaard's—rather than the pseudonymous Silentio's—views.

7. For a reading that argues that Abraham does not actually believe that God will require such a sacrifice, see Andrew Cross, "Faith and the Suspension of the Ethical in *Fear and Trembling*," *Inquiry: An Interdisciplinary Journal of Philosophy* 46, no. 1 (2003): 3–28.

8. *Fear and Trembling* and *The Sickness Unto Death* [*FT*], trans. Walter Lowrie (Princeton: Princeton University Press, 1968), 72. Unless otherwise noted, all citations for *Fear and Trembling* will be to this edition.

9. In Anthony Ruud's words, "This is the existentialist Kierkegaard, the spokesman for the free, lonely, responsible individual, whose voice, taken up and amplified by so many, from Ibsen through Sartre to the present day, has resonated so powerfully in our culture" (*Kierkegaard and the Limits of the Ethical* [Oxford: Clarendon Press, 1997], 118). Jacob Golomb's *In Search of Authenticity: From Kierkegaard to Camus* (New York: Routledge, 1995) represents this strain of commentary on *Fear and Trembling* (see esp. 61–62). For Golomb, "the demand for absolute conformity prevents the emergence of the unique individual" (59), thus warranting Abraham's transcendence of the ethical (and therefore violence against Isaac) on individualistic, existential grounds.

10. For example, see Kierkegaard's sermon notes to Galatians 4:1–7: "Christianity is a matter of being a man, Judaism of being a child. In dealing with a child, we do not place his whole childhood at his disposal and tell him that in 7 or 8 years he will be checked to see how he has used them. No, no every day, every week, every month we supervise the child. Judaism displays this childishness in the relationship to God. 'The Test' lasts for a time and then is all over—but please note, within this earthly life" (*Søren Kierkegaard's Journals and Papers*, 4 vols., ed. and trans. by Howard V. Hong and Edna H. Hong (Bloomington: Indiana University Press, 1967), 2:507). Subsequent citations to Kierkegaard's *Journals and Papers* are from this edition.

11. Emmanuel Levinas, "Useless Suffering," *EN* 91–101. Kierkegaard writes in his journal: "Thus in one sense Christianity is infinitely more rigourous than Judaism; letting go, giving up, and losing the things of this earth, sheer suffering, and dying to the world are literally in earnest. In another sense Christianity is infinitely more gentle, for it manifests eternity. But to be molded and transformed so that one is consoled solely by eternity means to become spirit, but to become spirit is the most agonizing of all the sufferings, even more agonizing than 'the test' in the O.T." (Hong and Hong, *Journals and Papers*, 2:506; abbr. Kierkegaard's). In another journal entry Kierkegaard asked, "In what sense the Jews can be called the chosen people is a big question. They were not the happiest of people; they were rather a sacrifice which all humanity required. They had to suffer the pains of the law and of sin as no other people. They were the chosen people in the same sense

as the poets and the like often are—that is, the most unhappy of all" (Hong and Hong, *Journals and Papers,* 2:504). Such a view should not remain unchallenged in a post-Holocaust world.

12. *PN* 74. See also Catherine Chalier, "Levinas and the Talmud," in *The Cambridge Companion to Levinas,* ed. Simon Critchley and Robert Bernasconi (Cambridge: Cambridge University Press, 2002), 100–19.

13. Levinas's unique sense of subjectivity is detailed in "Substitution," chapter 4 of *OB* 99–130. See also Philip J. Maloney's "Levinas, Substitution, and Transcendent Subjectivity," *Man and World* 30 (1997): 49–64.

14. *EI* 71; emphasis Levinas's. Here Philippe Nemo winnows down a longer quotation from Levinas in *TA* 82–87. See also *TO* 90–94. The relevant section can also be found in "Time and the Other," *LR* 52–54.

15. For historical analyses of child sacrifice in the Ancient Near East, see J. Day, *Molech: A God of Human Sacrifice in the Old Testament* (Cambridge: Cambridge University Press, 1989); Shelby Brown, *Late Carthaginian Child Sacrifice and Sacrificial Monuments in Their Mediterranean Context* (Sheffield: JSOT Press, 1991); Jon Levenson, *The Death and Resurrection of the Beloved Son: The Transformation of Child Sacrifice in Judaism and Christianity* (New Haven: Yale University, 1993); Frank Moore Cross, "A Phoenician Inscription from Idalion: Some Old and New Texts Relating to Child Sacrifice," *Scripture and Other Artifacts: Essays on the Bible and Archaeology in Honor of Philip J. King,* ed. J. Cheryl Exum, Philip J. King, and Lawrence E. Stager (Louisville, Ky.: Westminster/John Knox Press, 1994), 93–107; Susan Niditch, *War in the Hebrew Bible: A Study in the Ethics of Violence* (Oxford: Oxford University Press, 1995), 42–57.

16. *AT* 30. Compare Genesis 22:1,11. See also, *EI* 105–10: "It is what in my descriptions I have called the 'illeity' of the Infinite. Thus, in the 'Here I am!' of the approach of the Other, the Infinite does not show itself. How then does it take on meaning? I will say that the subject who says 'Here I am!' *testifies* to the Infinite. It is through this testimony, whose truth is not the truth of representation or perception, that the revelation of the Infinite occurs" (106; emphasis Levinas's).

17. *TO* 91–92. For another reading of the adult-child dynamic in Levinas (focusing on this same passage), see David Kennedy, "Parent, Child, Alterity, Dialogue," *Philosophy Today* 45, no. 1 (Spring 2001): 33–42. Kennedy's article has been helpful in my thinking about Levinas's critique of *Fear and Trembling* in terms of the analytics of childhood and age.

18. See Simone de Beauvoir, *The Second Sex* (New York: Bantam, 1970), xvi, and particularly Luce Iragary's "The Fecundity of the Caress," in *Face to Face with Levinas,* ed. Richard A. Cohen (Albany: State University of New York Press, 1986), 231–56.

19. In Kelly Oliver's excellent formulation, "for Levinas, the promise of paternity is a promise not of recognition but of nonrecognition, of strangeness, of an open future, of infinity, of singularity." Oliver continues, "It is not a promise from the past, a promise that returns to itself. Rather, the promise of paternity,

as Levinas describes it, is a promise of an open future, the promise that the son is to his father" ("Fatherhood and the Promise of Ethics," *Diacritics* 27, no. 1 [1997]: 47).

20. Mishnah Avot 5:3–4: "[3] There were ten generations from Noah to Abraham, to show how great was His patience, for every one of those generations provoked Him continually until Abraham, our father, came and received the reward of them all. [4] With ten tests was Abraham, our father, tested and he stood steadfast in them all; [they were] to show how great was His love." Many versions of the Mishnah are easily available online. This quotation comes from Mishnah Pirkei Avot, *The Ethics of the Fathers,* available online at http://www.shechem. org/torah/ avot.html#chap5. Rashi (Rabbi Shelomo Yitzchaki, 1040–1105) and Rambam or Maimonides (Rabbi Moshe Ben Maimon, 1135–1204) are the two great medieval commentators who have shaped talmudic thought into the present. Although Maimonides and Rashi identify trials 1 through 9 differently, the tenth, the *akedah,* is shared. Rashi's reading of Genesis 22:2 has been quite influential: "He did not say to him, 'Slaughter him,' because the Holy One, blessed be He, did not wish him to slaughter him but to bring him up to the mountain, to prepare him for a burnt offering, and as soon as he brought him up [to the mountain], He said to him, 'Take him down.'—[from *Gen. Rabbah* 56:8]." Rashi's commentary on Genesis 22 is easily available at http://www.chabad.org/library/article. asp?AID=8217&showrashi=true.

21. See Claire Elise Katz, "The Voice of God and the Face of the Other," *The Journal of Textual Reasoning* 2, no. 1 (June 2003), online at http://etext.lib. virginia.edu/journals/tr/volume2/katz.html. See also Katz's *Levinas, Judaism, and the Feminine: The Silent Footsteps of Rebecca* (Bloomington: Indiana University Press, 2003), 108–25.

22. "By a total transcendence, the transcendence of trans-substantiation, the I is, in the child, an other. Paternity remains a self-identification, but also a distinction within identification—as structure unforeseeable by formal logic" (*TI* 267).

23. In the Douay-Rheims, Isaiah 49:1–6 reads: (1) "Give ear, ye islands, and hearken, ye people from afar. The Lord hath called me from the womb, from the bowels of my mother he hath been mindful of my name. (2) And he hath made my mouth like a sharp sword: in the shadow of his hand he hath protected me, and hath made me as a chosen arrow: in his quiver he hath hidden me. (3) And he said to me: Thou art my servant Israel, for in thee will I glory. (4) And I said: I have laboured in vain, I have spent my strength without cause and in vain: therefore my judgment is with the Lord, and my work with my God. (5) And now saith the Lord, that formed me from the womb to be his servant, that I may bring back Jacob unto him, and Israel will not be gathered together: and I am glorified in the eyes of the Lord, and my God is made my strength. (6) And he said: It is a small thing that thou shouldst be my servant to raise up the tribes of Jacob, and to convert the dregs of Israel. Behold, I have given thee to be the light of the Gentiles, that thou mayst be my salvation even to the farthest part of the earth."

24. I will use the conventional spellings of Abraham and Isaac to refer to the biblical text (or Kierkegaard's and Levinas's readings) but Deus, Abraham, Ysaac, and the Angell to denote the Brome characters. All citations to the Brome play of *Abraham and Isaac* [*AI*] are from Davis, ed., *Non-Cycle Plays and Fragments,* 43–57. Line numbers are cited in the text.

25. In two articles, Norman Davis elaborates the history of this important form of address: "A Note on *Pearl,*" *Review of English Studies* 17 (1966): 403–05, and "Solacia in *Pearl* and in Letters of Edward III concerning the Death of his Daughter, Joan," *Notes and Queries* 31 (1984): 454–59. Davis identifies numerous examples in correspondences of the twelfth through sixteenth centuries, including at least 34 occurrences in the Paston correspondence. The formula is also found in the York *Noah,* and in the Chester, York, N-Town, and Brome Abraham plays, and in the Towneley *Isaac* (332–33). See *Pearl*: "In Krystez dere blessyng and myne" (l. 1208), in *The Poems of the Pearl Manuscript,* ed. Malcolm Andrew and Ronald Waldron, 4th ed. (Exeter: University of Exeter Press, 2004), 110.

26. *TI* 278–79: "The father does not simply cause the son. *To be* one's son means to be I in one's son, to be substantially in him, yet without being maintained there in identity. Our whole analysis of fecundity aimed to establish this dialectical conjunction, which conserves the contradictory movements. The son resumes the unicity of the father and yet remains exterior to the father: the son is the unique son. Not by number; each son of the father is the unique son, the chosen son. The love of the father for the son accomplishes the sole relation possible with the very unicity of another. But this relation of the father with the son is not *added* to the already constituted I of the son, as a good fortune.... He is unique for himself because he is unique for his father. This is precisely why he can, as a child, not exist 'on his own'" (emphasis Levinas's).

27. See *OB* 31.

28. Levinas writes in *Otherwise Than Being*: "This absolute passivity beneath the neutrality of things takes on the form of incarnation, corporeity — susceptibility to pain, outrage, and unhappiness. It bears in its susceptibility the trace of this *hither side* of things, as the responsibility for that of which there was no will, in the persecuted one, in ipseity, that is, as responsibility for the very persecution it suffers" (197, n. 26; emphasis Levinas's).

29. See, for example, "Diachrony and Representation," *EN* 158–77, esp. 166–67.

30. See Daniel T. Kline, "Jephthah's Daughter and Chaucer's Virginia: The Critique of Sacrifice in the *Physician's Tale,*" forthcoming in *The Journal of English and Germanic Philology.* For an example of reading passivity as acquiescence, see Milla C. Riggio's rather schematic anthropological and psychological reading of the Abraham and Isaac plays in "The Terrible Mourning of Abraham," *Medievalia* 18 (1995): 285–319. Levinas radically reformulates passivity in relation to uniqueness and chosenness (*OB* 56–57).

31. See James C. Scott, *Weapons of the Weak: Everyday Forms of Peasant Resistance* (New Haven: Yale University Press, 1985).

32. After all, near the end of the play Ysaac remarks, "I thank owre Lord euery dell, / That my wyt servyd me so wull" (408–09).

33. Davis accepts Manly's emendation to "fewe" at 230. Davis notes, interestingly, that the ms reads "feve" (as in perhaps five strokes of the blade?).

34. Levinas writes: "Signification is the ethical deliverance of the self through substitution for the other" (*OB* 164).

35. The most recent summation is René Girard, *I See Satan Fall Like Lightning*, trans. James G. Williams (Maryknoll, N.Y.: Orbis Books, 2001), but see also Girard's *The Scapegoat*, trans. Yvonne Freccero (Baltimore: Johns Hopkins University Press, 1989); *Things Hidden Since the Foundation of the World*, trans. Stephen Bann and Michael Metteer (Palo Alto: Stanford University Press, 1987); and perhaps most importantly, *Violence and the Sacred*, trans. Patrick Gregory (Baltimore: Johns Hopkins University Press, 1979).

36. Davis accepts Holthausen's emendation to "nowt" at 337. The ms reads "not зyt," which would indicate that Ysaac continues to believe he is to die. I am retaining the harsher language of the ms.

37. Davis accepts Holthausen's emendation, "And commawndyd yow yowre chyld to slayn" at 444, but I have retained here the harsher language of the ms.

38. The talmudic commentary is presented in Spiegel, *The Last Trial*.

39. Jacques Derrida, *Specters of Marx: The State of the Debt, the Work of Mourning, and the New International*, trans. Peggy Kamuf (New York: Routledge, 1994), 126; emphasis Derrida's. The parenthetical phrases are from Kamuf.

NOTES TO PAXSON, "THE PERSONIFICATIONAL FACE"

1. Mary Carruthers, "Allegory Without the Teeth: Some Reflections of Figural Language in *Piers Plowman*," *The Yearbook of Langland Studies* 19 (2005): 27–43.

2. Larry Scanlon, "Personification and Penance," *The Yearbook of Langland Studies* 21 (2007): 1–29.

3. Ibid., 2; 29.

4. William Langland, *Piers Plowman: the B Version* [*PP*], ed. George Kane and E. Talbot Donaldson (London: Athlone, 1975), 15.22–36.

5. Scanlon, "Personification and Penance," 26.

6. Angus Fletcher, *Allegory: The Theory of a Symbolic Mode* (Ithaca: Cornell University Press, 1964), 25–69.

7. See my discussion of the extrusion of a personified dream character into the diegetically encompassing, outer frame of Will's waking experience in *The Poetics of Personification* (Cambridge: Cambridge University Press, 1994), 120–21.

8. Catherine Chalier, "Levinas and the Talmud," in *The Cambridge Companion to Levinas*, ed. Simon Critchley and Robert Bernasconi (Cambridge University Press, 2002), 107.

9. See Bernhard Waldenfels, "Levinas and the Face of the Other," *The Cambridge Companion to Levinas* (63–81), for a good overview regarding the Levinasian face.

10. Susan Handelman, *Fragments of Redemption: Jewish Thought and Literary Theory in Benjamin, Scholem, and Levinas* (Bloomington: Indiana University Press, 1991), 212.

11. Paul de Man, *The Resistance to Theory* (Minneapolis: University of Minnesota Press, 1986), 48.

12. Best known are Paul de Man's studies of thematized *prosopopeia* in "Autobiography as De-Facement," in *The Rhetoric of Romanticism* (New York: Columbia University Press, 1984), 67–81; and "Hypogram and Inscription" and "Reading and History," in *The Resistance to Theory*, 27–53, 54–72, respectively. Note too that, following de Man's lead, J. Hillis Miller has coined the expression "paraprosopopeia" to convey the sense of the making and/or unmaking of a personification figure at a poem's narrative and thematic level; see *Versions of Pygmalion* (Cambridge: Cambridge University Press, 1990), 228. I myself had, in turn, applied de Man's self-reflexive rhetorical system of prosopopoetic semiosis, wherein "defacement" or the disfiguration of faces calls into epistemological question the poetic efficacy of the trope, in my reading of the violent destruction of Prudentius' Vices in the *Psychomachia*. See Paxson, *The Poetics of Personification*, 66–70. Shortly after my treatment, Gordon Teskey published his important declaration about the universal violence in all "allegory" that inculcates intensive bodily demolition at iconographic and diegetic levels; see *Allegory and Violence* (Ithaca: Cornell University Press, 1996). Teskey's approach and model of violent allegory I have called "Gírardian and Nietzschean"; see my "(Re)facing *Prosopopeia* and Allegory in Contemporary Theory and Iconography," *Studies in Iconography* 22 (2001): 5.

13. See for instance Laura Wyrick, "Facing Up to the Other: Race and Ethics in Levinas and Behn," *In Proximity: Emmanuel Levinas and the Eighteenth Century*, ed. Melvyn New, Robert Bernasconi, and Richard A. Cohen (Lubbock: Texas Tech University Press, 2001), 53–68.See page 63 for the resolution that the grisly climax of Aphra Behn's late-seventeenth century novel, *Oroonoko*, which stages the actual "severing [of Imoinda's] yet smiling face from [her] delicate body" lest the beautiful black slave girl fall into the hands of Oroonoko's enemies, a group of white slavers and Oroonoko's late owners, dramatizes at a literal level Levinas's concept of the face at the extreme moment of violence-bloody defacement.

14. Handelman, *Fragments of Redemption*, 216.

15. In their Introduction to "Meaning and Sense," Levinas's editors well establish the primacy of the three key tropes hyperbole, emphasis, and paradox, while enigma they show to likewise govern the rhetorical structure of Levinasian discourse (*BPW* 33–34).

16. Handelman, *Fragments of Redemption*, 213.

17. Gilles Deleuze and Félix Guattari, *A Thousand Plateaus: Capitalism and Schizophrenia*, trans. Brian Massumi (Minneapolis: University of Minnesota Press, 1989), 170.

18. Ibid., 170.

19. Such daemonic quality for Deleuze and Guattari is generated thusly: "We can even propose the following law: the more circles there are around a hole, the

more the bordering effect acts to increase the surface over which the hole slides and to give that surface a force of capture. Perhaps the purest case is to be found in popular Ethiopian scrolls representing demons: on the white surface of the parchment, two black holes are drawn, or an outline of round or rectangular faces; but the black holes spread and reproduce, they enter into redundancy, and each time a secondary circle is drawn, a new black hole is constituted, an eye is put in it" (Deleuze and Guattari, *A Thousand Plateaus,* 182–83). I initially had employed the Deleuzean scheme of the white wall/black hole machine to help describe the polyfaced devils of medieval manuscript and wall art; see "The Nether-Faced Devil and the Allegory of Parturition," *Studies in Iconography* 19 (1998): 155–57. The Mercier study adduced by Deleuze and Guattari is *Ethiopian Magic Scrolls,* trans. Richard Pevear (New York: Braziller, 1979).

20. According to Handelman, "Another contemporary Jewish Philosopher, Rabbi Joseph B. Soloveitchik, makes a similar argument [to Levinas] for a rational approach to philosophy and religion and for not divorcing religious knowledge from temporality and sensibility. Soloveitchik, like Levinas, is haunted by the collapse of reason in Europe in World War II and the subsequent atrocities." (Handelman, *Fragments of Redemption,* 215). See also Joseph B. Soloveitchik, *The Halakhic Mind: An Essay on Jewish Tradition and Modern Thought* (New York: Free Press, 1986), 50–53.

21. See Levinas, "Franz Rosenzweig: A Modern Jewish Thinker" *OS* 49–66.

22. Franz Rosenzweig, *The Star of Redemption,* trans. William W. Hallo (Boston: Beacon Press, 1964).

23. John Llewelyn, "What is Orientation in Thinking? Facing the Facts in *Robinson Crusoe,*" *In Proximity,* 79.

24. Ibid., 79.

25. As Levinas declares in "Ethics as First Philosophy": "Prior to any particular expression and beneath all particular expressions, which cover over and protect with an immediately adopted face or countenance, there is the nakedness and destitution of the expression as such, that is to say extreme exposure, defencelessness, vulnerability itself" (*LR* 83).

26. Jacob Bronowski, *The Ascent of Man* [*AM*] (Boston and Toronto: Little, Brown and Company, 1973); film, directed by Dick Gilling, Mick Jackson, David John Kennard and Adrian Malone, narrator and performed by Jacob Bronowski (BBC, 1973).

27. Ironically, the gigantic sculpted head of Borgrajewicz—rendered in its size simply so we could see some details (ears and slant of face) in accord with the meter-long lengths of radio waves—resembles the gigantic heads of Easter Island, effigies which Bronowski, in his final essay in the book and telefilm ("The Long Childhood"), declares to be representations of the impersonal, prescientific, authoritative, "ancestral," "crude" and "dead" personalities that rule nonscientific and nondemocratic societies. These Easter Island heads, in short, "even look like Mussolini" (*AM* 425), as Bronowski quips.

28. Walter Benjamin, *The Origin of German Tragic Drama*, trans. Robert Osborne (London: Verso, 1977), 166.

29. Is the personified entity in an allegorical text merely an animated noun, or is it an actual personage walking about? Such a radical and crucial distinction was first speculated upon by Morton W. Bloomfield, "A Grammatical Approach to Personification Allegory," *Modern Philology* 56 (1958): 73–81; and was fully put to application and test regarding Langland's poem in Lavinia Griffiths, *Personification in "Piers Plowman"* (Cambridge: D. S. Brewer, 1985).

30. See Susan Buck-Morss, *The Dialectics of Seeing: Walter Benjamin and the Arcades Project* (Cambridge, Mass.: MIT Press, 1992).

31. One of Bronowski's more brilliant and moving explanations of science as a human enterprise built up out of workable analogies and metaphors that we share as humans is *Science and Human Values*, rev. ed. (New York: Harper and Row, 1965), a book written as a response to his witnessing of devastated Nagasaki in 1945 when he served as a governmentally appointed civilian science advisor (3–4). "Knowledge and Certainty" proceeds directly from the findings and feelings expressed in this prior book. Bronowski's further philosophical ruminations on the violence of political and social irrationalism at mid-twentieth century take a title that is the chiasmus of one of Levinas's own significant titlings: see Bronowski, *The Face of Violence: An Essay and a Play* (Cleveland: The World Publishing Company, 1967); and of course, Levinas, "Violence of the Face," *AT* 169–82. This convenient chiasmus notwithstanding, my research is unique in linking Levinasian with Bronowskian thought and discourse.

32. See my discussions of Anima as an allegorical figure for ethically intransigent erotic and rhetorical pulsions, in line with Lacanian and various deconstructive procedures, at work in the genesis of poetic language and rhetorical play: "Gender Personified, Personification Gendered, and the Body Figuralized in *Piers Plowman*," *The Yearbook of Langland Studies* 12 (1998): 84–88; and "Inventing the Subject and the Personification of Will in *Piers Plowman*: Rhetorical, Erotic, and Ideological Origins and Limits in Langland's Allegorical Poetics," in *William Langland's Piers Plowman: A Book of Essays*, ed. Kathleen Hewett-Smith (New York: Routledge, 2001), 220–21. For a more rigorous and up-to-date reconsideration of Langlandian allegorical poetics in terms of Lacan, see Daniel M. Murtaugh, "'As myself in a Mirour': Langland Between Augustine and Lacan," *Exemplaria* 19, no. 3 (2007): 351–85.

33. My insinuation—practically that Langland *presages* the image of the modern X-ray—is admittedly playful in its insistence on a conceptual anachronism. So-called "X-ray art" does in fact, however, date to the "Paleolithic, shamanic" depictions, done on cave walls, of the skeletal structures inside the bodies of the animals sought in the Great Hunt: see Joseph Campbell, *Historical Atlas of World Mythology: Volume 1, The Way of the Animal Powers* (New York: Harper and Row, Publishers, 1988), 131. In deference to anachronism as a creative, master trope in its own right and in the context of imagining "imaging technologies" in the

Middle Ages, I note too that I follow James Sheridan who sees in the "writing tablet" of Nature, as Alan of Lille presents her, a prefiguration of modern motion pictures; see *Plaint of Nature,* trans. James J. Sheridan (Toronto: Pontifical Institute of Medieval Studies, 1980), 108, n. 1. I have pressed for a fully anachronistic, creative-critical understanding of a "medieval cinematography" in my essay, "The Anachronism of Imagining Film in the Middle Ages: Wegener's *Der Golem* and Chaucer's *Knight's Tale," Exemplaria* 19, no. 2 (2007): 290–309. At the same time, I can stand in line with a conservative, historically sanctioned view by taking the "defaced" figure of Anima as the mimesis of physically defaced mural art personifications on the actual church walls of Langland's northern English countryside as witnessed and studied by C. David Benson. See his "Piers Plowman and Parish Wall Paintings," *The Yearbook of Langland Studies* 11 (1997): 1–38.

34. Drawing upon the contemporaneous visual aesthetics of the famous *Luttrell Psalter,* I speculate as well that one of that manuscript's most arresting images—a figure that could be a macabre version of a ghost or liberated soul lacking tongue and teeth though possessed of blank eyes and fleshy ears—evokes the facialization evident in Langland's Anima. See Michael Camille, *The Luttrell Psalter and the Making of Medieval England* (Chicago: University of Chicago Press, 1998), 343; Camille calls this strange marginal figure a "winged death's head on a stick." On a related note, the "softness" or "subtleness" of Anima as a facialized figure suggests other, actual depictions of disembodied souls in contemporary allegorical texts: see Jean-Claude Schmitt, *Ghosts in the Middle Ages: The Living and the Dead in Medieval Society* (Chicago: University of Chicago Press, 1994), figure 22, for a depiction taken from Guillaume de Deguilleville's *Pelerinage de Vie Humaine* (Paris, B.N., MS Fr. 823, fol.89) of the souls of the dead as blankly white phantoms exhibited only by sharp black outlines marking facial, cranial and bodily lineaments. If Langland's Anima suggests X-ray Borgrajewicz, it likewise suggests, as do the figures in the *Pelerinage* ms, Bronowski's Ultraviolet Borgrajewicz. Yet the *Pelerinage* figures remind me again of the blobby-white, outline-only lineaments of Radarwave-Borgrajewicz.

35. See *PP* 20.191 for the actions against Will of another iconographic analogue of the Death's Head and of Anima as I am reascribing him in this essay, Elde or "Old Age": "He buffetted me aboute þe mouþ [and bette out my wangteeþ]."

36. J. A. Burrow, *Gestures and Looks in Medieval Narrative* (Cambridge: Cambridge University Press, 2002), 73, 101–05. Regarding a still further reduction of Anima possible via the antirationalist and antihumanist logic of the sort constituting Deleuzean or Lacanian analysis, see Masha Raskolnikov's speculation that my model in "Gender Personified" could lead to the tongueless-and-toothless orifice as a human *anus*: "Promising the Female, Delivering the Male: Transformation of Gender in *Piers Plowman," The Yearbook of Langland Studies* 19 (2005): 97.

37. Hearty thanks are due to Ann Astell for her encouragement, suggestions and patience during my writing and revising of this essay; and to my friend and (now retired) colleague of the University of Florida, Mel New, with whom my discussions about Levinas clarified the philosopher's thinking for me greatly.

NOTES TO JACKSON, "THE INFINITE DESIRE OF *PEARL*"

1. Theodore Bogdanos, Pearl: *Image of the Ineffable* (University Park: Pennsylvania State University Press, 1983), 103.
2. For Levinas's understanding of a responsibility before freedom, see *OB* 121–29.
3. All references to *Pearl* are taken from Malcolm Andrew and Ronald Waldron, eds., *The Poems of the Pearl Manuscript:* Pearl, Cleanness, Patience, Sir Gawain and the Green Knight (Exeter: University of Exeter Press, 1987). All translations from the poem are my own.
4. See, for example, Robert J. Blanch and Julian N. Wasserman, *From* Pearl *to* Gawain: *Form to Fynisment* (Gainesville: University Press of Florida, 1995), 111–47.
5. In *Ethics and Infinity,* Levinas writes: "The best way of encountering the Other is not even to notice the color of his eyes! When one observes the color of the eyes one is not in a social relationship with the Other. The relation of the face can surely be dominated by perception, but what is specifically the face cannot be reduced to that" (85–86).
6. Stephen Russell, *The English Dream Vision: Anatomy of a Form* (Columbus: Ohio State University Press, 1988), 163–68.
7. Bernhard Waldenfels, "Levinas and the face of the other," in *The Cambridge Companion to Levinas,* ed. Simon Critchley and Robert Bernasconi (Cambridge: Cambridge University Press, 2002), 67. Waldenfels cites *Totality and Infinity,* 190, 194, and 212.
8. Ibid., 67.
9. I am working from a model of mimetic desire developed by René Girard. See *Things Hidden Since the Foundation of the World,* trans. Stephen Bann and Michael Metteer (Stanford: Stanford University Press, 1987), 18, 26–27, 283–98.
10. Most pertinent to my study here with regards to the ethical and the political is chapter 4 in *OB* 99–129. For a complete analysis of the ethical and the political in Levinas, see Howard Caygill, *Levinas and the Political* (New York: Routledge, 2002).
11. See Saint Augustine, *Sermons on Selected Lessons of the Gospels* (87 [137 Benedictine]), in *Nicene and Post-Nicene Fathers: Second Series* (Peabody: Hendrickson, 1999), 6:517–23.
12. Russell argues that the Maiden assumes that the Dreamer "is not yet ready for such a frontal attack on sublunar logic and semantics" and that she supplies Paul's image of the body of the Church to avoid the Dreamer's rational questions regarding the hierarchy of the heavenly court: "the answer seems platitudinous and mildly evasive, not serving to answer the material question in material terms" (*The English Dream Vision,* 164–165).
13. For a discussion of the 144,000 brides in a medieval context, see Santha Bhattacharji, "*Pearl* and the Liturgical 'Common of Virgins'," *Medium Aevum* 64

(1995): 37–50. By placing her reading of *Pearl* into the context of the liturgy, in the Common Mass and Office of Virgins, Bhattacharji asserts that it will provide "the central image of the pearl of great price, and associates with it the theme of wisdom and with the imagery of a bridal procession" (39). With the *Pearl*-maiden as the central image of the poem, other concerns are brought to light—that the *Pearl*-maiden, who died at such a young age, has not "earned" her high place in heaven by works; the problem of male/female participants in the processional scene of the poem.

14. See Ad Putter, *An Introduction to the* Gawain*-poet* (London: Longman, 1996), 169–78; David C. Fowler, *The Bible in Middle English Literature* (Seattle: University of Washington Press, 1984), 214–16.

15. See, for example, Saint Augustine, *Sermons on Selected Lessons of the Gospels* (37 [87 Benedictine]), *Nicene and Post-Nicene Fathers,* 6:373–78.

16. Robert Ackerman, "The Pearl-Maiden and the Penny," *Romance Philology* 17 (1964): 615–23. Ackerman makes an especially strong case for the connection, citing a numerous exegetical sources and vernacular texts. See Heather Phillips, "The Eucharistic Allusions of *Pearl,*" *Medieval Studies* 47 (1985): 474–86.

17. I have borrowed this phrase, "unwarranted gift" from Russell, *The English Dream Vision,* 167. He distinguishes it from "a payment for services rendered."

18. For a nonontological reading of the gift, see Jean-Luc Marion, *Being Given: Toward a Phenomenology of Givenness,* trans. Jeffrey L. Kosky (Stanford: Stanford University Press, 2002), 161–82.

19. Rhodes also notices this movement from the earthly crucifixion to the vision of the Lamb as specifically part of the Maiden's lesson for the dreamer. See *Poetry Does Theology: Chaucer, Grosseteste, and the* Pearl*-Poet* (Notre Dame: University of Notre Dame Press, 2001), 142–43.

20. I am borrowing this phrase from Levinas (*OB* 117).

21. For an intelligent reading of Christ as Torah, see Matthew Levering, *Christ's Fulfillment of Torah and Temple: Salvation According to Thomas Aquinas* (Notre Dame: University of Notre Dame Press, 2002), 12–79.

22. Levinas writes: "Infinity is not the 'object' of a cognition (which would be to reduce it to the measure of the gaze that contemplates), but is the desirable, that which arouses Desire, that is, that which is approachable by a thought that at each instant *thinks more than it thinks* (*TI* 62). See also *OB* 108. For a reading of desire in *Pearl* both similar and contrastive to my own, see George Edmondson, "*Pearl*: The Shadow of the Object, the Shape of the Law," *Studies in the Age of Chaucer* 16 (2004): 29–63.

23. Pierson Prior, *The* Pearl *Poet Revisited* (New York: Twayne, 1994), 39. For varying treatments of the "extra stanza," see Andrew and Waldron, *The Poems of the Pearl Manuscript,* 94, n. to 841–912; Barbara Nolan, *The Gothic Visionary Perspective* (Princeton: Princeton University Press, 1977), 175–76. Sarah Stanbury argues quite succinctly: "The poem's uncanny resistance to closure, a feature that draws readers of this theological dream-vision back again and again, lies I believe in its elegiac foundations, its replay of a loss that can never be fully put aside" ("The Body and the City in *Pearl,*" *Representations* 28 [1994]: 37.

24. For a detailed account of the Dreamer's vision, see Stanbury, *Seeing the Gawain-Poet: Description and the Act of Perception* (Philadelphia: University of Pennsylvania Press, 1991), 12–41.

25. For liturgical readings of the poem, see Bhattacharji, "*Pearl* and the Liturgical 'Common of Virgins'," 37–50; John Gatta, Jr., "Transformation Symbolism and the Liturgy of Mass in *Pearl*," *Modern Philology* 71 (1974): 243–56.

26. Geoffrey of Auxerre, *On the Apocalypse*, trans. Joseph Gibbons (Kalamazoo, Mich.: Cistercian Publications, 2000), 21.

27. See Blenkner, "The Theological Structure of *Pearl*," *Traditio* 24 (1968): 43–75, esp. 64–66; Phillips, "The Eucharistic Allusions of *Pearl*," 474–86; Cary Nelson, *The Incarnate Word: Literature as Verbal Space* (Urbana: University of Illinois Press, 1973), 25–49.

28. Levering, *Christ's Fulfillment*, 109.

29. For a connection between the ethical and the anagogical, see Dante Alighieri, "The Letter to Can Grande," in *Literary Criticism of Dante Alighieri*, trans. and ed. Robert S. Haller (Lincoln: University of Nebraska Press, 1973), 103–05. Making an explicit connection between the contemplative and the teleological, Saint Bonaventure offers the following reading of a threefold spiritual meaning of Scripture: "the *allegorical*, by which we are taught to believe concerning the divinity and humanity; the *moral*, by which we are taught how to live; and the *anagogical*, by which we are taught how to cling to God. Therefore, the whole of sacred Scripture teaches these three truths: namely the eternal generation and incarnation of Christ, the pattern of human life, and the union of the soul with God. The first is concerned with *faith;* the second with *morals;* and the third with the *ultimate goal of both*." See *On the Reduction of the Arts to Theology*, trans. Zachary Hayes (St. Bonaventure, N.Y.: St. Bonaventure University, 1996), 45.

30. For a reading similar to my own, see Rhodes, *Poetry Does Theology*, 144–45.

31. Jim Rhodes, "The Dreamer Redeemed: Exile and the Kingdom in he Middle English *Pearl*," *Studies in the Age of Chaucer* 16 (1994): 129.

32. See Henri de Lubac, *Medieval Exegesis*, vol. 2, trans. Mark Sebanc (Grand Rapids, Mich.: Eerdmans, 2000), 188–93.

33. Contra my reading, Edmondson writes, "Thus the dilemma for the dreamer becomes, again like the shape of *Pearl*, circular. For it is only to the extent that he enlists himself in the Other's discourse, becomes God's 'homly hyne,' that the dreamer can gain access to the form of enjoyment with which he identifies; and yet it is that same enlistment, that same acceptance of sacrifice, which makes it impossible for him to regain his lost pearl as anything other than signifier" ("*Pearl*: the Shadow," 63).

34. *CPP* 3. For other treatments of Levinas and art/literature, see especially, Edith Wyshogrod, "The art in Ethics: Aesthetics, Objectivity, and Alterity in the Philosophy of Emmanuel Levinas," in *Ethics as First Philosophy: The Significance of Emmanuel Levinas for Philosophy, Literature, and Religion*, ed. Adriaan T. Peperzak (New York: Routledge, 1995), 137–48; Jill Robbins, *Altered Readings: Levinas and Literature* (Chicago: University of Chicago Press, 1999); and Gerald

R. Bruns, "The Concepts of Art and Poetry in Emmanuel Levinas's Writings," *The Cambridge Companion to Levinas,* 206–33.

35. A line famously attributed to Prince Myshkin in *The Idiot:* "The world will be saved by Beauty!"

36. I am of course alluding to David Hart's *Beauty of the Infinite: The Aesthetics of Christian Truth* (Grand Rapids, Mich.: Eerdmans, 2003). I think it is fair to say that Levinas finds little praise in Hart's book. Hart argues, "Levinas advances a view of the world that is perhaps a little depraved" (75). Or perhaps more to the point: "I confess that, with the exception of the obviously barbarous ideologies of this past century, I know of no modern philosophy of 'values' more morally hideous than that of Levinas" (81–82). I do not intend here to rebut Hart's reading of Levinas's philosophy but would simply point out that my reading of *Pearl* both employs a Levinasian excessiveness in terms of an otherwise than being and relies on, albeit in an unstated fashion, an aesthetic vision of an *analogia entis,* a theological premise at the very core of Hart's aesthetic and philosophical arguments. It should also be mentioned briefly that Hart sees no space for aesthetics in Levinas's system: "Obviously, from the Levinasian perspective, an 'ethics' allied with aesthetics would be monstrous, and an 'aesthetic ethics' a contradiction in terms" (80). In his footnote, he cites only Levinas's "very curious (and silly)" "Reality and its Shadow" (80n.80).

Notes to Mitchell, "Criseyde's Chances"

1. The best account of this view remains that of Jill Mann both in "Troilus' Swoon," *Chaucer Review* 14 (1980): 319–45, and in "Chance and Destiny in *Troilus and Criseyde* and the *Knight's Tale,*" *The Cambridge Chaucer Companion,* ed. Piero Boitani and Jill Mann (Cambridge: Cambridge University Press, 1986), 75–92. The argument is also set forth in her *Feminizing Chaucer* (Woodbridge, UK: D. S. Brewer, 1992), 18–24, 80–88, 129–32.

2. All citations of Chaucer's *Troilus and Criseyde* [*TC*] taken from *The Riverside Chaucer,* ed. Larry D. Benson (Boston: Houghton Mifflin, 1987).

3. To clarify the role passivity and good luck play in the realm of ethics consider the following everyday examples as observed by Derrida in "Passions: 'An Oblique Offering,'" in *On the Name,* trans. David Wood (Stanford: Stanford University Press, 1995): "One must not be friendly or polite out of duty" (7). Friendship must be passive and not simply the result of following rules in the vein of Kantian ethics, for if it derives from mere rule-following friendship is destroyed. Claudia Card in *The Unnatural Lottery: Character and Moral Luck* (Philadelphia: Temple University Press, 1996), 122–23, gives another example in her discussion of the debt of gratitude that cannot be a duty without contradicting itself: "A duty to *be grateful* sounds like a joke.... To be grateful, must I not first be in some measure gratified? I can hardly be bound to be that. That is, I can hardly be bound to be gratified by others.... To deserve my gratitude others must succeed in gratifying me somewhat. There is luck here, if only in the 'fit' between us."

4. For an account of the fortunes of Troilus see my 'Romancing Ethics in Boethius, Chaucer, and Levinas: Fortune, Moral Luck, and Erotic Adventure,' *Comparative Literature* 57, no. 2 (2005): 101–16.

5. I take my cue from Mark Lambert, "*Troilus,* Books I–III: a Criseydan Reading," in *Essays on Troilus and Criseyde,* ed. Mary Salu (Cambridge: D. S. Brewer, 1979), 105–25.

6. The term "courtly love" is problematic but apparently irrepressible in recent ethical theory, as will become evident in my discussion of Lacan, and Deleuze and Guattari, alongside Levinas. On the medieval phenomena see Roger Boase, *The Origin and Meaning of Courtly Love* (Manchester: Manchester University Press, 1977), and Peter Dronke, *Medieval Latin and the Rise of European Love-Lyric,* Vol. 1 Problems and Interpretations (Oxford: Clarendon Press, 1965).

7. Maurice Blanchot, *The Writing of the Disaster,* trans. Ann Smock (Lincoln: University of Nebraska Press, 1995), 25.

8. Cf. Catherine S. Cox, *Gender and Language in Chaucer* (Gainseville: University Press of Florida, 1997), 48.

9. David Aers, *Chaucer, Langland and the Creative Imagination* (London: Routledge, 1980), 129–31.

10. Carolyn Dinshaw, *Chaucer's Sexual Poetics* (Madison: University of Wisconsin Press, 1989), 57.

11. Priscilla Martin, *Chaucer's Women: Nuns Wives, and Amazons* (Iowa City: University of Iowa Press, 1990), 188.

12. Aers, *Chaucer, Langland and the Creative Imagination,* 129. Aers cannot avoid using the phrase "what happens" to describe events, and yet he is at pains to disavow the significance of happenstance. The figure has regularly been dismissed as a form of quietism that renders the social order inexplicable and the status quo inevitable if not desirable. The "problematic political value" of the concept has also been highlighted by Larry Scanlon, who argues that Fortune is a great leveler of history and is effectively a means of social control; see Larry Scanlon, *Narrative, Authority, and Power: The Medieval Exemplum and the Chaucerian Tradition* (Cambridge: Cambridge University Press, 1994), 123–26. Recently there has been renewed interest in the fortuitous and casual as such, though most studies address a later period: see Jacques Lezra, *Unspeakable Subjects: The Genealogy of the Event in Early Modern Europe* (Stanford: Stanford University Press, 1997); Hanna F. Pitkin, *Fortune is a Woman: Gender and Politics in the Thought of Niccolo Machiavelli* (Chicago: University of Chicago Press, 1999); and Michael Witmore, *Culture of Accidents: Unexpected Knowledges in Early Modern England* (Stanford: Stanford University Press, 2001); and Daniel Heller-Roazen, *Fortune's Faces: The* Roman de la Rose *and the Poetics of Contingency* (Baltimore: Johns Hopkins University Press, 2003).

13. As is made explicit in *Practicing New Historicism* (Chicago: University of Chicago Press, 2000), 452, in which Catherine Gallagher and Stephen Greenblatt urge "a wholly integrated and sequential account, a history of causes and effects."

14. Slavoj Zizek in *For They Know Not What They Do: Enjoyment as a Political*

Factor (London: Verso, 1991), lii–lvii, profitably resists the presumption that political critique is only possible and powerful when analyzing effects into their respective
causes: he urges that "true materialism" does not explicate historical change but
rather "consists in precisely accepting the chanciness *without* the implication of
the horizon of hidden meaning—the name of this chance is *contingency*." Political critique will regain its relevance only when it humbly acknowledges that there
is no deeper meaning to human history, no redeemable sense to suffering and
violence. Therefore, Zizek urges what he calls the "ethical struggle to sustain the
meaninglessness of the catastrophe." It is a painful post-Holocaust consciousness
of the inadequacy of historical explanation to our singularity as ethical subjects
(for on what grounds is it defensible to say we now understand such suffering?),
and it can go to inform a new materialist historiography, something several
recent theorists besides Zizek are attempting to inaugurate. Levinas speaks of the
way the interiority or secrecy of the subject (glimpsed, for instance, in the suffering
in the camps) cannot be *totalized:* "Totalization is accomplished only in history—in
the history of the historiographers, that is, among the survivors" (*TI* 55). Maurice
Blanchot in *The Writing of the Disaster,* trans. Ann Smock (Lincoln: University of
Nebraska Press, 1995), 143, is also preoccupied with this impossibility of history:
"How is it possible to say: Auschwitz has happened?" How can one write the
disaster? In a similar spirit Thomas Docherty in *After Theory* (Edinburgh: Edinburgh University Press, 1996), 253, calls for a radical ethical and epistemological
reorientation toward the singularity and alterity of historical events, promoting a
postmarxist position that "accepts the fundamental unknowability of the world
and its history." "The mere opposition advanced by Marxism is not enough for
a radical criticism; it must be fully implicated in the much more radical pursuit of
the unknown rather than the always-already-known-but-merely-forgotten; and it
must be fully implicated in the ethics of alterity" (253). Disasters, catastrophe,
alterities—we only do justice to history and its subjects by recognizing that such
untimely events remain inassimilable to explanation. The chief point of contention
here is that some recent forms of historiography have *not been historical enough*.

15. See Monica E. McAlpine, "Criseyde's Prudence," *Studies in the Age of
Chaucer* 25 (2003): 215. She is adopting a phrase originally used by Derek Pearsall,
but not his ironical conclusions as set out in "Criseyde's Choices," *Studies in the
Age of Chaucer,* Proceedings No. 2 (1986), 17–29. Whereas Pearsall argues that
Criseyde is evading responsibility by representing herself as moved inexorably by
forces outside herself, McAlpine correctly locates responsibility itself *within* the
recognition of agency as so constituted.

16. I am referring to *TO*, originally published in French in 1947, and *TI*, originally published in 1961. Levinas seems to have become increasingly circumspect
about the transcendence of love over the self, and already in *Totality and Infinity*,
in the section "The Ambiguity of Love," he describes its ethical ambivalence, to
which I will return below. Levinas drops the romantic model from his account
in *OB*. However, Levinas indicates the centrality of erotic experience even there
when he redescribes philosophy as the "wisdom of love," inverting the usual
etymological priority.

17. On the *à-venir* see Levinas's *TO* 10, 76–77, 89; and Derrida's *Politics of Friendship* and *Specters of Marx: The State of the Debt, the Work of Mourning, and the New International,* trans. Peggy Kamuf (New York: Routledge, 1994).

18. Zygmunt Bauman, *Liquid Love: On the Frailty of Human Bonds* (Cambridge: Polity, 2003), 3.

19. Simone de Beauvoir, *The Second Sex,* trans. and ed. H. M. Parshley (New York: Vintage, 1989), xxii. For essays, critical and commendatory, see *Feminist Interpretations of Emmanuel Levinas,* ed. Tina Chanter (Pennsylvania: Pennsylvania University Press, 2001). Simon Critchley, in *The Ethics of Deconstruction: Derrida and Levinas* (Oxford: Blackwell, 1992), 136, speaks of sexual politics as Levinas's "blind spot." See also Claire E. Katz, *Levinas, Judaism, and the Feminine: The Silent Footsteps of Rebecca* (Bloomington: Indiana University Press, 2003).

20. Luce Irigary, *An Ethics of Sexual Difference,* trans. Carolyn Burke and Gillian Gill (Ithaca: Cornell University Press, 1993): "Beloved woman. Not female lover. Necessarily an object, not a subject with a relation, like his, to time. She drags the male lover into the abyss so that, from these nocturnal depths, he may be carried off into an absolute future" (194).

21. Lacan, in his well-known remarks on courtly love in Seminars VII and XX, elaborates on the dialectic of desire. See Jacques Lacan's *The Seminar of Jacques Lacan: Book VII: The Ethics of Psychoanalysis, 1959–1960,* ed. Jacques-Alain Miller, trans. Dennis Porter (New York: W. W. Norton, 1992), esp. 146–52; and *The Seminar of Jacques Lacan: On Feminine Sexuality, the Limits of Love and Knowledge: Book XX, Encore 1972–1973,* trans. Bruce Fink (New York: W. W. Norton, 2000), 69. Other important psychoanalytic accounts are those of Slavoj Zizek, "Courtly Love, or, Woman as Thing", in *The Metastases of Enjoyment: Six Essays on Woman and Causality* (London: Verso, 1994), 109; and of A. O. Aranye Fradenburg, *Sacrifice Your Love: Psychoanalysis, Historicism, Chaucer* (Minneapolis: University of Minnesota Press, 2002), 18–24.

22. Quoting Simon Gaunt, *Gender and Genre in Medieval French Literature* (Cambridge: Cambridge University Press, 1995), 146; see also Sarah Kay, *Subjectivity in Troubadour Poetry* (Cambridge: Cambridge University Press, 1990), 84–85.

23. Martin Heidegger's *Mitsein* (Being-with) as defined in *Being and Time,* trans. John Macquarrie and Edward Robinson (Oxford: Blackwell, 1962), 149–68, stands behind my discussion of sociality here. Heidegger's influence on the thought of Levinas is considered by Robert John Sheffler Manning, *Interpreting Otherwise than Heidegger: Emmanuel Levinas's Ethics as First Philosophy* (Pittsburgh: Duquesne University Press, 1993). See Levinas discussing "sociality" (*EI* 79–81).

24. Gilles Deleuze and Félix Guattari, *A Thousand Plateaus: Capitalism and Schizophrenia,* trans. Brian Massumi (Continuum: London, 1987), 154–57.

25. The distinction between desire and need is crucial to understanding the novelty of Levinas's approach to courtly love. He defines desire in one place: "Desire 'measures' the infinity of the infinite.... This desire without satisfaction hence takes cognizance of the alterity of the other," (*CPP* 56). The other side

of human longing is "need," which satisfies itself by assimilating the other to the same, whereas "desire" is ever future-tending (*TI* 117). Ultimately, Levinas acknowledges the "ambiguity of love" (*TI* 254–55). But even here the "need" of love attests to the ethical relation lying beyond the self.

26. See Boethius's *Consolation of Philosophy*, 2m8; and Dante's *Purgatorio* 17.103–05: "Bethink thee then how love must be the seed / In you, not only of each virtuous action, / But also of each punishable deed." Here love is a matrix—comparable to the ethical relation—out of which both virtue and vice spring. Compare also the Augustinian ethical theory according to which evil does not exist in itself, but only as a privation of good. There are formal resemblances: Goodness, for Augustine and Levinas, is prior to evil.

27. McAlpine, in "Criseyde's Prudence," includes a brief review of the scholarship: "many tend to associate her with a high degree of regrettable or deplorable passivity—chosen, enforced, or both" (200).

28. Jill Mann, "Chance and Destiny in *Troilus and Criseyde* and the *Knight's Tale*," *The Cambridge Chaucer Companion*, ed. Piero Boitani and Jill Mann (Cambridge: Cambridge University Press, 1986), 75–92.

29. Cf. A. C. Spearing, *Chaucer: Troilus and Criseyde* (London: Edward Arnhold, 1976), 19; Elaine Tuttle Hansen, *Chaucer and the Fictions of Gender* (Berkeley and Los Angeles: University of California Press, 1992), 171.

30. Consent stands as one of the many conspicuous examples of the dissimulation of inner states of the mind, such as intention (*entente*) in this romance, as others have indeed observed. See, for example, Elizabeth Archibald, "Declarations of 'Entente' in *Troilus and Criseyde*," *Chaucer Review* 25 (1991): 190–213; and Jennifer Campbell, "Figuring Criseyde's 'Entente': Authority, Narrative, and Chaucer's Use of History," *Chaucer Review* 27 (1993): 342–58.

31. In other words, even what seems fortuitous is fated from the outset by virtue of its conventionality. For example, we might consider the possible sources of Antigone's song and the dream; see *The Riverside Chaucer*, 1034. But we should also bear in mind that the "courtly experience" of the love lyric is not restricted to late medieval court society: a lover's willingness to suffer and submit to the superior other has been discovered in many cultures and over a much longer period of time; see the first chapter of Peter Dronke's *Medieval Latin and the Rise of European Love-Lyric*.

32. Just think what little difference it would make to redefine the situation in which the courtly lover makes his or her choices, say by removing her from the medieval to any modern society. It will always be possible to redescribe ethics as politically determined by forces that are beyond the control of individual moral agents. Ethics—if it exists at all—is a *given* feature of intersubjective and political states of affairs; it is a gift of being "otherwise than being."

33. Simon Critchley, "The Other's Decision in Me (What Are the Politics of Friendship?)," in *Ethics—Politics—Subjectivity: Essays on Derrida, Levinas and Contemporary French Thought* (London: Verso, 1999), 263.

34. Derrida, *Politics of Friendship*, 68–69. I allude to Derrida's coy phrase, "as if it were possible to think a responsibility without freedom" (231), epitomiz-

ing the contingency of the ethics and politics of the *perhaps* he describes in this book.

35. Mann, "Chance and Destiny," 82.

36. The sense is the same as Christine de Pisan's reference to a virgin who once "was yolden in to" the Temple of Venus, in *The Middle English Translation of Christine de Pisan's* Livre du Corps de Policie, *ed. from MS C.U.L. Kk.1.5*, ed. Diane Bornstein (Heidelberg: Carl Winter, 1977), 53.

37. For these alternative views, see Fradenburg's discussion of Criseyde's consent as a form of traumatism and compensation in *Sacrifice Your Love*, 225–26; Hansen on Criseyde's consent as a means of saving face and surviving in *Chaucer and the Fictions of Gender*, 170; and Pearsall who argues in "Criseyde's Choices" that Criseyde effectively masquerades as passive in such moments only to preserve her freedom from responsibility: "She has discovered the great principle of survival, and the solace of the survivor: true freedom is the ability to convince yourself that you have no choice but to do what you want to do" (20).

38. Mann, *Feminizing Chaucer*, 87.

39. I am thinking of the Lacanian axiom: "man does not come (*n'arrive pas*), I would say, to enjoy woman's body," on which see *The Seminar of Jacques Lacan: On Feminine Sexuality, the Limits of Love and Knowledge*, 7. For extended comparisons of the two thinkers see essays in *Levinas and Lacan: The Missed Encounter*, ed. Sarah Harasym (Albany: State University of New York Press, 1998).

40. Thomas Usk, *The Testament of Love*, ed. R. Allen Shoaf (Kalamazoo, Mich.: Medieval Institute Publications, 1998), III.viii.933–35. In his discussion of the freedom and dependency of the will, Usk had *Troilus and Criseyde* in mind; see III.iv.558–64, 683–85, and 870.

41. Mann, *Feminizing Chaucer*, 23.

42. See Sarah Kay in *Subjectivity in Troubadour Poetry*, 84.

43. Mann has an acute sense of the issue when she observes that Criseyde "takes responsibility, fully and delightedly," for the casual chain of events lying outside her control ("Troilus' Swoon," 330). She observes that Chaucer "makes us alive to the *in*voluntary elements involved in the exercise of the will" ("Chance and Destiny," 83). McAlpine's point about the virtue involved in making the involuntary voluntary must have similar ramifications on the level of moral choice, conduct, and character. But fortune does not just give rise to discrete moral dilemmas, or extenuate guilt in difficult or marginal cases. Contingency and temporality are not just accidents to be anticipated and then corrected on the way to more equitable moral judgments. Part of the trouble with fortune is that it is unanticipated, singular, original—the sign of an event to come, a future adventure—without which moral judgments would not arise.

Notes to Kraman, "The Wound of the Infinite"

1. The habit of interpreting any given figure or theme from two diametrically opposed perspectives is part of the same medieval impulse that had scholars

attempting to synthesize Plato and Aristotle, and theologians aligning Christian and pagan wisdom. It also generates irony and complexity in the work of imaginative writers, such as Chaucer and Langland.

2. Bersuire (d.1362) redacted the Old French *Ovid moralisé*. His method is discussed by Alistair. J. Minnis and A. B. Scott, *Medieval Literary Theory and Criticism c. 1100–1375: The Commentary Tradition,* ed. A. J. Minnis and A. B. Scott, with the assistance of David Wallace (Oxford: Clarendon Press, 1988), 324.

3. Jean Jacques Rousseau, *Discourse on the Origins of Inequality,* trans. G. D. H. Cole, rev. ed. (New York: Everyman, 1973), 75. Rousseau finds rational philosophy corrupts man's natural compassion; Levinas would not.

4. See Emmanuel Levinas, "Dying For," *EN* 219–22.

5. *BPW* 70. In Greek, *ainigma* means an obscure or equivocal word, a riddle, something hard to understand or explain. I thank Ann Astell for calling this passage to my attention.

6. Origen, *The Song of Songs: Commentary and Homilies,* trans. R. P. Lawson, Ancient Christian Writers Series 26 (London: Longmans, Green, 1957), 61. The Latin translation by Rufinus of this passage in Origen's commentary appears in PG 13, c85.

7. Again and again Levinas contrasts his course with that of the emblematic sage Odysseus, who journeys into the world of experience, but for whom "self-consciousness is a return path" (*OB* 81). Richard A. Cohen explains: "Sacred history, the ethical time and significance of sociality, for Levinas, is not the voyage of an Odysseus, who ventures out courageously but only in order to finally return home, where he began his voyage; but the journey of an Abram, who leaves his ancestral home for good, who never returns and never arrives at his destination, who encounters and is subject to the absolute alterity of God, who overthrows the idols and is transformed to become his better self, Abraham" ("Translator's Introduction," *TO* 24).

8. On the allegorical status of the Song of Songs, see Ann W. Astell, *The Song of Songs in the Middle Ages* (Ithaca: Cornell University Press, 1990), esp. 25–41.

9. The outcry of *Yadayim 3:5* itself proves there was resistance, or R. Akiba would not have needed to protest. It was not only sexuality that was the problem. *Megilloth* 7a raises the point of this being a work by Solomon rather than God. But in *Abot de-Rabbi Natan,* chapter 1, one gathers, from the material debated, including the Song, that sex is a subtext of the debate. However, the famous Mishnaic discussion of *Yadayim 3:5* about the Song "rendering the hands unclean" is about altering the ritual status of one who touches a holy object, and has been misunderstood to have to do with sexuality. An Old French translation of the Song warns the text should not fall into the hands of children. See Landry de Waben and Cedric E. Pickford, *The Song of Songs, a Twelfth Century French Version* (London: Oxford University Press, 1974), 97.

10. See Marina Warner, *Alone of All Her Sex: The Myth and Cult of the Virgin Mary* (New York: Knopf, 1976).

11. Rabbi A. J. Rosenberg, ed., *The Five Megilloth*, vol. 1 (New York: The Judaica Press, 1992), 1–3.

12. Geoffrey Chaucer, *The Parliament of Fowls*, in *The Riverside Chaucer*, ed. Larry D. Benson, 3rd ed. (Boston: Houghton Mifflin, 1987), 385.

13. The medieval idea of the two Venuses is found in Chaucer's "Knight's Tale" and is well footnoted by Vincent J. DiMarco in his notes for lines 1955–66 in the *Riverside Chaucer*, 835.

14. *BPW* 140. Levinas provides references to Plato, *Symposium*, 192c and 192e, in footnotes 17 and 18, p. 191.

15. *BPW* 140. In note 19 (p. 190), Robert Bernasconi identifies the passage in Pascal's *Pensées* to which Levinas alludes.

16. Rosenberg, ed., *The Five Megilloth*, 5. Unless otherwise noted, all translations from the Song of Songs and Rashi are from this edition. Exterior brackets in Rosenberg's edition are used to indicate midrashic sources.

17. Midrashic commentary on the reaction of the Israelites to receiving the commandments first from God and then from Moses reveals that they, of course, prefer to hear them directly from God; hence the Song's "kisses of His mouth." See Yitzhak I. Broch, ed. and trans. *Shir ha-Shirim, The Song of Songs in Hebrew and English, with a Talmudic-Midrashic Commentary* (New York: Feldheim, 1983), 13. See also Michael Fishbane, *The Kiss of God: Spiritual and Mystical Death in Judaism* (Seattle: University of Washington Press, 1994), 15–20.

18. In Exodus 19:8, the people reply to Moses' report of God's commands with the words, "All that YHWH has spoken, we will do." In Exodus 24:3, the people repeat, "All the words that YHWH has spoken, we will do." Verse 7 of that chapter adds, "we will do and we will hearken!" The word "hearken" includes the meanings "to hear" and "to obey." See Everett Fox, trans., *The Five Books of Moses* (New York: Schocken Books, 1997), 391.

19. *Shir ha-Shirim (Song of Songs)/An Allegorical Translation Based upon Rashi, with a Commentary Anthologized from Talmudic, Midrashic, and Rabbinic Sources*, trans. Rabbi Nosson Scherman, ArtScroll Tanach Series (New York: Mesorah Publications, 1977), 98.

20. I wish to acknowledge Ann Astell's contribution to the development of my thoughts in the preceding three paragraphs.

21. Cf. *TI* 58: "The discontinuity of Cartesian time, which requires a continuous creation, indicates the very dispersion and plurality of created being."

22. Rosenberg, ed., *The Five Megilloth*, 6.

23. Julia Kristeva, "A Holy Madness: She and He" in *Tales of Love*, trans. Leon S. Roudiez (New York: Columbia University Press, 1987), 80.

24. Rosenberg, ed., *The Five Megilloth*, 55.

25. Divine Scrutiny, the continuous interest and influence of God in the life of each person, is a Jewish principle found in all liturgy and commentary.

26. Rosenberg, ed., *The Five Megilloth*, 56.

27. Ibid., 57.

28. The phrase is in line 186 in Andrew Malcolm and Ronald Waldron, eds.,

The Poems of the Pearl Manuscript, rev. ed. (Manchester: University of Exeter Press, 1989), 193. The editors note, "Sleep is often used in medieval religious writings to signify lack of moral awareness." Jonah's sleep at this point is specifically interpreted as the sleep of sin by the thirteenth century commentator Hugh of St. Cher, in his *Postillae.* See R. H. Bowers, *The Legend of Jonah* (The Hague: Martinus Nijhoff, 1971), 58.

29. See Claire Elise Katz, *Levinas, Judaism, and the Feminine: The Silent Footsteps of Rebecca* (Bloomington: Indiana University Press, 2003), 23–31. Katz investigates Levinas's treatment of the *il y a* from the perspective of Rashi's "claim that the nothingness before creation is actually the nothingness before separation" (25).

30. Rosenberg, ed. *The Five Megilloth,* 60.

31. Luce Irigaray, "The Fecundity of the Caress," in *Face to Face with Levinas,* ed. Richard A. Cohen (Albany: State University of New York Press, 1986), 231–56.

32. Rosenberg, ed., *The Five Megilloth,* 96.

33. The connection of the two is based, according to *Torah Temimah,* on a common root for the words "apple" and "mount." In addition, Sinai bore its fruit—the Torah—in the same season (Sivan) when the apple trees bear theirs.

34. Rosenberg, ed., *The Five Megilloth,* 96.

35. *Shir ha-Shirim, The Song of Songs,* ed. and trans. Scherman and Zlotowitz, 195.

36. Simone de Beauvoir, *The Second Sex,* ed. and trans. H. M. Parshley (New York: Vintage Books, 1989), xxii. See Tina Chanter, "Introduction," in *Feminist Interpretations of Emmanuel Levinas,* ed. Tina Chanter (University Park: Pennsylvania State University Press, 2001), esp. 1–5.

37. Catherine Chalier argues this, as well as for a positive, Levinasian evaluation of motherhood and the feminine in a domestic place, in "Ethics and the Feminine," in *Re-Reading Levinas,* ed. Robert Bernasconi and Simon Critchley (Bloomington: Indiana University Press, 1991), 119–29.

38. We read in Talmud Tractate Chulin 139b: "Where is the name Esther indicated in the Torah? (In the verse) 'I will hide, yes hide My face." The Talmud quotes Deuteronomy 31:18. Esther, we are told, comes from the same root as "hester" or hidden.

39. For a robust feminist critique see Luce Irigaray's essay "Questions to Emmanuel Levinas: On the Divinity of Love," in *Re-Reading Levinas,* 109–18.

40. Obviously, the male Jew always stands behind this allegorical female. But Rashi's insistence on characterizing her as a fully human woman, widow, beloved, is striking. Also, the nation includes women who are mentioned as a group and individually in the commentary. If one adds to this the fact that God in His female aspect, the Schechina, is part of Rashi's allegory (a topic omitted in this discussion as too esoteric), as well as the inextricably blurred assignment of "Lover" and "Beloved" to the actors in this drama, gender becomes rather fluid in Rashi's commentary.

41. For a discussion of the various lists of principles for both aggadic and halakhik material, lists which include the Malbim's 613 principles, as well as a presentation of the "most frequently encountered" principles, see Rabbi Adin Steinsaltz, *The Talmud, A Reference Guide* (New York: Random House, 1980), 147–54.

42. *The Traditional Prayer Book for Sabbath and Festivals,* ed. and trans. David de Sola Pool (New Hyde Park, N.Y.: University Books, 1960), 130.

43. For a discussion of this passage, see John Llewelyn, "Am I Obsessed by Bobby? (Humanism of the Other Animal)," *Re-Reading Levinas,* 239.

44. Irigaray, "Fecundity of the Caress," *Face to Face with Levinas,* 231–56.

45. See Rosenberg's discussion in *The Five Megilloth,* vii.

46. Saint Bernard of Clairvaux, Sermon 3:I.1, *On the Song of Songs I,* trans. Kilian Walsh (Kalamazoo, Mich.: Cistercian Publications, 1976), 16.

47. For my mother, Esther Sarah Kraman née Weinstock, 1922–2007. This essay was presented at the International Congress on Medieval Studies in 2005 in a slightly different form.

Notes to Goodhart, "'A Land that Devours Its Inhabitants'"

1. To some extent, every piece of writing, even one attributed to a single author, is a collaboration. That is especially true in this case. Ann Astell's linkage of my argument to Luke's Gospel and Levinas's essay on Claudel's *Emmaüs* (especially Claudel's prefigurative reading of Hebrew scripture), her introduction of the vast literature of the Middle Ages on Jacob's ladder and the monastic *lectio divina,* and in general her heightening of my argument about Levinas's performative reading of rabbinic (talmudic) scriptural commentary in context of the fourfold Christian versions of this ancient Jewish exegetical practice reflect her own astonishing erudition and intelligence, and her uncommonly good editorial sense. Her influence is present on almost every page of this essay—much too often to cite. Jewish and Christian scriptural readings genuinely meet in this textual land.

2. *The Holy Bible,* ed. John P. O'Connell (Chicago: The Catholic Press, 1950).

3. *DF* 119–20. On the influence of Jewish exegesis on Christian commentary, especially that of the Victorines, see Beryl Smalley, *The Study of the Bible in the Middle Ages,* 3rd ed. (Oxford: Blackwell, 1984), 103–05, 149–72, 361–65.

4. Quoted by Marc Hirshman, "Aggadic Midrash," in *The Literature of the Sages,* ed. Shmuel Safrai, Zeev Safrai, Joshua Schwartz, and Peter J. Tomson (Royal Van Gorcum: Fortress Press, 2006), 114.

5. On the distinction between compositional allegory and allegoresis, see Jon Whitman, *Allegory: The Dynamics of an Ancient and Medieval Technique* (Oxford: Clarendon Press, 1987), 1–5. The key role played by the Jewish exegete, Philo of Alexandria, in the systematic development of the allegorical interpretation of the Scriptures strongly suggests that Christian *allegoresis* has its primary origin not in

the Stoic commentaries on Homer but in the Hebraic commentary tradition. On the error of seeing the fourfold Christian allegoresis as a "Greek invention," see Henri de Lubac, *The Four Senses of Scripture,* Vol. 1, trans. Mark Sebanc (Grand Rapids, Mich.: Eerdmans, 1998), xv.

6. The "doctrinal" level is often called "allegorical," but that term is also used broadly to include all the levels of signification except that of literal meaning. Similarly, the term "midrashic" is used both narrowly, to refer to one level of hidden meaning, and broadly, to refer to all such levels.

7. See, for example, D. W. Robertson, Jr., "Historical Criticism" in *English Institute Essays, ed.* A. S. Downer (New York: Columbia University Press, 1951), 3–31, and *Preface to Chaucer: Studies in Medieval Perspectives* (Princeton: Princeton University Press, 1962). For an incisive commentary on the history of "Robertsonianism" in medieval studies, see Alan T. Gaylord's "Reflections on D. W. Robertson, Jr., and Exegetical Criticism," in *Chaucer Review* 40, no. 3 (2006): 311–33.

8. See, for example, Bernard F. Huppé and D. W. Robertson, Jr., *Piers Plowman and Scriptural Tradition* (Princeton: Princeton University Press, 1951).

9. The key book in Foucault's work for this analysis was, of course, *The Order of Things* (New York: Random House, 1970).

10. On "new historicism" see Harold Veeser, ed., *The New Historicism* (New York: Routledge, 1989).

11. See Laura Brown and Felicity Nussbaum, eds., *The New Eighteenth Century: Theory, Politics, English Literature* (New York: Methuen, 1987).

12. See Terry Eagleton, *The Ideology of the Aesthetic* (London: Blackwell, 1990). The analysis that literary historian Meyer H. Abrams undertook of the "art for art's sake" movement reflects similar interests. See "Art-as-Such: The Sociology of Modern Aesthetics," *Bulletin of the American Academy of Arts and Sciences* 38, no. 6 (1985): 8–33.

13. See Bernard F. Huppé, *A Reading of the Canterbury Tales* (Albany: State University of New York Press, 1964).

14. See Whitman, *Allegory;* Carolynn Van Dyke, *The Fiction of Truth: Structures of Meaning in Narrative and Dramatic Allegory* (Ithaca: Cornell University Press, 1985); Maureen Quilligan, *The Language of Allegory: Defining the Genre* (Ithaca: Cornell University Press, 1979); Ann W. Astell, *The Song of Songs in the Middle Ages* (Ithaca: Cornell University Press, 1990); *Political Allegory in Late Medieval England* (Ithaca: Cornell University Press, 1999). For Coleridge on allegory, see *Coleridge's Miscellaneous Criticism,* ed. Thomas Middleton Raysor (London: Constable & Co., 1936), 30–31, 33, 99.

15. See Paul de Man, "The Rhetorical of Temporality," in *Blindness and Insight: Essays in the Rhetoric of Contemporary Criticism,* 2nd rev. ed. (Minneapolis: University of Minneapolis Press, 1983), 187–228. See also Paul de Man, *Allegories of Reading: Figural Language in Rousseau, Nietsche, Rilke, and Proust* (New Haven: Yale University Press, 1979).

16. See Gerald Bruns, "Midrash and Allegory: The Beginnings of Scriptural Interpretation," in *Literary Guide to the Bible,* ed. Robert Alter and Frank Kermode (Cambridge, Mass.: Harvard University Press, 1990), 625–46. For a very different sense of allegory than our modern predispositions would condition us to expect, see Henri de Lubac's magisterial four volume *Exégèse médiévale: les quatre sens de l'écriture* (Paris: Aubiers, 1959), translated into English in two volumes: *Medieval Exegesis: The Four Senses of Scripture,* Vol. 1, trans. Mark Sebanc (Grand Rapids, Mich.: Eerdmans, 1998), and *Medieval Exegesis: The Four Senses of Scripture,* Vol. 2, trans. Edward M. Macierowski (Grand Rapids, Mich.: Eerdmans, 2000).

17. On the way the midrashic may be understood as not just an addendum to rabbinic interpretation but its very fabric, see Gerald Bruns, "Midrash and Allegory." See also our discussion below.

18. See, for example, *The Soncino Midrash Rabbah,* ed. H. Freedman and Maurice Simon (Chicago: Institute for Computers in Jewish Life, Davka Corp, 1995).

19. The literature of this field is massive. See Judith Baskin's *Midrashic Women: Formations of the Feminine in Rabbinic Literature* (Hanover: Brandeis University Press/University Press of New England, 2002), or Judith Plaskow's *Standing Again at Sinai: Judaism from a Feminist Perspective* (New York: HarperCollins, 1990), or Ellen Frankel's *Five Books of Miriam: A Women's Commentary on the Torah* (San Francisco: HarperCollins, 1998).

20. See Gerald Bruns, "Midrash and Allegory"; Geoffrey H. Hartman, "The Struggle for the Text," in *Midrash and Literature,* ed. Geoffrey H. Hartman and Sanford Budick (New Haven: CT Press, 1988); Michael Fishbane, *Biblical Interpretation in Ancient Israel* (Oxford: Oxford University Press, 1989), *Garments of Torah Essays on Biblical Hermeneutics* (Bloomington: Indiana University Press, 1992), and Fishbane, ed., *Midrashic Imagination: Jewish Exegesis, Thought, and History* (Albany: State University of New York Press, 1993); Susan A. Handelman, *The Slayers of Moses: The Emergence of Rabbinic Interpretation in Modern Theory* (Albany: State University of New York Press, 1982); David Stern, *Parables in Midrash: Narrative and Exegesis in Rabbinic Literature* (Cambridge, Mass.: Harvard University Press, 1991), and *Midrash and Theory: Ancient Jewish Exegesis and Contemporary Literature Studies* (Evanston: Northwestern University Press, 1998); Daniel Boyarin, *Intertextuality and the Reading of Midrash* (Bloomington: Indiana University Press, 1990.

21. See Harold Bloom's "Introduction" to Martin Buber's *On the Bible: Eighteen Essays,* ed. Nahum Glatzer (Syracuse: Syracuse University Press, 2000).

22. See Derrida's "Abraham, the Other," in *Judeites: Questions for Jacques Derrida,* ed. Bettina Bergo, Joseph Cohen, and Raphael Zagury-Orly, trans. Bettina Bergo and Michael B. Smith (New York: Fordham University Press, 2007), 1–35.

23. Boyarin, *Intertextuality and the Reading of Midrash,* 128.

24. This Midrash appears in *The Book of Legends, Sefer Ha-Aggadah: Legends from the Talmud and Midrash,* ed. Hayim Naham Bialik and Yehoshua Hana

Ravnitzky, trans. William G. Braude, with an Introduction by David Stern (New York: Schocken Books, 1992), 40.

25. Medieval schoolboys memorized the following distich: "The letter teaches events, allegory what you should believe,/Morality teaches what you should do, anagogy what mark you should be aiming for" (De Lubac, *Medieval Exegesis,* Vol. 1, 1).

26. I quote from the talmudic passage as it appears in this text.

27. Everett Fox, trans., *The Five Books of Moses: Genesis, Exodus, Leviticus, Numbers, Deuteronomy, The Schocken Bible,* Vol. 1 (New York: Schocken, 1997), 731. Unless otherwise indicated, I use this translation of the Hebrew text throughout the rest of this essay.

28. The maxim is often attributed to Rabbi Hanina, but it is a fairly common phrase. See Byron L. Sherwin, "Fear of God," in *Contemporary Jewish Religious Thought: Original Essays on Critical Concepts, Movements, and Beliefs,* ed. Arthur A. Cohen and Paul Mendes-Flohr (New York: Macmillan, 1987), 249.

29. *Tractate Sotah,* 34b–35a, *NT* 51.

30. André Chouraqui interestingly translates the first word from Numbers (*vayitrou*), as *prospecteront* and the second from Deuteronomy (*veyachperou*) as *fouilleront.* See *La Bible. Traduite et Commentée par André Chouraqui* (Paris: Desclée de Brouwer, 1989).

31. Michael Fishbane, "Inner Biblical Exegesis: Types and Strategies of Interpretation in Ancient Israel," *Midrash and Literature,* 20–21.

32. See *A Hebrew and English Lexicon of the Old Testament,* ed. Francis Brown, S. R. Drover, and Charles Briggs (Oxford: Clarendon Press, 1951), 343 (*chapar:* dig, search for) and 344 (*chapeir:* be abashed, ashamed).

33. See *Bava Metzia,* 58b.

34. See *Erachin,* 51a.

35. *Orchot Zaddikim,* ed. and trans. Seymour J. Cohen (New York: Ktav, 1982), 590.

36. See Emmanuel Levinas, *Du sacré au saint. Cinq nouvelles lectures talmudiques* (Paris: Editions de Minuit, 1977).

37. Sherwin, "Fear of God," *Contemporary Jewish Religious Thought,* 245, 253.

38. The Biblical passage does not say *how* Caleb calmed the people "before Moses" (13:30) and gained their attention. The rabbinic explanation, recorded in Tractate *Sotah,* is that he at first pretended to join in the general criticism of Moses. The story of the criticism of Moses' Cushite wife by his sister Miriam (12:1) shortly precedes the story of the explorers' mission, and the equally famous story of the rebellion of Korah comes immediately afterwards. In this rebellious atmosphere, the rabbis speculate, Caleb must have exercised a wily rhetoric. Joshua is curiously silent at this point. Since *Numbers* does not record any speech of his here, the rabbis provide a Midrash, saying that Joshua tried to speak, but the people would not let him, protesting that he had no children and therefore had little at stake in the matter of entering the land of Canaan.

39. Jacques Derrida, "Specters of Marx," in *The Derrida Reader: Writing Performances,* ed. Julian Wolfreys (Lincoln: University of Nebraska Press, 1998), 149. In "Diachrony and Representation," Levinas clarifies the difference between the promissory and the prophetic, between a perspective he identifies with theodicy, and a perspective he identifies with participation. See Emmanuel Levinas, "Diachrony and Representation," *TO* 97–120.

40. Is this similar to Derrida's democracy-to-come, or justice-to-come; is it a "messianism without a messianicity" as Derrida puts it? Perhaps, in so far as there is no quality, no messianicity, that can be determined as genuine as opposed to some false messianic mode. It is not as a promissory messianism, the promise of a promise; only as a prophetic messianism. See Derrida, "Specters of Marx."

41. Moshe Idel discusses this Midrash in *"Pardes: The Quest for Spiritual Paradise in Judaism,"* The Samuel and Althea Stroum Lectureship at University of Washington, Seattle, April 16, 18, and 22, 1991. For a discussion of the varieties of this tradition in Talmud and in the Tosefta, see Alon Goshen Gottstein, "Four Entered Paradise Revisited," *The Harvard Theological Review* 88, no. 1 (Jan. 1995): 69–133.

42. On Jewish hermeneutics, see Fishbane, *The Garments of Torah.*

43. Rav Mershasheya suggests that the inhabitants of Canaan may have been observing a local custom, "eating their funeral meal under the cedars," when they were observed by the explorers, who hid in the branches of the trees, and thus appeared to the people below like grasshoppers, feeding upon the leaves. The structure of eating below and above is mimetic, a matter of projection from one to the other (*NT* 53).

44. See Bialik and Ravnitzky, eds., *The Book of Legends,* 348. See also p. 386, where a similar verse of comfort (Jer. 30:10) is interpolated as a midrash into the story from Genesis. This midrash resembles medieval legends about The Fall of Princes and the turning of Fortune's Wheel, concerning which King Arthur, for example, dreams.

45. Bialik and Ravnitzky, eds., *Book of Legends,* 348.

46. Hildegard of Bingen, *Scivias,* trans. Mother Columba Hart and Jane Bishop (New York: Paulist, 1990), book III, vision 8, p. 425.

47. St. Catherine of Siena, *The Dialogue,* trans. Suzanne Noffke (New York: Paulist Press, 1980), 140.

48. On this complex image, see Mary J. Carruthers, *The Book of Memory: A Study of Memory in Medieval Culture* (Cambridge: Cambridge University Press, 1990), 236–38.

49. *Bonaventure: The Soul's Journey into God, The Tree of Life, The Life of Francis,* trans. Ewert Cousins (New York: Paulist Press, 1978), 54.

50. Ivan Illich, *In the Vineyard of the Text: A Commentary to Hugh's Didascalicon* (Chicago: The University of Chicago Press, 1996), 59. On the reference to Jewish mysticism, Illich cites George Steiner, "Our Homeland the Text," *Salamagundi* 66 (1985): 4–25.

51. Illich, *In the Vineyard of the Text,* 60.

Notes to Astell, "When Pardon Is Impossible"

1. Jacques Derrida, "On Forgiveness," *Studies in Practical Philosophy* 2, no. 2 (2000): 92.

2. Levinas, "Toward the Other," *NT* 29. Levinas refers specifically to the biblical way of mercy, compassion, and "individual sacrifice" on behalf of another, as illustrated in the maternal pity of the woman Rizpah (2 Sam. 21), a way that surpasses the strict demands of justice.

3. Samuel Moyn, *The Origins of the Other* (Ithaca: Cornell University Press, 2005), 2, 93.

4. Ibid., 95.

5. Ibid., 11.

6. For a discussion of this exegetical method of interpretation as employed by Levinas, see Cynthia Kraman's essay in this collection. I thank her for inspiring this insight.

7. Levinas finds great significance in this word-play. See, for example, his "Foreword," *GCM* xiii–xv. See Richard A. Cohen's remarks on this topic as an interpretive key for the Abrahamic/Odyssean journeys in his "Introduction," *TO* 23–24.

8. On the topic of atheism, see especially *TI* 58–60, 77–79, 88–89.

9. See, for example, "The Poet's Vision," *PN* 135–39.

10. All references to *Pardoner's Tale* are from *The Riverside Chaucer,* ed. Larry D. Benson, 3rd ed. (Boston: Houghton Mifflin, 1987), referenced by fragment and line numbers within the *Canterbury Tales* (*CT*).

11. His "bulles of popes and of cardynales/Of patriarkes and bisshopes" [VI.342–43] appear to be forgeries, as false as the relics he carries in his bag, although the text does not explicitly declare them to be such.

12. Levinas first gives prominence to the idea of the *hypostasis* in his 1947 work, *Existence and Existents,* 49, 70.

13. On the "mineness" of *Dasein,* see Martin Heidegger, *Being and Time,* trans. J. Macquarrie and E. Robinson (Oxford: Blackwell, 1962), 68.

14. Levinas, *Time and the Other,* 65, 69.

15. On this topic, see my "The *Translatio* of Chaucer's Pardoner," *Exemplaria* 4, no. 2 (1992): 399–416.

16. On the astrological significance of the Pardoner's poor memory, see my *Chaucer and the Universe of Learning* (Ithaca: Cornell University Press, 1996), 212–13.

17. Emmanuel Levinas, "Humanity Is Biblical," *Questioning Judaism: Interviews by Elisabeth Weber,* trans. Rachel Bowlby (Stanford: Stanford University Press, 2004), 78.

18. *OB* 75. See also Glenn Burger, "Kissing the Pardoner," *PMLA* 107, no. 5 (1992): 143–56; Anne Barbeau Gardiner, "The Medieval Kiss," *PMLA* 108, no. 2 (1993): 333–35.

19. See, for example, Gerhard Joseph, "The Gifts of Nature, Fortune, and Grace in the *Physician's, Pardoner's,* and *Parson's Tales,*" *The Chaucer Review* 9 (1975): 237–45.

20. On the topic of the centrality of the "Pardoner's Tale," see my *Chaucer and the Universe of Learning* (Ithaca: Cornell University Press, 1996), esp. 200–20.

21. On the ordering of the sins, see Morton W. Bloomfield, *The Seven Deadly Sins* (Lansing: Michigan State University Press, 1952). On Chaucer's source, see Siegfried Wenzel, "The Source of Chaucer's Seven Deadly Sins," *Traditio* 30 (1974): 351–78.

22. On the relationship between the end of the "Parson's Tale" and Chaucer's retraction, see Douglas Wurtele, "The Penitence of Geoffrey Chaucer," *Viator* 11 (1980): 335–59; Astell, *Chaucer and the Universe of Learning,* 196–97.

23. See especially Karla Taylor, "The Text and Its Afterlife," *Comparative Literature* 35, no. 1 (1983): 1–20; *Chaucer Reads "The Divine Comedy"* (Stanford: Stanford University Press, 1989).

24. I approach this position in my writings on the conclusion of the *Canterbury Tales* as a sacrificial offering. See Ann W. Astell, "On the Usefulness and Use Value of Books: A Medieval and Modern Inquiry," in *Medieval Rhetoric: A Casebook,* ed. Scott D. Troyan (New York: Routledge, 2004), 41–62; "Nietzsche, Chaucer, and the Sacrifice of Art," *The Chaucer Review* 39, no. 3 (2005): 323–40.

25. I gave an early version of part one of this essay as a paper at the inaugural meeting of the North American Levinas Society, held at Purdue University, West Lafayette, Indiana, in June 2006. I thank Daniel Kline, Sandor Goodhart, Cynthia Kraman, and the graduate student organizers of that meeting (Sol Neely, Michael Michau, Monica Osborne, Kathryn Ludwig, Rebecca Nicholson-Weir, Tavi Gabor, and Dara Fishberg) for their encouragement and insightful comments. The Chaucerian portions of the argument gained a vetting through a paper delivered at the meeting of the New Chaucer Society, held at Fordham University in New York City, in July 2006. I thank my auditors and co-presenters at that meeting, especially J. Allan Mitchell, George Edmundson, Mark Miller, Larry Scanlon, James Simpson, Louise Bishop, Peggy Knapp, Leonard Koff, Valerie Allen, Jennifer Summit, David Wallace, and Cynthia Kraman for their helpful remarks and moral support.

Notes to Gold, "Those Evil Goslings"

1. Emmanuel Levinas, "Reality and Its Shadow," *LR* 132.

2 The "shadows" here are not simply allusions to Socrates' allegorical story told over in Plato's *Republic*. I refer as well to skepticism, which would question my very attempt to perform in this essay what I will refer to as hyperbolic ethical criticism: "Philosophy is not separable from skepticism, which follows it like a shadow it drives off by refuting it again at once on its footsteps... Skepticism is

refutable, but it returns" (*OB* 168). I have borrowed the line, "toward apperceiving a non-allergic relation," from Emmanuel Levinas, *TI* 47.

3. *NT* 108. The Aramaic term "tanaim" (plural form of "tanna") indicates the teachers or sages whose sayings can be found in the Mishnah. Note also, a kabbalistic tradition attributes R. Shimon bar Yochai with the creation of the Zohar, a work that reveals, according to this tradition, usually hidden transcendent mysteries of the Torah. Quite a few stories portray R. Shimon bar Yochai as an extremely holy individual. During his life, one of the stories declares, there was no need for a rainbow (a "sign" from heaven), since R. Shimon bar Yochai was so suffused with holy radiance that he was a sufficient sign for his generation.

4. For a similar charge to Levinas scholars (one that concerns the problem of writing about ethics at the expense of enacting ethical criticism), see Adam Zachary Newton, "Versions of Ethics; Or, the SARL of Criticism: Sonority, Arrogation, Letting-Be," *American Literary History* 13, no. 3 (2001): 603–37.

5. See David Hartman's *A Living Covenant: The innovative spirit in traditional Judaism* (New York: The Free Press, 1985), 281–85. By not addressing the full story in the Babylonian Talmud, Hartman, I would argue, reduces the complexity of Rabbi Shimon bar Yochai's positions. Compare "In All Your Ways, Know Him: Two Modes of Serving God," the second chapter of *By His Light: Character and Values in the Service of God,* Based on addresses by Rabbi Aharon Lichtenstein, adapted by Rabbi Reuven Ziegler (Jersey City, N.J.: Ktav Publishing House, 2003), 27–48.

6. I am indebted to those who have written on Levinas and art before me, in particular, Jill Robbins, *Altered Reading: Levinas and Literature* (Chicago: University of Chicago Press, 1999); Colin Davis, "After Ethics: Levinas without stories," *After Poststructuralism: Reading, stories, and theory* (London: Routledge, 2004), and his "Hermeneutics and Ethical Encounters," *Ethical Issues in Twentieth Century Fiction: Killing the Other* (Basingstoke: Macmillan, 2000); Adam Zachary Newton, *Narrative Ethics* (Cambridge, Mass.: Harvard University Press, 1995), and his "Versions of Ethics"; Edith Wyschogrod, "The Art in Ethics: Aesthetics, Objectivity, and Alterity in the Philosophy of Emmanuel Levinas," *Ethics as First Philosophy: The Significance of Emmanuel Levinas for Philosophy, Literature and Religion,* ed. Adriaan T. Peperzak (New York: Routledge, 1995), 137–48; Robert Eaglestone, *Ethical Criticism: Reading After Levinas* (Edinburgh: Edinburgh University Press, 1997); Gerald L. Bruns, "The concepts of art and poetry in Emmanuel Levinas's writings," *The Cambridge Companion to Emmanuel Levinas,* ed. Simon Critchley and Robert Bernasconi (Cambridge: Cambridge University Press, 2002), 206–33; and Richard Cohen, *Ethics, Exegesis and Philosophy: Interpretation after Levinas* (Cambridge: Cambridge University Press, 2001). More than any of the other writers, Cohen serves as a constant reminder to me that performative interruptions risk turning, all too easily, into the kind of aestheticism/idolatrous rhetoric that Levinas takes to task severely and effectively. In addition, I greatly admire both Cohen's clarity and his vigilant awareness of the Jewish traditions raveling Levinas's discourses. While several of my concerns overlap with those addressed by all of these writers, my readings of Boccaccio, Levinas, and Rabbi

Shimon bar Yochai present significant challenges that, I hope to show, have not yet been addressed adequately by Levinasian criticism.

7. *TI* 47. For a nuanced reading of rhetoric in Levinas, see Susan E. Shapiro's "Rhetoric, Ideology, and Idolatry in the Writings of Emmanuel Levinas," *Rhetorical Inventions and Religious Inquiry: New Perspectives,* ed. Walter Jost and Wendy Olmsted (New Haven: Yale University Press, 2000), 254–78.

8. Scholars often recall this tale, perhaps because of the author's personal reappearance in the midst of all *The Decameron*'s tales, perhaps because of the author's direct responses to critics. At the very least, the first person singular form of "I" throughout the introduction to the fourth day (and the frame tale) refers to Boccaccio's implied author/personae.

9. Boccaccio, *The Decameron* [*TD*], trans. G. H. McWilliam, 2nd ed. (New York: Penguin Classics, 2003), 286. Hereafter cited parenthetically by page.

10. For a wonderful philosophical reading of this specific narrative (in particular, his chapter "The Nature of Desire"), see Gregory B. Stone, *The Ethics of Nature in the Middle Ages: On Boccaccio's Poetaphysics* (New York: St. Martin's Press, 1998). I have learned much about "nature" in the Middle Ages from Stone's work. However, whereas Stone connects his analysis of Boccaccio to Heidegger and Lacan, I read Boccaccio from within a response to interruptive sayings in the Talmud and Levinas. Whereas Stone's aim is to show reality imitating language and to argue "the birth of desire as the effect of language, lawgiving, and the name of the father" (76), my explorations attend to what Levinas would call "metaphysical desire." In other words, it is important that the son feels satisfied about objects in Florence, but his encounter with human others (and sexually different others), not "objects," begins to break apart the father's (and the son's) restrictive conceptions of existence and existents. More importantly, the entire cave narrative is the only story told by Boccaccio himself, and the interruptive story is addressed directly to his audience, in an attempt to create a sense of immediacy.

11. The most comprehensive close textual exegesis in English of this talmudic narrative remains Jeffrey L. Rubenstein's "Torah and the Mundane Life" in his *Talmudic Stories: Narrative Art, Composition, and Culture* (Baltimore: John Hopkins University Press, 1999). However much I gained by his "explication of the text"—as literary critics have often said—I feel that Rubenstein's focus on comparative versions of the story and particular historical contexts actually reduces the ethical significance and rigor of the overall text. A Levinasian approach to the suffering in story, and to those moments that require a critical rub, addresses significance in the story beyond the attention to historical exigencies of textual production. In addition, I am not sure that Levinas would agree with several of the generalizations Rubenstein posits, such as "the union of husband and wife is the most elementary human relationship" (112). As I will argue, Rashbi's wife actually enacts a primary ethical force in the narrative. Overall, whereas Rubenstein tends to desire mediations, I attempt to acknowledge ethical interruptions that go beyond reconciliation or mutual recognition. Nonetheless, despite significant differences, I remain indebted to his attentive reading of nuances in the Talmud's phrasing.

12. Pierre Hayat, "Introduction to the French Edition: Challenging History, Demanding Reflection," *Unforeseen History,* trans. Nidra Poller (Urbana: University of Illinois Press, 2004), 10.

13. Here I rub against the recent tendency to use pairs of opposed terms to explain Levinas. For example, the entire "Part One" of Michael B. Smith's *Toward the Outside: Concepts and Themes in Emmanuel Levinas* (Pittsburgh: Duquesne University Press, 2005), which Smith calls "Concepts," addresses seven splits, such as "Sacred/Holy" and "Totality/Infinity." However accurate any of these "concepts" might be (after all, Levinas himself uses these terms), the constant reinforcement of these oppositions often begs the critical question of how passage is possible from the Sacred to the Holy or from Totality to Infinity.

14. I have borrowed the line, "the nakedness of the face," from *TI* 74.

15. When "tza'ar" (her suffering) is coupled with "me-galyah" (revealing), the text suggests the forced sexual revealing of a woman (for critics interested in sufficient textual evidence, see Ketuvos 39a–b, Bava Kama 59a, and Nedarim 91b). For those critics interested in the textual evidence and variants, see Rubenstein.

16 The Mishnah is, among other things, a compilation of Oral Laws (edited probably in the end of the 2nd century CE).

17. Rubenstein nicely draws out the implications of the semantic constellation involving linguistic forms of "pleasantness" throughout the entire narrative.

18. For an intriguing perspective on what she calls "a tragic aspect at the heart of Levinas' Good" (80) see the last section of Bettina Bergo's third chapter of her *Levinas Between Ethics and Politics: For the Beauty that Adorns the Earth* (Dordrecht: Kluwer Publishers, 1999). According to Bergo, "If the violence of the Good is to be sought in its disruption of the order of being, it remains for all that, a violence—one which transforms immanence into the for-the-other of the prophet, and of any self or subject" (81). In general, Bergo's work is noteworthy for attending to the challenges of the biblical, prophetic, and talmudic inflections and—perhaps most significantly—the messianic consciousness of Levinas's writing in addition to what has become the more standard passages and emphases in Levinas criticism.

19. In the very last sentence of the first paragraph of the very last section of *Otherwise Than Being,* Levinas brings us back to Plato: "It is as though the Platonic Ideas themselves owed their eternity and their purity as universals only to the perishing of the perishable, before requiring a republic so as to come out of their bad idealism and be efficacious" (176). Might a revision of Plato's *Republic,* perhaps even the cave, keep haunting Levinas? Perhaps Levinas is even obsessed with bringing, so to speak, the Platonism (and utopianism) of Rashbi's cave out into the quotidian world of work and specific embodied existents?

20. For the existent's movement out of existence, see Levinas's *On Escape,* trans. Bettina Bergo (Stanford: Stanford University Press, 2003) as well as his *Existence and Existents.* See Bergo (especially at the beginning of her *Levinas Between Ethics and Politics*) for a particularly insightful exploration of this process.

21. See the work of Colin Davis for a more expansive treatment of these issues.

22. My reading of Boccaccio remains indebted to the thoughtful and critical discussion of "nature" in Gregory B. Stone's *The Ethics of Nature in the Middle Ages*. Stone effectively dismantles any reading of Boccaccio that would keep what is "natural" removed entirely from what is linguistically constructed. However, again, Stone's focus is on what is often called "natural desire," not what Levinas calls "metaphysical desire." If Stone is correct — if Boccaccio's interruptive story is a culturalist, not naturalist, manifesto, and if the boy does not start desiring until after he hears improper linguistic constructions ("goslings") — then Levinas's ethical claims would be even more important for reading Boccaccio: "metaphysical desire" can exist on a more basic level in the self than erotic desire or social constructions of desire do! A more significant dilemma arises once Irigaray's critique of Levinas enters any hyperbolic ethical criticism, but her question of an ethics of sexual difference deserves much more space than this essay will permit.

23. There is not enough space here to pursue the ethical implications, but perhaps I can suggest that Boccaccio here becomes, for a moment, more open to Irigaray's sense of otherness than Levinas's. That is, it might be possible to read Boccaccio's interruptive cave story as a critique of Levinas's position in *Totality and Infinity* that the son challenges the father's experience of time. In Boccaccio, the "young ladies" influence the son, who in turn, challenges the father's sense of time and obligation. The son, in other words, does not start the breaking open of the self's sense of time. Particular, embodied (sexually different) others first break open the son's sense of self.

About the Contributors

Valerie Allen is professor of English at John Jay College of Criminal Justice–CUNY. She specializes in medieval culture and literature, and continental philosophy. Her publications include essays on Emmanuel Levinas, Friedrich Nietzsche, and Martin Heidegger. Her essays have appeared in *English Studies, Review of English Studies,* and *Studia Neophilogia.* She has edited an anthology of essays on Chaucer (1997), is the author of *On Farting: Language and Laughter in the Middle Ages* (2006), and has a long chapter on the history of Middle English literature in *English Literature in Context* (2007).

Ann W. Astell was professor of English at Purdue University, where she chaired the program in Medieval and Renaissance Studies. In 2007 she joined the Department of Theology at the University of Notre Dame. The recipient of a John Simon Guggenheim Memorial Fellowship, she is the author of numerous articles and books, including *The Song of Songs in the Middle Ages* (1990); *Job, Boethius, and Epic Truth* (1994); *Chaucer and the Universe of Learning* (1996); *Political Allegory in Late Medieval England* (1999); and *Eating Beauty: The Eucharist and the Spiritual Arts of the Middle Ages* (2006).

Moshe Gold is associate professor of English and director of the Rose Hill Writing Program at Fordham University where he teaches courses in literary and critical theory, and pedagogy theory and practice. An editor of *Joyce Studies Annual,* his own essays on Shakespeare, Joyce, Plato, and Derrida have appeared in *Representations, Joyce Studies Annual, Criticism, James Joyce Quarterly,* and *ELH.*

Sandor Goodhart is associate professor of English at Purdue University where he teaches courses in "Biblical Reading: The Religious, the Ethical, and the Literary," "Structuralism and Poststructuralism," "Shakespeare," and "Greek Tragedy and Philosophy." He is a specialist in dramatic literature (Greek tragedy and philosophy, Shakespeare, modern drama), literary theory and criticism (structuralism and post-structuralism, the history of critical theory), and Jewish studies (Hebrew Bible, modern Jewish thought, Holocaust studies). He is the author of *Sacrificing Commentary: Reading the End of Literature* (1996) and *Reading Stephen Sondheim* (2000). He is at work on two books: *Moebian Nights: Literary Reading after Auschwitz* and *The Tears of Esau: Reading, Revelation, and the Prophetic*. He has published articles in *Diacritics, Philosophy and Literature,* the *Stanford Review, Modern Judaism, Contagion: Journal of Mimesis, Religion, and Culture,* among others. He is a member of the editorial boards of *Modern Fiction Studies, Contagion: Journal of Mimesis, Religion, and Culture,* and *Shofar: An Interdisciplinary Journal of Jewish Studies.*

J. A. Jackson is assistant professor of English at Hillsdale College where he teaches courses in Old and Middle English language and literature, and literary theory (René Girard and Emmanuel Levinas). He specializes in fourteenth century literature, Old and Middle English biblical narrative, and medieval exegesis. His research examines the depiction of violence in literature, focusing especially on the eschatological and the apocalyptic. This has led to his most recent publication in *Contagion: Journal of Mimesis, Religion, and Culture* (2006), on the deconstruction of mythological violence in the Revelation to John.

Eileen A. Joy is assistant professor of English at Southern Illinois University–Edwardsville. She is coeditor of three volumes: *The Postmodern Beowulf: A Critical Casebook* (2007), *Cultural Studies of the Modern Middle Ages* (2007), and *Premodern to Modern Humanisms: The BABEL Project* (2007), a special issue of the *Journal of Narrative Theory.* She regularly contributes articles to the *Old English Newsletter.*

Alexander L. Kaufman is assistant professor of English at Auburn University–Montgomery. He specializes in Middle English language and literature and has articles published and forthcoming on Malory's *Morte D'arthur,* medieval outlawry, and the Jack Cade Rebellion of 1450. His current book project, an examination of the historical representations of Cade's Rebellion, is forthcoming from Ashgate Press.

Daniel T. Kline is associate professor of English and graduate program director at the University of Alaska, Anchorage. He specializes in Middle English literature and culture, Chaucer, literary and cultural theory, and digital medievalism. His publications include essays in *Chaucer Review, Philological Quarterly, College Literature, Literary and Linguistic Computing, Comparative Drama,* and the chapter "Female Childhoods" in the *Cambridge Companion to Medieval Women* (2003). He edited *Medieval Children's Literature* (2003); is coediting *The Medieval in Motion,* a volume on contemporary film, TV, and video game neo-medievalism; and is author/webmaster of the Electronic Canterbury Tales (http://www.kankedort.net). Dr. Kline also has essays forthcoming in the *Journal of English and Germanic Philology* and in *Cultural Studies of the Modern Middle Ages* (2007). His research examines violence, sacrifice, and children and childhood in late medieval England.

Cynthia Kraman is associate professor of English at The College of New Rochelle. She has published on Chaucer in *Medieval Women in Their Communities* (1996) and on the *Pearl*-poet in *Time and Eternity: The Medieval Discourse* (2003). She is a poet with several collections including the recently reissued *Taking on the Local Color,* and her plays have been given staged readings in New York City. She presented on "Reconciliation and Levinas" at the North American Levinas Society in 2006.

J. Allan Mitchell is assistant professor of English at the University of Victoria, Canada. His work covers the fourteenth and fifteenth centuries with a particular focus on medieval rhetorical culture, philosophical ethics, and literary aesthetics. He is the author of *Ethics and Exemplary Narrative in Chaucer and Gower* (2004).

James J. Paxson is associate professor of English at the University of Florida where he teaches courses in medieval literature and literary theory, and is an editor of *Exemplaria*. Following the publication of his 1994 book, *The Poetics of Personification*, he has published many articles on medieval allegory, personification, the rhetorical "master tropes," gender, ethics, and on literature and science.

Susan Yager is associate professor of English and associate director of the Center for Excellence in Learning and Teaching at Iowa State University. Her area of specialization is Chaucer studies. Recent articles include "Howard's *Idea* and the Idea of Hypertext," in *Medieval Forum*, and "The BBC Man of Law's Tale: Faithful to the Tradition," in *Literature and Belief*.

Index